COMPARATIVE PERSPECTIVES OF THIRD WORLD WOMEN

♀

COMPARATIVE PERSPECTIVES OF THIRD WORLD WOMEN

The Impact of Race, Sex, and Class

edited by

Beverly Lindsay

PRAEGER SPECIAL STUDIES • PRAEGER SCIENTIFIC

Library of Congress Cataloging in Publication Data

Main entry under title:

Comparative perspectives of Third World women.

    Includes bibliographical references and index.
    1. Underdeveloped areas--Women--Addresses, essays,
lectures. 2. Minority women--United States--Addresses,
essays, lectures. I. Lindsay, Beverly.
HQ1870.9.C65   301.41'2   78-19793
ISBN 0-03-046651-2

Published in 1980 by Praeger Publishers
CBS Educational and Professional Publishing
A Division of CBS, Inc.
521 Fifth Avenue, New York, New York 10017 U.S.A.

© 1980 by Beverly Lindsay

123456789   145   98765432

Printed in the United States of America

PREFACE

During the late fall of 1976 and early winter 1977, a group of professional women educators and I began to formulate ideas for a panel at the twenty-first annual Conference of the Comparative and International Education Society. We observed that this organization, similar to many other professional ones, did not adequately address the roles of women in a comparative perspective. As an initial step we formed a panel focusing on fundamental social, economic, and educational institutions that hindered the overall humanistic development of select groups of Third World women in developing societies and the United States. Our research into the issues confronting these women revealed the severe paucity of material on this subject. Some material had been written by white male scholars, many of whom were insensitive to very fundamental areas that affect the lives of Third World women. Moreover, there was a very conspicuous lack of comparative literature. This is not to overlook the pioneering works by Ester Boserup, Irene Tinker, and others. Their works, however, usually focus on women in the traditional Third World countries and do not include minority or Third World women in the United States.

As Third World women ardently interested in the positions and roles of oppressed women everywhere, we reached the inevitable conclusion that it was our responsibility as women scholars to begin, albeit in a tentative manner, to rectify the situation. To portray both a scholarly position and our humanistic concerns as women, we decided to produce a volume comparing the positions of Third World women in developing countries with those of minority women in the United States. We were concerned with the scholarly content, but equally, perhaps more, concerned with having Third World women themselves address the issues. As the editor of the volume, I made a concerted effort to have Third World women scholars discuss their respective groups. Due to publication and other time commitments, I was not completely successful in all instances in locating such scholars. However, women who have been intricately involved with the lives of Third World women, in a very humanistic sense, also consented to write particular chapters.

As the major editor, I assume responsibility for the general direction of the volume; however, each chapter reflects its author's views. Some elected to write in an objective and scholarly genre, while others attempted to portray more humanistic and subjective views of crucial issues affecting respective groups. Both approaches are necessary to fully comprehend the dynamic social factors influencing the lives of Third World women.

This volume does not intend to provide encyclopedic coverage of any or all particular groups of Third World women. Neither does it purport to be an exclusive or definitive treatise viewed within the conceptual frameworks represented by disciplinary fields such as sociology, psychology, or education. It is offered as an introduction to vital issues that profoundly influence the lives of Third World women. It is hoped that this work will help fill the void in comparative material on the subject. It should raise as many questions as it seeks to answer. It should be helpful to scholars and students within the academic community as well as social planners and policy makers.

Our ultimate aim is to contribute to an egalitarian and humanistic world society for all—both men and women. As the proverb states:

> The world is possessed of two wings—the male and the female. So long as these two wings are not equivalent in strength, the bird cannot fly. Until womenkind reaches the same degree as man, until she enjoys the same arena of activity, extraordinary attainment of the world of humanity will not be realized; humanity cannot wing its way to heights of real attainment. [Writings of the Bahá í Faith]

Numerous scholars and individuals helped in the preparation of this work; some are cited in particular chapters. While we cannot mention all individuals, we do wish to express special appreciation to Fatou Sow, University of Dakar, Institute for Development Studies; Carolyn Wood Sherif, The Pennsylvania State University; and Richard Devon, The Pennsylvania State University. These persons continually provided constructive criticism. Special appreciation is also extended to Elaine Sipsky and Judy Leonard, who helped prepare the footnotes and bibliographies and did extensive typing for many chapters. As the editor, I sincerely appreciate the contributions and critiques of the authors.

We hope our work will help contribute to a humanistic understanding of people.

CONTENTS

1
PERSPECTIVES OF THIRD WORLD WOMEN: AN INTRODUCTION

Beverly Lindsay

The denial of women's rights and opportunities is at the
very root of our development problems and socioeconomic
ills—including illiteracy, malnutrition, [and] mass
poverty.

> Helvi Sipila,
> World Conference Documents

During the current decade the debate concerning the status of
women has been thrust into the national and international arenas.
Within the United States, various components of the women's movement have called for equality in employment, salary increments, and
promotions for females comparable to those of their male peers. At
the legislative and executive levels, several laws such as Title IX
(which forbids sex discrimination in public education) and executive
order Affirmative Action guidelines (11246 and 11375, which prohibit
racial and sexual discrimination in agencies with government con-
tracts) have been introduced to ameliorate the status of females. Another measure to improve the status of women is the Equal Rights
Amendment (ERA), which is currently before the state legislatures.
Through the framework of these national guidelines and the efforts of
state and municipal plans, various programs addressing the position
of women have also been initiated.

Minority women in the United States, while not always directly
affected by or involved in the drafting of such national or state guidelines and programs, have still been touched by some of the endeavors.
Puerto Rican and Black American women, who are frequently the
victims of poverty, have experienced partial assistance through wom-
en's development programs—often aimed at blue-collar and professional women. While some of their needs are comparable to those
of white women, there are very few programs for minority females.[1]

1

Further, because some programs for minority females have not been located in close proximity to their residences and/or places of employment, access to them has been limited. For minority females, programs must attempt to combat the dilemmas of sexism and racism that are inextricably linked with their depressed economic status, which often have a brutalizing effect on a woman's self-concept.

Depressed economic status of nations and its interactive effect within the social milieu profoundly influence the lives of women in the developing nations of Africa, Asia, Latin America, and the Caribbean. Many of these women are preoccupied with the most fundamental problems of human life—adequate food, decent shelter, elementary health services, and basic education, to cite a few examples. These oppressive conditions of acute poverty are their paramount concerns. Other concerns are often viewed in a secondary or peripheral manner.

While diverse variations exist among the lives of these women as well as women in North America and Europe, the denial of women's rights and opportunities is a common concern. Basic recognition and discussion of this common reality received attention in the United Nations during the early 1970s. That body acknowledged that the problems prohibiting women's rights and opportunities were, in fact, impeding human development and, hence, merited an international forum. Therefore, the body authorized the Committee on Social Development and Humanitarian Affairs, through Assistant Secretary-General Helvi Sipila, to formulate plans for an international conference to address issues impeding women's fundamental rights. Sipila stated, when asked about the International Women's Year Conference, that it is a great disadvantage to be born a female and that equality does not exist between the sexes. It is hoped that worldwide discrimination against females will become a major issue on the "world agenda," being deemed as important as problems of population, energy, and peace.[2]

Equality, development, and peace were the central themes of the International Women's Year Conference that convened in Mexico City in midsummer 1975. Women from the developed Western nations of North America, Europe, and Australia were present, as were delegations from the developing nations of Africa, Asia, Latin America, and the Caribbean. Various speeches were put before the conference, reflecting the concerns of diverse groups of women and the nations they represented. Mexico's President Luís Echeverría stated that the conference could not ignore the inequalities between males and females of more developed countries. But participants should recognize that three-quarters of the women in the world have more fundamental concerns for themselves and their children than do women in the developed world. He urged women of the more developed nations to

view the problems of their sex from a broader angle and
in a greater spirit of solidarity. It will avail humanity
very little if they improve their status without being aware
of the need to further the cause of the underprivileged
classes in the rest of the world, who lack medical care
for their children, hygienic housing in which to shelter
them and adequate training to prepare them for life.[3]

Statistics provide an initial insight into the stark realities facing
women in developing countries, conditions that more profoundly affect women due to their gender. During the 1970s, 110 million children will be born in Latin America, 5.2 million of whom will die before age one, while another 5.6 million will die by age five[4]—nearly
11 million young children. In parts of Africa 50 percent of the children die by age five.

Mortality rates for adults from developing nations also present
a gloomy picture. In Angola the life expectancies for adult males and
females were similar at 33.5 years in 1970, while it was 41 years in
Botswana. Figures for the same time period in Kenya were only
slightly higher—51.2 years for females and 46.9 years for males.
In the United States the expectancy for white females was 71.7 years
and nearly 70 years for males. Native American (Indian) males and
females have a life expectancy of 45.6 years; that is, their rates are
comparable to those of developing nations. In Sweden the figures
were 71.7 and 76.5 years for males and females, respectively.

Illiteracy rates are still another index of discrepancies between
the developed and developing nations. In the developed nations, 4.3
percent of the females are illiterate (2.5 percent for males), while
60.2 percent in developing nations are illiterate (40.4 percent for
males). In certain geographical areas of the developing world, the
illiteracy rates are much higher. In Africa 83.7 percent of the females were illiterate in 1970, while the figure was 63.4 percent for
males.[5]

With such statistics in mind, we can understand why the International Council of Social Welfare urged the International Women's
Year Conference to emphasize the importance of food, health, and
education for females. After considerable debate, the International
Women's Year Conference unanimously approved a ten-year plan of
action, which emphasizes improving these major areas. It also advocates changing the role of rural women so that the sheer drudgery
of their lives is eliminated. There are other wide-range provisions
calling for establishing child care facilities, giving equal rights to
unmarried mothers, combating prostitution, presenting more employment opportunities, and providing greater access to political offices
and policy-making positions.

There are some ostensibly built-in plans of action to help ensure
the plan's success, such as a timetable for action, regional programs,
and a second major conference to be convened in 1980. Regardless
of whether the ten-year plan and the conference attain all of their
goals, particular needs were noted: (1) bringing women's issues to
an international forefront in an unprecedented manner, (2) accentu-
ating differences among women, and (3) pointing out international
similarities in sexism. Understanding that one woman's stereotype
of her oppressed position is another's sense of security, identity, and
continuity is an insight that must be kept in mind.[6] Women of both
the developed and developing world are oppressed by gender. There
are, undoubtedly, common concerns; but those affecting a great majority of women in the developing countries frequently focus on survival or mere subsistence—or a level just above this. In short, the
International Women's Year Conference identified basic common features and variations between these women that may provide the groundwork for further policies and research.

A basic purpose of this volume is to examine these common features and variations with a specific focus on women from developing
nations and minority women in the United States, that is, Third World
women. We seek to raise fundamental questions and provide initial
responses. Some of the questions include the following: What are the
most crucial issues confronting women of Asia, Africa, Latin America, and the Caribbean and minority women in the United States?
What are the basic issues affecting Black, Mexican (Chicana), Native,
and Vietnamese American women? What does a rural Kenyan mother
have in common with a welfare mother in New York? What linkages
are there between Chicana women and West Indian women? What
mutual concerns may exist between West African women and the recent Vietnamese women immigrants to the United States? How important is women's socioeconomic position (classism)? Is sexism a
factor for all Third World women? Is racism also a factor? In
short, what are some of the fundamental issues confronting Third
World women everywhere? We hope to provide some material that
may help to explore responses to these and several other questions
pertaining to Third World women. Our ultimate aim is to contribute
to the attainment of those fundamental egalitarian goals that will enhance the lives of women and improve the status of all humans in a
world society.

The remaining portions of this introductory chapter begin our
endeavor. It is devoted to conceptual views to help explain Third
World phenomena. With these views, we cite working definitions of
the term Third World and discuss some of the most fundamental conceptual criteria associated with it—such as colonialism, neocolonialism, internal colonialism, internal neocolonialism, development, and

dependency—which place a nation or group within the category of the Third World. The impact of these criteria on Third World women and their interrelationships with social, educational, and economic patterns will serve as a basis for examining and raising questions about Third World women's positions.

CONCEPTUAL VIEWS

The Third World

To discuss Third World nations is generally to envision the geographical areas in Africa, Asia, Latin America, and the Caribbean. These nations are linked by various economic, sociocultural, and political features that are often manifested on vastly different levels from those of the white majority in North America and Europe. Irving Louis Horowitz contends that what really binds the Third World is not these features per se but, rather, the psychological unity built around them. [7] From the time the term came into vogue in the early 1950s to the present, there have been various conferences and symposiums that have defined and debated the common features of the Third World. Some prominent examples are the Bandung Conference of Colored Peoples in 1955, the Belgrade Conference of Non-aligned Powers in 1961, the Congress of African States in Addis Ababa in 1963, a Second Conference of Non-aligned Nations in Cairo in 1964, the Tri-Continental Conference in Havana in 1969, the Sixth Pan-African Conference in 1974 in Dar es Salaam, and several Organization of African Unity (OAU) Conferences of the late 1960s and throughout the 1970s that convened in various major African cities. [8] Despite the developing nations' recognition of diverse ideological, economical, and developmental orientations and policies among themselves, these conferences delved into a common feature—the various forms of exploitation by the more developed Western nations. The premise was that exploitation had, in fact, prohibited the development of the Third World.

During the 1960s and 1970s various minorities in the United States began to identify increasingly with the citizenry of Third World countries. The Civil Rights and Black Power movements served as impetuses and solidifiers for similar beliefs and premises identified in the conferences. Later, the La Raza, Puerto Rican, and American Indian movements echoed and contributed to this sense of identity with the Third World nations. The movements by American minorities emphasized the exploitative nature of their relationship to the white majority, particularly the ruling elite, in the United States. Hence, this relationship was expressed by both Third World people in the traditional developing nations <u>and</u> minorities in the United States.

Our purpose now is to provide a succinct overview of various components involved in the nature of these exploitative relationships.

Colonialism

> I am convinced that until the colonial problems . . . are
> constructively and wisely settled, there is not likely to
> be permanent peace, especially at a time when the darker
> people of the world are becoming more and more self-
> conscious, and are eager to play an increasing part in
> national and international affairs. [9]

W. E. B. DuBois, in making this statement, recognized the overwhelming problems of colonialism for the twentieth century. Permanent peace did not mean the mere absence of war but the right for colonies to exert their roles in world affairs—particularly those darker colonized people who had been prevented from doing so.

Perusing the economic impact on societies is a fundamental approach to examining traditional colonialism. DuBois contended that colonies are investment areas where the rate of profits is far greater than that from domestic ventures. Colonization is a method of engaging in industry and commerce and distributing wealth. Traditionally, the methods were accomplished by one nation exerting political control over another geographical region. But, the basis for this control was often inextricably linked to the phenomenon of color or other descriptive or identifiable physical or cultural characteristics. During the 1800s when colonial expansion was occurring, the belief prevailed that only a minority of people were capable of civilization, who by their inherent gifts, difficult trials, and experiences were the rulers of the world. This group, for the most part, was white. Thus, the darker people of Africa, Asia, Latin America, and the Caribbean were termed the "white man's burden." [10] They were a burden in the sense that darker people had to be taken care of, since they allegedly could not care for themselves. Such a rationale served as the justification of the nonindigenous racial or ethnic group for exerting economic and political control.

Once colonies were established, the ascribed characteristic of race became solidified into caste distinctions—that is, opportunity and mobility were influenced by race. Hence, within the colonial framework in these countries, for the most part, whites became and remained the dominant class and others became subservient. Persons of mixed ancestry served as a buffer class between the dominant classes and indigenous persons. Examples of buffer classes include the mestizos of Latin America, the coloreds of East and southern Africa, the mulattoes of the Caribbean, and to a certain degree, the mulattoes of the United States. (In Chapter 6, Gloria Joseph briefly discusses the phenomenon of mixed heritage with reference to women in several Caribbean nations.) Thus, persons of mixed ancestry and indigenous people did not benefit from the colonial experience to the extent that the whites did. * In short, color was a factor for Third World people, and it was linked to their economic class.

Colonialism, based on economic control, has ramifications that permeate all phases of colonial life. We shall cite examples of colonialism in Africa because this continent experienced the last vestiges of traditional colonialism (it is simply beyond the scope of this volume to provide a detailed comparison of colonialism in all of the Third World). Asian nations, for instance, became independent prior to most African nations. Yet, the harsh effects of colonialism were often similar despite the locale.

Neglected institutional social services and education are two prominent examples. Under colonial domination limited social services were extended to Africans. Angola, Guinea-Bissau, and Mozambique were Portuguese colonies for approximately 500 years, and they are the most recent to obtain independence—in 1974 and 1975. But during the entire colonial period, the Portuguese did not train a single African physician in Mozambique. The life expectancy was about 30 years in eastern Angola at the time of independence. With regard to Guinea-Bissau, the Portuguese themselves stated that this area was more neglected than Angola and Mozambique.

-----

*It should be pointed out, however, that colonialism has not always been practiced by whites alone upon peoples of color. A notable exception is the Japanese penetration into China and other Asian countries. In this instance all participants were people of color. Undoubtedly, the ethnic animosities among the groups of Asian people were significant factors in these colonial endeavors. Japanese influence in Taiwan, for example, was not identical to that practiced by white Western powers, but many similar manifestations comparable to racial discrimination and oppression were present (Patricia T. Surmuri, Japanese Colonial Education in Taiwan [Cambridge, Mass.: Harvard University Press, 1977]).

Moreover, we should clearly bear in mind that the invidious use of sociocultural ascriptive characteristics as basis for discrimination and oppression existed among groups of Asian (and African) people prior to the advent of colonialism. The caste system of India is an eminent illustration. It is being contended, however, that race, ethnicity, and/or other designated ascriptive characteristics served as a basis for justifying and explaining colonialism in the majority of the examples of Western colonial expansion.

The British did not do much more for their African colonies, which had extensive natural resources. In Ibadan, Nigeria, for example, there were approximately 50 Europeans in a city of over 500,000 Blacks. Yet, during the early 1940s there was one segregated 11-bed hospital for whites and only a 34-bed hospital for all of the Blacks.[11] The actual dynamics of such a situation can be seen through the following quote:

> African workers . . . produced for European capitalism goods and services of a certain (economic) value. A small portion of the fruits of their efforts were retained by them in the form of wages, cash payments, and extremely limited social services, such as were essential to the maintenance of colonialism. The rest went to the various beneficiaries of the colonial system.[12] [Emphasis added]

Education was also in a deplorable condition. The budget for education in French West Africa, based on the revenues for taxing Africans, was 4.03 percent of such revenues in the mid-1930s. During a similar period, it was only 3.4 percent in Nigeria and 2.26 percent in Kenya. By 1960 these figures had increased twofold or so; but these were still insignificant amounts.[13] These represent amounts from taxation of Africans; the educational budget was not determined by the amount of profits generated from overall national efforts. The overwhelming majority of the profit revenues was being returned to the colonizer in the respective country, or substantially more was being spent in the colony on the colons than on the indigenous populace.

Failing to educate one generation has obvious repercussions for the next. It becomes understandable why there are currently shortages of qualified teachers, inadequate school sites, and deficiencies in the curriculum. The inadequacies of social service coupled with shortages in education contribute to the phenomenon where 13 million African children have no opportunity to enter school. Of the 12 million who did begin primary education in the early 1960s, less than one-half completed it, and only 3 of every 100 entered secondary school.[14] Bear in mind that in the very early 1960s, most African nations were still colonies. Therefore, the African continent still has an illiteracy rate of over 80 percent. (There is also a severe shortage of physicians, nurses, teachers, engineers, architects, and technicians who are indispensable during current developmental efforts.)

Neocolonialism and Internal Colonies

Neocolonialism frequently denotes the economic, political, and sociocultural relationships of dominance and dependency by an independent nation that was a former colony (such as Jamaica, Kenya, or Senegal) with the former colonizers (such as the British or French). Under such a system, political sovereignty exists in the newly independent nations, but strong economic and sociocultural ties are present with the former colonizer. This type of neocolonialism is still very widespread. In some instances, one nation always may have been politically independent of another; yet, one country has substantial control over another's economy. The relationship between the United States and Panama is often presented as a prominent example.

The terms internal colonies and neocolonialism also have been used by many Black scholars and others referring to the relationship between minorities in the United States and the dominant white majority. With particular reference to the United States, several authors (such as Kenneth Clark, Stokely Carmichael, Charles Hamilton, Carter Woodson, W. E. B. DuBois, Samuel Yette, and Martin Carnoy) discuss neocolonialism in a manner somewhat analogous to the approaches taken in describing traditional colonialism and contemporary neocolonialism in developing nations.[15] Stokely Carmichael and Charles Hamilton, for example, contend that Black American ghettos and Puerto Rican and Chicano barrios are economic, political, social, and educational colonies. These racial minorities are in a dependent relationship with the white majority, particularly middle and upper socioeconomic classes, similar to those of the indigenous people of contemporary independent states such as Jamaica or Kenya where neocolonialism is present. (It should be pointed out that with the exception of Native Americans, other American minority racial groups did not form independent political entities in what is now the United States as did the indigenous people of Jamaica and Kenya.) American minorities exist for the purpose of enriching the dominant group. To paraphrase Carmichael and Hamilton, the dominant American group wants the goods of minority America, in this sense, for their cheap human labor as an economy saver and simultaneously for their purchasing power as consumers. The welfare of minority Americans is only a peripheral concern.[16] Chapters 11 and 12 by Sylvia Gonzales and Gwendolyn Randall Puryear, respectively, will provide additional examples of this phenomenon with respect to minority women in the United States.

Black scholars and others have sometimes used the terms neocolonialism and internal colonies interchangeably with reference to racial minorities in the United States. Although the terms have different meanings, they have been used interchangeably mainly because the oppressive effects experienced through neocolonialism and internal colonialism have been comparable in terms of institutional control by the dominant group.

Gail P. Kelly and Philip Altbach, editors, among others, present different views of internal colonialism:

> Internal colonialism is the domination of a "nation" (de-
> fined geographically, linguistically, or culturally) within
> the national borders of another nation-state by another
> group or groups. Some of the dominated "nations" may
> at one time have been independent, such as American
> Indian tribes, but they are not at this time independent.
> Part of the problem of clearly defining internal colonial-
> ism is in the fact that there is much disagreement con-
> cerning the definition of "nation" and of the role of such
> elements as class in the equation of domination. [17]

Thus, we can see that it is difficult to define, clearly and precisely,
internal colonialism. After all, it could be argued that Black Americans and Chicanos are culturally distinct from white Americans. In
the case of Chicanos, the different linguistic element is also present.
Neither group formed independent political entities as was the situation with Native Americans, even though, for example, Chicanos were
once part of Mexico. So, we will observe in Chapters 11 and 12 that
Sylvia Gonzales and Gwendolyn Puryear use (internal) colonialism and
neocolonialism somewhat interchangeably. The writers are focusing
on effects, although in some instances the initial political, economic,
and sociocultural causes differed somewhat, which help to explain the
contemporary status of Third World women in the United States and
elsewhere.

This writer contends that a more correct way of referring to
the condition of racial minorities in the United States may be internal
neocolonialism. Racial minorities in the United States have, indeed,
been oppressed as were the indigenous people in the traditional colonial areas (as will be documented shortly); in short, they were and
are internal colonies. However, their status relative to the dominant
majority has ostensibly improved in terms of political spheres—for
example, voting rights laws and access to education. Yet, such al-
leged improvements have not significantly changed their status, just
as, for example, the achievement of political independence in former
traditional colonies has not significantly altered the status of the more
recent ones. In the latter, neocolonialism still exists, and internal
neocolonialism is still present in the former groups. These ideas
will be further discussed in the final chapter by this writer.

During the period when African, Asian, Latin American, and
Caribbean people were experiencing the adverse effects of traditional
colonialism, American minorities were enduring what has been
termed colonialism through institutional control. In his poignant
work, The Mis-Education of the Negro, Carter G. Woodson discloses
some historical facts. From the late 1800s to the mid-1900s, Blacks
were actively prevented from entering certain professions that would

have definitely ameliorated their statuses. These included designing, drafting, architecture, engineering, and chemistry.[18] While there were Black institutions—Howard and Meharry universities—to prepare medical professionals, these could not teach all Blacks who were needed for vital health services. White educational institutions accepted few Blacks or none at all. Similarly, Native Americans during this period were also severely restricted in their educational options and subsequent opportunities to provide social services for their people. The majority were confined to reservations where education usually did not extend beyond elementary school. The few who did enter professional or graduate schools sometimes entered Black institutions such as Hampton Institute or a few white colleges. While the traditional colonialists were limiting health and social services in Africa, similar restrictions were being imposed in the United States.

Minorities also experienced neocolonialism and/or internal colonialism through lack of control over their institutions. Carter G. Woodson discusses how arguments were frequently made regarding Blacks' inability to administer their institutions or raise funds for expenditures or expansions. These arguments do not recognize the administrative abilities of Booker T. Washington and R. R. Moton at Tuskegee Institute or John Hope at Atlanta University—regardless of whether one agrees with these men's views toward Black American education. Apparently, the arguments carried considerable weight, since Howard University did not have its first Black president until 1926, that is, nearly 60 years after its founding in 1867. Likewise, it was not until the 1930s that Lincoln University in Pennsylvania had the first Black trustee. In 1945, almost 100 years after its founding, Lincoln elected its first Black president. Blacks were simply not in control at the institutional level; moreover, they were not on various philanthropic boards, such as the Carnegie Foundation and General Education Board. These boards donated substantial amounts to Black American colleges and universities, frequently with the stipulation that funds be allocated to practical or vocational education.[19] Such education was not designed to train Black American professionals. The failure to educate or provide adequate education meant that social and economic adversities for Black American people were not being addressed.

Again, the picture was similar, and even worse in many cases, for other American minorities. The issue on control of four-year postsecondary institutions did not arise for Asian, Mexican, and Native Americans, simply because such colleges did not exist until the mid-twentieth century. Minority professional training for these groups was limited to the few who attended select white institutions or a few Black colleges. If a racial or cultural group does not have trained professionals in various fields, control over them by others is inevitable. Note that this is not to suggest that professional education is the only type needed. Instead, a combination of professional and vocational education is necessary to ameliorate minority life in the United States.

The Choice, by Samuel Yette, provides a piercing analysis of what he calls neocolonialism in the United States, with special reference to Blacks. Yette identifies and juxtaposes four comparable areas in terms of the effects of neocolonialism. First, Blacks are people of color with identifiable racial characteristics. Racism is an inescapable and paramount factor. Second, there are forms of economic exploitation. In the United States, Blacks and other minorities in particular residential areas frequently pay more than whites for the same consumer goods that whites buy in other areas. (Michael Harrington, Sidney Wilhelm, and Thomas Pettigrew provide extensive information on these facts.)[20] Third, restricted housing patterns are still another example. Black Americans often live in ghettos, and banks have systematically denied home loans for building outside designated areas through the practice of red-lining. Fourth, the illusion of assistance is provided through some programs. Job corps programs assist persons in obtaining vocational positions. Yet graduates of job corps programs frequently retain approximately the same socioeconomic status as prior to training.[21]

Development and Dependency

Our discussion addressing components of these various forms of colonialism is directed toward the need for the eradication of such phenomena so that human development can occur, which involves the many economic, political, educational, and social facets interacting in an optimum manner. "Development cannot be seen purely as an economic affair, but rather an overall social process which is dependent upon the outcome of man's efforts to deal with his natural environment."[22]

Unfortunately, underdevelopment is the reality; development exists for a select group. Underdevelopment may be viewed as the product of the historical and contemporary exploitative relationship between nations or people within a nation.[23] It is an explanation of the exploitative relationship derived from the perspective of those who are exploited and is based upon the dependency relationship between the Third World nations (in the case of the United States, minorities) and the ruling elite in a developed nation. Dependency relationships also exist between the ruling elite in a Third World area and the majority of the people who are semiskilled and/or unskilled, who cannot partake of the benefits of development. The nature of the dependency relationship, indeed, is most important, particularly if it is explained in conjunction with various forms of colonialism, as will be discussed in Chapters 2 and 14 by Shelby Lewis and Beverly Lindsay, respectively. To liberate oppressed people, a central goal must be to move beyond the very nature of the dependency relationship and its various manifestations toward a more developed state. Development entails improvement in the quality and quantity of life. Quality can refer to social, health, and educational concerns, for example, while quantity may involve the amount of economic and political involvement.

The various forms of colonial exploitation developmentally affect all Third World people, both male and female. Yet their effects are much harsher for females. We shall now briefly describe how these several conceptual views help explain the status of Third World women.

THE DECLINING STATUS OF THIRD WORLD WOMEN

Colonialism exploitation in its many forms and dependency relationships has adverse effects upon the status of Third World women. We shall cite several examples with reference to the economic, sociopolitical, and educational status of African women.

Ester Boserup and Leith Mullings assert that the woman's role in agriculture and other activities, prior to colonialism, was based to a large extent upon equality with men, although there were some distinctions. In societies where men and women have engaged in similar activities, women's participation has given them equal access and control over their labor. When hunting and gathering were the primary means of subsistence, the distribution of resources was based on communal life and goods were distributed fairly equally. As women engaged in agriculture or related activities, they were still active participants in the distribution of such goods.[24] With the advent of colonialism, though, the Europeans demonstrated little desire to see women's farming continued. Examples may be cited whereby females were systematically excluded from various aspects of agricultural production—usually those involving cash crops. Examples from Africa aptly illustrate this contention. Ugandan women began cultivating cotton during the early 1920s. But the European director of agriculture stated that cotton production should not be left in the hands of women and elderly people. A decade later men were growing most of the cotton. To ensure that women did not participate in various farming sectors, they were not taught contemporary skills. Currently, females that continue farming are forced to use antiquated, traditional methods that are quite arduous and produce low yields. Moreover, women's farming activities are increasingly being restricted to food production, where crop yields are also lower than what they would otherwise be, reflecting differences in acquired skills and implements.[25]

In other economic activities, women also have been restricted. Various groups of West African women have historically engaged in trading and marketing. These activities were an integral part of precolonial life. Yet Boserup, Kenneth Little, and Mullings[26] point out that, while there are individual examples of successful market women, the vast majority are still petty traders. Many of their commodities are agricultural products, and the seasons (rainy or dry) and general climatic conditions often jeopardize their earnings. The bazaar represents an intermediate phase between agriculture activities and modern occupations. Eventually women will experience competition from imports and more modern components of the economy with which they are not equipped to deal. Simultaneously, they have limited educational and technical skills for entering other sectors. In short, women find themselves in a dubious position, where their traditional roles have been eroded and they are left with limited means to new avenues of production. Exclusion of females from relatively viable modes of production means they are unequal to men of the same social strata.

A division of labor and other distinctions existed prior to colonialism but within the context of communal societies. Ida Faye Rousseau has stated, "The role of women in traditional African societies can best be understood if we conceive of it in terms of the African woman's traditional integrity within a separate but not subordinate female community. . . . [It is] an interdependence without which the equilibrium of the natural order upon which traditional societies are based would be destroyed."[27] The traditional concept of a division of labor was disrupted during the colonial period. Mullings's discussion of the concepts of equality, inequality, symmetry, and asymmetry may clarify the distinctions between male's and female's roles and statuses.

Equality refers to the situation wherein all members of a society have the same relationship to the society's resources. Such a situation would exist in a truly communal society. Symmetry refers to a situation in which males and females have access to similar roles and statuses. Inequality occurs when society's resources are appropriated by certain social strata as private property, which limits access to resources for other strata. This increased throughout the Third World during the colonial period. In asymmetrical relationships, access to the same means of production may be equal, but males and females may not have access to the same roles and statuses. Sex roles may be differentially evaluated in some instances.[28] Historically, since there was a division of labor, relationships between the sexes were equal but asymmetrical in that males and females did not engage in the same roles. Asymmetrical roles served as a justification for producing and increasing the chasm between males and females during the colonial and contemporary periods. Men have increasingly accepted these role distinctions and thus feel comfortable with current differences in status, as will be shown in Lois Adams's chapter on Zaire.

Sociopolitical life represents another area where females' status deteriorated with the coming of colonialism. The Queen Mother or Queen Sister exerted considerable political influence in areas of Benin and Ghana. In Mozambique, the widow of an Nguni king was consulted by the reigning king on significant political matters that affected their clan or ethnic group. Other examples of women's political influence were witnessed in precolonial Niger, Chad, and northern Nigeria.[29] With increasing formal political organizations, many African women have found that the traditional criteria, upon which their authority had rested, crumbled. Gradually, authority and privilege disappeared. In Labadi, Ghana, for example, the manyei ("mother of town") represented women's issues. The position of mantse for men was transformed into the equivalent of a chieftainship and was buttressed by colonialism. On the other hand, the manyei is heading toward oblivion. One local chief even indicated that there was no current manyei because no woman had fulfilled the educational criteria that he had set for that office.[30] The chief, in this case, was seeing that asymmetrical roles actually became the basis of inequalities in the status of males and females.

We should point out that while some anthropologists and sociologists have presented these views of equality prior to colonialism, such views are currently being reassessed. Some social scientists now argue that what appeared as equality before the advent of colonialism may not have actually been that equal. (In Chapter 2 Shelby Lewis offers some additional insights regarding the issues associated with equality before colonialism.) Therefore, we must take into account the preceding views and still others. Most social scientists do agree, however, that colonialism radically altered the status of women, placing them in a more dependent position.

Differences in educational opportunities reveal still another area of inequality between males and females. The Belgians were notorious for their neglect in providing education for what was formerly the Congo. From 1948 to independence in 1960, there were only a few token secondary academic institutions for boys. But for females, only "concerned discussion" existed.[31] Colonial education was a sharp contrast to the traditional education that both males and females received. While educational opportunities were not as bleak in Tanzania and Kenya, discrepancies in education still exist between the sexes, which began during the colonial period. In 1968, for example, females comprised only about 38 percent of the Tanzanian primary school enrollment and approximately 15 percent of the enrollment at the University of Dar es Salaam. During the 1974/75 academic year females comprised slightly over 40 percent of the Kenyan primary school students, less than 25 percent of the student body at Kenya Science Teacher's College, and less than 30 percent of the undergraduate enrollment at the University of Nairobi.[32] Again, this imbalance is in contrast to the education received by both males and females in traditional Tanzanian and Kenyan societies.

Differences in access to education are a crucial barrier, particularly as societies move through the development process. Ostensibly, the purpose of education is to help people acquire knowledge so that they are capable of new or improved contributions. Education should also help people develop inventive and analytical abilities. If women cannot attend schools, how can they acquire the knowledge and skills that should enable them to move from restrictive roles and activities to the more modern sectors? Or, how can women assist themselves and others in social development, if they are unable to develop the critical and analytical abilities that are needed to examine the developmental process? A person still may not be an integral part of a society or contribute in an optimum manner with education; but one is guaranteed exclusion from key policy positions without it.

Perhaps the roles and statuses of Native American women in the United States parallel those of African women under colonialism more closely than those of other American minority women. Native American women and men originally formed independent sociocultural and political entities in North America. This general situation changed as group after group was subjugated through treaties, relegated to reservations, and subjected to various acts of genocide. The status of women in the Indian Council of Elders was eliminated, since the council itself often became a meaningless or defunct body through successful efforts to subjugate Native American people. Life on reservations radically curtailed the traditional roles and division of labor between the sexes. For example, domestic chores became just that, since Native American women frequently performed their roles around their individual houses. Traditional education was largely eradicated; it was frequently not replaced by any type of formal schooling. Even during the twentieth century, formal education usually has not extended beyond the elementary levels on the reservations. Laura Waterman Wittstock provides more information on historical and contemporary life for Native American Indians in Chapter 10.

By the early 1970s, a very dismal picture existed for Native American females. Native American women have the lowest income of any group in the United States. The median income then was $1,697 for all Native American women; it was even lower at only $1,356 for those in rural areas. Over one-third of all Native American women, both rural and urban, are employed in service occupations, that is nearly twice the national average.[33] The average life expectancy is in the mid-forties as mentioned previously.

SOCIAL, EDUCATIONAL, AND ECONOMIC PATTERNS

Our preceding discussion of the Third World, colonialism, neo-colonialism, internal neocolonialism, development, and dependency and the relationship of these phenomena to Third World women was provided to illustrate that forms of oppression and exploitation are basic features that link these women together. The general conceptual overview indicates that various forms of exploitation for Third World women are frequently manifested in social, educational, and economic institutional patterns. Institutions may be viewed as continuous significant practices, relationships, or organizations within a society. Collectively, institutional patterns provide a comprehensive view of Third World women's roles. Hence, this volume centers around such basic institutional patterns.

The institutional patterns are used in a broad sense to include various facets and ideas presented in several disciplines. Social patterns include, among others, such issues as the woman's position in the family in view of economic conditions within a particular locale, the effects of socialization patterns on interpersonal male and female relationships, and the effects of sex role activities upon women's political activities. Educational patterns involve factors within and directly related to formal school and university systems—curriculum tracks, presence of male and female schools, admissions programs, administrative policies, and society-school relationships. In developing nations, it can also include components of nonformal education such as literacy classes through the radio and other media. Economic or occupational patterns focus on the roles of women in rural agriculture, unskilled labor, market activities, general office work, and various professional spheres. Each chapter focuses on race, sex, and class (triple jeopardy) in light of the institutional patterns. Understanding the interactive effects of these patterns is of fundamental importance for comprehending the status of women.

Our basic goal is to contribute to a comprehension of the interrelationships among social, educational, and economic institutional patterns of Third World women within the context of various forms of colonial exploitation that encourage dependency and hinder development. Our discussion will examine various dynamic variables that have oppressed the status of Third World women as members of society. It is hoped that as a result of increased awareness fundamental institutional changes will result.

NOTES

1. Nadine Brozan, "A Life for Underprivileged Girls: Fantasies of Bright Futures," New York Times, March 26, 1977, p. L-9.

2. International Women's Year, World Conference Documents, OPI/CESI/Note IWY/13, September 13, 1974, p. 1.

3. International Women's Year, World Conference Documents, CIWY/9/E, June 18-19, 1975, p. 3.

4. International Women's Year, World Conference Documents, CIWY/9/E, June 18, 1975, p. 1.

5. International Women's Year, World Conference Documents, E/Conf. 66/3/add. 3, pp. 10, 11, 14, 15.

6. Ashraf Pahlavi, "And Thus Passeth International Women's Year," New York Times, January 5, 1976, p. 29.

7. Irving Louis Horowitz, Three Worlds of Development: The Theory and Practice of International Stratification (New York: Oxford University Press, 1972), p. 8.

8. For a discussion of these conferences, see ibid., chap. 1; Hoyt W. Fuller, "Notes from a Sixth Pan-African Journal," Black World 23 (1974): 70-88; and James Garrett, "A Historical Sketch, The Sixth Pan-African Congress," Black World 26 (1975): 4-20.

9. W. E. B. DuBois, Color and Democracy: Colonies and Peace (New York: Harcourt, Brace, 1945), p. 130.

10. Ibid., pp. 46, 56; and William J. Wilson, Power, Racism, and Privilege: Race Relations in Theoretical and Sociohistorical Perspectives (New York: Free Press, 1973), p. 20.

11. Walter Rodney, How Europe Underdeveloped Africa (Dar es Salaam: Tanzania Publishing, 1972), p. 224.

12. Ibid., p. 232.

13. Ibid., p. 265.

14. Ibid., p. 269.

15. Several writers discuss internal colonialism and neocolonialism in reference to various institutional conditions. Kenneth Clark discusses economic, educational, and social conditions of colonialism in relation to Black Americans. See Kenneth Clark's, Dark Ghetto (New York: Harper & Row, 1965). Stokely Carmichael and Charles Hamilton also discuss economic, social, and political

features of neocolonialism in their work, Black Power: The Politics of Liberation (New York: Random House, 1967). Carter G. Woodson and W. E. B. DuBois discuss some historical aspects of neocolonialism and internal colonialism. Woodson presents material on Black Americans in his work, The Mis-Education of the Negro (Washington, D.C.: Associated, 1933, 1969). DuBois's work is a comparative discussion; see DuBois, Color and Democracy: Colonies and Peace. Samuel Yette concentrates on contemporary effects of neocolonialism for Blacks resulting from federal executive policies and programs of the 1960s. See Samuel F. Yette, The Choice: The Issue of Black Survival in America (New York: Putnam, 1971). Martin Carnoy examines the relationship between education and neocolonialism; see Martin Carnoy, Education as Cultural Imperialism (New York: David McKay, 1974); and Martin Carnoy, ed., Schooling in a Corporate Society: The Political Economy of Education in America (New York: David McKay, 1975).

16. Carmichael and Hamilton, Black Power, p. 17.

17. Philip G. Altbach and Gail P. Kelly, eds., Education and Colonialism (New York: Longman, 1978), pp. 20-21.

18. Woodson, The Mis-Education of the Negro, p. 78.

19. J. M. McPherson, "White Liberals and Black Power in Negro Education, 1865-1915," American Historical Review 75 (June 1970): 1357-86; and J. John Harris et al., "A Historical Perspective of the Emergence of Higher Education in Black Colleges," Journal of Black Studies 6 (1975): 55-68.

20. For extensive documentation on this issue, see Michael Harrington, The Other America (New York: Macmillan, 1970); idem, The Twilight of Capitalism (New York: Simon and Schuster, 1977); Sidney Wilhelm, Who Needs the Negro? (Cambridge, Mass.: Schenkman, 1970); and Thomas Pettigrew, Racial Discrimination in the United States (New York: Harper & Row, 1976).

21. Yette, The Choice, pp. 90-168.

22. Rodney, How Europe Underdeveloped Africa, pp. 12, 21, 22.

23. James D. Cockcroft, Andre Gunder Frank, and Dale L. Johnson, Dependence and Underdevelopment: Latin America's Political Economy (New York: Doubleday Anchor, 1972), p. 3.

24. Ester Boserup, Woman's Role in Economic Development (London: George Allen and Unwin, 1970), pp. 53-56; and Leith Mullings, "Women and Economic Change in Africa," in Women in Africa: Studies in Social and Economic Change, ed. Nancy J. Hafkin and Edna G. Bay (Stanford, Calif.: Stanford University Press, 1976), pp. 242-43.

25. Boserup, Woman's Role in Economic Development, pp. 53-56.

26. Ibid., pp. 91, 92, 99, 178, 179; Kenneth Little, African Women in Towns (London: Cambridge University Press, 1973), pp.

29-30; and Mullings, "Women and Economic Change in Africa," pp. 248-50.

27. Ida Faye Rousseau, "African Women: Identity Crisis? Some Observations on Education and the Changing Role of Women in Sierra Leone and Zaire," in Women Cross-Culturally: Change and Challenge, ed. Ruby Rohrlich-Leavitt (The Hague, Netherlands: Mouton, 1975), p. 44.

28. Mullings, "Women and Economic Change in Africa," p. 240.

29. Rodney, How Europe Underdeveloped Africa, p. 248; and Denise Paulme, ed., Women of Tropical Africa (Berkeley: University of California Press, 1963), p. 94.

30. Mullings, "Women and Economic Change in Africa," p. 254.

31. Rousseau, "African Women: Identity Crisis?" p. 47.

32. Marjorie Mbilinyi, "The State of Women in Tanzania," Canadian Journal of African Studies 6 (1972): 373-75; Beverly Lindsay, "Sociocultural Factors Influencing Career Choices of Kenyan Women?" The Kenya Education Review 2 (1975): 120.

33. Beverly Lindsay et al., "Minority Women in America," in The Study of Women: Enlarging Perspectives of Social Reality, ed. Eloise Snyder (New York: Harper & Row, 1979).

REFERENCES

Altbach, Philip G., and Gail P. Kelly, eds. Education and Colonialism. New York: Longman, 1978.

Boserup, Ester. Woman's Role in Economic Development. London: George Allen and Unwin, 1970.

Brozan, Nadine. "A Life for Underprivileged Girls: Fantasies of Bright Futures." New York Times, March 26, 1977, p. L-9.

Carmichael, Stokely, and Charles Hamilton. Black Power: The Politics of Liberation. New York: Random House, 1967.

Carnoy, Martin. Education as Cultural Imperialism. New York: David McKay, 1974.

Carnoy, Martin, ed. Schooling in a Corporate Society: The Political Economy of Education in America. New York: David McKay, 1975.

Clark, Kenneth. Dark Ghetto. New York: Harper & Row, 1965.

Cockcroft, James D., Andre Gunder Frank, and Dale L. Johnson. Dependence and Underdevelopment: Latin America's Political Economy. New York: Doubleday Anchor, 1972.

DuBois, W. E. B. Color and Democracy: Colonies and Peace. New York: Harcourt, Brace, 1945.

Fuller, Hoyt W. "Notes From a Sixth Pan-African Journal." Black World 23 (1974): 70-88.

Garrett, James. "A Historical Sketch, The Sixth Pan-African Congress." Black World 26 (1975): 4-20.

Harrington, Michael. The Other America. New York: Macmillan, 1970.

_____. The Twilight of Capitalism. New York: Simon and Schuster, 1977.

Harris, J. John, et al. "A Historical Perspective of the Emergence of Higher Education in Black Colleges." Journal of Black Studies 6 (1975): 55-68.

Horowitz, Irving Louis. Three Worlds of Development: The Theory and Practice of International Stratification. New York: Oxford University Press, 1972.

International Women's Year. World Conference Documents. CIWY/9/E, June 18, 1975.

_____. World Conference Documents. CIWY/9/E, June 18-19, 1975.

_____. World Conference Documents. E/Conf. 66/3/add. 3, pp. 10, 11, 14, 15.

_____. World Conference Documents. OPI/CESI/Note IWY/13, September 13, 1974.

_____. World Conference Documents. Press Release, CIWY/10/E, June 19, 1975, p. 5. New York: UNIFO Publishers, LTD., 1976.

Lindsay, Beverly. "Sociocultural Factors Influencing Career Choices of Kenyan Women?" The Kenya Education Review 2 (1975): 120-28.

Lindsay, Beverly, et al. "Minority Women in America." In The Study of Women: Enlarging Perspectives of Social Reality, edited by Eloise Snyder. New York: Harper & Row, 1979.

Little, Kenneth. African Women in Towns. London: Cambridge University Press, 1973.

McPherson, J. M. "White Liberals and Black Power in Negro Education, 1865-1915." American Historical Review 75 (June 1970): 1357-86.

Mbilinyi, Marjorie. "The State of Women in Tanzania." Canadian Journal of African Studies 6 (1972): 371-77.

Mullings, Leith. "Women and Economic Change in Africa." In Women in Africa: Studies in Social and Economic Change, edited by Nancy J. Hafkin and Edna G. Bay. Stanford, Calif.: Stanford University Press, 1976.

Pahlavi, Ashraf. "And Thus Passeth International Women's Year." New York Times, January 5, 1976, p. 29.

Paulme, Denise, ed. Women of Tropical Africa. Berkeley: University of California Press, 1963.

Pettigrew, Thomas. Racial Discrimination in the United States. New York: Harper & Row, 1976.

Rodney, Walter. How Europe Underdeveloped Africa. Dar es Salaam, Tanzania: Tanzania Publishing, 1972.

Rousseau, Ida Faye. "African Women: Identity Crisis? Some Observations on Education and the Changing Role of Women in Sierra Leone and Zaire." In Women Cross-Culturally: Change and Challenge, edited by Ruby Rohrlich-Leavitt. The Hague, Netherlands: Mouton, 1975.

Surmuri, Patricia T. Japanese Colonial Education in Taiwan. Cambridge, Mass.: Harvard University Press, 1977.

Wilhelm, Sidney. Who Needs the Negro? Cambridge, Mass.: Schenkman, 1970.

Wilson, William J. Power, Racism, and Privilege: Race Relations in Theoretical and Sociohistorical Perspectives. New York: Free Press, 1973.

Woodson, Carter G. The Mis-Education of the Negro. Washington, D.C.: Associated, 1933, 1969.

Yette, Samuel F. The Choice: The Issue of Black Survival in America. New York: Putnam, 1971.

I
WOMEN IN DEVELOPING COUNTRIES

INTRODUCTION TO PART I

Beverly Lindsay

THE AFRICAN CONTINENT

Chapter 1 presented several conceptual views of colonialism, neocolonialism, internal colonialism, internal neocolonialism, dependency, and development and their related features. The lives of African women can be explained in part through these conceptual views as they relate to social, educational, and economic institutions. The combinations of social conditions evinced through the views vary and they are unique. Shelby Lewis's chapter on African women and national development challenges and further explains several of these conceptual views. In Chapter 1 the author cites several examples that anthropologists and sociologists have sometimes contended represented examples of relative equality between the sexes in social, economic, and political life prior to the advent of colonialism. Lewis presents several alternative and sometimes mutually exclusive views, beginning with the antitraditionalist perspective that reexamines some of the material regarding equality for African women.

Unfortunately, colonialism provided social transformations in African society that depressed the status of women, as we observed in Chapter 1. The positions of African women must be examined within the context of various African societies and, to a small degree, compared with those of more technologically advanced societies. Relative social context is an important view, as Lewis discusses in presenting the arguments of the relativist positions. Relativists provide some insight since they are critical of the tendency to compare the positions of African and other Third World women with those of women influenced by Western modes of development. Comparisons with the West can result in incorporating additional contemporary negative components of women's inequities into African society, and this can also be the situation in Asia, Latin America, and the Caribbean. In their respective chapters, Lewis, Lois Adams, and Beverly Lindsay concur that new approaches are needed to examine the roles of African women in various sectors of the society in relation to social development. Lewis focuses on women in the traditional sector of the African society; Adams discusses women in traditional and contemporary society; and Lindsay examines the roles of women in what has often been viewed as the modern sectors of society.

When examining current roles of African women in the traditional sector, it may be helpful to keep in mind that sexist views coupled with economic oppression have depressed the status of women. Lewis maintains that rural women have always comprised an indispensable component of the economy. Yet, colonial sexism, which was later supported by African men, often led to the exclusion of African women's direct participation in farming cash crops. As a result of being denied direct involvement, women's economic contributions may not be calculated in development plans and may be overlooked when agricultural, technological, or industrial programs and innovations are introduced to a locale. Men are the beneficiaries. Hence, women's oppressed economic status is further perpetuated by national development plans and men's views that their wives' activities should be confined to the home or related domestic activities.

In Chapter 3, which deals with women in Zaire, Lois Adams provides additional examples of sex and class subjugation of the position of African women. She presents material indicating that no single measure of status can be applied to the majority of Zairian women. Adams contends that many of women's economic and social activities are not always recognized in the public sphere. She also discusses how the educational system in Zaire perpetuates females' inferior socioeconomic status by automatically limiting employment options.

Beverly Lindsay's chapter (Chapter 4) on African professional women, with special emphasis on Kenyan women, enumerates the various laws, policies, and practices that restrict employment opportunities for women. She points out that closely related to these formal restrictions are the sociocultural views and attitudes of families, which may be sexist in that women's positions are often viewed in terms of their domestic roles, not their employment or public roles. Further, she examines the various ways in which their formal educational opportunities are limited. Thus, Lindsay demonstrates the interactions among social, educational, and economic institutional patterns that perpetuate the oppressed status of Kenyan women vis à vis sexism and economic conditions.

THE ASIAN CONTINENT

Moving to the Asian continent provides additional material supporting the perspectives that sex and class are paramount issues in the lives of contemporary Third World women. In Bee-Lan Chan Wang's chapter (Chapter 5) on Chinese women, sex and class are viewed within the context of the People's Republic of China, Taiwan, and Malaysia. These countries have differed during this century in their approaches to social and economic development.

During various periods in the development of the People's Republic of China since its independence in 1949, for instance, the position of Chinese women has shifted due to changing political and economic tenets. The Great Leap Forward in the late 1950s and the Great Proletarian Cultural Revolution in the middle and late 1960s ushered in periods of economic growth and production, and with them came opportunities for women to enter the agricultural and industrial labor forces. Wang maintains that, on the whole, the several ideological policies and subsequent programs have improved the status of women in the People's Republic of China since liberation.

On the island of Taiwan, she argues that sociocultural attitudes have encouraged inequities between the sexes and, further, suggests that the capitalist economic system has little need to provide equal employment/economic opportunities between the sexes; so capitalism encourages family views that advocate restrictive female roles.

Malaysia, Wang's third topic, is inhabited by a substantial percentage of Chinese people. The Chinese are more urbanized and economically advanced than the Malays and Indians. Sociocultural values associated with particular ethnic groups appear to account for some of the different groups' strivings for urbanization and economic advancement. As a result Chinese women are more frequent participants in the modern sectors of the economy than other ethnic women, although their participation is not comparable to that of men from the several ethnic groups. It appears, however, that Chinese girls in Malaysia are not as concerned with education as an economic investment as are males. Females have internalized social attitudes about their sex and also perceive restrictive social and economic roles in comparison with males.

The position of women in India is examined in light of the interplay between sex and class by Tonia K. Devon in Chapter 6, which examines political life in northern India. While women's political views and participation are influenced by the media (for example, radio and newspaper), family and work conditions also exert their influences. Women indicate that their families' and society's views of the female sex do not encourage their extensive involvement in political and related activities.

THE CARIBBEAN AND LATIN AMERICA

Similar to the presentation on Indian women, Gloria Joseph's chapter (Chapter 7) on Caribbean women describes their positions through case studies and empirical data. Caribbean women from several islands are represented in Joseph's case studies of Black women from various socioeconomic backgrounds. Race, sex, and

class discrimination—triple jeopardy—permeate the lives of Black
Caribbean women. Only a few have acquired advanced socioeconomic
positions. The situation, however, is considerably different in Cuba.

According to Johnnetta Cole in Chapter 8, which deals with women
in Cuba, dynamic social conditions in Cuba have produced some authentic changes in the status of women. The improved status of Cuban
women is due to its socialist political and economic system that advocates and promotes equal policies and programs for all, eradicating
invidious class distinctions based upon inequitable economic differentials. Further, the subsequent passage of laws establishing maternity benefits and child care facilities has enabled women to participate in the public economic sphere. Cole contends, however, that
much still needs to be done to liberate women domestically. But as
egalitarian views toward women gain a foothold in the domestic realm
and as comprehensive sociopolitical changes occur, the status of
women will improve even more.

In many other Latin American societies, Nora Jazquez Wieser
contends (Chapter 9) that sociopolitical and economic changes are not
occurring to enhance the status of women. In fact, she asserts,
repressive and stagnant social conditions are still the norm. Improving their status necessitates the eradication of oppressive economic
conditions. Yet all women are not supportive of changing economic
conditions, because current class distinctions among Latin American
women prevent those from affluent socioeconomic backgrounds from
identifying with peasant and other poor women. Perhaps if changes
in economic conditions were evinced in the society's internal scene,
there might be an increasing identification of affluent women with those
less fortunate, since sexism affects all women.

RACISM IN DEVELOPING COUNTRIES

Are race and racism still major factors in the lives of women
in developing countries? Racism is a distinct characteristic of colonialism and neocolonialism. Various writers have argued that
racism served as an initial justification for colonialism and later
neocolonialism.[1] Race may refer to a human group that defines itself and/or is defined by others as different from other groups by
virtue of innate and immutable physical characteristics. Hence, a
social view of groups based upon physical characteristics is important when defining race. Similarly, an ethnic group defines itself
and/or is defined by others based upon cultural characteristics such
as language or religion.[2] A powerful group espousing prejudiced
views is able to perpetuate racism, which may be viewed as a special
criterion of socioeconomic stratification. It was racism, not ethnicity,

which helped Europeans to subjugate African, Asian, Latin American, and Caribbean people.

We recognize, however, that ethnicity still plays an important role in domestic affairs of some developing nations. For example, the civil wars in Nigeria were based, to a large extent, upon ethnic animosities (during the civil war of the late 1960s, the Ibos wanted to establish a state, but the Yorubas wanted to maintain a viable nation —not colonize Ibos). Colonization in Africa was a European practice. Many atrocities committed under the recently deposed Idi Amin regime in Uganda were based upon ethnicity; however, colonization was not evident. Ethnic distinctions also exist among Asian people as observed in Wang's chapter. Again, colonization in Asia, for the most part, was practiced by Europeans.

As the formal colonial period recedes farther into the background, direct manifestations of racism seem to be less prevalent in the internal domestic affairs of nations, as policies and programs of indigenization are introduced, which racism prevented in the early stages of independence. One basic goal of indigenization is to ensure that indigenous persons occupy various rungs of the employment ladder, ranging from the positions of key policy makers, planners, and administrators to service and support personnel. It has resulted in African males, rather than white men, being employed in various positions. African men have usually been the beneficiaries of indigenization—not African women, as indicated in chapters by Adams and Lindsay.

Racism, however, still affects the lives of people in developing nations in relation to historical and contemporary international economic issues, profoundly influencing women in particular. It is hoped that these chapters will shed some light on the problems of Third World women and suggest ways in which they may be remedied.

NOTES

1. W. E. B. DuBois, Color and Democracy: Colonies and Peace (New York: Harcourt, Brace, 1945); Samuel F. Yette, The Choice: The Issue of Black Survival in America (Berkeley, Calif.: Berkeley Publishing, 1971); Donald J. Harris, "The Black Ghetto as Colony: A Theoretical Critique and Alternative Formulation," Review of Black Political Economy 2 (1972): 3-33; Robert L. Allen, Black Awakening in Capitalist America (Garden City, N.Y.: Doubleday/ Anchor Books, 1970); Walter Rodney, How Europe Underdeveloped Africa (Dar es Salaam, Tanzania: Tanzania Publishing, 1972); and Joan W. Moore, "Colonialism: The Case of the Mexican American," in Introduction to Chicano Studies, ed. Livie Isauro Duran and H.

Russell Bernard (New York: Macmillan, 1973). These writers do not argue that race is the <u>sole</u> factor per se that led to colonialism. Rather, race and/or ethnicity along with basic economic factors, for example, must be viewed in conjunction with each other—as discussed in Chapter 1 and later in this chapter.

2. Pierre L. van den Berghe, <u>Race and Racism: A Comparative Perspective</u> (New York: John Wiley & Sons, 1978), pp. 9, 10, 22, 24.

2
AFRICAN WOMEN AND
NATIONAL DEVELOPMENT

Shelby Lewis

> African women have always worked in the fields, in the
> markets and in the homes of our countries. We know this
> so well that we too often take for granted the enormous
> actual and potential contribution of women to the develop-
> ment of our continent and its people.
>
> Robert Gardiner,
> Women of Africa: Today and Tomorrow

However one views the status of women or their role in economic
activity in Africa, it seems clear that the position of women must be
placed in the wider context of the whole society. Women's emancipation is meaningless unless the social and economic myths throughout society are dispelled and exploitation of all groups ceases. We
cannot speak of the oppression and exploitation of women without at
the same time speaking of class and racial oppression. For the
emancipation of women is not simply an act of charity toward females;
it is not the result of a group of humanitarians changing their attitudes
and practices toward women; it is the prerequisite of the struggle of
any society to achieve liberation, democracy, and social progress.[1]
To pay little attention to the "problems of women" is tantamount to
ignoring one of the largest and most oppressed segments of society.[2]
For development to take place, women must share in the national effort (and the socialist revolution), and the improvement of the status
of women must become an integral part of national development programs if the natural and human resources of the nation are to be
utilized fully for economic and social progress.

Calls for the inclusion of women in national development began
in the early 1960s* and will, undoubtedly, continue until women have

---

*Similar calls resulted from such conferences as the Seminar
on the Status of Women in Family Law, Bogotá, Colombia, 1963;

31

become completely integrated into both the tasks and benefits of national programs. Largely resulting from UN efforts, many national, regional, and international programs have been initiated to reverse the effects of centuries of misdirected policy and practice. Many of the new programs, however, reflect an absence of systematic research about women and the reality of their conditions. They also reflect the presence of improper analyses and generally fail to incorporate the changes in systems, delivery services, and allocations necessary to modify attitudes and practices for reversing the effects of historic neglect.

Of critical importance in this connection is the realization that these recent efforts to integrate women into national economies are based on the false (but widely subscribed to) premise that women do not presently play important roles in national development. Seldom considered is the fact that improper assessments of the role of women in development and failure to acknowledge women's contributions have biased the outcome of development studies and plans. In addition, it should be pointed out that the uncritical acceptance of the Western definition of work and development has led to the omission of women from development programs and a lack of recognition by planners of their work activity. As a result, the agricultural and home-related responsibilities undertaken by rural African women have been defined as noneconomic activity.

A number of contemporary publications[3] on Third World women provide excellent commentary on the manner in which development planners, scholars, and governmental officials have historically neglected, excluded, underestimated, and misrepresented women across the globe. And, in spite of the abundant data[4] that indicate that the women of Africa grow, harvest, process, market, and cook the food that feeds the nation, development plans never seem to reflect women's activities accurately. Why is this so and what are the implications of this reality?

This chapter aims at exploring basic assumptions extant about women and development and indicating reasons why it seems logical to reject these assumptions as invalid for African development. An attempt will be made to discuss such factors as development theories;

Seminar on the Status of Women, Lomé, Togo, 1964; Seminar on Measures Required for Advancement of Women, Manila, Philippines, 1966; International Conference on Human Rights, Tehran, Iran, 1968; Seminar on Civic and Political Education of Women, Accra, Ghana, 1968; Seminar on the Status of Women and Family Planning, Istanbul, Turkey, 1972; and International Conference of Women, Mexico City, Mexico, 1975.

theories about the role of women in society; the actual contributions of African women to development; possible explanations for the historic exclusion of women from the tasks and benefits of development programs; and, finally, the commitment of African states not only to recognizing the role of women in development but to inducing the social, economic, and political changes that lead to the improvement of their condition. In effect, the following types of questions will be posed and addressed: What is the level or degree of female participation in national development efforts in Africa? To what extent is that participation recognized by observers? What accounts for the failure to acknowledge the contributions of women to development? How do African women view their role? What measures are suggested by women to improve their status in society? What efforts are national leaders making to provide women with the benefits enjoyed by males in their states? What are the deficiencies inherent in the present approaches to development? And, what are the consequences for national and continental development?

DIFFERENTIAL PERSPECTIVES ON DEVELOPMENT

As background for framing this analysis, it might be useful to look at the variety of existing views and misconceptions regarding the concept of development. Understanding what development is and who is of necessity a part of the development effort might alleviate some of the problems that lead to erroneous assumptions about the roles of specific groups in national development.

Unfortunately, development is all too often seen as a function of how such factors as capital formation and technological skills interact. Since the capital and technology are usually "Western," development is, therefore, seen as the process of Westernization.[5] Most mainstream economists equate development with economic growth. This view pits the economic and social conditions of developing areas against those of the West and measures growth by the degree of likeness. The distribution of income and the relative position of groups within the economic and social structure are not seen as important in determining whether a given nation is developing (or growing). The Western orientation for describing and analyzing development places primary emphasis on the growth of the society's industrial sector. Such development is determined by indexes of real wealth, capital growth, improved living conditions, and the like. Societies themselves do not develop; rather, certain leading sectors develop that, in turn, cause a change in societal patterns.[6]

Progressive scholars find this restricted conceptualization of development unacceptable. Samari Amin, for example, notes that there is a critical error—namely, the essential fact is left out. The underdeveloped countries form part of a world system and the history of their integration into that system forged their special structure. This structure, he contends, has nothing in common with what prevailed before their integration into the modern world.[7] Amin and other critics[8] of the Western model feel that the concept should not be limited to industrial factors. Instead, it should be seen ultimately as the "development" of human resources with the real test of success being whether the majority of the people benefit by a particular change or advance.[9] The way change is brought about, the direction of that change, and the ultimate beneficiaries of the change are pertinent concerns for the measurement and evaluation of development.

If terms such as dependency, developing, and underdevelopment are pitted against terms like developed, imperialist, and Western, the corresponding relationship between the deterioration of conditions in the Third World and the improvement of conditions in the Western world may be shown. To assume that new nations will develop as long as they remain dependencies of the "developed" nations is to misunderstand the reason for their underdevelopment and the nature of "development." Thus, the concept of dependency should be tied to exploitation. And, it should be concluded that the absence of exploitation is one step toward development. Added to this should be the realization that the importation of technology does not necessarily lead to development; and the technology imported should benefit the majority rather than a few. The principal objective of development (this alternative use of the term) is the activation of all sectors of the population and economy in the interest of the nation. People must be involved. As Walter Rodney notes:

> The capacity for dealing with the environment is depen-
> dent on the extent to which the people understand the
> laws of nature; on the extent to which they put that un-
> derstanding into practice by devising tools (technology),
> and on the manner in which work is organized.[10] [Em-
> phasis added]

If development was viewed in this manner, it seems that the role of women in development might be perceived and recorded differently. Presently, the concept is consistently used to exclude women and their activity from the development sphere. Reasons for this vary. Some authors suggest that this exclusion is due to the prevailing social formation that defines women and their contributions in a sexist and class-biased manner. Oppression and discrimination against women, it is felt, are characteristics of the exploitative social-economic formations of slavery, feudalism, and capitalism.[11]

An alternative explanation suggests that development plans tend to by-pass the rural populations in Africa where most women are found. In the absence of a conscious rural-agricultural development policy, the female majority is relegated to a position of relative unimportance. Even in cases where agriculture is consciously designed, those selected for participation in the development effort are largely men.[12] But, for whatever reason, women are neglected in development plans, and the conceptualization of "development" leads to the exclusion of women's activities in development programs. Perhaps an exploration of the views of women in developing areas, accent on Africa, will divulge the rationale underlying the development theory and policies characteristic of African states.

BASIC ASSUMPTIONS ABOUT THE STATUS OF WOMEN IN AFRICAN SOCIETY

There are several basic assumptions in the literature about the status of women in African society. These assumptions dictate the status of and specific roles assigned to women in development as well as the nature of the recommendations for improving the conditions of the African woman. Though a variety of subtheses logically grow out of these assumptions, we will examine only those that have utility for explaining the neglect and/or exclusion of women from development tasks and benefits.

Basic Assumption One: The Degredation Thesis

Assumption one is that women in Africa are oppressed, backward, and marginal. We will discuss three variant subtheses of this basic assumption.

Subthesis One: The Antitraditionalist Perspective

Those scholars who equate Westernization with development and progress usually see African culture and traditions as primitive and negative and, therefore, basic causes of the backward, oppressed, and marginal status of women. These scholars are generally anti-traditionalists. They assert that among the characteristics common to most African communities that give a certain degree of homogeneity to the continent the one that stands out most is the social inferiority of women.[13]

As a general rule, antitraditionalists see Christianity and the influences of the West as providing significant improvements in the lot of African women. But this is not the case, as they occupy a very

minor place in the social systems of Africa, which can be shown in
many ways. For example, the system of polygamy is seen as one of
the practices that are incompatible with equality. [14] Attitudes, customs, and some legal acts legitimate the unequal status of women in
Africa, and the rights guaranteed women in many African constitutions
do not change this reality very much. The attitudes, customs, and
traditions must be changed, contend the antitraditionalists. Further,
they argue, legislative changes are a precondition for equality in Africa, but they do not guarantee women equality. When laws change,
they must be accompanied by revolutionary efforts to change the
habits, customs, practices, and beliefs rooted in the minds of men
and women for hundreds of years[15]—that is, traditions must change
if women are to gain equality in Africa. Traditions that allow too
early marriages, the use of small girls as household and agricultural
helpers who are kept from school, and the setting up of a scale that
lowers the value of wives who are educated and designates women as
water carriers and beasts of burden are seen as contrary to equality
by the antitraditionalist. [16] By changing these customs, it is felt,
society can be transformed so that women can engage in gainful employment, take advantage of educational opportunities, improve their
health, and view themselves as valuable human beings.

Subthesis Two: The Anti-Western Perspective

Anti-Westerners feel that the encroachment by colonialists on
land owned by Africans had direct repercussions for women, namely,
the undermining of their economic power. While the traditional economic role of women did not give them political dominance, it guaranteed them power over the allocation of resources. [17] Traditionally,
African women owned as personal property the fruits of their labor.
The coming of Western man and capitalism have increased their dependency on husbands, fathers, and sons. Capitalism reinforced the
emerging patriarchal system. With the Western invaders, women's
traditional roles were relegated to social and domestic categories. [18]

Ivy Matsepe suggests that the evidence that the integration of
Africa into the capitalist system has produced social and economic
setbacks is overwhelming. [19] Westernization did not alter the rigidity
of the family structure as regards women; instead it led to even
greater sexual inequality characterized by diverse manifestations of
discrimination and oppression bound up with the private ownership
of property and the division of society into social classes. [20]

The anti-Westerners' recommendation for improving the conditions of women is a return to the communal system. Some suggest
the replacement of the capitalist system with socialism.

Subthesis Three: The Socialist Perspective

The socialist theory proposes that women are indeed oppressed and marginal in African societies; but their conditions result from both traditionalism and capitalism. They contend that traditional attitudes of men toward women, religious beliefs and practices (especially Islamic practices), and customary laws contributed to the exploitation of women, while capitalism through Western colonialism increased the exploitation, extended the discriminatory customs, and even initiated new discriminatory laws. Legislative changes, education, employment opportunities, and a change in attitudes are necessary but not sufficient to ensure equality and justice for women. It is essential, they hold, to understand the exact nature of female oppression in order to analyze it meaningfully. And, the underlying factor behind female oppression, whatever the variations in its manifestation, is private property.[21]

In order to gain freedom for women, socialists contend the individual family unit must be abolished. This enables the reintegration of women into production. Private housekeeping should be transformed into a social industry, domestic economy should be collectivized, kindergartens should be created for children, and popular restaurants should be opened for feeding the population. In essence, the present economic order must be changed and a socialist order put in its place if women are to gain equality in African society.[22]

Analysis

In sum, basic assumption one—namely, that women in Africa are oppressed, backward, and marginal (in a state of degradation)— is shared by both reformists and revolutionaries. The significant difference is that the two groups posit different causes and solutions for female degradation. The antitraditionalists see the primary cause of female oppression in traditional customs and practices and would opt for remedying the problem with legislation, education, and general reform of rural productive methods. The movement, as they see it, should be from primitive culture and technology to modern culture, that is, Westernization. Policy changes and improvements in working conditions and opportunities are keys to ending discrimination against women. On the other hand, the anti-Westerners see nothing wrong with the status of women in traditional African society. They hold that communalism was an equitable way of life, not deserving of harsh criticism. For them, Western influences, the capitalist mode of production, and a monied economy led to the undermining of women's valued roles in Africa. Anti-Westerners feel that improvements in working conditions, improved educational opportunities, and the transfer of technology and legislative changes will provide women with a certain degree of equality in African society; but a return to the communal way of life is necessary if full equality is to accrue to them. The socialists, however, are not content with the explanations or solutions offered by the other critics. They see the failure of African society to reach the right stage of productive relations—that is, to institute socialist systems—as the cause of female oppression. They assert that revolution and the transformation of the entire society and its structures will gain for women the freedom that they seek.

Basic Assumption Two: Relativism Thesis

A less championed assumption about the status of women in African society asserts that women in Africa are no worse off than women elsewhere in the world, and in some respects they are better off—the relativism theory. [23] The argument is that women had equal status with men in traditional society, especially in the economic realm. Second, African women have virtually the same constitutional status as do other women, and, thus, under the law they are no more degraded than Western women. Third, women are unequal in Africa primarily because of the influences of colonialism, which resulted in the assignment of Western roles to African women. Finally, the introduction of Western technology led to a shift in emphasis from the rural to the urban areas such that the real position and power of rural women is simply not recognized—even by most women themselves. The relativists assert that a number of serious misconceptions exist about the status and role of African women because of the comparison with Western society. Many of the misconceptions were spread by missionaries, colonial administrators, and anthropologists who misunderstood the African scene and/or opposed what they saw because it did not fit into their Christian/Western model of how men and women should relate.

Duties and roles were based on communal living in traditional African society and social relations were equitable. The arrangement provided security and clearly defined positions for all members of the society (including men) without attributing inferiority or superiority to the role of any group. Women's rights could not be abridged by men, and kinship and descent were often determined through the female line. However, the relativists note that with the evolution of the system of patriarchy antagonisms began to develop between the sexes and between groups. [24] Western influences aided the development of this system, and, like the anti-Westerners, the relativists blame the West for the decline of women's status in Africa. They further contend that it is difficult to generalize and characterize African women. They resent the lumping of them together as huddled and deprived masses. It should be recognized, they argue, that African women have various habits, attitudes, and values, depending upon the section of the continent where they live. In addition, there is little doubt that women have been at the center of production and family life in all areas of Africa. To see them as doomed to the silence of the unseen and as a group relegated to the lowest rung of the social ladder is to misunderstand the African reality. [25]

Most people are so caught up in the swiftness of change in Africa that they are unable to place African women in proper perspective. African women themselves appear to have lost sight of their actual roles and statuses in their respective societies. And, as Lusibu Nkanga warns:

> As long as African women don't realize that they can act without men, that they constitute a social force, a pres-sure group, there will be no change. And I say this whatever their traditional background. But this spe-cifically applies to those who have basic economic power (that is, produce food, work the fields) they must understand that their society cannot eat without them. [26]

In summary, the relativists contend that sexism exists through-out the "civilized" world and the relative development of technology and political institutions determine the way that sexism is manifested in the working conditions and social position of women. The status of women is relative. African women play crucial roles in the economic and social life of their countries, but the analyses of these roles by the West have been lacking in facts and understanding. What faces African women, they hold, is a problem of acknowledgment, recog-nition, and introduction of technology into areas where women can benefit. The relativists would recommend action to relieve the in-equalities that presently exist in Africa (and they admit that there are inequalities) through policy changes, improved working conditions, education, modernization, and improved economic opportunities for women.

CONTRIBUTIONS OF AFRICAN WOMEN TO DEVELOPMENT

Development and modernization theorists have neglected the vital role of women, especially rural women, in the economic life of African nations. This neglect has obfuscated the nature of national development and has resulted in failures to prescribe national solu-tions to economic and social problems. It has also caused the real nature of capitalist exploitation to be overlooked, underestimated, and oversimplified.[27] And, not only is the economic role of women underestimated, it seems clear that their political, cultural, and social contributions are also overlooked. The problem is most acute in the rural areas where approximately 80 percent of African women work in agriculture. Prominent in this group of rural women are those who must find means to either fully support or partially assist in the financing of their households.

Rural women have always formed the most productive sector of African society. They are indispensable, yet they are marginalized in development plans. An example of such marginalization is the manner in which modern equipment and skills for farming have been geared to the expressed needs of males, resulting in more, rather than less, work for women.

Statistics compiled concerning work activity done by women are biased. The figures fail to indicate the ratio of women to men workers in Africa. They often fail to show that women make up one-half to two-thirds of the total African work force. Further, they seldom give significance in data gathering to the fact that women are land cultivators, usually with primitive implements[28] and are also found in the professional and urban work forces. However, the fact that their numbers in the modern work force are insignificant compared with their percentage of the population is taken to mean that women do not work.

In the rural areas of the continent where a majority of the women live, African women are fully active in economic activities but are not recorded as such by those who compile economic data for the states. Family food production is the most common task undertaken by women. Even in areas where men once played a role in clearing the land, male migration to urban areas or to other countries for employment has left the entire responsibility to women. Many women are in fact, if not in law, household heads and have sole responsibility for family welfare.[29]

This set of circumstances is part of the reason why it is necessary to reexamine the actual role of women in development and harness all development potential. Over 50 percent of the potential to be harnessed is female—women who are only marginally touched by the benefits of technological change and represent an unassessed force for the new social orders of "developing" African societies.[30]

In addition to being a food producer, rural and some urban women are distributors of goods. Approximately 60 percent of the market trade in Africa is done by women. But the perceptions and role definitions of these female entrepreneurs are distorted. Evidence points to the historical pattern of development in the market trade prior to the twentieth century being predominately female. As one

African woman noted about the historical and contemporary importance of market women in Zaire: "If one day the market women decided not to go to market, Kinshasa, the capital city, would close down. The economy would be paralysed."[31]

Women also are employed in nonfarming occupations in Africa. They are engaged in various levels of commercial activity, but few are found outside the local and national trading areas due to the attitudes, restrictions, and constraints they face when attempting to go into large-scale businesses. But, they are very active in the prescribed areas. Usually without a fixed stall or shop, market women sell the quantities of goods that people can afford and thereby offer a needed service to the society. Governments have exercised insufficient imagination regarding the small-scale industries that women run, especially in the rural areas. Women seldom have the opportunity to acquire the skills necessary to enlarge their businesses or share in the benefits of modernization.

The introduction of technology in Africa may have had the unanticipated and unrecognized effects of increasing women's problems and their work loads while giving them few if any monetary rewards. At the rural level, new managerial methods have had no effect on women. The actual division of labor is not understood nor taken into account as a factor in development; thus, new techniques and tools have unforeseen impacts on the family labor force.[32] In fact, it is fair to say that very few changes that were of real benefit to women were introduced along with the transfer of technology. Those changes that were introduced aided in the perpetuation of the dominance of men. Caroline Williams notes that, "A paradoxical situation now exists in which the women, on one hand, as major producers of subsistence crops . . . are expected to cope with the increasing demand of subsistence food brought about by population growth and technological progress while on the other hand, they are denied the technical and social opportunities to do so."[33]

If we examine the attitudes that accompany the introduction of new technology into Africa, we might discover some clues as to why certain jobs are already identified by policy makers, technicians, and planners as "feminine" and others are open for men only.[34] This new technology, it would appear, has not been sufficiently adapted to the realities of Africa, and Western attitudes concerning male and female roles have been adopted along with the technology, usually to the detriment of women.

Even when surveying the modern sector of the economy, employment is defined in a manner that discriminates against women. When traditional sectors of the economy are surveyed (and the work that women do is quite impossible to overlook), it is the cash crops, especially export crops, that are classified as agricultural economic employment areas. Food produced by women is for subsistence purposes—it feeds the families of the nation. But because it is not generally sold, it is not measured in production figures; so, female producers are not "employed." In addition, work in the home in rural and urban areas is not considered employment. And, since women are largely found in household-related work and the production of food for local consumption, they are not counted in the work force of the nation. It is this sort of biased conceptualization of work that leads to the conclusion that women do not play a significant role in the development of their countries. If development planners continue to identify women as solely occupied in domestic duties, their true situation will remain hidden. Consequently, many possibilities for speeding up the pace of development will be overlooked.[35] As Marie-Helene LeFaucheux points out, "The many tasks a woman must perform, and above all her role as a mother, may ensure that she receive protection, respect, affection . . . but never authority."[36]

In summary, the issue that we are faced with in identifying the role of women in development is not the exclusion of women from participation in the economic sector, but the character and quality of that participation and the lack of recognition of women's contributions to economic development. Institutionally, women participate under discriminating conditions with unequal access to education. Economically, they receive minimal rewards for jobs performed. Thus, as a group, women are integrated into the economic life of the country but under highly disadvantageous conditions. An example of this is the classification of water and fuel portage, jobs performed by women, as household activities and not economic activities, while the men who lay the water pipes are always said to be economically active.[37] The traditional role of women in economic life is neither evident nor acknowledged in the national development plans for African countries. In addition, agricultural production by women within the subsistence sector of the economy is virtually ignored by Marxist and non-Marxist because it is not part of the modern industrial, wage-earning system. The role of women workers, their contributions, and their economic power are ignored or dismissed under conventional economic categories.[38] Changes in this conventional manner of analysis is essential if total development and participation of all sectors of the society are to occur. If men do not realize that it is to their benefit to integrate women at all levels in the process of development—not just by co-optation or tokenism—the only alternative for women is the exertion of pressure through use of their collectivity as a social force.[39]

Reasons for Nonrecognition of Female Contributions

Early development plans did not address the question of women's roles in national development. At the time that they were drawn up, in the early 1960s after the euphoria of independence, it was felt that all citizens were given equal rights in the various constitutions. This was assumed to be sufficient, as most nations sought to incorporate the sense of the Declaration of Human Rights in their legal statutes. For example, the Cameroon Constitution states that there will be no distinction based on sex, and so on, while the Central African Republic was explicit about men and women being equal under the law. The former French colonies generally cite the fundamental rights of all persons and/or the Universal Declaration when declaring that all citizens will be equal under the law. These legal provisions, like those in the West, are contradicted by numerous local statutes or customs and deal too broadly with the problem of sexism. Social, economic, and political attitudes and practices, informal agreements, and prejudices all conspire to prevent women from enjoying legally acknowledged rights. So, the assumption that legal provisions were sufficient to bring about equality of the sexes was obviously in error.

In African states that underwent protracted liberation struggles, the advance of social and economic rights for women is higher than in other states. For, as freedom fighters and participants in the struggle, women and men were transformed as part of that struggle.[40] The rights and dignity of each individual in the struggle were generally recognized by all concerned, and when independence was won, these transformed attitudes made the practice of sexism less of a problem than it proved to be in the areas where independence was negotiated.

In the countries where transformation through struggle did not take place, the legacy of oppression carried over into the independent period, where women faced additional barriers to advancement; they were now excluded from development planning and their work became characterized as noneconomic activity.

Another reason why the question of women was not addressed by early developers is the emphasis of these early plans on industrial development or modernization, while the activity of most women took place in the rural, agricultural area of the economy. When the move toward rural development became serious in the late 1960s, the question of the role of women was not so easy to avoid.

These early developers failed to understand, also, that the adoption and transfer of Western technology did not necessarily lead to development or prosperity. Most of this technology was transferred to the modern sector of the economy, and women, being in the traditional sector, were not considered essential to the development scheme.

The New Thrust

Faced with the false steps toward development and the discriminatory practices against women, African women today have begun innovating ways to consolidate and support each other. Mutual interest groups have been formed. In Nigeria, for instance, women have instituted a system where everyone in the group contributes to each person something that is needed until everyone gets what is needed (for example, house, loan, and so on).[41] These systems of mutual help are necessary because the political and economic institutions of African societies do not provide loans or encouragement in the way of training or legislation for women to advance.

Between 1963 and the International Women's Year, a number of UN conferences on the status of women were held in various Third World countries.* Recommendations following those conferences were similar. For example, women who attended the Regional Conference for women in Rabat in 1975 and those who attended the seminar on the status of women in Istanbul in 1972 called for the establishment of national and regional machinery to assist in promoting and influencing governmental and voluntary action in the advancement of females within the context of national development. The setting up of permanent national secretariats or technical women's bureaus to ensure participation of women in development planning and their integration into various sectors of the economy was also seen as essential to African women at the Rabat Conference.[42]

At about the same time that UN action began affecting African countries, many developed nations began to take up the women's cause. It should be noted, however, that prior to this period these "developed" powers sanctioned (directly or indirectly) and encouraged development policies that contributed to the neglect and exclusion of women from development planning, training programs, and plan implementation. However, UN agencies formed the vanguard in the international women's rights campaign.

In addition, the problems of the First Development Decade made clear the need to include women in the Second Development Decade planning. This meant that new approaches to development and new attitudes toward women were necessary to achieve the goals of the Second Development Decade, including recategorization of work to include nonwage earning activity. Redefinition of economic activity and special provisions for training workers who had been neglected in the past—women primarily—were to result from the new approaches.

FEMALE DEVELOPMENT:
THE CHALLENGE FACING AFRICAN NATIONS

What seems to be attempted at the national level is the integration of women into the economy. But, perhaps it is not integration

---

*A partial listing of these conferences was given earlier in the chapter.

per se that is called for, since such a move seems still to be based on the assumption that women are now outside the development effort. What appears to be needed is a thorough analysis of the work done by women and recognition and acknowledgment of the central role being played by African women in development. Once this is done it will be easier to develop plans that ensure for these women the benefits that others gain from change. Women are in need of concerted efforts to relieve the problems associated with the work that they do. By providing the skills and resources needed to improve the working conditions and productivity of women, the nation gains. There is a need to challenge boldly the narrow view of development that abounds. Women should and must demand a view that recognizes their role in the process and one that provides plans and programs that benefit them.

There are still a number of misconceptions about women's roles. While African nations espouse the notion of self-sufficiency, especially in food production, the group that now feeds most of the families—women—is still only marginally included in the decision-making process and only cursorily considered when estimates and plans for self-sufficiency are programmed. An accurate assessment of the female role suggests that they do the work and contribute significantly to political and social advancement in their nations. They are entitled to the power that goes along with the role.

Today, many African women are calling for a radical break with the sexism of the past. They are calling upon their governments to establish departments that address the concerns of women. They feel that they, and their countries, would benefit directly from a policy aimed at upgrading the basic knowledge of the thousands of women who toil in the rural areas and live in the urban areas but because of illiteracy and lack of skills never reach their full potentials. These women assert that the integration of women into national development should not be based on former myths, for it can, they realize, mean that co-optation may still become part of the established order and, therefore, controlled by it. "You can be well integrated into your economy as a slave."[43] The critical point here is whether the new developmental thrust in Africa and the integration of women into the economy will restrict instead of enhance or harm instead of benefit women.

Special efforts by governments, voluntary agencies, and international organizations are necessary to the productive integration of women into the social, political, and economic order in their respective countries. They are necessary for a number of related reasons. To begin with, the role of African female entrepreneurs will expand and enhance local and national market flows only if there is a degree of understanding on the part of planners and legislators about the significance of women's contributions to the economy.[44] Second, more creative aspects of the "indigenous economic system" in relation to women may not only inform but will also help to sensitize central planners to the needs of local populations. Further, the degree to which women make specific contributions to economic development programs is directly related to their involvement in program planning as well as implementation. Finally, unless special efforts are made to bring about holistic planning that includes contributions and benefits for women, the same old stereotypes, misconceptions, and prejudices will hinder full participation by women. Unless efforts are made to right misconceptions about the significance of present female roles, developmental thrust and programs will continue to neglect the enhancement of skills and ignore the fact that women need to become even more productive.

The perception that planners have of women and their role in general is important as a key to understanding how they have excluded women in the past and why they might include women in the future. Margaret Mungo observes that, "Men talk a lot about the equality of women, but in their hearts they are not prepared to give women any real position."[45] This attitude must be changed if a national development effort is to be successful. Moreover, Margaret Snyder* contends that the pressure from ineffective First Decade Development plans, international pressure from voluntary and UN agencies, unilateral pressure from aid donors, and the growing recognition by women of their rights and by men of women's contributions to national development combined to make possible a new thrust in development strategy in African states. The new emphasis led naturally to a shift from a total emphasis on modern sector development to rural development. Since it is in the rural areas of Africa where the majority of African women spend their lives and carry on their activities, the new emphasis on the rural or female domain was important to women. All of these factors led to the passing of some new legislation aimed at removing remaining legal barriers to female development. In some states, special programs were established to train women and provide the necessary tools to improve their working conditions. With the establishment of the African Training and Research Center for Women as part of the United Nations Economic Commission for Africa (UNECA), it became clear that some small steps were being taken to nourish the new thrust in development planning.

SUMMARY

All of the data available on the role of women in development point to an absolute need to redefine and assess the terminology and

---

*Margaret Snyder is director of the UNECA African Training and Research Center for Women, which is located in Addis Ababa, Ethiopia.

structure of development. In order to portray accurately women's work activities and lay the foundation for a holistic approach to development that would utilize all human resources and adapt development plans to the appropriate needs of the environment, such a rethinking is critical. This act alone would lead to better development planning and include all sectors of the economy and society in the national development effort.

There is now a general consensus among development scholars that national development planning should be inclusive rather than exclusive of women or any other group in a given society. Goodwill is often prevented from action because the actual facts of women's present work for development are unknown and we are short on vision for proposing specific projects to meet the real needs of women.

On the whole, in the present situation women are rural workers contributing primarily to the traditional sector. Their contributions are being restricted by insensitivity and lack of commitment and imagination. They process, produce, and distribute goods on a small scale; all but a few are in these categories. Even the few educated women are often excluded from the modern sector of the economy. There is a need to analyze these trends and the attitudes that perpetuate them.

Women must recognize their value and press for changes, and men must acknowledge and reward women for their contributions to development. Unless there is cooperation, respect, and understanding, societal transformation cannot take place. Even if the leadership is committed to social change, it must realize that all members of the society must be included in the work and fruits that the society has to offer. Change without female participation and benefits will nurture the oppression of women.

NOTES

1. "The Exploitation and Oppression of Women in Ghana," African Red Family 3: 35. See also Linda Jenness, Feminism and Socialism (New York: Pathfinder Press, 1977).

2. Le Duan, On the Socialist Revolution in Viet Nam, vol. 2 (Hanoi: Foreign Languages, 1967).

3. See such works as May Rihani, ed., Development as if Women Mattered: An Annotated Bibliography with a Third World Focus (Washington, D.C.: Overseas Development Council, 1978); Irene Tinker and Bo Bromsen, Women and World Development (Washington, D.C.: Overseas Development Council, 1976); and Ester Boserup and Christina Liljencrants, Integration of Women in Development: Why, When and Why (New York: UN Development Programme, 1975).

4. United Nations, Economic Council for Africa, Women's Programme: National Commission on Women and Development and Women's Bureaux (Addis Ababa, Ethiopia: UNECA).

5. See Gloria Braxton, "Adult Education and Rural Development in Ghana" (Ph.D. diss., Atlanta University, 1978); Irving Horowitz, Three Worlds of Development 2d ed. (New York: Oxford University Press, 1972); and Frederick Harbison, Human Resources as the Wealth of Nations (New York: Oxford University Press, 1973).

6. Excellent critiques on development theory are found in Harry Magdoff, Age of Imperialism (Englewood Cliffs, N.J.: Prentice-Hall, 1969); and Paul Sweezy, The Theory of Capitalist Development (New York: Monthly Review Press, 1968).

7. Samari Amin, Accumulation on a World Scale, vol. 1 (New York: Monthly Review Press, 1974), p. 8.

8. Notable among critics of the Western model are Andre Frank, Capitalism and Underdevelopment in Latin America (New York: Monthly Review Press, 1969); George Beckford, Persistent Poverty: Underdevelopment in the Plantation Economies of the Third World (London: Oxford University Press, 1972); Amin, Accumulation on a World Scale; and Walter Rodney, How Europe Underdeveloped Africa (Washington, D.C.: Howard University Press, 1974).

9. See, for example, Rodney, How Europe Underdeveloped Africa; and Samari Amin, "Underdevelopment and Dependence in Black Africa: Their Historical Origin and Contemporary Form," Journal of Modern African Studies 10, no. 4 (1972): 503-24.

10. Rodney, How Europe Underdeveloped Africa.

11. See Gobena Wale, "On Some Aspects of the Oppression of Women in Ethiopia," African Red Family 3: 40-50; and Le Duan, "We Must View the Woman Question from a Class Standpoint" (Speech delivered at the National Conference of Women Activists, February 1959).

12. United Nations, Economic and Social Council, Report on the African Social Situation (Second Conference of African Ministers Responsible for Social Affairs, Alexandria, Egypt, 1977). See also Ellen Johnson-Sirleaf, "The Role of Women in African Societies," and Caroline Williams, "The Rural Woman: Her Problems and Possibilities," both in Conference Proceedings: The African Woman in Economic Development (Washington, D.C.: African-American Scholars Council, 1975).

13. See Marie-Helene LeFaucheux, "The Contributions of Women to the Economic and Social Development of African Countries," International Labour Review 86 (July 1962): 17-28.

14. Ibid., p. 17.

15. See Ida Rousseau, "African Women: Identity Crisis," in Women Cross-Culturally: Change and Challenge, ed. Ruby Rohrlich-

Leavitt (The Hague: Mouton, 1975); Shelby Lewis, "Women in Developing and Industrialized Societies," Conference Papers: Race, Culture and Societies (Nashville, Tenn.: Fisk University, 1979); and Johnson-Sirleaf, "Role of Women in African Societies."

16. LeFaucheux, "Contributions of Women"; United Nations, Economic Council for Africa, Women's Programme; and idem, Plan of Action for the Integration of Women in Development in Africa (Addis Ababa, Ethiopia: UNECA, 1974).

17. A number of works on women in development make this point as do women who attend the various UN-sponsored conferences on women. They consistently call for the elimination of traditional burdens and the initiation of programs to improve economic and social opportunities for women. See Tinker and Bromsen, Women and World Development; and Nancy Hafkin and Edna Bay, Women in Africa (Stanford, Calif.: Stanford University Press, 1976).

18. "Women: The Neglected Human Resource for African Development," Canadian Journal of African Studies 1, no. 2 (1972): 360-61.

19. Ivy Matsepe, "Underdevelopment and African Women," Journal of Southern African Affairs 21 (April 1977): 6.

20. Ibid.; and Conference Proceedings: The African Women.

21. Wale, "On Some Aspects."

22. Ibid. See also H. Soffioti, Women in Class Society (New York: Monthly Review Press, 1978); and Jenness, Feminism and Socialism.

23. See Tinker and Bromsen, Women in World Development; Boserup, Women's Role in Economic Development (New York: St. Martin's Press, 1970); and Rohrlich-Leavitt, ed. Women Cross-Culturally (Chicago: Aldine Press, 1975).

24. Among the works espousing this view are "Women: The Neglected Resource for African Development," pp. 359-70; Sonia Mills, "An Interview with an African Woman," Essence, July 1978; and Kathleen Cloud, "Sex Roles in Food Production and Food Distribution Systems in the Sahel" (Special paper, U.S. Agency for International Development contract, Washington, D.C., December 1977).

25. Isabel Larguia, "The Economic Basis of the Status of Women," in Women Cross-Culturally: Change and Challenge, ed. Ruby Rohrlich-Leavitt (The Hague: Mouton, 1975).

26. Lusibu Nkanga of Zaire made this comment during an extensive interview. See Mills; "Interview with an African Woman."

27. For an excellent discussion of this point, see Matsepe, "Underdevelopment and African Women."

28. LeFaucheux, "Contributions of Women."

29. The incidence of de facto female-headed households is high in a number of countries in Africa. Because of migratory employment

in South Africa, for example, 42 percent of households are headed by women. See UN reports on seminars and conferences sponsored by the Economic Council for Africa, African Training and Research Center for Women, Addis Ababa, Ethiopia, for statistics on female-headed households (UNECA publications).

30. Johnson-Sirleaf, "Role of Women in African Societies"; Margaret Mbilinyi, "The State of Women in Tanzania," Canadian Journal of African Studies 6 (1972): 361.

31. Mills, "An Interview with an African Woman."

32. "Women: The Neglected Human Resource."

33. Williams, "The Rural Woman: Her Problems and Her Possibilities"; and United Nations, Economic Council for Africa, Women's Programme.

34. Ibid.

35. Snyder, "African Woman in Economic Development."

36. Lefaucheux, "Contributions of Women."

37. Ruth Hamilton develops this point in an article dealing with market women, "The African Woman as Entrepreneur," Conference Proceedings: The African Woman in Economic Development (Washington, D.C.: African-American Scholars Council, 1975). See also Barbara Lewis, "Female Strategies and Public Goods: Market Women in the Ivory Coast" (Paper presented at the Conference on Women and Development, Wellesley College, Wellesley, Mass., June 1976).

38. Matsepe, "Underdevelopment and African Women"; Jenness, Feminism and Socialism; and Hafkin and Bay, Women in Africa.

39. The international movement for women's liberation is based on this premise. Works on The International Women's Year and regional and national conferences indicate the need for women to organize for the purpose of forcing men to recognize their concerns and rights. See Marianne Githens and Jewel Prestage, A Portrait of Marginality (New York: Longman, 1977); Mills, "An Interview with an African Woman"; and Anne Koedt et al., Radical Feminism (New York: Quadrangle Press, 1973).

40. See special reports on the Zimbabwe African National Union (ZANU) women in the Guardian, February 14 and 21, 1979. See also Zimbabwe News, an organ of ZANU, for views on women's liberation and armed struggle, Zimbabwe News, vol. 10, no. 2 (1978).

41. Hafkin and Bay, Women in Africa; and United Nations, Economic Council for Africa, Women's Programme.

42. "Women: The Neglected Human Resource." See also UN reports on seminars and conferences sponsored by The Economic Council for Africa, African Training and Research Center for Women, Addis Ababa, Ethiopia.

43. Ibid. See also Mills, "An Interview with an African Woman"; and Emmy Simmons, Economic Research on Women in

Rural Development in Northern Nigeria (Washington, D.C.: Overseas Liaison Committee, 1976).

44. Hamilton, "African Woman as Entrepreneur"; and United Nations, Economic and Social Council, Report on the African Social Situation.

45. See Mbilinyi, "State of Women in Tanzania."

REFERENCES

Amin, Samari. Accumulation on a World Scale. Vol. 1. New York Monthly Review Press, 1974.

_____. "Underdevelopment and Dependence in Black Africa: Their Historical Origin and Contemporary Form." Journal of Modern African Studies, 10, no. 4 (1972): 503-24.

Beckford, George. Persistent Poverty: Underdevelopment in the Plantation Economies of the Third World. London: Oxford University Press, 1972.

Boserup, Ester, and Christina Liljencrants. Integration of Women in Development: Why, When and Why. New York: UN Development Programme, 1975.

Braxton, Gloria. "Adult Education and Rural Development in Ghana." Ph.D. dissertation, Atlanta University, 1978.

Cloud, Kathleen. "Sex Roles in Food Production and Food Distribution Systems in the Sahel." Special paper, U.S. Agency for International Development contract, Washington, D.C., December 1977.

"The Exploitation and Oppression of Women in Ghana." African Red Family 3: 35.

Frank, Andre. Capitalism and Underdevelopment in Latin America. New York: Monthly Review Press, 1969.

Githens, Marianne, and Jewell Prestage. A Portrait of Marginality. New York: Longman, 1977.

Guardian (New York), February 1979.

Hafkin, Nancy and Edna Bay. Women in Africa. Stanford, Calif.: Stanford University Press, 1976.

Hamilton, Ruth. "The African Women as Entrepreneur." In Conference Proceedings: The African Woman in Economic Development. Washington, D.C.: African-American Scholars Council, 1975.

Harbison, Frederick. Human Resources as the Wealth of Nations. New York: Oxford University Press, 1973.

Horowitz, Irving. Three Worlds of Development. New York: Oxford University Press, 1972.

Jenness, Linda. Feminism and Socialism. New York: Pathfinder Press, 1977.

Johnson-Sirleaf, Ellen. "The Role of Women in African Societies." In Conference Proceedings: The African Woman in Economic Development. Washington, D.C.: African-American Scholars Council, 1975.

Koedt, Anne, et al. Radical Feminism. New York: Quadrangle Press, 1973.

Larguia, Isabel. "The Economic Basis of the Status of Women." In Women Cross-Culturally: Change and Challenge, edited by Ruby Rohrlich-Leavitt. The Hague: Mouton, 1975.

Le Duan. On Socialist Revolution in Viet Nam. Vol. 2. Hanoi: Foreign Languages, 1967.

_____. "We Must View the Woman Question from a Class Standpoint." Speech at the National Conference of Women Activists, February 1959.

LeFaucheux, Marie-Helene. "The Contributions of Women to the Economic and Social Development of African Countries." International Labour Review 86 (July 1962): 17-28.

Lewis, Barbara. "Female Strategies and Public Goods: Market Women in the Ivory Coast." Paper presented at the Conference on Women and Development, Wellesley College, Wellesley, Mass., June 2, 1976.

Lewis, Shelby. "Women in Developing and Industrialized Societies." Conference Papers: Race, Culture and Societies. Nashville, Tenn.: Fisk University, 1979.

Little, Kenneth. African Women in Towns: An Aspect of Africa's Social Revolution. London: Cambridge University Press, 1973.

Magdoff, Harry. Age of Imperialism. New York: Monthly Review Press, 1978.

Matsepe, Ivy. "Underdevelopment and African Women." Journal of Southern African Affairs 1 (1977): 6.

Mbilinyi, Margaret. "The State of Women in Tanzania." Canadian Journal of African Affairs 6 (1972): 361.

Mills, Sonia. "An Interview with an African Woman." Essence, July 1978.

Rihani, May, ed. Development as if Women Mattered: An Annotated Bibliography with a Third World Focus. Washington, D.C.: Overseas Development Council, 1978.

Rodney, Walter. How Europe Underdeveloped Africa. Washington, D.C.: Howard University Press, 1974.

Rohrlich-Leavitt, Ruby, ed. Women Cross-Culturally. Chicago: Aldine Press, 1975.

Rohrlich-Leavitt, Ruby, ed. Women Cross-Culturally: Change and Challenge. The Hague: Mouton, 1975.

Rousseau, Ida. "African Women: Identity Crisis." In Women Cross-Culturally: Change and Challenge, edited by Ruby Rohrlich-Leavitt. The Hague: Mouton, 1975.

Simmons, Emmy. Economic Research on Women in Rural Development in Northern Nigeria. Washington, D.C.: Overseas Liaison Committee, 1976.

Snyder, Margaret. "The African Women in Economic Development: A Regional Perspective." In Conference Proceedings: The African Woman and Economic Development. Washington, D.C.: African-American Scholars Council, 1975.

Soffioti, H. Women in Class Society. New York: Monthly Review Press, 1978.

Sweezy, Paul. The Theory of Capitalist Development. New York: Monthly Review Press, 1968.

Tinker, Irene, and Bo Bromsen. Women and World Development. Washington, D.C.: Overseas Development Council, 1976.

United Nations, Economic Council for Africa. Plan of Action for the Integration of Women in Development in Africa. Addis Ababa, Ethiopia: UNECA, 1974.

_____. Women's Programme: National Commission on Women and Development and Women's Bureaux. Addis Ababa, Ethiopia: UNECA.

United Nations, Economic and Social Council. Report on the African Social Situation. Second Conference of African Ministers Responsible for Social Affairs, Alexandria, Egypt, 1977.

_____. Women of Africa: Today and Tomorrow. Addis Ababa, Ethiopia: UNECA, 1974.

Wale, Gobena. "On Some Aspects of the Oppression of Women in Ethiopia." African Red Family 3, no. 2: 40-50.

Williams, Caroline. "The Rural Woman: Her Problems and Possibilities." In Conference Proceedings: The African Women in Economic Development. Washington, D.C.: African-American Scholars Council, 1975.

"Women: The Neglected Human Resource for African Development." Canadian Journal of African Affairs 1, no. 2 (1972): 359-70.

3
WOMEN IN ZAIRE:
DISPARATE STATUS AND ROLES

Lois Adams

INTRODUCTION: STATUS VERSUS ROLE

Zairian women's lives are disrupted by status and role ambigui-
ties. The Zairian Constitution and its Legal Code prescribe one mode
of behavior; customary law and actual practice contradict this. These
contradictions between law and social life tend to make Zairian women
dependent on men. The resulting conflicts pervade social life in Zaire
today.

Operational definitions of the concepts of status and role expose
the limitations and problems inherent in the measurement of Zairian
women's status and roles, which are described in the literature reviewed in this chapter.

Discussion of women's status itself brings about a value judgment
that simultaneously ranks the position of women relative to that of men
and differentiates their positions in terms of prestige, power, and esteem; it defines women's place in the social structure. A chief limitation in operationally defining status in this chapter is that no single
measure of status can be applied to the majority of Zairian women.
They are not in the public view, and their more ordinary activities are
not highly visible. Therefore, the positions of those who carry out
such activities are frequently ignored. Their behavior remains unre-
corded and unmeasured, and the group as a whole has low status. How-

I discussed my ethnographic information with as many Zairian informants as could be found. Not all those persons are listed in the references nor are the many brief conversations that were held. All the
informants answered questions fully and with visible concern to help
me form a balanced picture of the roles and status of urban Zairian
women. My warmest appreciation goes to my Zairian informants. I
give special thanks to Jan Vansina and M. Crawford Young for their
help and encouragement.

ever, there probably are gradations of status, according to what are perceived as relevant indicators. Indicators determine the prestige of social positions within any group and must be considered.[1]

A role is the set of actions that the occupant of a social position carries out in keeping with the cognitions that help the actor define the range of actions sanctioned by a society. Role expectations consist of the rights, privileges, duties, and obligations of the occupant of a status in relationship to persons occupying other statuses in the society. Thus, role is a simultaneous realization of a status as well as a personal interpretation of what is socially acceptable. There may not always be a perfect correlation between attitudes and actions. Then, the measures of deviancy from traditional attitudes or norms may be a guide to explaining how women assimilate and accommodate to changing conditions.[2]

Having had no opportunity for field research in Zaire that would allow firsthand formulations of definitions of women's status and role, I have been forced to accept less satisfactory operational definitions. Women's status is defined here in terms of those provided by customary and civil law, though these are at best theoretical constructs. Women's role is defined in terms of their recorded activities in specific areas of behavior. My observations are limited to recorded behaviors that have been subject to popular commentary or formal study. (Field research is needed to investigate how and what rankings are made by the members of the different, small groups that constitute the Zairian majority.) Thus, this chapter should be read with caution as a provisional assessment of a complex, little-known subject. It stands as an invitation to further research.

Conflict between status and role is bound to occur: role expectations may vary, while at the same time everyone has more than one status, which creates a balancing problem. Any status may function in more than one social system. The conflict may have positive or negative effects.

Max Gluckman's enculturation theory explains how social conflict may be generated. Gluckman (1964) suggested that social conflict is inherent. A fundamental social conflict centers on the position of women. Although females produce children and play the larger part in organic transmission, the social transmission of property, power, and position tends to be from male to male. Power and property belong to men principally; younger males succeed to senior males' power, position, and goods. Yet, women transmit social as well as organic endowments.[3] Thus, the experiences and expectations of parents are passed on to their children. The experiences and expectations of the parents of today's generation of Zairians affect them differentially according to sex.

Further problems arise when new values are emerging and all individuals do not share the same values. Individuals are compelled to redefine their roles when their statuses are uncertain, and there is no one standard of behavior to guide self-definition. The conflict inherent in such disparate statuses leads to differences in formal and informal behavior and official and unofficial traditions.[4] These differences have not been articulated, but they should be so that they may be resolved.

The position of women in postindependence Zaire stems directly from their situation in colonial times. The colonial period created a break in traditional patterns of interaction between Congolese women and men and conferred new disabilities on rural and urban women. For example, women were described in law as the dependents of men, and they were subject to the wishes of their relatives, especially their parents, husbands, and husbands' relatives.[5] Legislation regulated the lives of Congolese women without their direct participation or consent, forcing changes in behavior so that their roles conformed to this new legal status. Men were brought to urban centers selectively for work and schooling. The colonial government permitted families to move to urban areas only by the late 1920s. Migration policies remained sexually selective until the 1950s.

On the eve of independence women in the Congo were still treated unequally by law and everyday social life. Although many women may have been treated as equals in some aspects of their lives, and though some men may have recognized the equal importance of women, their legal status and roles were unequal. Moreover, the position of Congolese women reflected Belgian beliefs and practices, which were imposed on the Congo, and which had incompletely and imperfectly interlocked with traditional practices to severely disadvantage women.

Customary rather than civil law affected most Congolese at that time. Civil law primarily affected the évolués* and those females associated with them. This group represented between 1 and 2 percent of the total Congolese population. Civil and customary law tended to overlap in jurisdiction. Although legislation often embraced both customary and civil law, there is considerable evidence that the system of categories used in the legal system did not reflect the underlying social structure; the dual legal system was not created by the individuals it governed but by the colonial powers.

Few Congolese women could have been aware of their rights during the colonial period. Few women were literate, and women's general level of education was low. Few would have had the means to bring any dispute before a tribunal. In this respect, colonial legislation had import in theory but not in fact; some of the legislation that purported to modify the status of women changed very little. Legislation of the period is an instance of an official tradition invalidating it-

---

*An évolué was an individual Congolese, one who was deemed by the Belgian colonial government to be an evolved—that is, civilized and/or Europeanized—person.

self from its inception. The real position of Congolese women—their informal position and role as uneducated and uninformed individuals—contributed to the invalidation of the legislation before independence. The dual legal system and the social dialectic it reflects persist. Nowadays, while all Zairians are governed by civil law, they may still choose to be governed by customary law. [6]

Prior to the 1960s Congolese women probably would not have experienced or have been expected to achieve much outside the home. More recently, in the 1960s and 1970s, indigenous and foreign observers have reported with increasing frequency situations that suggest that values and behavior may be changing. Therefore, I have chosen to review recent findings about modern Zairian women, focusing first on their primary area of orientation, marriage, and then considering women in education, employment, and public life, to encourage a redefinition of their status and roles.*

MARRIAGE AND RELATED INSTITUTIONS

Congolese independence from Belgium did not signal a revolution in law and custom. The postindependence government has tended to perpetuate the colonial government's treatment of women. [7] Legislation from colonial times to 1970, and seemingly even to the present, did not directly modify marriage laws except in regard to divorce. [8] Many of the laws governing marriage were made in the 1940s. A decree of January 31, 1947, prohibited polyandry. [9] The most important decree of those times was the decree of April 4, 1950, which repealed polygamy.

Although the decree of April 4, 1950, was a step toward making men and women equal before the law (just as women were prohibited from practicing polyandry, men were prohibited from practicing polygamy), female partners in a polygamous relationship were, and are, protected by the Legal Code only in regard to their children's rights in customary law. † Nevertheless, the fact that many women

---

*An extensive study of the literature and anecdotal materials collected by myself and others from Zairian informants form the major sources of information for this chapter. M. Crawford Young's and Thomas Turner's data (for the period 1965-76) on Zaire's political elite—leaders of the Mouvement Populaire Revolutionaire (MPR) and ministers—were made available to me. Because of the composition of the sample (more about this later), the statistical analyses did not often yield significant correlations between data on sex compared with other variables. Thus, my remarks on these and other matters reflect my impressions gathered from the literature and interviews with Zairians.

†There is a loophole in the decree of April 4, 1950. Article 3 upholds the effects of customary law on the rights and privileges of

seem to have entered voluntarily into such relationships suggests that this may have added to their social standing and been experienced as a social benefit.[10] I found no record of court prosecution for infractions of the marriage laws, including polygamy.

A recent newspaper article,[11] confirmed by informants, bears witness to the continued prevalence of polygamous relationships in a form called deuxième bureau ("second office"). A distinction must be made between the use of the terms wife and deuxième bureau in modern Zaire. The term wife is ordinarily applied to those women who have contracted legal marriages, or to a woman with whom a man has a regular relationship. The more regular the relationship and the more the couple's behavior resembles that of legally married couples, the more likely it is that the woman will be called "wife" rather than "deuxième bureau": the term deuxième bureau may carry the connotation "wife" and mean "second wife," or it may mean "concubine" or "mistress."[12] One difference between marriage and the bureau is that legal wives of a single husband would typically interact with one another and share the same household, while bureaux do not.*

This institution seems to be specific to the cities. It seems to be the practice only of wealthy men (and their female companions), and it may be the relatively new form of polygamy that the decree of April 4, 1950, sought to prevent. In this form of relationship, a man's role as husband has some publically inadmissible aspects that lead to its being called "informal" or "illegal." Yet, all the reports I have heard or read give evidence that this behavior is widespread, has widespread social recognition, and is largely uncriticized by women and men. The precise terminology describing this behavior and the frequency of its use also indicate that such behavior is common, although few men are rich enough to maintain completely more than one household. (Only those with the highest incomes are able to afford the bureau.) Although habitually called informal, it is regular and formulized, and even sanctioned "unofficially." Above all, it represents the continuation of female Zairian dependency on males; males make the laws and females succumb to their (male) customs. There is some female complicity in this, of course, but apparently many women find that circumstances do not give them another choice.

---

children. This article may have provided sufficient protection to any children who were a product of polygamous relationships so that the majority of adults may have felt free to disobey a law that went counter to social pressures created by kinship groups and peers and to contract polygamous alliances.

*I have not found any comparable terminology for women's behavior, although some women may have "unofficial" husbands and a deuxième and even a troisième ("third") bureau.

It seems that women themselves find the status of <u>bureau</u> acceptable,[13] and those who have the status of mistress or concubine may also find it acceptable. Are Zairian women just giving in to circumstances that favor polygamy? The proportion of women to men in Kinshasa (and other urban areas) may be in better balance currently than in 1961, when out of ten communes in the Kinshasa District of the former city of Léopoldville, there were only 77.3 women to every 100 men.[14]

Literature on bridewealth suggests that during the 1960s the population rates were just beginning to alter. In the early 1960s women were still in short supply. Bridewealth, still obligatory in postindependence Zaire, was a controversial topic by the mid-1960s, primarily because of its abuse. A colloquium (November 1966) recommended moderate changes in the institution—for example, that the government set a limit. (Such discussions seemed to foreshadow the creation of a new domain of Congolese law, regulation of the pecuniary conventions of marriage.)[15] An increasing number of reports of the abuse of bridewealth indicate that women had been in short supply until just about that time, but that the supply may have been reversing. Hence, Susanne Comhaire-Sylvain (1968) was able to report (referring to 1965) that people tried to evade payments; concubinage of long duration seems to have been established as a means of avoiding some marital financial obligations. Comhaire-Sylvain may have actually described practices pertaining to <u>deuxième bureau.</u>

Yet, it is hard to say whether Zairian women have great difficulty finding husbands today. They probably do have some trouble, because now the number of women in urban areas is greater than the number of men. This and the social factors mentioned previously may be sufficient to preserve the status quo.

One indicator of changing Zairian behavior may be the treatment of <u>les femmes vivant théoretiquement seules</u> ("women living theoretically alone").[16] Article 12 of the 1974 Constitution says:

> No Zairian may be the subject of a discriminatory measure, in the field of education or public functions, whether it results from the law or an act of the executive, because of religion, ethnic origin, sex, or place of birth or residence.[17]

Nevertheless, there is a tax levied on women who live alone. Single men living alone are not so taxed. The term for single women living alone specifies that according to the legal, public conception such women live alone in theory but not in fact. It implies that they are living with men or at least have male visitors with whom they presumably engage in sexual activity and may either be promiscuous or dishonest if they describe themselves as independent. Why does the law appear to support a negative view of women living theoretically alone?

More and more Zairian women may be gaining salaried employment, which would enable them to live independently. The threat of being classified among the "women living theoretically alone" could discourage any woman from attempting to live alone, other than those who are admittedly concubines or mistresses, or who are engaged in prostitution. "But, Madam, that isn't normal," explained one Zairian male. He added that women may live alone and have boyfriends who visit them, or may live with only one man, or may be prostitutes, but, of course, they do not actually live alone.[18]

While some of the laws pertaining to this heterogeneous group are probably inoperative[19]—and in this sense the law seems to go against the will of the people—they are not opposed by others, and public sanctions do take their toll against the group. At the very least women must pay an inequitable tax. But are those taxes collected? To what extent is the legislation regulating women who live alone an invalid official Zairian tradition today? Comhaire-Sylvain studied this problem in regard to the women of Kinshasa in the mid-1960s (when Kinshasa was still a district within Léopoldville); it is time for further research on this subject.

Child rearing is another aspect of the traditional family role of Zairian women that hinders their participation in education, work outside the home, and public life. As Anatole Romaniuk says in Fécondité des populations congolaises (1967), "One may say without exaggeration that a woman's value is measured by her reproductive capacity."[20] Romaniuk cautiously remarked that the procreative behavior of city dwellers expresses a strong progenitive desire, which also characterizes rural milieus. The 1955–57 inquiry revealed a slight advance of urban over rural birthrates.[21]

The Zairian government has suggested a standard of naissances désirables ("desirable births")—the ideal family has five children. One indicator of official support of such a standard is President Mobuto Sese Seko's declaration that 1975 would be called "The Year of the Momma."[22] Elsewhere it was being designated as "The Year of the Woman."

If this is a primary orientation of Zairian society, it may preclude a woman's choosing other activities. Kikassa Mwanalessa (1974), director of Zaire-Afrique (a main Zairian journal), observed that there are numerous sociopolitical advantages to large families.[23] However, he questioned the benefits of having many children and criticized the African marriage goal of procreation for the sake of the clan without regard to the interests of either spouse. As clan ties weaken, marriage tends to become a more personal matter.[24] Couples should have more say in family planning. Nevertheless, many Zairian families have the recommended number of children or more. This tends to keep women out of the public sector as does their lack of training and job shortages. Those few women who participate in public life usually come from families that are financially better off than the majority. They have maids or other household help, so their number of children may not keep them out of public life. Most urban families cannot afford maids or support resident relatives who could care for children while a mother engages in outside activities. Thus, the persistence of traditional views is likely to continue to deter women from extrafamilial activity, just as it supports the government's natalist ideology and policies and the many families with five or more children.

Recently, the population trends that Romaniuk observed in the 1950s have altered. Now the trend is for birthrates to increase in rural areas and decrease in urban areas in proportion to the female population. One observer suspects that there may be a sharper decline of pregnancies among women of the wealthier urban families; these families may have just begun to measure a woman's productivity in terms of such qualities as the ability to trade, management skills, and so on.[25] Such a trend may also indicate an emerging value in national economic and political life. Similarly, the recent heavy influx of women into urban areas could have a significant impact on social life. These matters deserve further investigation.

EDUCATION

During the colonial period, Congolese women had few opportunities to gain a Western education; it was usually inferior to that of men, consisting mainly of training in homemaking skills, and did not equip women to enter the modern world as men's education did. Developments in the postindependence education system have been more sweeping and positive than those in the judiciary, but the effects of inadequate women's education during colonial times linger on.

Authorities did not seem to have the same interest in girls' education as in boys'. Female education in Léopoldville was poor in quality (overcrowding, lack of supplies, weak curricula). Higher education was not open to women[26] until after independence but was open to men by the end of the 1950s. After World War II women's general education was furthered by increasing the number of schools for women and enrollments.[27]

Just after independence, while there was a surge in school enrollment of girls (and boys), there was a sharp reduction in both native and foreign personnel. Classes were crowded; academic deficits of the preceding years could not readily be repaired. Selection for secondary school was not rigorous; political influence and nepotism reigned over selection criteria. Girls were often directed toward homemaking programs despite their real aptitudes for general studies.[28] Teachers' strikes damaged the prestige of the teaching profession and disrupted learning. These kinds of conditions prevailed at least five years after independence.

Education statistics for that period are meager and conflicting. For example, in 1966 the United Nations Educational, Scientific and Cultural Organization (UNESCO) only reported total public and private primary school enrollment and total higher education enrollment (only reported for Université Louvanium) for the academic year 1960/61. Girls were sent in great numbers to secondary schools instead of home economics schools only after 1960.[29] Other education statistics were available for 1961/62 by 1966, but UNESCO had revised those figures.[30] UNESCO's figures for girls' secondary education in 1961/62 are lower than the figures given by M. Crawford Young et al. (1969). Young's figures for total secondary school enrollment for that year are also higher.[31]

After the mid-1960s education statistics show an increase in enrollments, including an increase in female enrollments. While it is not feasible to analyze the education statistics for the postindependence period accurately, the attitudes of young women and men in Kinshasa toward women's education can indicate developments in this area. Young et al. observed that:

> To a remarkable extent, the educational system . . . defines and allocates social status. . . . Perception of this phenomenon is generalized throughout the society. . . . The near perfect correlation between level of education and social status is reinforced by the central importance of government and parastatal organizations as an employment outlet for secondary and post-secondary graduates. Pay scales are totally bound to number of years of formal education completed.[32]

Regardless, poor education for women defeated their interest in pursuing it. Comhaire-Sylvain's (1968) study shows how motivation to gain an education was shaped among young women in Kinshasa. For example, their reading ability tended to be low, owing to inadequate instruction and little social support for reading, and their attitudes toward reading tended to be negative. Young women retained little of what they had read; they preferred to read romances, biographies of famous women, or novels about problems of conjugal life.[33] Their education suffered accordingly.

Although this negative attitude may indicate disinterest in education, Young et al. (1969) reported education statistics for the whole

Congo that give a contrary indication: the number of girls attending secondary school changed greatly between 1961/62 and 1967/68. In 1961/62 "13.8% of . . . students in secondary schools were girls. This . . . increased to 15.4% by 1963-64 and to 16.8% by 1965-66, and was 18.9% in 1967-68."[34] As mentioned before, however, UNESCO's 1961/62 figures are lower.

Education statistics, though scant overall, indicate that by 1967/68 there may have been some reason for optimism about women's progress in education. Reportedly, the government made every possible effort to close the gap between boys' and girls' schooling. The results were "still far from meeting the needs of women and by implication the Congo,"[35] and most Congolese women were having great difficulty gaining a sound education. Social pressures were handicapping women's educational performance and enrollment. Their behavioral model did not support positive academic performance.

Therèse Verheust's later study (1972) of Kinshasa schoolgirls showed how these negative conditions continued to curb women's ambitions in the early 1970s.[36] Her subjects used feminist criteria in discussing the exercise of a profession but often worried about and had trouble formulating plans for work after marriage and choosing a profession. Female emancipation remained a theoretical motivation for young women as a result of opposing social forces. Choosing a career placed them in conflict with the many men who feared that working women would not be good wives. There were few openings in "suitable" professions. Yet, the majority of young women in Kinshasa envisioned entering the world of work.[37]

The scarcity of education statistics on women even today indicates the relative unimportance of women in academic life. Even external sources have not been able to obtain reliable and comprehensive statistics on female education in Zaire. Internally, the colonial administration did not take much interest in women's education, and the postindependence government has sometimes lacked the interest and means to obtain such statistics.

EMPLOYMENT AND PUBLIC LIFE

If women and men are equal before the law and job discrimination is illegal, there should be as many job openings for women as for men. Instead, Verheust (1972) suggested that, as Comhaire-Sylvain found, the general problem of unemployment in Zaire does not account for women's relative rate of unemployment. One male Zairian stated that job openings are even better for women than for men owing to a government campaign to promote women; however, it seems to be untrue that most educated women find suitable jobs. The campaign to promote women is more nominal than real.

Many Zairian beliefs contribute to female unemployment. Women lack the option of holding a job and being a wife, though men may hold a job and be husbands; most Zairians do not think regular employment is a "proper" woman's activity. One Zairian male indicated that a nonprostitute living alone would need to work to "get by," and that there should be nothing to prevent her from being a secretary or typist. He volunteered a description of the proper role of a wife—attending to housework and caring for children. He stressed that the care of children is a very important female function; men are not equally able to care for children. When asked leading questions, he did not conceive of an exchange of roles between women and men nor a man's temporarily taking over some facet of the traditional female role.[38]

Mary Collins (1976) found that some women have negative attitudes toward women's employment. Many Zairian women do not want to work outside the home and consider themselves lucky not to have to work. Collins's informants believe work disrupts marriage.[39] One woman said they take pride in their lives and think American ways, such as planning the number of children in a family, are "rather funny."[40] Another woman told her that there was gossip about a woman in a community who worked to supplement her husband's income. Other women sympathized with her having to work and leave her children with outsiders and also keep house.[41] (The implication is that her husband did not have a double task.) The woman advocated that women work and earn success based on their abilities; yet, she implied that all women who work are perceived of as sexually permissive and manipulative.[42] She recognized that these perceptions blocked women's employment. Her remarks suggest that the best way to protect one's reputation (and one's person) is not to work. Can one ever prove one's job success does not stem from distributing sexual favors? This kind of reasoning about working women is similar to the popular reasoning about women of independent means living alone, which denies women their right to sexual relations outside of marriage while allowing it to men.

Young women like those studied by Comhaire-Sylvain, Verheust, and Collins are subject to all those Zairian points of view on proper conduct. Such views discourage their education and employment. Alternate recommendations are a long way from being realized.

Not many women finish secondary school. The latest available statistics, provided by Young et al. for 1967/68, show that women made up 22 percent of the total first-year secondary school population but only 9 percent of the sixth or final year. Low employment figures for women[43] correlate well with these statistics.

Now, as in the past, there are undoubtedly more women and men in the work force than statistical reports reveal. Comhaire-Sylvain showed that from 1945 until 1965 many women in the Kinshasa District merely "got by"; they may have had no reported, salaried work and their work may have been varied and irregular, but they did work.[44] This continues today. Georges Bokamba's (1969) findings were similar to Comhaire-Sylvain's and Collins's, but he concluded that Zairian women's employment had progressed markedly from 1960 to 1967. There was a de facto prohibition against women's employment in colonial times. Zaire's postcolonial constitutions have given women the (somewhat qualified) right to be employed. We could expect Zairian women to experience increasing job success in the 1970s. However, all of the negative attitudes and prejudices against women have not evaporated. Two recent articles document this.

Malulu Mitwensil muns Mukil (1978) described gross inadequacies in recruitment procedures and employment conditions in Bukavu's Department of Public Administration, 1970-72. According to Mukil, Zaire has witnessed the massive entry of women into public employment since independence, evidence that Zairian women's role is undergoing a fundamental transformation.[45] Nonetheless, although by law recruitment must be through competitive qualifying examinations, most women were appointed by recommendation or for reasons unrelated to any objective criteria and were unqualified either by education or training.[46] Most women saw their jobs as a pastime, were often late or absent, and performed poorly.[47] Male attitudes and behavior reinforced this. Meanwhile, women were often treated as sex objects or otherwise abused on the job.[48] Mukil recommended that more care be given to fair selection of personnel.

Terri Gould (1978) during 1973-76 found conditions paralleling those described by Mukil. Only about 3.2 percent of all women in Lubumbashi were employed. Only 3.8 percent of these had professional jobs. As Gould said, these women "are degraded and discriminated against both socially and economically. . . . They are treated by men as sex objects, forced to be non-assertive so as to avoid threatening those they work with, and are rarely given power or authority. When they are permitted to be supervisors it is usually of other women." Moreover, the Legal Code required that a married woman must have her husband's permission to accept a job.[49]

Although Zairian women may have experienced increased job success in the 1970s, the increase is small. Job market conditions aggravate women's problems. The market calls for unskilled heavy labor—for example, mine workers. Many sectors—the petty office clericals and domestics—are primarily a male domain. Women face fierce competition against large numbers of male "school leavers."

Despite the increase in women's associations, some of which were quasi-political during the 1940s and 1950s, and although more and more women have entered the Congo's prepolitical life,[50] Zairian women today do not have a very advanced role in public life. Bokamba

(1969) found traditional attitudes prevalent concerning women in politics; they were considered to be unready for it because it is too risky and only for men.[51] Collins (1976) found that although several women have held political posts this is tokenism and seemingly has had no significant effect on women's further entry into political life.[52] My Zairian informants agree.

M. Crawford Young and Thomas Turner's forthcoming study of Zaire's political elite confirms many of the impressions of women's life in modern Zaire described previously, including their role in politics. Young and Turner's sample was composed of 212 politicians in the Mouvement Populaire Révolutionnaire (MPR), including 17 women. Though the comparison of female with male subjects was sometimes statistically insignificant, something may be gained from examining the data.[53]

Zairians have a better chance of becoming politicians if they were born at the same time or after Mobutu. Education is a major channel toward political careers for politicians born after 1946, but the entrance of women into politics is made possible essentially through political decisions rather than on merit. These decisions are aimed partly at correcting the discriminatory treatment of women that was widespread during the colonial period.[54]

Data on sex by occupation show that female politicians do not enter many areas of employment compared with male politicians. Female politicians are younger than males because of differential education opportunities during the colonial period. After this period there is a significant change in education enrollments and employment figures for females, but these figures remain low.[55] (Figures for entry into business suggest that political appointments help women enter business, although they may not have the other support necessary for business activities.)[56]

Younger women more recently active in politics have better chances for political appointment than other women, but poor chances compared with men. Very few women have had leadership roles in associations compared with men.[57] Women in politics seem to have less of a chance of being rehabilitated than men after dismissal from public office. Although favoritism seems to play some role in women's appointments to political positions, once they are found to be politically disloyal, they are more severely punished than men.[58]

In general, then, all the publications reviewed here show that women in modern Zaire, whether private citizens or politicians, have limited opportunities compared with men. Their best avenue to eventual success is through education, but for now their success tends to depend on the whims of men.

NEW DIRECTIONS FOR ZAIRIAN WOMEN

Is a women's liberation movement needed or wanted in Zaire? Modern, urban Zairian women are currently prevented from realizing their full potential in social life, education, employment, and public life—their roles and counterroles and status and counterstatus constrict their choices and their activities. Zaire's legal institutions do not support—but do not prevent—males holding rights in females. Popular sentiment and the Zairian government's social ideal of large families have compromised the law and made it more likely that women's efforts to reduce the demands for parenthood will be opposed and women will be coerced into giving up their other rights to men. Evidently, they are compelled to let men hold their rights and deprive them of the exercise of those rights.

The system works subtly outside the law. Women rarely perceive that their rights have been co-opted. For example, Collins' informant reasoned as follows: All women workers succeed because they are sexually permissive and manipulative; therefore, I must not work; however, women should enter the work force on their own. Her logic is faulty, but her feelings are strong.

Greater insistence on women's right to work or receive an equal education cannot fully resolve this predicament. Kikassa Mwanalessa (1974) argued that each couple should reinterpret the policy of "desirable births." Collins' informants would reply that planning births is rather strange. Collins warned that because Western feminism is a group effort to free each woman as an individual, it would not be readily accepted where communal and kinship ties are important,[59] as in Zaire. These ties influence the number of desirable births and Zairian women's and men's attitudes toward equal opportunities for women. Under these circumstances how can Zairian women remedy their condition so that they may enjoy equal rights?

Baleka Bamba Nzuji (1973) advocates that women function with a value relatively equal to that of men, in sexually neutral domains. She believes that a common goal of all women is love and maternity but asks women to act self-confidently and preserve independent values vis-à-vis men. Nzuji assumes that women are biologically passive organisms; she pictures women and men tied to a relentless biological nature, but she envisions a form of woman's liberation that presupposes individual counterambition.[60]

Nzuji hopes that increasing numbers of a new class of young women will bring about Zairian women's liberation. Education, she contends, is almost the only way to achieve it, accompanied by a decrease in economic class differences. Those Zairian women who would profit most from education and are closest to liberating themselves are from among the most privileged socially and the group immediately below them. They are already knowledgeable and ready to learn about and act on the affairs of their husbands and national affairs.[61]

Nzuji's remarks recall more traditional and male-oriented social values. The realization of some of her more idealistic suggestions lie far into the future, requiring liberation as a precondition. Her efforts to come to terms with the problems of modern Zairian women are laudable, but she seems to have expressed her own conflicts and theirs more than resolved them.

The government ideology of "authenticity" offers some support for a solution. It has as one emphasis a return to one's sources, which could be a hindrance; in the past, women's rights and rights in women were held by men. It could have positive effects; some past societies honored women and recognized their independent abilities and contributions. A second emphasis of authenticity is that Zairians express themselves naturally without undue deference to other cultures and without ignoring what others are or have achieved.[62] This also draws on the past but suggests that Zaire's citizens move into a new and as yet undiscovered future. What incentives, then, can the Zairian government provide? Without concrete incentives, the ideology of authenticity will remain merely another form of statement that past and present conditions in Zaire continue to interact, a mere wish that Zairians look to the future, lacking the force of law or any special social impetuses.

A review of some of the available literature shows that the status and roles of Zairian women cannot be described in terms of particular aspects of social life; they are a function of complexly interrelated social conditions. Government programs to increase female school enrollments or revise discriminatory legislation cannot immediately change the wider environment or even ensure that programs are carried out and laws enforced.

The prevailing standards in Zaire define women's role as being the handmaidens of men. These standards are incompatible with modern Zairian women's emerging status as the equals of men. Social interaction is difficult because each female occupant of a particular legal status (equal to men) that is contradicted by a different social status (deuxième bureau, for example) must decide which of the two statuses is the appropriate basis for social interaction at any given moment. Internal conflicts may arise. Moreover, interaction between two persons with incompatible statuses becomes negatively charged. Zairian women must reassess their positions and redefine their roles each time they engage in behavior that encroaches on areas of status and role ambiguity.

The constitution grants equality to Zairian women and men. The double standard in Zairian life operates against women to make them legally and socially dependent on men. This double standard affects females of all ages in most areas of their lives, whether they live in rural or urban areas. The conflict between the legal status and actual roles of Zairian women disrupts and handicaps their lives, and Zairian life in general. Urban women are the most visibly affected.

Even if the Zairian society were to choose to curtail sexually discriminatory attitudes, beliefs, and practices, something more would be needed: time and the incentives to reaffirm such a choice. What can Zairian women hope for in the future?

Historical conditions have changed. The statuses and roles of Zairian women may be expected to change accordingly. The possible direction of social change is hinted at in Mwanalessa's, Mukil's, and Nzuji's articles, Jan Vansina's observations concerning urban population trends, and the 1974 Constitution. A noticeable increase in the number of females enrolled in schools or regularly employed probably indicates a new valuation of women emerging in Zaire. Although there is no organized socially progressive force within Zaire, scattered individuals and groups have had some small impact over the years since independence. Additionally, modern technology and international pressures for political reform may be expected to create more favorable opportunities for Zairian women, enabling them to participate more fully and equitably in society. This goal is in the future, but the future is just ahead.

NOTES

1. Mayra Buvinić et al., Women and World Development: An Annotated Bibliography (Washington, D.C.: Overseas Development Council, 1976), pp. 1-4.

2. Ibid., pp. 4-7.

3. Max Gluckman, Custom and Conflict in Africa (New York: Barnes and Noble, 1964), pp. 65-66, 73.

4. Jan Vansina, Oral Tradition: A Study in Historical Methodology, trans. H. M. Wright (Chicago: Aldine, 1965).

5. See Georges D. Bokamba, "An Aspect of Social Change: The Emancipation of the Congolese Woman," mimeographed (Seminar paper, African 983: "Social Change in Congo-Kinshasa," University of Wisconsin, Madison, March 27, 1969), pp. 18-19; and A. Sohier, Le mariage en droit congolais (Brussels: Institut Royal Colonial Belge, 1938), cited by Bokamba, "An Aspect of Social Change," p. 23.

6. Pierre Piron and Jacques Devos, Codes et lois du Congo Belge, I, Matières Civil, Commerciales, Pénales, 8th ed. (Brussels: Maison Ferdinand Larcier, 1960), p. 187. Chapter 4, Article 7 explains how the Legal Code applies to customary law. See the prelimi-

nary notes to the decree on monogamous indigenous marriage and the repression of bigamy and adultery. See also the ordinance of May 16, 1949, cited by Bokamba, "An Aspect of Social Change," p. 24.

7. Bakonzi Agayo, "The Formation of Modern Political Elites in Zaire: 1945-1959," mimeographed (Seminar paper, African 983: "Social Change in Zaire," University of Wisconsin, Madison, Spring 1977).

8. Pierre Piron, Supplement aux Codes Congolais: Legislation de la Republique Democratique du Congo (Brussels: Ferdinand Larcier, 1970), should be consulted for vague references to such changes —for example, a change in the procedure for divorce by Congolese living abroad. There has not been any specific law governing a situation in which one of the parties to a divorce fails to obey its terms.

9. Peron and Devos, Codes et lois du Congo Belge, p. 197.

10. See Suzanne Comhaire-Sylvain, Femmes de Kinshasa hier et aujourd'hui (Paris: Mouton et Compagnie, 1968); and A. Sohier, "Notes sur l'évolution du mariage des Congolais," Bulletin des séances, no. 21 (November 1950), pp. 857-68.

11. "Pourquoi tant de soins dans l'entretien des 'IIme bureau'?" Elima 52 (October 1977): 2-4.

12. Although some men allow at least joking application of the term bureau to men, not all permit this. One urban Zairian male (who had lived in Kinshasa for three years) asked if the concept of bureau attached to men, exclaimed, "No!" He explained that only a man has a bureau because men possess women and pay household expenses. He agreed, however, that a wealthy woman may pay the household expenses for some men. He said it is his belief that whomever controls the purse controls the relationship between a man and a woman, and it is very rare for a woman to control a man. Anonymous male Zairian source, interview in Madison, Wisconsin, May 1977.

13. Anonymous but reliable male Zairian source, interview in May 1977.

14. Jean S. LaFontaine, City Politics: A Study of Léopoldville, 1962-63 (London: Cambridge University Press, 1970), table 3b, p. 34.

15. A. Lamy, "La dot congolaise et ses prolongements direts et lointains," Problèmes sociales congolaise, no. 80 (March 1968), pp. 28, 38. The operative legislation for this area of law may be found, for example, in Piron, Supplement aux codes congolais, under legislation on a married couple's savings, June 10, 1950, Section 2, p. 162, which gives husbands the greater control over funds whether deposited by wife or husband (Article 32). Between 1950 and 1970, the Zairian courts had not seemingly passed other legislation governing the pecuniary conditions of marriage.

16. Comhaire-Sylvain, Femmes de Kinshasa, p. 15; but see pp. 14-16 for discussion of the term.

17. Democratic Republic of Zaire, "Law 74-020 of 15 August, 1974 Amending the Constitution of 24 June, 1967," Constitution of the Republic of Zaire (n.p., n.d.), p. 2.

18. Anonymous but reliable male Zairian source, interview in Madison, Wisconsin, during May 1977.

19. Registration of prostitutes and their certification with a clean bill of health are irregularly enforced regulations, according to an anonymous male Zairian source, May 1977.

20. Anatole Romaniuk, La fécondité des populations congolaises (Paris: Mouton et Compagnie et I.R.E.S., 1967), p. 220.

21. Ibid., p. 189.

22. Terri F. Gould, "The Educated Woman and Social Change: A Sociological Study of Women Students at the National University of Zaire," Papers in Education and Development (Dar es Salaam: University of Dar es Salaam, Department of Education, 1976), p. 136.

23. Kikassa Mwanalessa, "Politique de population au Zaire--Experience des 'naissances désirables basées sur la maternité,'" Zaire-Afrique, no. 86 (June-July 1974), p. 342. Although he states that the government encourages families of five or more children, a male Zairian observed that while the government does give incentives to having several children, five is an inflated figure. Interview in Madison, Wisconsin, September 1, 1978.

24. Romaniuk, La fédondité des populations congolaises, p. 188.

25. Jan Vansina, interview in Madison, Wisconsin, May 16, 1977.

26. Comhaire-Sylvain, Femmes de Kinshasa, pp. 11-21, 25.

27. United Nations Educational, Scientific and Cultural Organization, "Congo (Léopoldville)," World Survey of Education, IV: Higher Education (New York: UNESCO, 1966), p. 362.

28. Comhaire-Sylvain, Femmes de Kinshasa, p. 234.

29. Ibid., p. 233.

30. United Nations Educational, Scientific and Cultural Organization, "Congo," pp. 361-62; and idem, "Democratic Republic of the Congo," World Survey of Education, V: Educational Policy, Legislation and Administration (Paris: UNESCO, 1971), pp. 333-40.

31. M. Crawford Young (chairman) et al., Survey of Education in the Democratic Republic of the Congo (Washington, D.C.: American Council on Education, August 1969), p. 67.

32. Ibid., p. 17.

33. Comhaire-Sylvain, Femmes de Kinshasa, pp. 93-95.

34. M. Crawford Young et al., Survey of Education.

35. Bokamba, "An Aspect of Social Change," p. 26.

36. Therèse Verheust, "La jeune fille kinoise face à la profession," Zaire-Afrique, no. 70 (December 1972), p. 600.

37. Ibid., pp. 603-4. Verheust recommended job counseling (p. 604). This could help women make practical career choices, but

other social factors are clearly the stronger and more immediate determinants of women's academic performance and future work.

38. Anonymous male Zairian source, interview in Madison, Wisconsin, May 1977.

39. Mary Collins, "Women in Zaire and Indonesia" (Paper for Political Science 653, University of Wisconsin, Madison, April 23, 1976), p. 20.

40. Ibid., n. 30, no page.

41. Ibid., p. 14.

42. Ibid. This footnoted material indicates that the report is from the same informant who mentioned the plight of the working woman.

43. United Nations, Economic Commission for Africa, African Statistical Yearbook, Part 4: Central Africa/Others in Africa, 1974 (New York: United Nations, 1974), p. 40-41.

44. Comhaire-Sylvain, Femmes de Kinshasa, pp. 171-215.

45. Malulu Mitwensil muns Mukil, "La femme zairoise: Recrutement et conditions d'emploi dans l'administration publique de la Ville de Bukavu (1970-1972)," Revue de recerche scientifique 1 (January-March 1978): 56.

46. Ibid., pp. 61-64.

47. Ibid., pp. 62-68.

48. Ibid., pp. 66-68.

49. Gould, "Educated Woman and Social Change," p. 134.

50. Diamant, Association Récreative, was founded in Léopoldville in 1943. The Association Nationale des Femmes Protestantes, founded in 1946, also had a Léopoldville chapter. Many provincial women's associations were founded in the late 1940s; for example, L'Union des Femmes du Katanga was founded in 1948 (reported by Bokamba, "An Aspect of Social Change," p. 18). Patrice Lumumba's Association Libérale was apolitical, interethnic, and composed of 20 women and 20 men after its establishment in 1956. M. Mogenda founded the Association des Femmes Evoluantes Kinoise in 1957 (reported by Comhaire-Sylvain, Femmes de Kinshasa, p. 277). Bokamba, "An Aspect of Social Change," p. 23, citing Comhaire-Sylvain, reported that a woman was nominated to Léopoldville commune's city council in 1956.

51. Bokamba, "An Aspect of Social Change," pp. 27-31.

52. Mary Collins, personal interview in Madison, Wisconsin, May 28, 1977.

53. See M. Crawford Young's forthcoming work in collaboration with Thomas Turner, Political Change in Mobutu's Zaire, on Zaire's political elite, 1965-75. Data were collected on 212 persons who held ministerial posts or positions in the top MPR party organs from 1965 to 1975. The biographical data were obtained primarily from the

Centre d'Etudes et de Documentation Africaine (CEDAF), in Brussels, and encoded with the help of a panel of Zairian doctoral candidates. Women listed in CEDAF's file tend to emerge from relative obscurity. Their cards seem to begin abruptly with political appointment and the sudden onset of their political activity.

54. Ibid., computer printout; see computations for "age by sex," "sex by education," and "sex by immediate background." Bakonzi Agayo, commentary, July 25, 1978, and August 3, 1978.

55. Ibid., see under "sex by occupation."

56. Ibid.; see under "sex by entry into business" and "politics and business by sex."

57. Ibid.; see under "sex by associational activity," "sex by leadership position in associations," and "sex by pre-Independence leadership roles."

58. Ibid.; see under "political disgrace by sex" and "rehabilitation by sex."

59. Mary Collins, personal interview of May 28, 1978; and also Collins, "Women in Zaire and Indonesia," passim.

60. Baleka Bamba Nzuji, "Que signifié au juste la liberation féminine," Cultures au Zaire et en Afrique, ONRD, no. 1 (1973), pp. 186-88, 193.

61. Ibid.

62. Siradiou Diallo, Le Zaire aujourd'hui (Paris: Editions Jeune Afrique, 1975), p. 56, quoting President Mobutu in the N'Sele Manifesto.

REFERENCES

Bakonzi, Agayo. "The Formation of Modern Political Elites in Zaire: 1945-1959." Seminar paper, African 983: "Social Change in Zaire," University of Wisconsin, Madison, Spring 1977. Mimeographed.

Bokamba, Georges D. "An Aspect of Social Change: The Emancipation of the Congolese Woman." Seminar paper, African 983: "Social Change in Congo-Kinshasa," University of Wisconsin, Madison, March 27, 1969. Mimeographed.

Buvinić, Mayra, Cheri S. Adams, Gabrielle S. Edgecomb, and Maritta Koch-Weser. Women and World Development: An Annotated Bibliography. Washington, D.C.: Overseas Development Council, 1976.

Collins, Mary. "Women in Zaire and Indonesia." Paper for Political Science 653, University of Wisconsin, Madison, April 23, 1976. Mimeographed.

Comhaire-Sylvain, Suzanne. Femmes de Kinshasa hier et aujourd'hui. Paris: Mouton et Compagnie, 1968.

Democratic Republic of Zaire. "Law 74-020 of 15 August, 1974 Amending the Constitution of 24 June, 1967." Constitution of the Republic of Zaire. N.p., n.d.

Diallo, Siradiou. Le Zaire aujourd'hui. Paris: Editions Jeune Afrique, 1975.

Gluckman, Max. Custom and Conflict in Africa. New York: Barnes and Noble, 1964.

LaFontaine, Jean S. City Politics: A Study of Léopoldville, 1962-63. London: Cambridge University Press, 1970.

Lamy, A. "La dot congolaise et ses prolongements directs et lointain." Problèmes sociaux congolaise, no. 80 (March 1968), pp. 3-91. Also, in "Chronique du CEPSI: Colloque sur la dot, situation actuelle et son avenir." Problèmes sociales congolaises, no. 74 (September 1968), pp. 97-117.

LeBlanc, Maria. Personalité de la femme katangaise: Contribution a l'étude de son acculturation. Louvain: Publication Universitaires, 1960.

Mwanalessa, Kikassa. "Politique de population au Zaire—Experience des 'naissances désirables basées sur la maternité.'" Zaire-Afrique, no. 86 (June-July 1974), pp. 341-49.

Nzuji, Baleka Bamba. "Que signifié au juste la liberation féminine?" Cultures au Zaire et en Afrique, ONRD, no. 1 (1973), pp. 185-95.

Piron, Pierre. Supplement aux Codes Congolais: Legislation de la Republique Democratique du Congo. I, Matieres Civiles, Commerciales et Penales. Brussels: Maison Ferdinand Larcier, 1960-70.

Piron, Pierre, and Jacques Devos. Code et lois du Congo Belge. I, Matieres Civil, Commerciales, Penales. 8th ed. Brussels: Maison Ferdinand Larcier, 1960.

"Pourquoi taut de soins dans l'entretien des 'IIme bureau'?" Elima 52 (October 1977): 2-4.

Romaniuk, Anatole. La fécondité des populations congolaises. Paris: Mouton et Compagnie et I.R.E.S., 1967.

Sohier, A. "Notes sur l'évolution du mariage des Congolais." Bulletin des séances, no. 21 (November 1950), pp. 857-68.

United Nations, Economic Commission for Africa. "Zaire." African Statistical Yearbook, Part 4: Central Africa/Others in Africa, 1974, pp. 40-41 to 41-21. New York: United Nations, 1974.

United Nations Educational, Scientific and Cultural Organization. "Congo (Léopoldville)." World Survey of Education, IV: Higher Education, pp. 361-62. New York: UNESCO, 1966.

_____. "Democratic Republic of the Congo." World Survey of Education, V: Educational Policy, Legislation and Administration, pp. 333-40. Paris: UNESCO, 1971.

Vansina, Jan. Oral Tradition: A Study in Historical Methodology. Translated by H. M. Wright. Chicago: Aldine, 1965.

Verheust, Thérèse. "La jeune fille Kinoise face à la profession." Zaire-Afrique, no. 70 (December 1972), pp. 593-604.

Young, M. Crawford. Politics in the Congo: Decolonialization and Independence. London: Oxford University Press, 1965.

Young, M. Crawford (chairman), William M. Rideout, Jr., David N. Wilson, George V. Corinaldi, L. Gray Cowan, and John S. McNown. Survey of Education in the Democratic Republic of the Congo. Washington, D.C.: American Council on Education, August 1969.

Young, M. Crawford, and Thomas Turner. Political Change in Mobutu's Zaire. Forthcoming.

Interviews with Zairian Informants

Bakonzi, Agayo (male). April 18, 1977, interview of 1 hour. April 20, 1977, interview of 2 hours. Also, at various other times. Translator of tape recorded interview with Empegne Djele (see below) of May 18, 1977. Further interviews of July 25, 1978, and August 3, 1978, to discuss the statistical analyses of data collected by M. Crawford Young and Thomas Turner for their forthcoming book on Political Change in Mobutu's Zaire, for which Bakonzi prepared the computer program.

Empegne Djelo (male). Professor of Law, National University of Zaire, Kinshasa. May 18, 1977, interview of 1 hour and 30 minutes, with the assistance of Edwin Whitman, escort provided by the U.S. Department of State, who did a partial translation at the time of recording the interview, in Madison, Wisconsin.

Toumba Diambu Yamvu (female). February 22, March 3, March 22, March 31, April 14, April 21, 1977. Each interview lasted about 1 hour and 15 minutes and was conducted at the subject's house in Madison, Wisconsin.

Yamvu Makasu a M'Teba (male). April 19, 1977, interview of 3 hours; and, at other times, in Madison, Wisconsin.

4
ISSUES CONFRONTING PROFESSIONAL AFRICAN WOMEN: ILLUSTRATIONS FROM KENYA

Beverly Lindsay

> The position of women provides an excellent measure
> of the development of that society.
>> Evelyne Sullerot,
>> Woman, Society and Change

Reading many contemporary publications from the developing African nations—ranging from national development plans and ministry reports to newspapers and popular magazines—reveals an ardent appeal for indigenous populace participation in national development. Special appeals are frequently made to women citizens. Depending upon the indicators we wish to identify, women are participating to a greater or lesser degree in the development of their respective societies. From the historical to the current periods, there are the rural agrarian women who till the soil, carry the water, and prepare the family's food. There are the young women who attend higher education institutions, studying educational, scientific, and technical subjects, which the national government has designated as priority areas. And, there are the professional women engaged in positions that require the utmost mental alertness and stamina. Women are contributing to national development in diverse sectors. Yet, we can quickly see that the sociocultural benefits of development award

The research for this chapter was sponsored, in part, by a Ford Foundation Grant. This chapter is a revised version of a paper presented at the 1978 Association for Study of Afro-American Life and History 63rd Annual Conference in Los Angeles, California. The author wishes to express appreciation to Martha Whiting and Abigail Krystal for providing many documentary references and to Sheila Walker for her critique.

different benefits to males and females; for example, only 16 percent of the wage labor force are females.[1] In a society, where a continual source of financial income is important to the individual, participation in the labor force is quite important.

Examination of participation in the wage labor sector and traditional areas such as subsistence farming immediately discloses the dual nature of the African economy. One sector is characterized by the presence of workers with various levels of education and skills, which permit them to be involved directly in the monetary component of the national economy. Such persons would include, for example, teachers, attorneys, engineers, and physicians. The other historically traditional sector includes persons involved in barter, exchange, and subsistence agriculture, and such persons frequently have limited or no formal educational training. Often the traditional sector is not fully taken into account in official estimates of national economic statistics, such as the gross national product (GNP). This chapter focuses on various sociocultural conditions, policies, and programs that have hindered women's participation in this monetary realm. The central concern revolves around the transformation of women into the modern economic sector.

The absence of participation in the modern sector seems rather paradoxical when we recall quotes such as "to educate a girl is to educate a whole nation." Are women educating a nation without educating themselves? Or are women and men educating male and female children in distinct manners, so that the ultimate results are different benefits in terms of social development between the sexes? There are few immediate answers to such initial questions. Surely, we could not argue definitively that women are responsible solely for their situation regarding national development. For instance, many women have not participated in formal education to the extent that males have, because there are more male than female secondary boarding schools.[2] When women do participate, problems confronting them are usually quite dissimilar to those confronting their male peers.

Various issues are quite distinct among the many African nations; however, the positions of Kenyan women may serve as basic indicators of variables present in other developing African nations. A fundamental purpose of this chapter is to delve into some of the select issues confronting African women in Kenya. Because focusing on all women in Kenya is beyond the parameters of this chapter, mainly we shall discuss the professional women in Kenya. Professional Kenyan women are in a unique position. To paraphrase the Kenyan woman anthropologist, Achola Pala, the professional Kenyan woman must utilize her knowledge and expertise for presenting a different perspective to examine the problems of women in local societies in relation to national development.[3]

After a preliminary discussion of the terms professional women (used in a comprehensive sense) and roles, this chapter will peruse fundamental issues affecting Kenyan women. The first major section of this chapter focuses on a discussion of sociocultural factors that influence their roles. These factors have often been perceived as phenomena affecting individual women; yet they permeate the lives of many professional women. We shall observe sociocultural factors in relation to the family, education, and employment that influence the roles and positions of Kenyan women. A second major part of this chapter discusses the pivotal position of social policies and is integrated with our presentation of the three sociocultural factors. The chapter concludes by discussing the relationship between sociocultural issues and roles in relation to social policies aimed at national development.

SOCIOCULTURAL FACTORS AFFECTING PROFESSIONAL WOMEN

Professional Women

Providing a comprehensive definition of the term professional women can prove to be a rather elusive task within the Kenyan context. Definitions and views of professional women derived from the Western hemisphere do not suffice for our purposes, because they have often focused upon women who have completed the baccalaureate degree or its equivalent; often graduate or professional education has also been completed. Women's positions as physicians, professional nurses, engineers, university professors, or social workers and the income associated with them are also indicators of professional status. Personal earnings are usually higher than the modal incomes for most women in the society. [4] In the United States, professional women earn from 10 to 40 percent more than other women. Based upon income, for example, actresses and other professional entertainers would be included in the category of professional women. In Kenya only a small proportion of African women have completed the baccalaureate degree and may be engineers or professional entertainers. Instead, we should focus on somewhat different criteria for professional Kenyan women, since they may not be viewed precisely in the same manner in Africa as they are in the West.

The completion of secondary education or its equivalent usually defines an "educated" person. [5] Completion of four to six years of secondary education and/or two to four years of tertiary education is normally a prerequisite for entrance into the professional world of teachers, lawyers, professional nurses, as well as medical technologists, laboratory assistants, executive secretaries, and secretarial supervisors. The latter categories have also been termed technical and kindred workers and are included in the category of professional women for reasons cited later. Basically, we contend that the lives of these professionals are characterized by participation in the modern economic sector.

Achola Pala and Kenneth King provide some succinct and insightful cues concerning the modern sector. The presence of a cash salary is one major feature of the modern economic sector, which usually accompanies formal employment.[6] It implies a contrast to the traditional, largely self-employed economic activities of the rural areas and the small-scale trading of the towns and urban areas. Regular or systematic cash exchanges may not always be evident in the traditional areas; instead we see the prevalence of barter and exchange along with subsistence agriculture. Positions that comprise the bulk of the labor force as constituted in national surveys of salaried employees in public services, private firms, and large-scale farm operations are the usual illustrations cited in the modern economic sector.[7]

The completion of some form of postsecondary formal education and employment are two criteria for viewing women as professionals. We can also include women who are in positions whereby they may influence policies affecting significant portions of the society. They may view themselves as professional and/or others may perceive them in this light. Women in this category include political leaders, influential wives of ministers, and major officeholders in national women's organizations such as Maendeleo ya Wanawake. A sense of responsibility as professional women appears to characterize this third category.

As we can see, providing a working definition of professional Kenyan women encompasses several dimensions. Indeed, we realize that we have not identified all types of professional women; but a variety of illustrative examples within the modern economic sector have been cited. We have suggested some factors that may distinguish facets of the lives of "professional women" from those of the rural traditional women—hence we use the term professional women.

Roles

Roles may be viewed as a set of expectations applied to one who holds a particular position. Expectations associated with the position assume crucial characteristics since they may be derived from the views of the incumbent within the role or from the views of others regarding a role. An ideal situation would be for the incumbent and others to hold the same expectations regarding roles. A potential or actual conflict may arise when the professional woman is ambivalent about her roles.[8] For example, the professional woman may be quite concerned about care for her young children. Yet, she may perceive that her professional roles dictate, on occasions, that she leave the care of her young children to others while she completes a major report. Or another potential source of role conflict may develop when her spouse asks her to care for the children and delay completion of the report. Or her employer may express still other expectations regarding her position as an employee. These conflicts may be of a temporary nature but are frequently recurrent.

In essence, we are contending that professional women confront a variety of sociocultural conditions that influence their personal or domestic roles and their professional or public roles. Perhaps women may view these issues as phenomena that are unique to the individual. Yet, we shall cite illustrations that portray prevalence of various sociocultural conditions that influence these roles. The primary illustrations revolve around the family, the education system, and the career. Or stated in another manner, we may view family influences and the education system as sociocultural conditions that are external to the career per se, though such issues are intricately related to it. Still other factors are directly related to the career, such as working conditions and compensations.

The Family: Domestic Roles and Social Conditions

Women are socialized by their families during their childhood. The socialization process imparts a different set of roles and expectations for females and males; different expectations about roles based on gender are internalized. One of these internalized expectations concerns the difference between the roles of females as wives and mothers—that is, domestic or personal roles versus their professional or public roles. The early socialization process helps instill the view that females should opt for domestic roles or at least be cognizant of the expectation that domestic roles be paramount in their lives. Women learn these expectations from their families and later perpetuate similar expectations in their children during the socialization process.[9]

Marriage and motherhood (domestic roles) and career (professional roles) responsibilities often become a double burden for professional women. As issues associated with the domestic role emerge, women may often confront several options. A first of these options may be to commit themselves tentatively to professional roles, which may initially begin with the choice of a secondary or college/university major restricted to certain areas. A second may be to accept a role defined in terms of traditional female occupations such as nursing or teaching. And a third may be to allow themselves to be incorporated into the work force predominately in lower-level professional positions that do not permit individual creativity nor the opportunity to make innovative contributions to the society. [10] The first two options appear to be personal choices made by individual professional women influenced, undoubtedly, by their early socialization. Yet the choices are inextricably bound to social conditions. Rates of participation and entrance into low- and high-level positions are beyond the control of individual professional women and their families as shown by the following national statistics from Kenya.

In 1976, as mentioned previously, women comprised only 16 percent of the wage labor force. On the one hand, women were concentrated in secretarial work, nursing, and teaching, which were the most feminized fields. Over 90 percent of secretarial workers and nurses were females—two positions with more female than male employees. (Percentages of female teachers will be discussed in the next paragraph.) On the other hand, less than 5 percent of lawyers, physicians, and engineers were women. Here, the first and second options may be operative. A woman may be expressing her commitment to a career, albeit in a tentative manner, by preparing for and opting for secretarial work or nursing—professions that may be periodically interrupted more easily than if one is an engineer or physician. Overall rates of participation in the professions, nevertheless, are beyond the control of individual women. It is doubtful that only 16 percent of the employees in the modern sector are women because additional females do not desire employment. Participation rates are related to formal education, for example, as demonstrated in the following section on education institutions.

The percentage of female teachers in Kenya also provides some insight concerning levels of participation for professional women. In 1964, 25 percent of the primary schoolteachers were women; by 1976, 30 percent of the teachers were women. Of the secondary schoolteachers, 35 percent were women in 1964; by 1975, 30 percent of these teachers were women. [11] The increase in the percentage of female primary schoolteachers may be due, in part, to women's increasing identification with this position as a female profession despite historical dominance of males in this field. Historically, formal education was provided more often to males than females. The differences between the percentages of women teachers in primary and secondary schools may be related to the amount of formal education required—that is, a social condition that women do control. To be a qualified primary schoolteacher, one must complete primary education and three or four years of teacher training; or one must complete two to four years of secondary education and an additional two to three years of teacher training. To be a qualified secondary schoolteacher, one must complete at least four years of secondary education and three years of teacher training. Continued participation as a student in formal education is not solely determined by females. For example, parents may be willing to spend monies for a career in primary teacher education, but they may be somewhat reluctant or unable to provide funds for extended years of schooling.

Attendance at formal education institutions (and later participation in a career) is related to both the socioeconomic background of students and the education system. Males whose fathers are either farmers or professionals are represented in postprimary education, although the percentage from professional backgrounds is somewhat higher. Various studies have shown, however, that the socioeconomic background for females in terms of attendance at the postprimary level in Kenya and other East African nations portrays a somewhat different picture. [12] The payment of school fees for secondary education serves as a deterrent for female attendance, especially if there are limited resources and a male is also of school age. [13] During 1975 this writer conducted studies of women attending higher education institutions. Over 50 percent of the women students' fathers were from high socioeconomic backgrounds as defined within the Kenyan context. [14]

Education Institutions

Of equal, if not of more, significance are factors associated primarily with the education system. Female enrollment figures present initial insight. Approximately 34 percent of the primary school enrollees were females in 1963. By 1974 almost 43 percent of the enrollees were females. A notable increase has occurred; yet this increase is tempered by the realization that in 1975 over 7,000 more male children were attending government schools than female children. Government schools, as opposed to private schools, are the main vehicle for formal education. With each successive class, the number of female children continues to decline. At government secondary schools, the percentages of female enrollees remained fairly constant from 1963 to 1974 with women students constituting about 34 and 33 percent, respectively. [15]

Somewhat similar to secondary school enrollments are the figures for higher education. Approximately 28 percent of the students in primary teacher training colleges were females in 1964; the number was about 31 percent in 1975. Although enrollment began in the late 1960s, by 1975 female enrollees constituted only about 28 percent of the student body in the country's only secondary science teacher training institute that offers diploma courses. At the national university, women enrollees constituted about 21 percent of the total in 1966 and around 18 percent in 1977. [16] Female university enrollment in the several faculties varied. The largest numbers, about 36 percent and nearly 30 percent, were enrolled in the Faculty of Education and Faculty of Liberal Arts, respectively. Less than 3 percent were enrolled in the Faculty of Engineering. Enrollment in a faculty is basically equivalent to majoring/concentrating in a subject. Thus, with the majority of female enrollees in education and teacher training colleges, it is not surprising that a significant percentage of professional women are teachers as mentioned earlier.

The differences in primary school enrollment between males and females are influenced by parental attitudes and socioeconomic status. Yet the presence of some concerted national priorities regarding primary school education has served as one method of increasing female access to education. The government has constructed new primary schools and has gradually eliminated school fees at the primary level. That is, national priorities have served as the impetus for specific policy and program changes, which have increased female enrollment. The national government has not designated universal secondary education as significant a priority as universal primary education. In this instance, policy and program priorities (taking into account limited national economic resources) for secondary education have not been clearly set; therefore, the situation curtails changes comparable to those at the primary level. Female access to education is still limited by the small number of schools and the failure to construct new ones. There are 54 boys' schools, 31 girls' schools, and 15 mixed schools at the higher secondary level. [17] Many mixed schools have a substantially higher percentage of male than female students; in some cases, only 20 percent of the enrollees are females. In essence, more financial resources for male schools have limited the opportunities for females to attend secondary schools and major or concentrate in various curriculum offerings. For example, boys' and mixed schools offer more science and mathematical courses, whereas female schools offer more liberal arts subjects.

Moreover, the absence of policy and program changes within education institutions per se has also stifled female enrollments and opportunities. The schools have inadequate counseling and guidance programs, so students in general, and females in particular, may not receive much formal guidance in making decisions. Alliance Girls' School is one of a select few that offers a rather comprehensive counseling program to its students. Students from this school have often expressed more career ambitions than those from other schools. Yet, less than 1 percent of secondary female students attend this particular government school. Hence, for most females, career pursuits are probably based on haphazard or erroneous information, since there are not other systematic means for obtaining accurate information on careers.

Another factor that limits female enrollment is the repeating phenomenon. Repeating is a method of prolonging study in order to gain additional instruction and time to prepare for the Certificate of Primary Education exam (CPE). This phenomenon is distinct between the sexes: more males than females "voluntarily" decide to repeat standards or grades in primary school to prolong their study for the CPE. During 1972, 49,125 or 58.35 percent of the boys repeated, while 35,064 or 41.65 percent of the girls repeated. Hence, males take additional opportunities to repeat curricula and enhance their prospects for passing the CPE. Passing the CPE and placing in the top percentiles are necessary for entering a government secondary school.

Students who do not score a high percentage on the CPE are usually forced to abandon their formal academic training or enroll in secondary harambee schools, second-chance institutions seriously inadequate in curriculum and instruction. Such schools provide only a remote opportunity for reentering government academic schools and continuing career opportunities. Indeed, studies by Edmond J. Keller indicate that the overwhelming majority of harambee school students do not complete the equivalent of secondary education. [18] The fact that well over 50 percent of harambee school students are female is related to the higher percentage of girls who do not repeat and/or pass the CPE. [19] The nature of educational curricula and performance on primary and secondary (East African Certificate) school examinations determines who enters higher secondary schools and postsecondary institutions. Absence of policy changes for and within these educational realms coupled with the ways financial resources are allocated depresses the enrollment of females and affects their entrance into professional careers.

Career Conditions

Although professional women may surpass many of the hurdles associated with the educational system and the family, career conditions still confront them. Until mid-1976 one basic obstacle to women's employment was the Employment of Women, Young Persons, and Children's Act. This act forbade the employment of women between the hours of 6:30 P.M. and 6:30 A.M. unless a formal petition was filed with and granted by the Minister of Labor. Exceptions were provided for women in medical fields and managerial positions. [20] In short, the working hours of women were being restricted—a particular burden for those seeking career advancement, especially for those women who may have been school administrators or secretarial or office supervisors.

Salary differentials are a second obstacle confronting professional Kenyan women. With the assistance of legal regulations, employers have hired women in lower positions than males, although they possess the same qualifications, and many females have received lower compensation for performing the same work as their male peers. To conceal this discriminatory pattern, some employers have attempted to provide different names for similar positions. For example, if a woman is a secretarial employee, a male may be a personnel employee; different titles result in different compensation. The result of establishing different salary scales is a continual source of frustration for women and helps perpetuate men's sense of superiority. One result of different salary scales is demonstrated by the fact that less than 13 percent of all monetary benefits were paid to women employees in 1975. A gap is established between the two sexes' earnings in a society where money translates into influence and substantive material rewards.[21]

Social security programs for employees are a third obstacle reflecting differential treatment for professional males and females. In June 1963, just prior to formal political independence, a social security bill was enacted, which was in effect until January 1975. (An independent Parliament approved the bill in toto during 1965.) Only employed men over 16 years were legally required to be registered contributors. Women who had the same attributes as men were excluded from the registration. On January 17, 1975, this legal constraint was abolished. By March 1976, however, no directive had been provided to require women to make financial contributions and, hence, receive many of the benefits—although nominal registration had begun. Benefits would be available to the individual in the event of serious illness or death (death benefits to survivors), reaching age 60, or permanent migration outside East Africa.[22] It should be kept in mind that we are not stating that women do not participate in any of these benefits; rather, there are legal loopholes that can curtail benefits to women based upon their contributions, despite their participation.

The Widow's and Young Children's Pension Act as amended in 1971 is a fourth obstacle facing professional women. The act stipulates that a man, married or not married, upon attaining the status of a "public officer" (for example, a district officer), is eligible to contribute voluntarily to a fund for the benefit of his widow or orphans. A woman public officer, on the other hand, may contribute only after passing a strenuous selection process. The law states that a married woman may participate "on proof, to the satisfaction of the President, that her husband is wholly or mainly dependent on her."[23] Moreover, a widow forfeits her benefits if she cohabits with a male, although she is not married to him nor is he supporting her. The issue of women public officers (although "public officers" is a nebulous term) must be addressed in order to ensure equity. Regardless of marital status, women, along with men, should be able to contribute and partake of the benefits.

A fifth and perhaps most crucial obstacle affecting professional women (and women in general, for that matter) involves maternity benefits. Through May 1976 employers were not legally required to provide paid maternity leaves. In fact, it was explicitly stated that female employees, regardless of marital status, are eligible for unpaid maternity leaves. Childbirth was not regarded as a sickness; hence benefits were not paid as in the case of illness. In 1975, the president decreed that all women should be provided paid maternity leaves; however, a presidential decree is not a law in Kenya except during a state of emergency. On May 3, 1976, a new employment act stated that, "A woman shall be entitled to two months leave with full pay: Provided a woman who has taken two months maternity leave shall forfeit her annual leave in that year."[24]

The five issues enumerated regarding career conditions for professional women indicate that employment policies at the national and local levels have curtailed or prevented women's participation in professional positions. To ensure women's participation is to continue changing national and local policies. Changing policies requires a fundamental examination of the roles of professional Kenyan women. Hence, we must again devote some attention to the family, the education system, and the career in relationship to sociocultural views toward professional women as we assess policy implications for national development.

SOCIOCULTURAL ISSUES AND ROLES: POLICY IMPLICATIONS FOR NATIONAL DEVELOPMENT

As we portrayed earlier, professional Kenyan women usually confront a double burden—their domestic roles and their professional roles. Although statistics are sketchy, the evidence seems to indicate that the majority of professional women are married; the exception may be young women who are under 25. With reference to their domestic roles, the issue of household administration (for example, cleaning and marketing) is ever present. To obtain some general views regarding household administration, the author asked Kenyan women students their views on the subject. Well over one-half of the women stated that they did not anticipate receiving assistance from their mothers or other female relatives as was the situation in more traditional households. Many of these women generally expected to administer their household affairs with the assistance of paid employees. Receiving assistance from spouses was not often mentioned as a viable option. Moreover, approximately 84 percent of these women students (who were unmarried) did not believe that their profession would hinder marriage prospects; however, it should be kept in mind that almost three-fourths were preparing for professions in what are increasingly being identified as new traditional women's careers (for example, primary teachers).[25]

Although comparable data is not available for women actually in the professions, the women students' responses may provide some insigtful cues. These young women anticipate both marriage and careers. (Nearly 75 percent of the women in this study indicated that they expected to be a wife and work.)* If this becomes a reality, how will the issue of household administration be addressed? Will the professional woman perform the necessary tasks? Or will she seek assistance from other "less educated" women? The current trend is to have servants involved in the routine household assignments. Indeed, it is rather rare for a professional Kenyan couple not to have household servants. However, socioeconomic differences will arise and be perpetuated between the two groups of women—the professional and the unskilled. In essense, professional women may enhance their individual positions at the expense of their unskilled cohorts. As this occurs, an inevitable result is a class cleavage that may be even wider than that between professional Kenyan women and men. Surely, professional women would not "consciously" argue that they are bettering their positions by exploiting less skilled women (and men) servants. Moreover, with the increased use of domestic appliances, many professional women may not rely as heavily on household personnel to assist them as they have in the past.

As mentioned earlier in this chapter, the care of children is another crucial area confronting professional women. Many of the child's immediate physical needs may be taken care of by household servants. If some other options become available for persons who are household servants, the care of young children may not be approached in this way. Perhaps parents may desire that their children have a variety of social and educational experiences that they cannot provide (nor the servants) due to professional commitments. What options may be available? In Kenya there are few nursery schools. The majority are in Nairobi, where nursery schools are under the auspices

---

*Obtaining additional information regarding careers and marriages was recently undertaken in a follow-up study with Kenyan women in higher education. Data analysis is currently under way.

of the city council. Elsewhere in the country, they are conspiciously absent. Will there be consideration of or is there a need to consider national and/or provincial policies for establishing nursery schools for young children? If so, what are the implications for mothers as professional women, their families, and their children? What are the sociocultural ramifications of more institutionalized settings for young children? Will there be a variety of negative experiences in this setting? Or will the institutionalized setting provide a variety of positive experiences that will offset the negative ones? Mothers and their families must concern themselves with such questions from a sociopsychological perspective. The national and provincial governments are concerned from the perspective of social/national development and the ensuing planning with respect to finances, locations, facilities, and the like.

General sociocultural ambivalence regarding the roles of women as professionals and as wives and mothers may still be present despite the fact that national and/or local policies may address the area of child care.[26] Married males may still believe that their wives' primary or sole role is a domestic one. Such perceptions overlook the possibility of androgynous sex roles, that is, a mutual sharing of responsibilities regardless of sex. We recognize that historically Kenyan males have not been primarily concerned with child care; this was the role of women. But with the move toward modernization, a reassessment of male and female roles is occurring. Child care and domestic work can be performed by both sexes. Both partners can share responsibilities, which include socialization and early childhood education. By sharing, the eminence of the quote "to educate a girl is to educate a nation" could assume a new meaning. Girls and boys could be socialized into more interchangeable roles. Interchangeable roles would mean that both sexes can be educated to participate in and contribute to national development.

The implications of androgynous roles extend immediately into the professional and public spheres. If either sex can perform in a variety of fields, employers must change existing policies to ensure equality for both sexes. Some of these were discussed earlier with reference to different employment policies and practices between the sexes—policies that have frequently discriminated against women. Equitable policies should be the goal. It is incumbent upon the national government to initiate specific policy changes within a variety of professional fields. For instance, national policies regarding work conditions, benefits, and promotions in priority employment realms (science and technology) should undergo alterations. In short, policy changes instrumental to encouraging women to enter these priority areas of development should occur at the national government level.

To enter the professions, women must first be aware that such professions exist and that there are viable professional opportunities in the areas. Changes could occur through the establishment and extention of counseling and career information programs within the education system. Simultaneously, the examination system, nature of the curricula, and female access to education should undergo policy changes. It is not very realistic to encourage women students to enter fields necessary for national development if they have had limited preparation for pursuing these careers. It would not be pragmatic to encourage female students to pursue areas that they have not passed on the East African Advanced Examination, unless the examinations are changed and access to education is expanded, especially in priority fields (for example, in scientific and technological spheres). Educational policy changes are necessary.

There must be a serious reassessment of the roles—both domestic and public—played by professional Kenyan women. The assessment should contribute to a critical examination of sociocultural issues affecting all women's roles. Women's roles should be changed in the domestic sphere, and simultaneous changes should occur in public roles that are often beyond the control of individual women and their families. National and local policy changes within education and employment must be initiated to buttress and enhance individual women's roles. Hence, women's changing roles may begin to reflect and support the appeals of government officials to participate in vital areas of development, since there would be concrete opportunities for them to participate in national development. Women and men could participate and benefit through employment in the modern sector—the sector that has historically been dominated by males. Direct benefits would accrue to women themselves by their acquiring professional positions and contributing to national development as part of their inalienable rights as citizens. In essence, professional women's roles and the expectations associated with these roles would be consistent with the aims of national development. Thus, improving the positions of women would begin to provide a more excellent measure of development for all Kenyans.

NOTES

1. Social Perspectives, Women in Kenya (Nairobi: Ministry of Finance and Planning, Central Bureau of Statistics, April 1978), p. 1.

2. Achola Pala and Abigail Krystall, "Women in Rural Development" (Bureau of Education Research Paper, Nairobi, 1978).

3. Achola Pala, "Definitions of Women and Development: An African Perspective," Signs Journal of Women in Culture and Society 3 (1977): 13.

4. Alice Rossi and Ann Calderwood, Academic Women on the Move (New York: Russell Sage Foundation, 1973); and Jessie Bernard, Academic Women (University Park, Pa.: The Pennsylvania State University Press, 1964).

5. Patricia L. McGrath, The Unfinished Assignment: Equal Education for Women (Paper no. 7, Worldwatch Institute, Washington, D.C., July 1976), p. 25.

6. Achola Pala, "A Preliminary Survey of the Avenues for and Constraints on Women in the Development Process in Kenya" (Discussion paper no. 218, Institute for Development Studies, Nairobi, June 1975), p. 1.

7. Kenneth King, Jobless in Kenya: A Case Study of the Educated Unemployed, Bureau of Education Research, Monograph Series (Nairobi: University of Nairobi, 1976), p. 3.

8. Nora Scott Kinzer, "Sociocultural Factors Mitigating Role Conflict of Buenos Aires Professional Women," in Women Cross-Culturally: Change and Challenge, ed. Ruby Rohrlich-Leavitt (Chicago: Aldine, 1975), pp. 182–85.

9. Rene DuMont, "Development and Mounting Famine: A Role for Women," in Women Workers, International Labor Organization (Geneva: International Labor Office, 1976), p. 47.

10. Elsa M. Chaney, "The Mobilization of Women: Three Societies," in Women Cross-Culturally: Change and Challenge, ed. Ruby Rohrlich-Leavitt (Chicago: Aldine, 1975), p. 475.

11. Figures were not readily available regarding the participation of female professionals at the higher education level between the mid-1960s and mid-1970s. However, during the 1974/75 academic year, less than 10 percent of the faculty at the University of Nairobi were women. Social Perspectives, Women in Kenya, pp. 6–7; and Social Perspectives, The Development of the Teaching Profession (Nairobi: Ministry of Finance and Planning, Central Bureau of Statistics, November 1977), pp. 11, 18.

12. H. C. A. Somerset, "Educational Aspirations of Fourth-Form Pupils in Kenya," in Education, Society and Development: New Perspectives from Kenya, ed. David Court and Dhraim Ghai (Nairobi: Oxford University Press, 1974); and Marjorie Mbilinyi, The Education of Girls in Tanzania (Dar es Salaam, Tanzania: University of Dar es Salaam, 1969).

13. Abigail Krystall, "The Education of Women since Independence" (Bureau of Educational Research Paper, University of Nairobi, Nairobi, 1975).

14. Beverly Lindsay, "Education and Career Choices for Kenyan Women," Journal of Negro Education, in press.

15. Social Perspectives, Ministry of Finance and Planning, vol. 1, no. 1 (Nairobi: Central Bureau of Statistics, 1976), p. 10; and Lindsay, "Education and Career Choices."

16. Social Perspectives, Women in Kenya, pp. 4-5.

17. Krystall, "Education of Women"; and Somerset, "Educational Aspirations."

18. Edmond J. Keller, "The Role of Self Help in Education for Development: The Harambee School Movement in Kenya," in What Government Does, ed. Mathew Holden, Jr., and Dennis L. Dresang (Beverly Hills, Calif.: Sage, 1975).

19. Ministry of Education, Annual Report—1972 (Nairobi: Government Printing Office, 1972), p. 39; Martin Hill, "Harambee Schools in Kitui," Kenya Education Review 1 (1974): 61-68; and Joyce Moock, "Pragmatism and the Primary School," in Education, Society and Development: New Perspectives from Kenya, ed. David Court and Dhraim Ghai (Nairobi: Oxford University Press, 1974), p. 117.

20. Achola Pala, "A Preliminary Survey of the Avenues for the Constraints"; and S. B. O. Gutto, "The Status of Women in Kenya: A Study of Paternalism, Inequality and Underprivilege" (Discussion paper no. 235, Institute for Development Studies, Nairobi, 1976), p. 63.

21. Gutto, "Status of Women in Kenya," pp. 64, 67.

22. Ibid., pp. 43-44.

23. Ibid., pp. 48-49.

24. Ibid., pp. 53-55, 76.

25. Beverly Lindsay, "Comparative Perspectives of Kenyan Women on Career Choices," International Education Journal 5 (1976): 30.

26. McGrath, Unfinished Assignment, p. 36.

REFERENCES

Bernard, Jessie. Academic Women. University Park, Pa.: The Pennsylvania State University Press, 1964.

Chaney, Elsa M. "The Mobilization of Women: Three Societies." In Women Cross-Culturally: Change and Challenge, edited by Ruby Rohrlich-Leavitt. Chicago: Aldine, 1975.

DuMont, Rene. "Development and Mounting Famine: A Role for Women." In Women Workers, International Labour Organization. Geneva: International Labour Office, 1976.

Gutto, S. B. O. "The Status of Women in Kenya: A Study of Paternalism, Inequality and Underprivilege." Discussion paper no. 235, Institute for Development Studies, Nairobi, 1976.

Hill, Martin. "Harambee Schools in Kitui." Kenya Education Review 1 (1974): 61-68.

Keller, Edmond J. "The Role of Self Help in Education for Development: The Harambee School Movement in Kenya." In What Government Does, edited by Mathew Holden, Jr., and Dennis L. Dresang. Beverly Hills, Calif.: Sage, 1975.

King, Kenneth. Jobless in Kenya: A Case Study of the Educated Unemployed. Bureau of Education Research, Monograph Series, Nairobi: University of Nairobi, 1976.

Kinzer, Nora Scott. "Sociocultural Factors Mitigating Role Conflict of Buenos Aires Professional Women." In Women Cross-Culturally: Change and Challenge, edited by Ruby Rohrlich-Leavitt. Chicago: Aldine, 1975.

Krystall, Abigail. "The Education of Women since Independence." Bureau of Educational Research Paper, University of Nairobi, Nairobi, 1976.

Lindsay, Beverly. "Comparative Perspectives of Kenyan Women on Career Choices." International Education Journal 5 (1976): 30.

_____. "Education and Career Choices for Kenyan Women." Journal of Negro Education, in press.

McGrath, Patricia L. The Unfinished Assignment: Equal Education for Women. Paper no. 7, Worldwatch Institute, Washington, D.C., July 1976.

Mbilinya, Marjorie. The Education of Girls in Tanzania. Dar es Salaam, Tanzania: University of Dar es Salaam, 1969.

Ministry of Education, Annual Report—1972. Nairobi: Government Printing Office, 1972.

Moock, Joyce. "Pragmatism and the Primary School." In Education, Society and Development: New Perspectives from Kenya, edited by David Court and Dhraim Ghai. Nairobi: Oxford University Press, 1974.

Pala, Achola. "Definitions of Women and Development: An African Perspective." Signs Journal of Women in Culture and Society 3 (1977): 9-13.

_____. "A Preliminary Survey of the Avenues for and Constraints on Women in the Development Process in Kenya." Discussion paper no. 218, Institute for Development Studies, Nairobi, June 1975.

Pala, Achola, and Abigail Krystall. "Women in Rural Development." Bureau of Education Research Paper, Nairobi, 1978.

Rossi, Alice, and Ann Calderwood. Academic Women on the Move. New York: Russell Sage Foundation, 1973.

Social Perspectives. The Development of the Teaching Profession. Nairobi: Ministry of Finance and Planning, Central Bureau of Statistics, November 1977.

_____. Ministry of Finance and Planning. vol. 1, no. 1. Nairobi: Central Bureau of Statistics, 1976.

_____. Women in Kenya. Nairobi: Ministry of Finance and Planning, Central Bureau of Statistics, April 1978.

Somerset, H. C. A. "Educational Aspirations of Fourth-Form Pupils in Kenya." In Education, Society and Development: New Perspectives from Kenya, edited by David Court and Dhraim Ghai. Nairobi: Oxford University Press, 1974.

5

CHINESE WOMEN: THE RELATIVE INFLUENCES OF IDEOLOGICAL REVOLUTION, ECONOMIC GROWTH, AND CULTURAL CHANGE

Bee-Lan Chan Wang

INTRODUCTION

This chapter will present a broad account of changes that have occurred in the roles of Chinese women in Asia, attempting to answer the question: "Does ideology and the politicoeconomic system make a difference regarding women's social, educational, and occupational aspirations and opportunities?" Politicoeconomic system refers to the differences between the Communist model, as represented by mainland China (the People's Republic of China), and the capitalist model, as represented by Taiwan and Malaysia. A description of the traditional place of women in Chinese culture will be followed by an analysis of the changes that have taken place in the People's Republic of China, Taiwan, and West Malaysia. These three countries, respectively, represent the three main kinds of influences on Chinese women's roles in the world today: Communist ideology and politicoeconomic system, capitalist economic development without cultural discontinuities, and capitalist economic development accompanied by extensive Westernization.

Mainland China has never been directly colonized, and although it was powerless in the face of demands from Western nations during the nineteenth century, de facto Western control extended to economic matters and Western cultural influence was confined to such cities as Canton, Shanghai, and Peking. Since the establishment of the People's Republic of China in 1949, a conscious attempt has been made to transform women's roles in conjunction with the ongoing politicoeconomic revolution. The struggle on the mainland has been more

I am grateful for the help of Henry Huang. Thanks are also due to Greg Dolezal, Eva Lu, and Pauline Roelofs.

against traditional ways of thinking and extremely poor economic circumstances inherited by the Communist government than against Western or colonial influences.

Taiwan, in contrast, is generally hailed as one of the success
stories in economic development and maintains a strong emphasis on
Chinese culture. It has never been under <u>direct</u> Western control.
While Japanese colonial rule began just before the turn of the century,
the Japanese did little to alter the traditional Chinese social system
until the 1930s. In fact, they initially even attempted to prevent fundamental cultural changes. The decade or so of "Japanization" (mainly
through education) that began in the 1930s was soon neutralized by the
influx of Chinese from the mainland after Chiang Kai-shek lost the
civil war to the Communists.[1]

West Malaysia, on the other hand, underwent educational and
politicolegal Westernization at the same time that the infrastructure
for modern economic developments was being laid down. Different
states came under British rule at different times over the eighteenth,
nineteenth, and early twentieth centuries. The state of Penang and
Province Wellesley, where the research to be reported below was done,
was the earliest to pass under British control, in 1786. The first
English secondary school was built there, followed by many others
including schools for girls, mostly the result of Western missionary
work. The author's hometown, Georgetown, comprises about 90 percent of the population of the state, which indicates the urban nature of
this economically developed area.

TRADITIONAL POSITION OF CHINESE WOMEN

Traditional Chinese beliefs and norms regarding women's character and roles were extremely oppressive, as evidenced by conversations I have had with most middle-aged or older Chinese persons in
Asia. Sayings such as, "All day long a woman moves between three
terraces: the <u>kang</u> ("stone bed"), the kitchen stove, and the millstone"
reveal the limited daily life of hard housework that was the accepted
lot of the vast majority of Chinese women. Women's low status in society as a whole was but a reflection of their lack of status within the
family, by far the most important unit in Chinese society. Girls were
liabilities to their families of origin, since they would marry and become part of their husbands' families. Hence the Chinese proverb:
"A boy is born facing in; a girl is born facing out."[2] Baby girls were,
therefore, not as valued as boys. Indeed, mistreatment of girls and
female infanticide were serious enough that an imbalance of sex ratios
in the population of China early in this century has been documented.[3]

Marriages were arranged by parents, the prime consideration being the socioeconomic interests of the families concerned. Marriage

often took place at an early age among the better-off families, since parents were anxious to see their offspring settle down and, on the groom's side, to hasten the arrival of a male heir. The partners to the marriage often were unacquainted with each other until the wedding day. The bride was therefore a virtual stranger in her husband's household. She was also cut off from her own family, with visits home only for occasional ceremonial purposes. Weddings were elaborate and expensive affairs, paid for by the groom's parents. This fact, and "the parents' . . . letting the son use the family property to start his married life reaffirmed both to the son and to the daughter-in-law who was boss and who was subordinate."[4] The young age at marriage also made it easier for the mother-in-law to exercise control over her son and daughter-in-law.[5]

"Officials depend on seals [instruments of authority], tigers on mountains and women on their husbands." "Married to a chicken, a woman must fly; married to a dog, a woman must walk." "If I buy a horse I can beat it; if I buy a wife I can do as I like." These sayings are self-evident. The idea that wives were bought was common. Women had no property rights within the family—women were property. Neither did they have legal rights nor recourse to justice if they were mistreated. It is not an overstatement that the woman's only sanction against ill treatment by her husband's family was suicide or attempted suicide.[6] Such episodes are rather common in the literature of ancient China. Due to the division of labor by sex, the young married woman's lot would be improved only when she in turn bore a male child.

The women of wealthy families lived in isolation, with little association even with women of other families and limited contact with male family members. They were, therefore, uninformed about the outside world and economic matters. Peasant families, however, could not afford the luxury of completely secluding their women, who had to perform physically demanding tasks such as carrying water, washing, and gathering firewood, as well as helping in the fields. Despite her role in the economics of the household, however, the death of her husband meant destitution, since she did not own land in her own right.

Confucious taught that the virtue of a woman lay in her being untalented, unskilled, and ignorant. Too much knowledge would lead to unsubmissiveness and submissiveness was the ideal of feminine propriety. The most dramatic evidence of attempts to achieve these ideals was, of course, the practice of foot binding, which was not eliminated until after the turn of the century.[7] In Asia examples of Chinese women who had undergone this treatment are not hard to find even today. Binding girls' feet from infancy and thus preventing the feet from growing beyond a couple of inches in length ensured a womanly life of physical and economic dependence. It follows from this kind of philosophy that women were not educated, much less expected to engage in remunerative work or careers outside the home.

A few of the more progressive families in large cities such as Shanghai, which served as one of China's major gateways to the Western world during the nineteenth and early twentieth centuries, did educate their daughters. The author's mother-in-law was one of those early women to be educated through high school in a Western-type missionary institution. The presence of older Chinese women in the professional world in Asia today is evidence of these exceptional cases and should not be taken to mean that Chinese women as a whole were or are liberated, as some writers have done.[8] What, then, are the social, educational, and occupational positions of Chinese women in Asia today? The following sections examine the extent and nature of the changes that have taken place in Chinese women's roles.

COMMUNIST CHINA: IDEOLOGY AND ECONOMIC MOBILIZATION

The Communist position on women is basic to the changes in the lot of Chinese women on the mainland since the Communist take-over of 1949. Frederick Engels taught that the rise of private property was responsible for the change in women's status from fully participating members of society to dependent wives whose major role was to bear male heirs to productive property, which belonged only to men. "The emancipation of women . . . [is] impossible . . . so long as women are excluded from socially productive work and restricted to housework, which is private."[9] "Socially productive work" is work that produces a surplus for exchange. Thus, housework and other work that supplies the subsistence needs of the family are excluded. The main reason for the man's status in the traditional family was that he alone owned and controlled whatever means of production (land, capital) that belonged to the family. When communal ownership replaces private family ownership, then women can participate as equals with men in socially productive work. Therefore, the Maoist program for women's liberation in China has not been separate from the socialist transformation of society that started in 1949 but an integral part of the continuing revolution. The emancipation of women from oppression in their family roles can be accomplished only as a result of basic changes both in the people's thinking and the economic relations of production and ownership of property.

As a result of decades of international and civil wars, economic production was at a virtual standstill in China at the time of the Communist take-over. Unemployment was extremely high and inflation rampant. Restoration of industrial production in the towns was therefore a high priority. The All-China Democratic Women's Federation adopted a policy for urban women to become involved in industrial production and urged all women to contribute to the task of nation building.[10] Thus, the mobilization of women for economic roles outside the home was launched.

Women's roles in the family were also drastically redefined, and women were given many basic rights for the first time by the New Marriage Law promulgated in May 1950. Marriages were to be effected through the free will of the two individuals involved and not dictated by parents, and the family would be founded on mutual respect between husband and wife as equals. Child betrothal,[11] bigamy, concubinage, and exaction of money at marriage, all of which were expressions of the view that the woman was property, were outlawed. Husbands and wives were held equally responsible for the care of their children and were both to perform productive labor and contribute to the building of the new society. Article 9 of the law established the right of women to the free choice of occupations and participation in work or social activities. Equal rights concerning ownership of property and divorce were also established.[12]

It was, of course, one thing to proclaim a new order of things and another to see it put into effect. Traditions and ingrained attitudes die very hard, particularly in rural areas. During the first year or two under the New Marriage Law, efforts to implement it took rather radical forms, with disruptive consequences. For example, marriages arranged by parents—the majority of marriages—were subject to dissolution, and after divorce wives were allowed to withdraw their share of the property. The economic havoc this would have wreaked on the villages if large numbers of families were thus affected, together with the resistance of even party cadres to pushing implementation of the law so far, led to a moderation of tactics by late 1952. Persuasion and public discussions of family issues were used instead.[13] The Women's Federation was given the task of informing women of their new legal rights and encouraging them to demand and use them. In the town, local residents' committees or street associations played a role in providing opportunities for women to be involved as individuals in the sociopolitical world outside their families. In addition, these committees also looked after the health and general welfare of their members.[14]

Thus, some fundamental changes in the position of women were beginning to be achieved in the early years of Communist Chinese society. However, the Marriage Law began to lose its position as an up-front issue about 1953, when the First Five-Year Plan went into effect. Political struggle was in many ways inimical to economic reconstruction, and the latter became the top of the agenda. Economic conditions were such that it was not possible to provide all women with outside jobs. High urban unemployment continued through the 1950s because of high rates of urban population increase. Further, development priorities in the First Five-Year Plan emphasized heavy industry, an area where women were least equipped to compete for jobs because of lack of skills and education, as well as because of traditional conceptions of female aptitudes and the usual "double burden" of having the primary responsibility for housekeeping in addition to outside jobs. What industrial employment opportunities there were for women were, therefore, confined to the traditionally female-oriented textile and tobacco industries. [15]

The glorification of industrial labor in the mid-1950s probably had the effect of devaluing other types of work. The new ideology, however, emphasized selfless service to the people over earnings. Since, contrary to Marxist ideals, most women were still unable to participate in industrial production, attempts were made to reconcile realities and ideology by glorifying the role of the housewife as one who provided important supportive, unpaid services to her husband, who was thus enabled to be directly involved in production. [16]

Women's direct participation in economic activities probably took its first quantum jump during the Great Leap Forward of 1958, a monumental experiment attempting to promote rapid economic development and social change through ideological motivation and mass mobilization. Under the aegis of the Great Leap philosophy and goals, women were required to enter into production and engage in political activities together with men. Given the lack of capital and low level of mechanization in Chinese industry and agriculture, human labor was seen as a substitute, and women's labor was certainly not excluded. While the emancipation of women was not a major focus of the Great Leap Forward, the fact that for the first time women were being mobilized to work on a large scale raised many issues related to the condition of women.

Women comprised 50 percent of the agricultural labor force in 1958, but this did not mean that sex equality had been achieved. The idea of women having their primary responsibilities away from home still met with considerable opposition, especially from the older generation. Further, work points or credits, the primary remuneration in collectivized agriculture, were awarded unequally to men and women. This aroused some political conflicts at the level of the commune when local women's federations took up the issue. The inequality of work point awards, however, resulted not merely from male chauvinism but from actual conditions of rural work, which relied mainly on manual labor and physical strength; remuneration depended on the amount of work accomplished, and men with their greater physical capabilities naturally were more productive. [17] At any rate, the fact that women were performing tasks deemed important by the country's leaders and bringing home income probably contributed to a new sense of worth independent of their roles as housewives and mothers, a consequence whose significance could be very far reaching though difficult to assess. Participation in economic production also served to increase women's knowledge and skills. As a by-product of their involvement in agricultural production, collectivized services such as mess halls, nurseries, and kindergartens became institutionalized, although not to as great an extent as in the towns. Also, health and welfare services and benefits for women, previously neglected, became necessary in order to ensure a healthy labor force for production.[18]

In urban areas, women's participation in the efforts of the Great Leap Forward mostly took the form of small-scale, local, light industries producing simple consumer items and providing basic social services, so that men could be freed to undertake heavier enterprises. Street industries, organized on the initiatives of women themselves, were based on skills related to homemaking that the women already possessed. Thus, economic participation by urban women enabled them to acquire only the simplest economically relevant skills. The regular industries were unable to absorb female labor because of women's poor training and lack of education. The urban communes of 1958 and neighborhood factories a decade later were therefore a kind of compromise between ideals and reality. These workshops were not very productive, and their workers were poorly paid and had few supplemental benefits. However, since workers were from the same locality, women with family responsibilities found it easier to work under these neighborhood arrangements. Thus, despite difficult economic conditions, there was a rising trend in female nonagricultural employment. Women formed about 17 percent of total nonagricultural employment in 1957 and 25 percent in 1962.[19]

Although women were still nowhere near equality with men in urban employment, as was the case in rural areas, there were some positive side effects from the increased involvement of women in economic activities outside the home, however simple or poorly paid. The street industries, although characterized by poor equipment and highly labor-intensive, provided women with the opportunity to acquire some skills and be paid. Services such as mess halls and nurseries also became institutionalized. More important, perhaps, was that, together with their participation in residents' committees looking after matters affecting living conditions and social services, their involvement as individuals contributing to the public good independently of their husbands probably promoted more "liberated" attitudes and a sense of self-confidence.[20]

The role of women in urban communes freed the men for jobs in newly established heavy industries and other more demanding state enterprises. Since jobs in heavy industry paid the highest wages and carried the most prestige, this meant that the advancement of large numbers of men had been made possible by the newly acquired roles of women in light industry. Thus, while the economic status of women has advanced in absolute terms, equality between the sexes is yet to be achieved, since men have the opportunities for more remunerative work.[21] Men retain close to a virtual monopoly of the topmost levels of skill and experience. Political committees that are organized in conjunction with places of work are predominately male in membership and leadership, even in industries where women comprise the majority of the workers. Male dominance of committees was problematic enough in Shanghai, for example, that quotas requiring 20 to 30 percent minimum female participation were set.[22]

A few women, however, those with high education, have secured places among the professional elite. By 1960 it was reported that 25 percent of the researchers in the Chinese Academy of Sciences, 50 percent of those in the Chemical Industry Research Institute, 40 percent of the doctors in Peking, and 30 percent of the student body of major universities were women.[23] However, it is this author's opinion that this is not necessarily the result of communist ideology or the socialist transformation of Chinese society. In the modern history of the Chinese people, there have been a few avant-garde women who broke out of the traditional mold and, because they acquired higher education and badly needed technical skills, were involved in important leadership roles. When only a very tiny minority among a society's population has higher education, that society cannot afford to deny highly educated women the opportunity to use their skills.

Ideology regarding women's roles was itself subject to economic conditions and political conflicts in the Chinese leadership. The pendulum of Chinese economic policy has swung between what is now known as radicalism and pragmatism, and so have political pronouncements regarding women. When it became clear in the mid-1950s that there were not enough jobs for women as well as men, housework was extolled as being of social value because, it was reasoned, the salaries of men actually contained the value of their wives' labor, too. Women were also said to be contributing to future socialist reconstruction through their part in the upbringing of children. During the ideological fervor of the Great Leap Forward, a massive propaganda campaign was launched in support of the idea that women were as capable of work as men. During the post-Leap period, however, economic policies reverted to conservatism, and women were once again exhorted to keeping house with industry and thrift in support of their husbands. In fact, from 1961 to 1964, when the country was attempting to recover from the disastrous economic consequences of the Leap and three years of bad harvests, propaganda stressed such traditional family values as respect for the aged, kinship obligations, and the importance of women as mothers and housewives. Then, during the mid- and late 1960s, the emancipation of women was said to be a very integral part of the Great Proletarian Cultural Revolution, and any attempt to see the women's issue as a separate, sexist problem was viewed as being counterrevolutionary. Traditional family structure, hierarchical social relations, and sex roles were again seen as obstacles to the revolution. This line of thinking led to renewed emphasis on political activism among women and the advancement of many women to positions of leadership. [24]

It is clear that women's opportunities in China have reflected the tensions between theory and practical reality. Generally, periods of intensive attempts at altering social values and mass mobilization, such as the Great Leap Forward and the Cultural Revolution, were also times when special attention was paid to the position of women. Maoist thought has proved itself correct in that economic realities have been determinative of the extent of women's participation in society. Mao would, of course, claim that any inequalities between men and women in present-day China are there only because the socialist transformation of Chinese society has yet to be completed. In fact, an article in Peking Review in 1972 made this very point. [25] The same article claimed that all healthy women under 45 years of age had work. However, even if this were true, deeply ingrained cultural attitudes regarding the sexual division of labor still had to be changed. The article pointed out the lack of universal implementation of the equal pay principle, the fact that many parents still valued sons over daughters, and that there were fewer girls than boys enrolled in schools.

In summary, while total emancipation of women in Communist China is yet to be attained, some permanent, institutionalized progress has been achieved. The New Marriage Law, though difficult to enforce, at least put the moral force of government legislation behind the concept of women's equal rights. Women found new economic and political roles on their own right outside the home; this taste of freedom must have given them new aspirations and a new sense of confidence. Periods of mass mobilization brought collectivized services such as child-care facilities into being; the idea that household responsibilities must necessarily prevent women from outside work was thus proved false and the way paved for women to enter economic production when and if such opportunities exist. [26]

TAIWAN: CULTURAL CONTINUITY
AND ECONOMIC DEVELOPMENT

The impact of the Japanese occupation of Taiwan on family structure was basically conservative. In fact, in the late 1960s, it could still be said that in many of the most technologically modernized rural areas in Taiwan "traditional family organization remains supreme."[27] One reason given was the labor requirements of new crops such as tobacco and the demands of double-cropping, which required that daughters-in-law contribute to the work. Further, the requirement that all young men serve two years in the military depletes the rural household of its most able-bodied members, and often the role of the young daughter-in-law is to help out at home and in the fields while her husband is away.[28] Thus, in the rural areas, modern economic and political developments have not served to emancipate women from family-based responsibilities.

Legislation regarding women's rights has not been absent. After 1948 the law in Taiwan specifically gave equal rights and opportunities to women in such areas as divorce, education, government service jobs, the holding of public office, and equal pay for equal work.[29] However, no concerted nationwide effort was made to inform women of these rights or to encourage or to facilitate their use of them, as was done on the mainland. In fact, it is likely that many women in Taiwan today are still unaware of these rights.[30] In this regard, it is interesting to note that even in the years before World War II on the mainland, laws had been passed giving daughters and sons equal rights to the family inheritance, but women were unaware of them. In 1938 it was reported that "one lawyer [in Shanghai] was doing a highly lucrative business by watching the newspapers and other sources for deaths where the man had a daughter or daughters and then going to inform them of their rights with an offer to obtain their share of the inheritance."[31] It is clear that de jure equality between the sexes is a paper tiger, to use a phrase popularized (in another context) by the late Chairman Mao.

However, what about the area of popular opinion? The evidence is spotty, but what data there are reveal the rise of some typically modern attitudes. In 1961 more than 90 percent of Taiwanese who were respondents in a survey expressed the opinion that the choice of a marriage partner should not be in the parents' hands alone but should be initiated by the son or daughter and approved by the parents or vice versa.[32] Opinion and actuality vary, though. In 1962 another survey found that fewer than 60 percent of the university students in the sample expected to choose their own mates.[33] In 1972 in another survey of university students, 87 percent indicated a desire to choose their future spouses, but the percentage expecting to be able to do so had not changed—it was 58 percent.[34] Unfortunately, these data were not broken down by sex. Neither are there comparable data from the mainland. But they do indicate that in Taiwan the authority of parents in such an intimately vital matter as the choice of a life partner is still very strong despite desires for greater freedom on the part of the younger generation.

Parental control over marriage also means lack of status for the young bride, especially if marriage is patrilocal. However, the majority of marriages in Taiwan today evidence neolocal residence, where the young couple maintains a separate household away from the authority of the husband's parents. In this context, the woman appears to enjoy a fair amount of intrafamilial authority. In 1962, 71 percent of Taiwanese families were said to share authority equally between father and mother, while 91 percent of high school students in a survey believed that this ought to be the norm.[35] In 1972 it was reported that 92 percent of husbands would discuss major decisions with their wives, although the same study showed that husbands were less liberal in their tendency to allow their wives to go to movies alone (71 percent would) or join clubs by themselves (67 percent). The degree of liberality correlated significantly with both family income and education.[36] Thus, while wives have a good amount of authority within the household, their freedom to engage in activities outside appears to be somewhat curtailed.

This is consistent with the fact that the large majority of wives have no occupation outside of housework,[37] something that is true even though about 94 percent of all girls aged 6 through 14 were enrolled in school as early as 1960.[38] The function of education for girls in Taiwan, however, is not so much to equip them for lifelong occupations or careers as to enable them to marry well-qualified men. The working life of a woman, especially in the case of salaried work, is confined largely to the years between high school and marriage. While about 30 percent of the work force are women, they are confined to low-skilled jobs such as sales and office work and positions such as assembly-line workers in traditionally female-oriented industries such as textiles and electronics. Nursing and teaching are about the only professions open to the more highly educated woman. Other than these, few women in Taiwan are to be found in professions or high administrative posts. Those who are are mostly older women who were exceptional in their day in educational attainment and commitment to career.[39]

Views regarding the function of education for women have apparently changed in the conservative direction over the past generation. While very few parents in traditional China would even think of educating their daughters, those who did had the view that education was for service to society. Therefore, the exceptionally well-educated women of today's older generation are much more likely to have had unbroken careers. Even if they married, their husbands were most likely to have been equally progressive in allowing their wives to continue working. Today, however, education for the woman is viewed as being for self-improvement and service to her future family. It is also a status symbol. Educated women are likely to marry into the urban middle class, whose values hark back to those of the upper classes in traditional China, where the leisurely woman of the house was the norm and the ideal. If a woman works outside the house, the implication might be that her husband does not earn enough, which is of course to be avoided. [40]

Unfortunately, present realities do not entirely conform to past ideals. The modern middle-class housewife is not quite a lady of leisure, for several reasons. Servants were common in the old days, but in present-day Taiwan they are very expensive even if one could get them, because the new industries absorb most of the working-class women. In addition, mothers are required to act as tutors for their children, for whom educational success is a highly prized goal in the competitive Taiwanese school system. Indeed, the tutor role is seen as a major reason for women to obtain education, so that they can ensure their children's success. This extends the number of years of a mother's child-rearing responsibilities, in that she cannot consider herself free to return to outside work even after the children enter school. Popular opinion in Taiwan is that a mother who works is selfish and her children are likely to become delinquent. [41]

Taiwanese society does not hold the view that women are as capable as men. The belief in female inferiority pervades the schools as well; evidence of equal or better performance on examinations is explained by saying that this is due to rote memorization and plain hard work on the part of girls, rather than native ability. Not surprisingly, girls themselves grow to believe this and opt for the humanities rather than the sciences in junior high school. [42] While the female share of college enrollment rose from 15 percent in 1957 to more than 40 percent in 1972, [43] there is no commitment to increase female participation or encourage women to enter male-dominated fields. On the contrary, there is a tendency to restrict the number of women entering higher education or even to reduce it. A report on women to a conference on manpower in 1972, prepared by Taiwanese, also recommended shunting female high school students into general liberal arts programs rather than scientific, vocational, or technical tracks. Although the same report recommended raising women's participation in the work force to 40 percent, it envisaged the increased participation to be only in service, sales, and low-skilled factory jobs, which are poorly paid and offer no long-term career prospects. Young, unmarried women do not have to be paid at the same rate as men with families to support, and so female workers are much in demand for low-level jobs in the rapidly developing economy of Taiwan. [44]

At higher levels of employment and social participation, it is probably true that Taiwan boasts of proportionately more women professionals and political leaders than many Western countries. In 1972 there were 301 women out of 1,446 members in the National Assembly, 82 out of 773 in the Legislative Yuan, and 19 out of 233 in the Control Yuan.[45] Yet, these figures reveal the familiar pattern of greater and greater inequality as one goes up the ladder of power and prestige. Likewise, while about 40 percent of university graduates are women, women junior faculty comprise about one-sixth of the ranks, and the percentage of women professors declined from 9 percent in the late 1960s to 6 percent in the early 1970s.[46] Indeed, it appears that this decline was probably indicative of a widespread trend, since the spread of education among women has not been accompanied by increases in opportunities to use that education. Rather, there has been a change in ideology regarding the reason for women to become educated.

Thus, we see in Taiwan a situation where rapid economic development has resulted in increased opportunities for women to attend school even up to the college level, but where there has been no official encouragement of the emancipation of women or even the acknowledgment of such a need. Instead, public opinion seems to have taken a conservative turn, and the educated woman today is far less liberated than were those of her mother's generation who, though a rare breed, nevertheless put their education to full use in careers outside the home. One might speculate on the societal functions of such a waste of educated womanpower, but it does appear that a capitalist economy has no necessary interest in providing opportunities for women equal to that of men. If an ideology that says women should quit work upon marriage means that low wages for women can be justified on the basis of their being only temporary workers, then why should those benefiting from a system based on private profits change it?

MALAYSIA: WESTERNIZATION AND ECONOMIC GROWTH

Chinese migrated to Malaya* as early as the eighteenth century, settling mainly in the coastal ports of Penang, Malacca, and Singapore, which came under direct British control during the late eighteenth and nineteenth centuries. The early Chinese immigrants often adopted native customs, dress, and even language, sometimes intermarried with native Malays, and evolved a Malayan Chinese subcul-

---

*Malaya was the name of the peninsula south of Thailand on the Asian mainland, which included the inland of Singapore. It is now joined with the northwest portion of the island of Borneo to form the Federation of Malaysia.

ture that combined elements of Malay and Chinese cultures. These Straits Chinese, as they came to be called, were later joined by much larger numbers of Chinese immigrants in the first few decades of the twentieth century. By now, however, the vast majority of Chinese in Malaysia are native born.

The immigrants were mostly young men, as is typical of most migrant populations. Those who were married came first without their wives. After they were economically established, they either sent for their wives to join them or married new wives in Malaya, if they were not particularly fond of their first wives. Bigamy was not frowned upon in Chinese culture, and neither was concubinage, which was a status symbol in old China. The law in Malaya allowed marriages to be effected either under the civil code, which was based on British laws and therefore allowed only one wife, or under customary ethnic laws. Chinese marriages were most often effected under the latter until after the Second World War, when women began to realize the disadvantages to themselves of Chinese customary law marriages, and they or their families began to demand registration under the civil code as well. Therefore, there are still a few examples of bigamous marriages among the middle-aged generation today. Sometimes both wives live under one roof; sometimes each wife lives in a separate household; and sometimes the first wife still lives in China. However, bigamy is nonexistent among the younger Chinese in Malaysia.

There is also a marked difference between the older and younger generations in terms of choice of marriage partner. Matchmaking is still a "profession" practiced by a few older ladies, but it is a dying one. Even if one's mate were to be picked by one's parents, with or without the benefit of a matchmaker, it is rare today for either the bride- or groom-to-be not to have final veto power. Marriage is also often neolocal, so that the young couple is not under the constant observation, if not supervision, of the groom's parents. Divorce is available to either party on equal grounds if the marriage was registered under the civil code, and inheritance laws treat sons and daughters equally. However, sons are still considered special because they carry on the family name.

The Chinese are more advanced in the education of girls than the other ethnic groups in Malaysia, the Malays and the Indians, though this does not mean that the Chinese culture favors girls more than Malay or Indian cultures. Rather, the Chinese are simply the most economically advanced group and were by far the first to be urbanized. The education of girls is therefore something that most Chinese parents would take for granted at least until grade six. After elementary school, some rural Chinese and a few of the lower economic classes in the towns may withdraw their daughters from school, particularly if they have not been very good students. The reason often given is that they are needed at home to help with chores or that the parents cannot afford to pay the fees (a nominal sum) and other expenses. Voluntary withdrawal does not happen as a rule. In the area in which the research to be reported below was done, there were as many Chinese girls as boys in the last year of high school.

Often, girls who have finished schooling will go to work as domestic help for middle-class families or, more and more frequently, as assembly-line workers in the new consumer goods industries. Such jobs obviously do not offer a line of advancement, and their wages would be inadequate for men who have to support families—hence, the prevalence of young, unmarried girls in these low-skill, dead-end jobs, as in Taiwan. Married women may or may not work, depending on the economic status of their husbands, their educational level, and the presence of grandparents to act as babysitters if a paid helper cannot be found or is too expensive for the family.

Unlike Taiwan, the Chinese middle class in Malaysia does not appear to have a nostalgia for the idealized role of the upper-class woman in traditional China. In Malaysia the more eduated the woman the more likely she is to have a job. However, the reason is not attributable to education per se. The main reason lies in the salary structure, which, because government is the single most important employer of educated persons, is largely dictated by government pay scales. There is a vast gap between the pay of college graduates and that of high school graduates, in the ratio of at least three to one among liberal arts graduates up to six to one among professionally trained graduates. There, the incentive for a college graduate to work is great, especially given an increasingly consumer-oriented society where conspicuous consumption and keeping up with the Wongs are important elements of middle-class life.

Some things are changing, however, that may have an effect on the extent to which married women with children can work. The amah or unmarried older Chinese lady who made a career (complete with guilds and retirement associations) of being a household servant was very common a generation ago, but the cutoff in immigrants from China since World War II has meant that this kind of professional servant is no longer available. Instead, present-day middle-class families have been relying on young, unmarried girls of working-class and rural backgrounds. However, the recent growth of new industries has absorbed most of these girls, and complaints about "the servant problem" are common in Malaysian middle-class households today. Because of this, many married women are postponing motherhood in order to be able to work as long as possible. There are also increasing instances of college-educated women staying home after their first babies are born, for lack of help. Since geographical mobility is increasingly a fact of middle-class life, grandparents are also ceasing

to be available as babysitters. Therefore, a trend toward postpone-
ment of motherhood and nonparticipation in the labor force among
middle-class mothers is beginning, the primary reason being the lack
of facilities for child care.

Whether an ideology regarding women's proper roles as mother
and housewife will arise in order to rationalize or justify this development is an interesting speculation. In any case, it is unlikely that
the values of traditional China will be evoked for such an ideology.
Educated Chinese women in Malaysia are too far removed culturally
from old China. It is possible that the incentive to work might be so
great that privately run nurseries or preschools will develop to accommodate the needs of working mothers. Private kindergartens are
already common, and there is no reason why the age at which children
are sent to such facilities could not decrease. However, even if such
facilities became more available, they take care of children for only
part of the day. Mothers who depend on them will have to work only
part-time or at jobs whose hours are amenable. Clearly, teaching
fits the bill very nicely. As in Taiwan and most other countries,
teaching and nursing are the two professions in Malaysia that are un-
questionably open to women.

Despite the extent of Western influence and relatively greater
orientation toward careers on the part of educated Chinese girls in
Malaysia, research conducted by this author in 1972 revealed some
typically traditional patterns of educational and occupational choice
and attitudes. A stratified, random sample of secondary schools in
the state of Penang and Province Wellesley was taken, and in each
school all the final year (Form Five) students were given a questionnaire. There were 452 Chinese boys and 450 Chinese girls in the survey who were either in general academic schools or in the highly selective technical school. The rate of response was 97 percent.[47]

Students in general academic schools are divided according to
track or stream of studies. The science stream is the most selective
and emphasizes mathematics and science subjects. Next in selectivity
is the arts stream, which provides a general academic education.
Then come various vocational streams in which one or two courses in
practical skills are included in the curriculum. The technical school
is different from general academic schools in that all of its students
emphasize science and technical subjects not usually available in general schools. Its students are overwhelmingly male, reflecting the
fact that few girls choose to apply. The relative female bias against
science subjects is also seen in the composition of science and arts
streams in the general schools as revealed by the survey. There
were fewer girls than boys in science streams, while the opposite was
true in arts streams. Girls were also present in slightly greater proportion in vocational streams than were boys, but vocational means

domestic science and needlework in girls' schools and woodworking, mechanics, and other industrial skills in boys' schools.

In response to a question asking whether they preferred another stream to the one they were in, over 90 percent of the students in science and vocational streams indicated satisfaction with where they were. Among art students, however, there was considerable dissatisfaction, especially among boys. More than one-half of the boys in arts preferred another stream compared with just more than a quarter of the girls. What are the reasons for the relative unpopularity of the arts stream? Students were asked what they liked best about the stream they were in.* Generally speaking, beyond the arts stream being considered an easy stream or "interesting" (a rather vague reason often given by Malaysian students when they cannot think of anything else to say), it does not appear to hold any particular attraction to students. Even though it is an academic stream, only 5 percent of the Chinese students in it believed they had good higher education prospects. This is not surprising, since arts is a poor cousin to science in selectivity. Further, scholarships awarded to Chinese by the government or by private firms for higher education are almost all in areas of high-level manpower shortage—that is, in technical and scientific fields. About half the science students said that what they liked best about their stream were the higher education prospects. Given the definite superiority of the science stream over the arts stream in this respect, the fact that fewer girls than boys were dissatisfied with arts indicates a lesser concern with higher education on the part of the girls.

Table 1 shows student aspirations toward the different fields of study common at Malaysian universities.† The most obvious sex dif-

---

*The question was worded as follows: "Let us talk about the stream that you are now in. What is it that you like best about this stream?"

1. The work in this stream is easy.
2. The subject(s) is/are useful for me to find a job next year.
3. The prospects for higher education are very good for people in this stream.
4. The subjects in this stream are really very interesting to me.
5. Students in this stream have high status and prestige.
6. Other (say what).
7. There is nothing I like about this stream.

†Responses to the question: "Let us say you are offered a scholarship to go to University three years from now and you can choose to study any subject you like. What courses would you choose to study?"

TABLE 1

Preferences for University Courses by Sex
(in percent)

	Male	Female
Arts	4.3	19.0
Science	13.7	11.9
Engineering	46.0	4.8
Medicine	11.3	18.7
Law	3.6	7.3
Agriculture and pharmacy	4.6	9.5
Economics	7.2	12.0
Other	9.4	16.8
Total number (100 percent)	442	448
Chi-square p	< 0.001	

Source: Compiled by the author.

ference is the extremely high popularity of engineering among boys,
while it was the least popular choice among girls. Instead, girls who
did choose professional fields tended toward the less "hardcore technical" ones such as the biologically oriented fields of medicine, agriculture and pharmacy, or law, which is not related to the natural
sciences.

Almost three times as many girls as boys chose the nonscientific,
nonprofessional fields of arts and economics. Graduates of these fields
typically go on for the one-year Diploma of Education course to become
certified teachers. This indicates that Chinese female college graduates in Malaysia are not different from most of their international
counterparts in being the major source of recruits for the teaching
profession. Indeed, the higher percentage of girls than boys choosing
"other" fields of study was largely the result of choices for "education" or "nursing" listed by respondents themselves, even though these
are nondegree or nonuniversity courses. That almost as many girls
as boys chose science is not surprising, therefore, as most women
with the Bachelor of Science degree end up in the teaching profession.
In brief, it is clear that Chinese women in Malaysia show a marked
avoidance of hardcore technical fields such as engineering, in extreme
contrast to men. If they are professionally oriented, it is largely toward the field of teaching.

Social class differences in preferences were found only among
the boys. One-quarter of high-status boys chose unusual professions

or fields, compared with only about 9 percent of their middle- or low-status peers, who were more likely to prefer engineering (49 percent compared with 30 percent). Boys from better-off families are probably both more cognizant of newer (and a greater variety of) occupations and readier to launch out into the less secure professions than are working-class boys. At the high school level, social class differences in preference of stream were also found only among boys. More working-class than middle- or upper-class boys in the arts stream were unhappy with it, and almost twice as many working-class as middle- or upper-class boys preferred the vocational stream. The reason is that working-class boys are more concerned with job prospects after high school, and the vocational stream for boys teaches industrial skills believed to be in demand in the job market. Among college graduates, engineers are likewise believed to be in great demand. The same social class differences are not observed among girls because job considerations are not as salient as among boys.

Table 2 shows the reasons given by students for their choices, controlled for the type of field chosen. There were few significant motivational differences between the sexes among those who chose arts fields. Girls were somewhat more likely than boys to give their presumed aptitude or current stream of studies as the reason, but that was to be expected since more girls than boys were in the arts stream in upper-secondary school. Both among those who chose arts fields and those who chose science fields, proportionately three times as many boys as girls gave job or money prospects as the reason for their choices. The greater concern of boys than girls for their further educational or earning prospects, reflected not only in their expressed motivations for choices of higher educational options but also in their attitudes toward the various streams of study at the secondary level, is understandable since boys will have the role of primary breadwinners in their future families and also since working-class parents are dependent on their sons for financial help.

Economic investment is not as salient a factor in the educational motivation of girls, for whom traditional conceptions of the female role are more important. Thus, highly educated women may indeed be economically active, but only in occupations that do not conflict too much either with their obligations as housewife and mother or with ideas regarding the female personality as being nurturant and affect-oriented. Teaching is an ideal profession in both regards. Nursing and medicine, both professions involved in caring for people, are also popular with Malaysian girls. Only the most academically capable, however, will be offered admission to medical school, so that nursing is a much more realistic aspiration.

The fact that economic considerations are not as important as traditional role assignments in determining girls' occupational choices

TABLE 2

Reasons for Choice of University Course by Sex,
Controlling for the Type of Course Chosen
(in percent)

	Those Who Chose Arts Field[a]		Those Who Chose Science Field[b]	
	Male	Female	Male	Female
Interest or liking for field	31.1	37.9	47.6	57.7
Good job/money prospects	14.4	4.2	24.4	8.0
Few people in field in Malaysia/service to country	12.4	7.8	13.1	16.7
Personal aptitude or present field of studies	25.2	33.1	7.0	8.3
Easy course/will lead to easy job	2.2	0.9 }	7.8	9.3
Other reason	14.7	16.1 }		
Total number (100 percent) percent)	56	156	294	177
Chi-square p	> 0.10		< 0.001	

Note: In Malaysia, "Arts" refers to the humanities and social sciences. In this table, the university courses included under this heading are arts, economics, and law. Those included under "Science" are science, engineering, medicine, agriculture, and pharmacy. This table excludes those who chose fields other than those listed above.

Source: Compiled by the author.

is further demonstrated by another set of data from the same study. Students were asked to indicate what they thought were the average wages of five jobs: clerk, customs officer, technician, motor-mechanic, and skilled factory worker. They were also asked to choose between going on to postsecondary education after Form Five and taking up an offer of a job as a clerk, customs officer, and so on (there were five questions, one for each job offer). If financial considerations were salient, one would expect the acceptance rates of the jobs to correlate with their perceived salaries. This was found to be true among boys but not girls. Indeed, the girls' responses were highly irrational economically. The clerk's job was accepted by the highest percentage (55 percent) of girls, even though clerks were perceived to have the lowest wages, about M$220 per month.* Fewer than 11 percent of the girls would accept a job as a motor-mechanic, even though they estimated the job to earn about $290 per month, and only 35 percent would accept the technician's job, which was thought to earn $370 per month. The figures for the skilled factory worker and the customs officer were, respectively, 20 percent and $240 and 43 percent and $290. In general, girls avoided the "dirty" or blue-collar jobs regardless of pay.

Further, the data show that girls tended to perceive wages of given jobs to be lower than boys did. This is probably indicative of the fact that women generally receive lower pay. Even in the supposedly achievement-based government services, remunerative differences between the sexes apply in the cost-of-living and housing allowances. These differences reflect the view that it is men who support their families—therefore women do not need as much pay. Clearly, there is no official endorsement of sex equality nor policy to encourage more women to work either through pay incentives or an ideology of serving the people. Instead, there is an unquestioning adherence on the part of the whole society, including women themselves, to things as they are or have been, despite the fact that this is a society where the education of Chinese girls has almost kept equal pace with that of boys, at least through high school level.

CONCLUSIONS

Societal conceptions of feminine roles and abilities that affect the educational and occupational choices of Chinese women in Asia are not necessarily peculiarly Chinese. Malaysian and Taiwanese women's predilections toward "softer" academic fields and occupations such as teaching, nursing, clerical and sales work, and low-skill jobs in light industries are typical of their international sisters as well. In this regard, the mainland Chinese ideology stands alone in promulgating the view that "whatever men comrades can accomplish, women comrades can too."[48] Thus, the literature out of China is replete with examples of women overcoming their lack of experience by persevering in trial-and-error methods in such male provinces as aviation, oil drilling, and bridge building.[49] It is hard to believe that three decades of concerted attempts to do away with the old beliefs have not had their effect. What stands in the way of full attainment of the new ideals is economic reality—there just are not as many meaningful job opportunities as there are people—more than cultural belief. Nevertheless, women have gained a place—even if it is more in the subjective realm of values than in objective reality–in Communist China that few would have dreamed possible 30 years ago.

Taiwan, in contrast, has been a model of essentially capitalist economic development, and women have had the opportunity for higher education in unprecedented numbers at the same time that techniques of the Green Revolution have increased agricultural productivity and many factories have mushroomed in urban areas. Ideology regarding women's roles, however, has undergone little change. While women have gained more freedom and status in family matters, their roles relative to men in regard to the outside world remain the same. The lack of freedom and status in their own right among women is especially evident in the relatively affluent middle class, since these women have been educated but do not have the options to use that education outside the home. Instead, modernization has added to their responsibilities as mothers in the roles of tutor and primary moral caretaker because of increased competitiveness in the educational system and isolation of the nuclear family.

The Chinese in Malaysia are generally much more removed from Chinese cultural traditions than their counterparts in Taiwan, both in terms of length of time and exposure to Western values. Thus, there has been no invoking of the traditional ideal to justify housebound roles of mother and housewife. Indeed, continuing educational expansion has provided many opportunities for educated women to be gainfully occupied as teachers, a job that does not conflict much with mothering responsibilities. Educated women have also engaged in other occupations in large numbers since their salaries, though often unequal to those of men in comparable jobs, have been more than adequate to pay for full-time domestic help. However, their educational and occupational choices remain limited by internalized conceptions of what is feminine and beliefs regarding what women are or are not capable of. These beliefs determine women's job and educational decisions to a much greater degree than does financial remuneration.

The comparison of contemporary Chinese women's positions in China, Taiwan, and Malaysia in this chapter does not always fit the conceptual framework of colonialism, neocolonialism, or internal colonialism as outlined in Chapter 1, mainly because direct external control was for relatively short periods. However, the concepts of development and dependency may be of relevance. While it may be arguable whether Taiwan and Malaysia are in a position of dependency on the West, it is clear that neither of these countries has been anywhere near China in its commitment to a total, continuing, societal transformation irrespective of international opinion and, indeed, of "pragmatic" economic considerations. If one theme stands out in these descriptions of women's roles in the three countries, it is the inertia of traditional ideas that have become institutionalized in the functioning of the family, schools, and the economy. This being the case, it takes a radical commitment to revolution to unseat the pervasive influence of old values. This has been true in China but not Taiwan or Malaysia. This author believes that if China had had economic resources comparable to the latter two countries, its women would have advanced much more toward equality with men in socially productive labor and hence in overall status.

NOTES

1. George Kerr, Formosa: Licensed Revolution and the Home Rule Movement, 1895-1945 (Honolulu: University Press of Hawaii, 1974).

2. Joseph C. Wong, "Relationships between Husband and Wife," Journal of the China Society 10 (1973): 31.

3. Delia Davin, Woman-Work: Women and the Party in Revolutionary China (New York: Clarendon Press, 1976), p. 72.

4. C. K. Yang, The Chinese Family in the Communist Revolution, 2d ed. (Cambridge: Massachusetts Institute of Technology Press, 1965), p. 25.

5. Ibid., p. 28.

6. Ai-Li S. Chin, "Mainland China," in Women in the Modern World, ed. Raphael Patai (New York: Free Press, 1967).

7. Davin, Woman-Work, p. 75.

8. For example, Albert O'Hara, "The Position of Women in Modern China," Journal of the China Society 9 (1972): 78.

9. Frederick Engels, The Origin of the Family, Private Property and the State (New York: International, 1942), p. 148.

10. Davin, Woman-Work, p. 156.

11. In this custom, a girl at about ten years of age was bought by the family of her designated future husband and lived in that family as a bond-maid until her marriage. Paul Chao, Women under Communism (Bayside, N.Y.: General Hall, 1977), p. 132.

12. The Marriage Law of the People's Republic of China, as published in ibid., app. 2.

13. Janet Weitzner Salaff and Judith Merkle, "Women and Revolution: The Lessons of the Soviet Union and China," in Women in China, ed. Marilyn B. Young (Ann Arbor: University of Michigan, Center for Chinese Studies, 1973), pp. 165-68.

14. Davin, Woman-Work.

15. Phyllis Andors, "Social Revolution and Woman's Emancipation: China during the Great Leap Forward," Bulletin of Concerned Asian Scholars 7 (January-March 1975): 33-42, 55-79. Also Davin, Woman-Work.

16. Shelah Gilbert Leader, "The Emancipation of Chinese Women," World Politics 26 (October 1973): 55-79.

17. Jane Barrett, "Women Hold up Half the Sky," in Women in China, ed. Young.

18. Andors, "Social Revolution and Woman's Emancipation."

19. Barry M. Richman, Industrial Society in Communist China, pp. 303-6, as cited in Davin, Woman-Work, p. 166; and J. P. Emerson, "Employment in Mainland China, Problems and Prospects," in U.S., Congress, Joint Economic Committee, An Economic Profile of Mainland China, p. 465, as cited in Davin, Woman-Work, p. 165.

20. Ibid.

21. Ibid.

22. Barrett, "Women Hold up Half the Sky."

23. Andors, "Social Revolution and Woman's Emancipation," p. 40.

24. Salaff and Merkle, "Women and Revolution"; Leader, "Emancipation of Chinese Women."

25. Ching-ling Soong, "Women's Liberation," reprinted from Peking Review, no. 6 (February 11, 1972), as cited in Women in China, ed. Young, pp. 201-4.

26. Yu-lan Lu, "Liberation of Women," reprinted from Peking Review, no. 10 (March 10, 1972), as cited in Women in China, ed. Young, pp. 205-9.

27. Myron L. Cohen, "The Family in Transition in Taiwan," in The Family in Transition, Proceedings of the Fogarty International Center, no. 3 (Bethesda: National Institute of Health, 1909), p. 103.

28. Joseph C. Wong, "Marriage," Journal of the China Society 10 (1973): 32.

29. O'Hara, "Position of Women in Modern China," p. 78.

30. Norma Diamond, "The Status of Women in Taiwan: One Step Forward, Two Steps Back," in Women in China, ed. Young, pp. 211-39.

31. O'Hara, "Position of Women in Modern China," p. 78.

32. Martin C. C. Yang, "Changes in Family Life in Rural Taiwan," Journal of the China Society 2 (1962): 68-79.

33. Albert O'Hara, "Changing Attitudes toward Marriage and the Family in Free China," Journal of the China Society 2 (1962): 57-67.

34. Wong, "Relationships between Husband and Wife," p. 31.

35. Ibid., p. 40.

36. Wen-Hui Tsai, "The Transitional Chinese Family Relationship in Taiwan," Journal of the China Society 9 (1972): 51-62.

37. Wong, "Marriage," p. 55.
38. O'Hara, "Changing Attitudes," p. 60.
39. Diamond, "Status of Women in Taiwan."
40. Ibid.
41. Ibid.
42. Ibid.
43. O'Hara, "Positon of Women in Modern China."
44. Diamond, "Status of Women in Taiwan."
45. O'Hara, "Position of Women in Modern China."
46. Diamond, "Status of Women in Taiwan."
47. For details on the methodology, see Bee-Lan Chan Wang, "Governmental Intervention in Ethnic Stratification: Effects on the Distribution of Students among Fields of Study," Comparative Education Review 21 (February 1977): 110-23.
48. Mao Tse-tung, as cited in New Women in New China (Peking: Foreign Languages Press, 1972), p. 4.
49. New Women in New China. Also, various issues of China Reconstructs.

REFERENCES

Andors, Phyllis. "Social Revolution and Woman's Emancipation: China during the Great Leap Forward." Bulletin of Concerned Asian Scholars 7 (January-March 1975): 33-42, 55-79.

Barrett, Jane. "Women Hold Up Half the Sky." In Women in China, edited by Marilyn B. Young. Ann Arbor: University of Michigan, Center for Chinese Studies, 1973.

Chao, Paul. Women under Communism. Bayside, N.Y.: General Hall, 1977.

Chin, Ai-Li S. "Mainland China." In Women in the Modern World, edited by Raphael Patai. New York: Free Press, 1967.

Cohen, Myron L. "The Family in Transition in Taiwan." In The Family in Transition. Proceedings of the Fogarty International Center, no. 3. Bethesda, Md.: National Institute of Health, 1909.

Davin, Delia. Women-Work: Women and the Party in Revolutionary China. New York: Clarendon Press, 1976.

Diamond, Norma. "The Status of Women in Taiwan: One Step Forward, Two Steps Back. In Women in China, edited by Marilyn B. Young, pp. 211-39. Ann Arbor: University of Michigan, Center for Chinese Studies, 1973.

Emerson, J. P. "Employment in Mainland China, Problems and Prospects." In An Economic Profile of Mainland China. U.S., Congress, Joint Economic Committee. (Taken from Woman-Work: Women and the Party in Revolutionary China, edited by Delia Davin, p. 165. New York: Clarendon Press, 1976.)

Engels, Frederick. The Origin of the Family, Private Property and the State. New York: International, 1942.

Kerr, George. Formosa: Licensed Revolution and the Home Rule Movement, 1895-1945. Honolulu: University Press of Hawaii, 1974.

Leader, Shelah Gilbert. "The Emancipation of Chinese Women." World Politics 26 (October 1973): 55-79.

Lu, Yu-lan. "Liberation of Women." In Women in China, edited by Marilyn B. Young, pp. 205-9. Ann Arbor: University of Michigan, Center for Chinese Studies, 1973. (Reprinted from Peking Review, no. 10 [March 10, 1972].)

New Women in New China. Peking: Foreign Languages Press, 1972.

O'Hara, Albert. "The Position of Women in Modern China." Journal of the China Society 9 (1972): 78.

_____. "Changing Attitudes toward Marriage and the Family in Free China." Journal of the China Society 2 (1962): 57-67.

Richman, Barry M. Industrial Society in Communist China. (Taken from Woman-Work: Women and the Party in Revolutionary China, edited by Delia Davin. New York: Clarendon Press, 1976.)

Salaff, Janet Weitzner, and Judith Merkle. "Women and Revolution: The Lessons of the Soviet Union and China." In Women in China, edited by Marilyn B. Young. Ann Arbor: University of Michigan, Center for Chinese Studies, 1973.

Soong, Ching-Ling. "Women's Liberation." In Women in China, edited by Marilyn B. Young, pp. 201-4. Ann Arbor: University of Michigan, Center for Chinese Studies, 1973. (Reprinted from Peking Review, no. 6 [February 11, 1972].)

Tsai, Wen-Hui. "The Transitional Chinese Family Relationship in Taiwan." Journal of the China Society 9 (1972): 51-62.

Wang, Bee-Lan Chan. "Governmental Intervention in Ethnic Stratification: Effects on the Distribution of Students among Fields of Study." Comparative Education Review 21 (February 1977): 110-23.

Wong, Joseph C. "Marriage." Journal of the China Society 10 (1973): 32.

_____. "Relationships between Husband and Wife." Journal of the China Society 10 (1973): 31.

Yang, C. K. The Chinese Family in the Communist Revolution. 2d ed. Cambridge: Massachusetts Institute of Technology Press, 1965.

Yang, Martin C. C. "Changes in Family Life in Rural Taiwan." Journal of the China Society 2 (1962): 68-79.

Young, Marilyn B., ed. Women in China. Ann Arbor: University of Michigan, Center for Chinese Studies, 1973.

6

UP FROM THE HAREM?
THE EFFECTS OF CLASS AND SEX
ON POLITICAL LIFE IN NORTHERN INDIA

Tonia K. Devon

INTRODUCTION

Interview data for the following study were collected in 1971 in two industrial towns of northern India, Faridabad in the state of Haryana and Modinagar in Uttar Pradesh, and are part of a larger study that also includes data on males, children, and the elementary school curriculum. The 80 interviews referred to in this chapter were with Indian working-class women; half worked only in their homes and the others were employed in factories. The mean age was 29 for factory workers and 30 for housewives. The sample of women who worked in factories was stratified by age (anyone over 40 was eliminated) and otherwise randomly selected for the interview data from the female employee rolls. The sample of housewives, who were all spouses of factory workers, was stratified by age and then selected randomly from every third house in the workers' quarters of the factories. However, in the latter case several houses were eliminated owing to the reluctance of the women or the presence of other adults. Like most women of India, whether urban or rural, the housewives of the sample were engaged exclusively in homemaking and were confined to a neighborhood comprised of a few homes.

The interviews consisted of 88 open-ended questions and 3 closed-ended questions in Hindi. Two questions that referred to factory experiences were omitted from the interviews with housewives. This chapter, drawn in part from those interviews, is an exploration of the ways in which the political life of the Indian working-class woman is molded by the forces of her class and sex.

THE POSITION OF WOMEN IN INDIA

In the last century and a half considerable material has been written by Indians about the position of women in their society, some assessing that position as positive and others as negative. Because Indian culture is so varied and rich, arguments can be made from traditions to show either that Indian women, especially the elders, are powerful within the family and the object of great respect or that they are oppressed drudges and little, if anything, more than chattel.[1] In the Hindu pantheon they can be found to embody benevolent givers of wealth and knowledge as well as the most malevolent and feared of all gods. The idea that women can be political leaders is present in Indian political history—for example, the famous stories of Chandbibi and the Rani of Jhansi, who led their people and even died on the battlefield. In each general election there have been some female candidates running for Lok Sabha (Parliament) seats. In 1962, 69 out of 1,935 candidates or 3.6 percent were women; in 1967, 67 out of 2,369 or 2.8 percent; in 1970, approximately 80 out of 2,782 or 2.9 percent. By 1967, 29, or 5.9 percent, of the members of the Indian Lok Sabha (House of the People) were women and 24, or 10 percent, of the Rajya Sabha (Upper House) were women. Throughout the 1960s India had more women in the national legislature than did the United States, the United Kingdom, or Japan. Further, while the percentage of women relative to men in the top political executive ranks in India was low in 1965, it was higher for India than for the United States, United Kingdom, USSR, Japan, Sweden, or Israel.[2]

The appearance of female politicians does not, however, symbolize an increasingly positive attitude toward women in politics among the general public or the male political elites. At one time the Congress party, which has a women's wing, had a provision for 15 percent representation for women, but that was removed by the time of the 1967 election. Before the 1971 campaign Indira Gandhi, through the women's wing of the Congress, sent out a letter to the party leaders in the states asking them to seek out qualified women candidates. As one commentator put it, "There would be no dearth of such candidates but the Congress (N) bosses were not obliging."[3]

> If despite Mrs. Indira Gandhi's effort for a larger number
> of women candidates for her party their party number has
> remained disappointingly small it is partly because of
> Congressmen's hardened attitude towards women. . . .
> As things are, they say, there is already istree raj in
> the country.[4]

The problem persists. In January 1977 the Indian Housewives Federation submitted a resolution to Mrs. Gandhi demanding as many seats for women as men in Parliament. The resolution said that "women should be given their due share of 'political power' and be treated on a par with men in Parliament, State Assemblies, municipalities and panchayats."[5]

Female candidates often are set against other females; thus, they are not allowed by the parties to compete in the campaigns as equals with men. At least in part, this is because a female would have many votes cast against her on the basis of sex alone if she were running against a man.

Still, by their very nature these statistics speak merely of a small group within Indian society. Only a very minute portion of the population can enter into politics as representatives, and none among the author's housewife or female-worker sample is ever likely to be among them. For the average Indian woman as compared with the average Indian male there is little, if any, expectation that, except for voting, she will or should be politically active on any level, that she should participate as do males of the same educational and socio-economic level, or that she has the intelligence to even discuss politics.

The aspects of South Asian tradition that allow women power in various ways might be used to justify their equality with men, but the fact remains that it is only a drop in the monsoon that constantly floods the lives of most Indian women. Only the socioeconomic elites, and then only a select few of them, can participate on any level approximating the opportunities allowed to men, provided they are willing to wade through the ubiquitous flood of sexism. Even a Nehru's daughter was "handed" very little; she fought for everything, against great odds.

Women are the servant class of India both to their own families and others.[6] Their position as such is partly justified by the idea that they are intellectually as well as spiritually inferior. In the rounds of birth and rebirth it is, everyone agrees, better to be born a man than a woman. As the chairman of the political science department of a large and prominent Indian university told an American secretary in an unsolicited and impromptu lecture, "It is the place of the woman to serve the man, and, who knows, if she does it well she has the hope of being born a man in the next life." Such attitudes are applied also in strictures concerning female participation in yoga. Being male is to be in a higher state of life, closer to truth and the Absolute. Although women are on a lower rung of spirituality, in their lives they are expected to be of high moral character—that is, their spiritual and intellectual levels, which are lower than that of men, do not justify any moral laxness. There are several theories that might be offered to explain why this attitude has developed and functions. But, the point to be made here is that the respect shown to Indian women in some aspects, though by no means all, in literature, theology, and social practices should not be confused with the attitudes toward their intellectual or rational capabilities, which are generally assumed to be well below those of a man. As one respondent of an earlier study put it, "It is a common proverb that 'Women's wits are only in their feet.' . . . the men are taught that women are subservient, and the women just follow along."[7]

The demands of moral standards and belief in the lower intelligence of women militate against political participation for females. In terms of moral sanctions, it is not proper for a woman to wander loose among a company of males. If she does, she is immediately branded a loose woman, indeed a charge that is not infrequently heard from Mrs. Gandhi's detractors. How, then, can the women of India attend political speeches, meetings, rallies, and similar activities?

Second, aside from difficulties of mere attendance at political functions, social and intellectual expectations as to the female role make it extremely difficult for her to participate. Because of the assumption of lower female intelligence, most men will not listen to females when they talk about politics but simply cut them off. Even if they were willing to listen, it is hard for men to take them seriously. It takes an extremely forceful woman to gain an audience. In general she could not make a better argument or suggestion than a male because she is sui generis less capable in such matters. Thus, due to social expectations, attendance and more active types of participation are difficult for a female.

Both general social attitudes toward women in politics and interview data indicate that political socialization is different for Indian women than for Indian males. What then is life, and particularly political life, like for these women?

HOUSEWIVES

There is no doubt that the lives of housewives revolve totally around domesticity and that their identities, hopes, and satisfactions are centered around the family. Margaret Cormack found this to be the view of a small sample of ten Indian women who were studying in the United States. If it is true for them, how much more true is it for those Indian women of whom it can literally be said that they have rarely stepped outside of their homes? The following quotes from two educated Indian women should be illuminating.

She is the efficient server of the family, not a thinking
individual. Her unquestioned future is marriage, so
that her security lies not so much in the love of her
husband as in his regard for her in her role as efficient

housewife and mother. . . . The result of all this is that
an Indian woman doesn't want for herself. She thinks
only of the family. [8]

A second variation on this theme reads as follows:

A girl learns that she must be a good housewife, a good
follower of her husband, a good manager of the home.
This is negation, but it is not withdrawal. It is good, and
it is done with pride. Women are proud of their position
as women. Many have more than two or three children,
but even then they want to do everything. This is a limited view of the self. . . . An Indian woman's security is
entirely in her home and her husband, not in herself. For
instance, few Indian women are interested in political
rights. They don't think about rights. They don't think
that way, although they did work for independence. [9]

The absorption of self into family was indicated in interviews
with the housewives in their replies to the question "What is the subject of your thought on desires for your own future and your family's
future?" The replies of all centered exclusively around their children.
Given this general setting for life, what is the political profile
of the housewives in the sample and what are the sources of their political socialization? First, and most obvious from the description
above, usually a housewife is not expected to be politically involved.
The strongest source of political socialization for the housewife comes
from her circumscribed position in society. Ordinarily she is taught
to think of herself in terms of family rather than in any way separate
from family. Her skills and duties in life are all centered around
perpetuation and nurturing of the family. With the exception of voting,
she simply is not offered the opportunity for political participation by
her society. Second, and very important for political socialization,
she fulfills her duties physically within the confines of the home.
Table 3, taken from an urban study done in northern India, reinforces
this description of the geographical boundaries of work for housewives.
Not withstanding the socialization that confines her largely to
domesticity, the housewife is not altogether unaware of politics and
in one area, namely voting, she often participates in politics. In the
national election of 1967, 152,724,611 women cast their votes. That
was 55.5 percent of the total female electorate in India, and it was
only 11.3 percent less than the male voting record. [10] In the Fifth
General Election (1970) 49.2 percent of the female electorate voted,
which was, once again, 11 percent less than the male record for the
same election. [11] Aside from the mere fact of voting, the data offer

TABLE 3

Distribution of Families by the Type of Tasks Performed by Women

Type of Work	Number of Families	Percent
Women do their household work, handle daily cash, do their own shopping, and look after children's studies	16	4
Women do household work, handle daily cash, and do their own shopping but do not look after children's studies	33	8
Women do household work and handle daily cash but do not do their own shopping nor look after children's studies	47	12
Women do housework only	300	75
Question not asked	3	1
Total	399	100

Source: D. Narain, "Growing Up in India," Family Process 3 (March 1964): 144.

further information about the voting behavior of housewives. Since in so many ways they are dependent upon their spouses, is that dependence reflected in casting the ballot?

When asked how they made the decision to vote, 18 percent stated that they voted for whomever their husband or friends recommended or else they voted randomly.* No one in the male sample indicated voting randomly, but, rather, all related their voting decision to candidate or party. This finding may be taken as some support for the idea that females vote as they are told by their husbands or

---

*A few Indian women of the working class, but not in the sample, informed me in a confidential tone that they did not follow their husbands' dictates at the polls but that they would never let them know this. In turn, some males suspected this.

they vote indiscriminately. But a figure of 18 percent is certainly not strong support; what is more noteworthy is the fact that 82 percent of housewives expressed their answers using the language of modern electoral politics. They _are_ becoming initiated into electoral politics. The majority of the housewives reported that they voted on the basis of assessments of the candidates. However, before it can be determined definitively whether females cast their votes, or at least pay more attention to candidates than issues or parties, a larger sample of men and women in India is needed. Some evidence was found that the responses of women vary with the particular locality in which they live, as do the responses of men. In one of the towns both males and females reported almost exclusively that they voted on considerations of party and issue, and in the total female sample 30 percent gave this answer. In the other town, both males and females made voting decisions principally on the basis of candidates. This may mean that housewives do partake of the political culture of their particular locality, and in this respect do not necessarily form a group with all women as compared with men. This hypothesis might be fruitful in attempts to construct a theory for the political behavior of Indian women. It is hoped that other researchers will bring data to bear on it.

Aside from the fact that she does vote, there are other elements in the political profile of the housewife as culled from the interview data, and they illuminate the ways in which she learns about politics. The main sources of political information for the housewife are, in order of frequency, neighbors, radio, and husband. In addition, a few women indicated that they gained some political facts from their children who were studying politics at school. Once again, the general social position of a women is a predominant ingredient in her political socialization. Her life is spent almost exclusively in her immediate neighborhood, and it is mainly from the sources present there that she obtains political information. This circumscribed political environment is also the case for the village women of India.

Females working at home have contact with neighbors more than do women working in the factories, and it is to their neighbors that they talk most about politics. The following sketch of one housewife, an unusually well-informed one, should provide some further insight into the political profile of an Indian working-class women—how her contact with the world outside the neighborhood is severely limited, but how her life need be by no means devoid of political concerns.

Lata, A Working-Class Mother

Lata, who is 33 years old, lives in Modinagar with her husband, a worker in a textile mill, and four children. Given the circumscribed

location of her activities (she does not even leave their compound to do the grocery shopping), the fact that she talks mostly to other females, and the fact that she is illiterate, Lata is representative of the housewives whom I interviewed. Lata is happy with her station in life—that is, she is happy to raise the children and be a good wife. *
Her desire for the family's future is typical of the total adult sample —she wants to give the highest possible education to her children.
The family can only be barely sustained by her husband's salary, and Lata would like to do some work to help. In this regard she mentioned knitting or embroidery work, which she could do at home. She is not a woman who wishes to extend her life beyond home and family and would not like to work outside the home.

In view of Lata's total lack of formal schooling and her neighborhood-centered daily life, one would expect that she would score low on political knowledge. And, it is true that on the most difficult questions, those concerning socialism, the Five-Year Plan, and the difference between the government and the nation, Lata could not answer. But beyond those three questions, the expectations of a low political knowledge score for Lata were proved wrong. The mean score on historical political knowledge for Uttar Pradesh males was 11.12; Lata scored 11.00 (one point equaling one correct answer). In addition, she knew all of the national anthem, could identify Rajendra Prasad (the first president of India), Jawaharlal Nehru (the first prime minister) and his teachings, and Bahadur Shastri (the second prime minister) and the slogan he promulgated, "Jai Jawan, Jai Kisan" ("Glory to the Soldier, Glory to the Farmer"). She knew who Bhagat Singh was (a patriot executed by the British), and she was one of the only two people in the combined male and female samples who could tell me that the Ashok pillar was the national symbol of India. Even more impressive, when asked what the name of the ruling party was, Lata replied:

> It is the New Congress of Indira Gandhi. In the recent elections to the Lok Sabha the New Congress got 351 or 352 seats out of 518. Members of the Government are Swaran Singh, Defense Minister Jagjivan Ram, President V. V. Giri, Prime Minister Indira Gandhi, Vice-President Pathak, Railway Minister Hanuman and the Congress President is Sanjivayya.

She also volunteered the name of the chief minister of her state, Uttar Pradesh. The mean score on responses to the question about the im-

---

*The interview schedule included several questions about the attitudes of women toward their place in life, desires for the future, and perceptions of how they might fulfill those desires.

portant current leaders of the ruling party was 2.7 for males; Lata named 8.0.

Without formal education and limited to a small circle of friends with whom to talk, Lata's high level of political knowledge was unexpected. It is doubtful whether many Americans educated to a high school level could respond as completely to a question about the leaders of their government as did Lata. Where did she gain all this knowledge? The answer is quite simple. Although she has learned some things about politics from her children and her sisters, the main source of Lata's information is the family radio. In her restricted environment where lines of communication with the political world outside are few, the radio was a powerful source of political learning and sufficient to bring her knowledge level up to or beyond the level of those who moved in a physically larger environment.

Although she has never attended a political rally (though she has heard political speeches on the radio), Lata has voted in all elections since she was old enough to do so. Despite all of the political information that she gains from the radio, Lata says she votes for "whoever has the same ideas as my husband, or the one he recommends." Without a doubt, she was sincere in saying this and probably does follow her husband's advice at election time. Like most people, she brings the traditions and modes of thought that she has learned from her general life into politics. This can be seen in Lata's reply to the question of what she thought about strikes: "Yes, there should be strikes, because without crying even a mother will not hear her child. I am a peace-loving person but if they will not listen then we must strike."

The fact that many aspects of a person's general socialization may be elements in political socialization is brought to the fore by Lata. And this is what makes the study of political socialization so difficult. Each person has many experiences, some common to most of society's members and some specific to the individual, and always put together in a unique fashion by each person. It was ascertained that the main source of information for Lata is the radio and that she brings her other roles as wife and mother to bear on her political attitudes and behavior. However, it is not known what made her listen to the news on All India Radio rather than to popular Hindi music or why she takes a charpoy (string bed) outside her home and sits there obviously seeking conversation with neighbors and steering them into political discussions and enjoying her role as "Prime Minister of the neighborhood," as one neighbor put it humorously but not sarcastically.

General Political Profile of Housewives

After having presented a specific case, the discussion will now return to the general political profile as it emerges for women. The

TABLE 4

Knowledge Items for Uttar Pradesh Adults

Knowledge Items	Percentage Who Did Not Know the Item	
	Female	Male
Party	53.6	6.3
Slogans	82.1	43.3
National anthem	67.0	30.0
Gandhi	17.9	3.3
15 August	39.3	6.7

Source: Compiled by the author.

interviews included questions about the ruling party, political slogans, the national anthem, Mahatma Gandhi, and Indian Independence Day (see Table 4). Because they were either emphasized in schools or were easily obtainable from the local environments, these subjects were termed "well-known facts." As it turned out, however, those who in a large percentage of cases had never attended school and had never entered into the local environments beyond their neighborhoods did not have this knowledge. The responses of the housewives indicated that these subjects are not well-known among them. The mean education level of the housewives in the sample is 3.4 years of formal schooling and 50 percent of them are illiterate. Thus, the majority of housewives had little or no opportunity to learn these "simple" facts at school and over half of them cannot read newspapers.

Housewives are both less educated and more confined to home than males, and so their lack of political knowledge cannot be attributed clearly to the influence of one or the other. However, with the exception of Lata, the few women who did score highly were the more educated of the group. Education likely accounts for this knowledge —that is, education broadly interpreted. Education does not merely mean facts learned in school. Except for a very few items on the questionnaire, the knowledge tested did not appear in the textbooks from which these women studied. What education has possibly done for them is to give them skills and confidence, so that they seek out and/or remember information concerning politics. Their main source of current information is the radio or conversation with neighbors who have listened to the radio. The ability to read that was learned in school does not seem to add much in terms of political socialization, since the women rarely have access to newspapers or books.

For a second category of question representing more complex political knowledge, which will not be detailed here, the housewives were largely uninformed and less knowledgeable than their male counterparts. (Although in some cases, such as naming political leaders, the differences were slight. The mean scores were 2.0 for females and 2.3 for males.)

In addition to voting behavior and political knowledge, an attempt was made to discover if politics and political outcomes have enlarged the expectations of housewives. As Rajni Kothari says of India as a whole:

> The broadening of India's political community is a direct consequence of the enlargement of the role and status of government as a factor in social development. This is true not only in terms of the penetration of the governmental system and its key resources, but also in terms of government-mindedness among the people at large. [12]

Among the male sample it was clear that politics politicizes, that the government is a main agent of political socialization, and that males do exhibit a government-mindedness. What of the women?

Almost one-quarter of the housewives said that they thought that the government could help them fulfill their desires for their families. Compared with males (nearly 100 percent) who thought that the government could help them succeed in their aims, this is low; but, given housewives' low level of knowledge about the government, this is notably high. All but one of those who thought the government could help could state specifically how help might be given. (Sixty-seven percent of the males could give details in this regard.) Those who did specify methods of governmental aid mentioned money for building a new home, land, clothing for their children, and scholarships for education. Only one mentioned the latter form of aid, and, even though housewives' desires are overwhelmingly concerned with the education of their children, they do not make the link between that desire and the activities of the government.

In considering the governmentalization of political socialization, it is noteworthy that the idea of getting government loans enters into replies. Only a few years ago, before the government instituted policies to give loans to individuals who wish to attempt self-employment, such a reply would have been extremely unlikely from either workers or housewives. The fact that 60 percent of the males and 12 percent of the housewives mentioned this signals an expansion of perceptions of possibilities, as well as a change in the methods perceived available for fulfilling desires. This new possibility is filtering down to generally uninformed housewives. Some of them, at least, are beginning to be aware of the government as it might affect their personal futures.

"WORK IS WORSE"—FACTORY WORKERS

Although during the last 25 years or so "development" has been viewed as an improvement, there is growing concern that even when gross national product (GNP) does increase, the economic position of a large proportion of the population may be worsening. Discussions in this regard until very recently have largely ignored women, but some authors are beginning to amass evidence about the effects of development (or modernization) on women. [13] Most recently Alex Inkeles and David H. Smith have written about the process of "becoming modern" in six of the poor countries of the world, and they cite the factory as one of the main schools in modernization. [14] They too ignore women, however. This section addresses the issue of how factory life may affect the female worker in India, particularly how it may alter her political knowledge and activities.

In general, female workers exhibited slightly less knowledge of and participation in politics than did males and housewives. Voting was one exception; females reported voting more often than the males. The mean for females was 3.3 votes cast and 3.2 for males.

Once the women leave the factory they are not free for relaxation but have other jobs, those of housewife and mother, awaiting them at home. Given this work schedule, then, it is not surprising that they have little time for political participation (lack of time should not be slighted as a pressure, as it contributes to lower female political participation). Nonetheless, during the course of the day the women do talk to other people—family, friends, and workers —and, although this conversation time might be more limited for women than men, it might nevertheless be utilized for discussion of politics. To some extent, women did report that they talked about politics: 22.1 percent said that they talked to family members about politics, 11.1 percent to friends, and 44.4 percent to other workers. These percentages are not especially lower than the respective percentages for males. Still, going to work outside the home may not necessarily mean a change in political socialization for those women involved. The value prevalent in Indian society that politics is not a subject for women does not disappear for women who enter the factory. Furthermore, in the case of the factory workers in the sample, entering the factory did not mean that they had a chance to talk with males about politics or that politics became more important to their lives. The main effect of their employment was to leave them with less time for talking and hearing about politics than had they remained at home. The female workers had no time to listen to the news on the radio or talk with neighbors, while those are two of the main vehicles for dispersion of political information for housewives. Let us follow two female workers home and glimpse their normal lives after a day at the factory.

Devi and Premila

After the factory day ended in Faridabad, a respondent, who will be called Devi here, walked an estimated three miles home, taking a detour along the way to stop at a stall to buy vegetables and cooking fuel. She does not live in a joint family, as is the case with many workers who have joined the move to the cities this generation. Her family consists of six children and the parents. The husband works at a hotel washing dishes, but Devi explained that none of his pay went toward supporting the family. Devi and her daughter both made R 100 per month, approximately $13, which is obviously a subsistence wage for the family. Devi is in debt so that she can pay the school fees for her eldest son, who is in the eleventh grade.

Three of the children greeted her as she approached their home, and she talked to them as she took a few items of clothing, which she had washed even before the early morning light, down from a door top on her way to the kitchen. Devi then proceeded to light the coals for the fire in order to make tea for me, an added activity for the occasion that she did not ordinarily do. Upon my repeated insistence, she proceeded with her work while the tea was heating and as I was later sipping it. In between talking to her children and lending a cooking pot to a neighbor, she peeled and finely chopped the vegetables and mixed some spices. A good deal of this time, her youngest child rested on her hip. By the time dinner was arranged and cooked, it was seven in the evening and Devi had not paused in her work. An hour earlier her oldest daughter had also come home from work, which was a lengthy distance away, and she rounded up the younger five siblings for dinner. Together mother and elder daughter served the guest and the children and then ate their own meal. By the time the meal was over and the dishes and utensils washed and scoured, it was eight o'clock and time to get the children into bed. The elder daughter took care of this task, although perhaps Devi would have been involved in that also had I not been there. Devi rises at 4:30 A.M. to bath the children, cook a morning meal and sometimes food for other meals during the day, and sweep. If Devi had time to think or talk about politics, surely it was not during the working week.

Devi has voted four times in parliamentary elections (until 1969 there were no municipal elections in Faridabad). She says that she never talks about politics because she has no time. Likewise, she has never attended any kind of political meeting due also to lack of time. It was a fond desire of hers to see Indira Gandhi, but, again, she never had the time.

Despite her lack of time for politics, Devi was able to answer the generally known political information questions. She reported that she got this information from her seven years of school as a young girl in what is now Pakistan. Her political information scores were no lower than the average male score. But her political participation was much lower, except for voting, which was slightly above the mean. It is probable that she gained from education the knowledge that she had no opportunity to gain from the environment of her adult life.

Premila, another factory worker in Faridabad, follows much the same routine as does Devi. She has four children, the oldest of whom is a son who has a job, and her husband is unemployed. She, too, makes R 100 per month and, along with her son, supports the family. Despite the husband's presence in the home, Premila does all the domestic work with the exception that some of the child care falls on her husband. Premila's brother is a member of the Legislative Assembly, and she has an interest in politics as was obvious from her enthusiasm while talking with me about politics. She is a member of the factory Works Committee, and, even though her brother is involved in politics, it is with her fellow workers and especially the other members of the Works Committee with whom she speaks most about politics. From my visit to her home, I can make a reasonable guess as to why this is. Whenever I asked Premila a question about politics or tried to discuss some political issue with her, it was her husband who answered for her. Thus, although she can presumably listen, when convenient, to the political conversations among the male members of her family, she is probably not expected or allowed to participate. (I did not observe any family discussion of politics, so the husband's reaction to my presence may not be generalizable when husband and wife are alone.)

Premila had voted an above-average five times, but she has never been to hear a political speech, although she says that she would like to go. She also volunteered that she would like to be active in the Home Guard but that because of her little children and lack of time she cannot. Premila was in school for four years, but she scored very low on the generally known political information. Premila expressed "an inclination to participate in politics," but, like Devi, she has no time.

Life Chances and Political Participation

Factory women live in a state of despair about their life chances and do not even hold out the hope that a paternalistic government can help. To the question of "How successful are you in fulfilling your desires?" the reply "Not at all" was given by the women in 78 percent of the cases, "Partly" in 22 percent, and none in the optimistic category "50-100 percent fulfilled." Of the males in the same factory, 58 percent felt they had attained 50-100 percent of their goals. In part, this reflects the fact that women are paid less than the males who work beside them, and they know it. And, also, they have the added burden of a second job awaiting them at home. In addition, female workers are influenced by the social attitude that it is both unfortunate and improper for a female to work outside the home. This leads them to feel more dissatisfied with their station in life than males, for whom it is accepted that they participate in such employment. The initial response of one woman to the goal attainment questions was "Women have never worked in factories but I have to work." The statistics above mask the choking voices and even tears with which the women discuss the bleak lives that they lead. (I was cautioned by one of the male personnel supervisors at a factory not to ask questions that would upset the women and was told of a case where an interviewer brought a woman to tears—as if it were the fault of the interviewer rather than a reflection of the life situation of the women.)

The theories that have been put forward about the groups that participate and protest in politics throughout the world rarely discuss the activities of women, and so it is difficult to gather any information on the conditions under which women have participated in political movements in any part of the globe. In general, in India as a whole, social attitudes discourage political participation of almost any kind for women. In connection with student politics in India it has been noted that "less than one percent of the incidents of indiscipline involved women's colleges, while 15 percent of all colleges are female institutions. Female college students are under much more severe pressure to comply with conventional social norms than are men, are under much closer surveillance and control, and are generally more compliant to the expectations of educational authorities."[15] There are some exceptions to the generally low level of female political participation, the main exception being voting. Also, educated, urban women have organized effective pressure groups that deal directly with elected officials at state and national levels, and there are some signs as recent as 1977/78 that their organizations are beginning to encompass women of the working class. Occasionally women are involved in union leadership, and, of course, a few are elected and appointed to fill government positions. Such hopeful exceptions notwithstanding, factory women in the sample are encumbered by social attitudes against their participation as well as the scarcity of time to get involved because of their work loads. Both of these pressures militate against their political participation other than voting. In the body of political science literature about why men rebel, it has been suggested that in order to participate in politics a person must possess some degree of hope of success and some regard for one's efficacy through participation. Women in the sample have a higher sense, by far, of failure in fulfilling their life's desires than do men, and also they do not perceive (even less than men) that the government can help them in fulfilling their desires. The data clearly show that women do not connect their state of well-being or hopes for improvement with the activities of the government. The hopes for the future expressed by the women all related directly to economic problems, but theories of how economic level and economic satisfaction vary with political protest must be developed further to encompass the responses of working-class women in India and elsewhere.

SUMMARY

In sum, even though the women are less educated than the males and though they are confined physically to a few houses along their residential block, or to the path between factory and home, political information does filter in to them. Occasionally they might read, or have read to them, newspapers, which in India are filled with political information. Sometimes they learn things about politics from their children who pass on the lessons they have in school. Other family members bring new information to them, as do neighbors and coworkers, and this is especially true during political campaigns, when interest in the election is high, or times of unusual events, such as the struggle of the East Bengalese for independence. Finally, for housewives, the political world is substantially enlarged by the All India Radio station. The radio, along with education, was the most prominent source of political information for housewives. The fact that they lead a rather circumscribed life limits the sources of political socialization with which they have contact, but it also allows them the opportunity to listen to the radio while they work.

Women are deterred from taking part in politics—talking about politics, amassing political knowledge, and entering into campaigns, as well as voting—more by the widespread idea that politics is not a fit subject for their interest than they are by their lack of education and narrow range of experiences. The same kind of political attitudes affects most of the women of the world. To cite just one example, the authors of The American Voter comment that:

> Decades after the first successes of the suffragettes many
> wives wish to refer our interviews to their husbands as
> being the person in the family who pays attention to poli-
> tics. Or the woman may say in so many words: "I don't
> know anything about politics—I thought that business was
> for men, anyway."[16]

I, too, had this experience in interviewing in India and had to abandon,
for obvious methodological reasons, any interview when a man was
even in sight.

While I am afraid the female factory workers are, for purposes
of this discussion, to be left in a dismal state of affairs, I would like
to include one addendum. In their manner there is an aura about these
women of a <u>person of the world</u> and not merely of the home. They
have entered into a man's world and are functioning there as skillfully
as are the men. Their lives as factory workers, on the one hand,
create abilities to move in the world at large and, on the other, place
upon them a concrete physical burden that limits the possibilities of
expanded movement. It has been said of the United States, and could
as well be said of India, that "Society is geared to socialize women
to believe in and adopt as immutable necessity their traditional and
inferior role."[17] But the women in the factories are no longer totally
convinced of this. To their dismay, they do not know what the concrete possibilities for improvement might be, but they are on the
"lookout" for them. This is true also of the more educated among the
housewives. In this sense they are at the same time becoming modern
and carrying the burden of that modernization, which, at least in the
short run (though one hopes not in the long run), is heavier than before.

Lata, out of her own resources, was able to become more well
informed about politics than were the males of her immediate social
group. But the stereotypes and pressures to keep her out of politics
still bear heavily upon her. The Indian government has attempted to
foster education for the young girls of India. The girls who do make
it to school (perhaps 50 percent of the relevant age group attend the
first few grades) and are able to remain in school for several years
(the highest estimate would be that 20 percent of the relevant age
group attain high school)[18] have the chance to learn about politics
and gain some organizational skills, which, if given equal support
and opportunity by society, would fit them for active political participation, campaigning, protesting, and so forth. Lata, Devi, and
Premila are not able to run for political office or become policy
makers at any level. The same will apply to the girls, even those of
the working class who make it to high school; they will not be given
the opportunity to think and do in politics. This has nothing to do with
merit but is a function solely of their class and sex.

It was not the purpose of this study to detail all the ways in which women do participate in politics in India but to look closely at one sample of blue-collar, working-class women. One must conclude that their participation is slight, though they are learning about politics. There are, however, women who are active in unions and the politics surrounding those activities in India. There are also women's pressure groups, which do have an effect at times on government policy—the Women's Vigilance Committees and the Indian Housewives Federation, to name two. But thus far such pressure groups have been dominated by educated women who have more support from family and social group for their political participation than do working-class women, either factory worker or housewife. Hopefully, the story of the spread of those activities to blue-collar, working-class women will be written one day. For now, however, one need not be unaware of male problems of class nor unsympathetic about the drudgery of male lives to note, nevertheless, that it is worse to be a woman.

The worker is the slave of capitalist society, the female worker is the slave of that slave. [19]

NOTES

1. The latest of this genre is Doranne Jacobson and Susan S. Wadley, Women in India (Manohar, 1977).

2. Chandrakala A. Hate, Changing Status of Women in Post-Independence India (Bombay: Allied Publishers Private Limited, 1969), p. 230.

3. Hindustan Times, March 7, 1971. The notation "(N)" represents that portion of the Congress organized with Indira Gandhi as leader in 1969, the time when the Congress party split into two separate parties, Congress (Old) and Congress (New).

4. In Hindi istree raj means "female rule"; the reference is to the former prime minister, Indira Gandhi. Hindustan Times, March 7, 1971.

5. Statesman, January 29, 1977.

6. The job of being domestic servant to nonrelatives may even be increasing in India. In two comparable surveys taken of Poona City in 1936/37 and 1954, the lone statistic pointing to any change in the labor market for women was the fact that while in the first survey women domestic servants were a little less than half the total, in 1954 they were 90 percent. See D. R. Gadgil, Women in the Working Force in India (Bombay: Asia Publishing House, 1965).

7. Margaret Cormack, The Hindu Woman (New York: Columbia University Press, 1953), p. 193.

8. Ibid., p. 187.

9. Ibid., p. 188.

10. Hate, Changing Status of Women, p. 225.

11. Government of India, Election Commission, Report on the Fifth General Election, 1971-72 (Delhi: Election Commission, n.d.), p. 120-21.

12. Rajni Kothari, Politics in India (Boston: Little, Brown, 1970), p. 285.

13. See, for example, Rayna Reiter, Towards an Anthropology of Women (New York: Monthly Review Press, 1975); and Ester Boserup, Women's Role in Economic Development (London: George Allen and Unwin, 1970).

14. Alex Inkeles and David H. Smith, Becoming Modern: Individual Change in Six Developing Countries (Cambridge, Mass.: Harvard University Press, 1974).

15. Lloyd I. Rudolf, Susanne Hoeber Rudolf, and Karuna Ahmed, "Student Politics and National Politics in India," Economic and Political Weekly 6, nos. 30-32 (Special Number 1971): 1663.

16. Angus Campbell et al., The American Voter (New York: John Wiley & Sons, 1964), p. 255.

17. Kirsten Amundsen, The Silenced Majority: Women and the American Democracy (Englewood Cliffs, N.J.: Prentice-Hall, 1971), p. 4.

18. Government of India, Ministry of Information and Broadcasting, India 1974, a Reference Annual (New Dehli: Ministry of Information and Broadcasting, 1974), p. 54. In 1969-70 the percentage of females of high school age (14 to 17) was listed as 9.5 percent, in contrast to the 1974 figure of 20 percent. Government of India, Ministry of Education and Social Welfare, Education in India 1969-70 (Delhi: Ministry of Education and Social Welfare, n.d.), p. 21.

19. Connolly, James. Labour in Ireland: Labour in Irish History: The Reconquest of Ireland (Dublin: Maunsel, 1917), p. 292. Connolly was an Irish patriot executed by the British in 1916.

REFERENCES

Amundsen, Kirsten. The Silenced Majority: Women and the American Democracy. Englewood Cliffs, N.J.: Prentice-Hall, 1971.

Boserup, Ester. Woman's Role in Economic Development. London: George Allen and Unwin, 1970.

Campbell, Angus, et al. The American Voter. New York: John Wiley & Sons, 1964.

Connolly, James. Labour in Ireland: Labour in Irish History: The Reconquest of Ireland. Dublin: Maunsel, 1917.

Cormack, Margaret. The Hindu Woman. New York: Columbia University Press, 1953.

Gadgil, D. R. Women in the Working Force in India. Bombay: Asia Publishing House, 1965.

Government of India, Election Commission. Report on the Fifth General Election in India 1971-72. Delhi: Election Commission, n.d.

Government of India, Ministry of Education and Broadcasting. India 1974, a Reference Annual. Delhi: Ministry of Information and Broadcasting, 1974.

Hate, Chandrakala A. Changing Status of Women in Post-Independence India. Bombay: Allied Publishers Private Limited, 1969.

Hindustan Times. March 7, 1971.

Jacobson, Doranne, and Susan S. Wadley. Women in India. Manohar, 1977.

Kothari, Rajni. Politics in India. Boston: Little, Brown, 1970.

Narain, D. "Growing Up in India." Family Process 3 (March 1964).

Reiter, Rayna. Towards an Anthropology of Women. New York: Monthly Review Press, 1975.

Rudolf, Lloyd I., Susanne Hoeber Rudolf, and Karuna Ahmed. "Student Politics and National Politics in India." Economic and Political Weekly 6, nos. 30-32 (Special Number 1971): 1663.

Statesman. January 29, 1977.

7

CARIBBEAN WOMEN: THE IMPACT OF RACE, SEX, AND CLASS

Gloria I. Joseph

INTRODUCTION

An examination of published research and popular interest in Africa and the Black diaspora reveals that the Caribbean has been the most neglected of three areas, Africa, Black America, and the Caribbean, and that women have been the "neglected of the neglected." For the past four years our research team has been engaged in a major research project concerning the sociopolitical status of women in the Caribbean. A major purpose of this study is to contribute to the meager body of information on Caribbean women and to combat the abundance of misconceptions about them. The research team of scholars and indigenous people from the various islands systematically examined the similarities and differences among women throughout this area, recording the extent to which these women were jeopardized and exploited because of their race, sex, and class—triple jeopardy.

The geographic spread of the islands and the complexities of women's roles and statuses necessitated a long-term study of over four years. Islands visited included Puerto Rico, Haiti, the Dominican Republic, Guyana, Trinidad, Jamaica, Curaçao, Anguilla, Virgin Islands (Saint Croix, Saint Thomas, Saint John), Martinique, Barbados, and Cuba.* Methods of data collection included participant observation, structured interviews, archival sources, and current literature representative of various local groups from each island. Participant observation and interview procedures are most obvious in the material presented.

---

*The condition of Cuban women in the Caribbean is exceptional. Cuba has fully embraced a different economic pattern. Cuban women will be discussed in Chapter 8.

The accumulation of data was overwhelming and instructive. The results and findings depicted an overview of the Caribbean that made the researchers acutely aware of the fact that on a certain level one must be extremely cautious about generalizing the findings of one island to another, and equally important, not to generalize the similarities of several islands to the entire Caribbean. For example, there are degrees of poverty on all the islands, but the poverty in Haiti remains unsurpassed and is not an accurate reflection of the entire Caribbean. Haiti's per capita income in 1976 was $100. There are high unemployment rates on many of the islands but none comes near to that of Anguilla: 18 percent of the population was employed![1] However, with the exception of Cuba, one fact was found to be very consistent from island to island—the similarity within each island of extremes in economic, social, and educational conditions.

Considering the potential within the female population of the Caribbean for the development of movements aimed at producing social change was a major concern. After several months of intensive interviewing and research, one major hypothesis was challenged: the concept that those who experience the severest of triple jeopardies are more conscious of their oppressed state and this provides the greatest impetus for uniting with others in similar circumstances to work for improvement of their common condition. This concept was not an actuality among this particular group of Third World women. From island to island, the degree of political consciousness among the women showed as much variance as did color, complexion, and income. That oppression does not automatically generate a revolutionary consciousness will be demonstrated. A necessary precondition is that the oppressed become aware of the exploitative bases of their situation under imperialist domination and patriarchy and, consequently, take action. Comparing the development of this political awareness reveals sharply differing perspectives among Caribbean women.

These women suffer to varying degrees from the oppressive nature of racial, sexual, and economic exploitation. To say that the majority of Caribbean women suffer class exploitation very simply means that their economic level dictates their life-style, and in this case it means experiencing hardships, extreme deprivations, and denial of access to desired goals. It also means that they are grossly exploited in terms of their labor and are more intensively victimized because of their greater vulnerability. The majority lack economic stability; many exist at a bare subsistence level, and the poverty that they face denies them vital schooling, occupational choice, and needed health care and housing. There are some rare exceptions to these situations: the Black female Trinidadian physician, the Haitian market woman who has built up a lucrative trading business, the Black woman university professor in Jamaica, and the woman provincial governor in the Dominican Republic. These cases remind us that it is possible for some Black women to attain middle-class status in the Caribbean Islands. The vast majority, however, do not have access to upward mobility. The services they perform are largely to the advantage of bosses, an owner, or a corporation. The pay and/or returns received by the women for their services are cruelly unjust.

The term sexual oppression within Caribbean society calls for some elaboration. In most societies, women are allocated certain roles owing to their biological status. Unfortunately, most women have accepted and internalized their assigned roles. Women are often crushed by cultural restraints, abused by illegitimate power structure, and referred to by many as domestic slaves. They are regarded as commodities and are, in many instances, considered to be the private property of men. Research by Frances Henry and Pamela Wilson on the status of women in Caribbean societies stated:

> We came to this project somewhat objectively since our aim was to have a careful but dispassionate look at Caribbean women and to see the extent of the multitudinous roles they play in society. Gradually, however, our readings convinced us that Caribbean women, by and large, play a subservient role to men particularly in economic and social areas; that a double standard of sexuality exists; and that women frequently are forced to hide their potential talents and abilities.[2]

These are the conditions and situations that are regarded as oppressive and are the direct consequence of being female. Women in Caribbean societies, like their sisters in other Western societies, do not contribute an appropriate amount nor substantive quantity of their real resources to their society, nor are they sufficiently recognized for the contributions they do make.

The third jeopardy, racial oppression in the Caribbean, will be discussed, to some extent, and compared with views of racial oppression in the United States. Black women in the United States have been affected by racial oppression throughout history, and it still influences their daily lives. H. Rap Brown once remarked that "Racism is as American as apple pie." It is simply a part of the daily routine of living—this includes both institutional and individual racism. Toni Cade Bambara aptly said in the preface of The Black Woman (1972):

> We are involved in a struggle for liberation; liberation from the exploitive and dehumanizing system of racism, from the manipulative control of a corporate society; the

Black American woman, whether by coming face to face
with whites and racism on a daily basis, or acutely feeling
the results of the absent white capitalist or liberal, is in
a position where she cannot avoid dealing with the oppression of race.[3]

In the predominantly nonwhite societies of the Caribbean, the
manifestations of racism may seem less obvious. At least many of
our interviewees in the Caribbean failed, refused, or were reluctant
to identify facets of their daily lives as aspects of racial oppression.
There seemed to be a "false" lulling on the feeling of the question of
color. Those for whom interracial contact is frequent and regular—
for example, employees in hotels and restaurants or domestics in
white homes—have little difficulty in describing incidents of overt
racism. Institutional racism is the most oppressive force in the
Caribbean, as in the United States. Such racism is often most subtle
and difficult to identify where it is taking its greatest toll. Institutional
racism does not need on-site white agents. In fact, it is probably
most effectively perpetuated where the direct agents are indigenous
leaders.

Neocolonialism serves to divert the discontent of Caribbean
women and men. In its subtle and more dangerous form, women are
often unaware of the insidious manner in which it affects their lives;
for example, there is the skillful control of economic resources by
agencies and forces located outside the region. There is also the
treacherous control and regulation of the educational systems. The
educational systems with their colonial structures have successfully
alienated the emerging indigenous intelligentsia from the thousands
of untrained people at the bottom of society. Those who are trained in
in the higher educational processes are simultaneously drained of humanitarian qualities. It is practically impossible for the intelligentsia
to identify with the lower socioeconomic groups. The racist, classist,
and sexist educational systems serve to help maintain a colonial mentality, thus ensuring the continuation of neocolonialism.[4]

Color caste still plays a dominant and peculiar role in Caribbean nonwhite society.* It is an intragroup phenomenon that functions
in a manner parallel to racism. On the one hand, skin color impunes
notions of superiority—the lighter the skin the more favorable. On the
other hand, in certain cases, skin color is ignored as a criterion for
racial identification. The very dark-hued Indian woman who identifies
herself as white is a case in point. In the United States the Cape Ver-

---

*It also plays a role in the white society of the Caribbean; how-
ever, this discussion pertains to the nonwhite society.

deans offer similar examples. Dark-skinned Cape Verdeans who appear to be Black will call themselves non-Black and have their birth certificates to offer as proof. On their birth certificates their racial category is stated as white. Manifestations of this color caste syndrome, with lighter skin being preferable, can be seen in places of employment. For example, practically all bank employees will have cream-colored complexions.

Being labeled as white or nonwhite on the basis of pigmentation or other physical characteristics is not what is of importance here. It is only the social significance bestowed on racial distinctions and the psychological significance thereby invested in racial identity that gives the fact of race its impact on human lives. Accordingly, social and psychological considerations become important in the definition of race. In many Caribbean communities dark-hued women declare themselves as white. Society refuses to grant them this status. It may consider them non-Black, but it does not accept them as white. Therefore, Caribbean women who are socially recognized as being nonwhite, who consider themselves to be nonwhite publicly and are accepted as such, are the focus of concern. Thus a very dark-hued Indian woman from Trinidad who may declare herself to be white would fall outside the purvey of this study. The incongruity between her social label and her self-perception sets her apart from the vast majority for whom social definition and self-concept coincide.

With these basic conditions of class, race, and sex as unifying factors, it becomes possible to understand Caribbean women through individual portraits, highlighting the political realities of four distinct and varied profiles. Each profile includes a description of the economic conditions in each woman's environment, how these women view themselves, and how the world views them; all of this information is combined in an analysis based on these unifying factors.

SISYPHUS WOMEN

If we begin at the Sisyphus stratum* of the economic-social ladder, we find the misery woman. She is born into poverty, knows nothing else, hence has no expectations of changing her condition in the world. She might be called Mavis and would certainly be found meandering through the streets of Haiti, "cotching and scuffling" on

---

*Sisyphus stratum is the author's original term for those persons endlessly toiling at the bottom of socioeconomic classifications (equal to the low-low class in sociological jargon).

the dungle* in Jamaica, or tucked away in the shadows of the corners of Antigua. Her salient feature is ignorance; it is hard to say how much her gender is relevant to her extreme state of suffering.

Mavis lives in housing so dilapidated that it might not even be recognized as such by passing tourists; her housing might be corrugated metal or even a bundle of rags. In the morning she can be seen shuffling out to buy or beg one or two cigarettes. Then she settles for the day, sitting next to a wall in any empty lot. She begs food from tourists and other native folks who are better off than she seems to be. Or she might be playing a "slide game": she disappears after a successful morning of begging to change into a better set of clothes. But Mavis has very little, even if she does manage a change of clothes. A tourist might spot her picking up grains of coffee in the street and find it incredulous that anyone could be so desperately poor.

Childbearing for Mavis involves considerable suffering: she suffers from vitamin deficiencies and is likely to have diabetes and/or malaria. She will die young, looking much, much older than her chronological age. The women in this category suffer the greatest triple jeopardy. They beg, suffer, breed, bleed, and die!

For Mavis the misery woman, life equals oppression. Physically and emotionally she is drained. What is political consciousness? What is potential as a revolutionary force? Can we measure her revolutionary potential on the basis of whether she steals or begs? Begging or stealing in the case of Mavis does not contribute to the political goals of the oppressed and superexploited. In Mavis's condition she could just as easily become a stoolie or junkie. Her activities are not directly connected with any social movement, nor do they inadvertently contribute to revolutionary struggle. Mavis's prime aim in life is to exist. Her world view of society is one of stark oppression. Society does not need, want, or care to view Mavis. Her sex is immaterial. So is her race. She was/is made virtually useless since she cannot participate as a consumer for others' profit or as a producer.

---

*The term <u>dungle</u> was employed by Orlando Patterson in his book <u>The Children of Sisyphus</u> and refers to an area in Jamaica near Spanish Town inhabited by members of the Ras Tafarians (a cult). This area is described as being inhumanlike, literally comparable to living in a garbage heap—for example, the lowest imaginable housing exists here and the main food source is the garbage itself.

LABORING WOMEN

Several rungs above the Sisyphus stratum of the economic ladder is the laboring woman. The laboring woman is recognized, of course, as a working-class woman. The usage of the word laboring is deliberate. The purpose is to distinguish the type of work done by those women in contrast to the traditional menial job categories. There is no glamorous association with these occupations. These domestics, factory workers, field workers, and the like experience hard labor, degradation, inequities, and injustices to a greater extent than any other group in the islands. They are exploited as workers and as women:

> Because while the merry wicked are making all the Black masses see plenty hell, the women seeing even more hell. Either husband gone and woman stranded, or husband pay pocket too small to make ends meet, or something. But every day is more of us looking for jobs, very often unprepared like hell in terms of skills or the way we were brought up, and less of us finding them. [5]

This woman also adds that when homes disintegrate under the pressure of the slavelike existence, nine out of ten times it is the woman who is left to scramble for the survival of the children. Many women are forced to seek some form of paid employment, regardless of young children and other family needs.

The laboring woman profiled here might be called Leona. Her house is small, possibly of cinder block construction, and she does her cooking out in the yard. She fixes a tiny corner to hang up her clothes on a string; there is a pump in the yard; old calendars decorate the walls of the house. The floors in her house might be dirt, but she keeps them swept, just as she does the dirt in the yard.

Leona realizes that she is mistreated, but to some extent her religion allows her to accept suffering and blame herself. She also expects to serve her man, although she tends to blame him rather than society for their economic condition. Leona values reproducing: she has children for her husband, her self-esteem, and her old age. An extended family system cooperates in child care. Leona earns less than $72.50 per month. Although on practically every island females outnumber males, the males who are "economically active" far outnumber the females. For example, according to the Year Book of Labour Statistics for 1972, 38.4 percent of the males in Guadaloupe were economically active, while only 19.5 percent of females were. [6] Leona has no recourse for grievances. As a domestic worker for tourists, hotels, or white "continentals," she has no way to limit the chores required of her. In many homes the attitude toward the domestic is one of contempt. As rising consciousness affects more and more domestic workers and they react to the dehumanizing conditions, the employers seek out "green" victims from the countryside, who are more easily exploited.

Leona's sister earns $8.00 for sewing 70 crinoline dresses in a Trinago garment factory; the dresses will be sold for $55.00 each. Companies are allowed considerable leeway. Town and Country Garment, a subsidiary of Sears and Roebuck, was able to dismiss over 500 women without question when they attempted to join the Transport and Industrial Worker Trade Union. Five hundred new workers were hired and forced to join a union set up over night by the company itself; other companies, which engaged in similar employment measures, formed like unions.[7] So, the laboring woman finds herself struggling among company, government, and union with the three forming a vicious alliance. Leona and her fellow laborers' material oppression is integrally related to their sexual and psychological oppression. Their life-styles dictate the way they think, feel, and act. The majority of them have very little experience outside of the demanding drudgery of labor, childbearing, child care, and husband or mate servitude. Being psychologically and emotionally locked into family relations and on-the-job slavery, these women have no freedom to pursue alternatives. They feel driven, compelled to provide and care for themselves and other family members, and know no other means of functioning.

You may not hear erudite explanations from these women of the role that bourgeois capitalism plays in their lives, but an awareness of their condition and the reasons behind it are emerging. The Trinidadian domestic expressed this attitude earlier, and the words of a Dominican woman, aged 32, further exemplifies this type of awareness.

She is a cleaning woman for a "very nice family who treats her very well." She has 2 siblings from the first marriage of her father and 11 from the second. This is not unusual she said, since there are often 16 to 18 children. Her father works in a chemical factory, her mother in a chocolate factory. She is married, with a 12-year-old daughter, and emphatically stated that she will have no more! During an interview with this domestic, the following questions and answers were recorded in 1974:

Q. If you had enough money would you still want to work?
A. Yes! One's body needs it.

Q. What do you want for your daughter?
A. She's intelligent—she should stay in school, get a degree, then a profession.

Q. Is it difficult for women to have good jobs in the Dominican Republic?

A. Most people get jobs through friends, but it's still easier for a man to get a job. It's still difficult for an educated woman to get a job.

Q. Do you know any of the women in the government? And who controls the government? [In 1966 Joaquin Balaguer, newly elected president, appointed women to the governorships of all 26 provinces of the Dominical Republic. Since that time women have held numerous government positions.]

A. Military controls. Men control!

Q. In the market the men whistle and hiss. Is this just for foreigners?

A. Just be glad they didn't do anything obscene! I hear that in Puerto Rico and parts of N.Y. they're even worse. More aggressive. There is more respect here. The whole world goes the way N.Y. and Puerto Rico behaves [sic].

Q. Is food expensive?

A. Things used to be cheaper, rice, beans, even meat, but everything has soared. Food up, salaries down. Out of our salaries money is taken for the party, insurance, taxes, etc.

Q. Is there prostitution? Drugs?

A. Drugs is only men. Just marijuana. Prostitution because the government is spending all its money on construction of government buildings and tourism. No industries, no employment for women, thus the streets.

Q. Is the situation where women stay home and man goes out and does as he wants getting any better? What kind of woman does a Dominican man like? Prettiness, etc.?

A. It's getting worse. Traditionally, man would want woman from the country, one who would stay home, not look at another man. Now, things are more updated, women work, and have more schooling. The woman with money is untouchable unless a man has more money than she. Difficult to cross this social barrier. Men like Indian women more than Black. There is intermarriage in the northern part of the island among descendants of the Spaniards [in San Francisco de Macoris] to keep the lineage pure [sic]. Many deformed children as a result.

Q. If you were president of the Dominican Republic, what would you do?

A. Get rid of armed forces! The strong man. Get rid of jobs where people don't exist—are mere names on the payroll and that's where all the money goes. Someone's daughter comes along, gets a job over someone more prepared, and she never comes to work.

The oppressed Leonas represent a group with potential for bringing about social change. The revolutionary leadership that is within them must be further developed, and consciousness raising must be a first step.

INDEPENDENT STRIVERS

Another group of women attempt to maintain their independence. Major earnings for this group come from self-employment. Kathlyn, as she might be called, has a more positive self-image than Leona or Mavis, but she, too, is having a difficult time.

The Jamaican higgler and market women are largely represented in this group. The Jamaican higgler is a term used by Jamaicans to describe a particular type of agricultural petty trader. The higgler, usually a woman, is the link between the isolated small farmer and the market. She walks and buys produce from the country people (those who sell produce grown by their own household personnel) to take to the market. Some country higglers spread their goods in the markets and sell directly to house buyers, and other sell to town higglers, town residents who rent stalls in the markets where they buy at wholesale and sell at retail.[8] These West Indian women are remarkable in their ability to make a living in an impoverished environment. Most West Indians are rural people and still depend on making a living from the land or related occupations closely tied to peasant agriculture. With limited capital, hard work, and small profits, these women utilize agriculture for their main source of survival. The market is the center of their economic existence.

Many central markets are located in places that require transportation, yet adequate provision for cheap public transport is not available. Hence, many women walk for miles with their produce. It is not uncommon to see a Haitian woman walking steep and narrow paths through the night with her children and herself laden down with produce in order to get to the market by daybreak. On a very few occasions a donkey may also be a part of the procession, overburdened with both produce and a sleeping child.

Supermarkets offer substantial competition for the market women, and particularly when they violate the one-mile radium law. For example, supermarkets are not to be located less than one mile from the market in Trinago. When vendors continue to operate their stalls closer to the town activity, to avoid sitting next to trays of decaying fruit and vegetables, they are hunted by the police who brutally destroy their stands, arrest them, and take them to court where they are fined. The situation discussed occurs specifically in Trinago; however, it is not unique to Trinago. In Anguilla the "market" consists of a large tree where two or three days a week a few vendors display a meager sprinkling of goods. The minisupermarket is very close to this tree market. And so it continues. In almost every area where the Black Caribbean working woman is seen, she is struggling to make ends meet.

On the other hand, she shares in a special community with other women. Kathlyn and the other market vendors share their pride in the family tradition of their trade, they enjoy a commonality of bawdy stories and rivalries, and in this sharing they are more spirited than the women previously discussed and so more independent from their men.

Kathlyn might be seen by tourists or white continentals as simply a poor Black woman, but in her community she is respected and given important economic status. Her family has probably been in the business of street vending for generations. By establishing a trustworthy reputation in the marketplace, Kathlyn achieves a gratifying position of importance in her community. She is not only streetwise, but is literate as well (she probably has gone through elementary school).

Kathlyn is not likely to be a victim of sexual exploitation in the same way as Leona. For Leona, there is an ever present demand for the surrender of her body—in obtaining a job, keeping a position, and earning a promotion. Kathlyn does not have to succumb to sexual exploitation to get her basic rights. For her daughters, usually with her where she sells her produce, she may be a role model of strength and independence.

The astute, witty, independent, yet cooperative, spirit of the Kathlyns of the Caribbean speaks well for their potential as a moving force in the drive for equality and liberation for women. They may voice distrust and indifference toward American feminism, but their behavior belies their indifference to a movement for equality. Their attitude toward work is positive; their management and organizational skills excellent; and their awareness of the exploitative nature of capitalism growing. They are becoming more vocal in their protestations against the debilitating effects of the influence of multinational corporations.

ERSATZ SOCIETY WOMEN

In the Caribbean societal structure, like the American one, there is no Black counterpart to the super rich—the Vanderbilts, Mellons, Duponts, Gettys, Rothchilds, or Rockefellers. But there is a bourgeois class of working people who are located on the top rungs of the economic scale among the Caribbean peoples. Agatha, the professional woman, belongs to this group. Women in this category are both professional and semiprofessional workers and include the "hi-sidditys"* of the Caribbean.

Agatha is a semiprofessional and can neither recognize nor acknowledge that she is similar to working-class women. The majority of the so-called middle- and upper-class Caribbean women—those who have reached some level of eminence either through marriage, education, or corruption—are consciously and unconsciously protecting their privileges. They are actively and inadvertently reinforcing their separation from the uneducated, menial job-holding or jobless masses.

Agatha is a government worker and identifies herself in the class of women that includes nurses, doctors, teachers, entertainers, university-affiliated women (including students), and wives of professional men. She has fewer children than the misery woman, the laboring woman, or the independent self-employed woman. She, like Kathlyn the market woman, might be more enlightened on the issue of sterilization than her working-class sisters, but her opinions would be shaped by her attitude of superiority to other women. Agatha might feel responsible for "bettering the conditions of the other women," but she would be unlikely to see herself as oppressed because of her gender. She would suffer more conflict concerning whites: she is seduced by the middle-class life-style but could identify with racial struggles. On the other hand, Agatha is likely to be more European-identified than Black-identified.

Agatha is more knowledgeable about the women's movement than Mavis, Leona, or Kathlyn and is a member of the Women's Political Organization, which recently sponsored a seminar on "The Study of Women and Family Planning." Women came from all over the Caribbean and Latin America—even Cuba. But, ironically and unfortunately, there were no Mavises present, nor was the topic of Mavis even considered. Too many Caribbean women in the upper strata are unmitigatingly guilty of elitism. They cannot identify with the women in the working classes. They feel a rightness and righteous-

---

*Hi-siddity is the colorful term popular in Black communities in America. It refers to certain characteristics associated with Blacks who are a part of Black "high society."

ness in their positions and operate primarily on the "pull yourself up by the bootstrap" philosophy, not realizing that most of the women do not even have "boots."

One of Agatha's fellow club members in the Business and Professional Women's Club teaches at a university. She proudly revealed the statistic that in her country in the past 15 years the percentage of women students had grown from 24 percent to 47 percent. However, there were no daughters of the Leonas, and very few of the Kathlyns, among the increased number of women enrolled. Again, this point to the deficits in the mentalities of the women in the upper stratas. They are the ones who are in the position to effect changes on the governmental level, and they are the ones who are in the forefront of the popular women's organization. The criticisms leveled at the women's organizations in the United States, particularly during the early stages of the movement, can be leveled against Agatha and her fellow club members. Personal liberation and the hope to create a better living situation on the personal level, but within the same societal structure, are their goals.

Agatha's younger cousin, a registered nurse, is representative of another distinctive type within this category. She is usually younger, feels closer ties to Black women in other societies, and her self-perception is more cosmopolitan. However, she, too, has the problem of not recognizing the similarity between her life and those of other women who do not control or own means of production. The following is taken from an interview with her concerning the women's question:

Q. What do you consider to be the single most important problem for women?
A. Education. Education is the only way, because through education you can be engaged in a productive field. And if you produce and have money, you can get your independence anyway. And your own self-estimation is higher—self-esteem, you know.

Q. Is there a family program here and how does it work?
A. In the past year there has been a considerable improvement in the hospital—the condition. The hospitals are cleaner, more personnel, but still a shortage of instruments. There is now a volunteer body of diplomatic women—you know, all rich women—the women from the bourgeoisie try to serve, do their charity thing. There had been a thousand babies born in six days. We have a problem in the country of family planning— a national problem. We have a United Nations Population Foundation—a national Family Council. But there is a noticeable change in the women's attitude

> towards having children. They want at least three or
> four children. No more. This is a drastic change
> from the accustomed 10, 12, 15 and 20. They say
> there are more than 100,000 women engaged in the
> program. I think it's more like 50,000.

Q. How do you see the difference between what they're
talking about in the U.S. that they call "women's liberation" and what the women in your country are trying
to do?

A. Even though there are women here who identify with
the women's movement in the U.S., I do not. U.S.
is a consumers' society and capitalists' and imperial-
ists' society. And really, we are undeveloped, we belong to the Third World. We are a poor country. We
live here not for consumers, even though there is a
sector of our society who lives for that. And we are
an island. Everything gets here two years late. I
haven't been out of the country in three years. You
don't know what's happening in the world. I feel just
fed up to here.

Q. You have one child, a baby girl, right?

A. Yes, but I would like to have a boy child so he could
be a new man. We have to have a new kind of man for
the new generation. Men who are not chauvinistic—
ones that will respect women as equals.

The comments of the young nurse reflect the conflicts that exist
within this group of women. She recognizes major inequities and has
a negative attitude toward those women in her category whom she considers "bourgeois." On the other hand, she fails to identify with the
labor women and misery women when she says that she feels education
is the single most pressing problem for women. Agatha and her
friends could provide the leadership via their education to lessen the
oppressive material conditions in the lives of Mavis and Leona.
Kathlyn has proved that she has intelligence equal to anyone. She
should not be denied educational opportunities, but that is certainly
not her major problem.

The categories of women discussed are not exclusive ones.
For example, you may find a domestic running a small lottery on the
side. "Pay three dollars for a pot, make your own lottery, sell tickets
and make seven dollars. Everyone weekly pays $2.50 and a number
is drawn, the winner gets the week's money. Helps you get a little

capital. "* A number of women take in sewing in addition to working elsewhere.

Regardless of the category, women feel the impact of sexual oppression. The impact of class, however, proves to be the most incisive, divisive factor among them.

MOVEMENTS OF THE 1970s
AND CARIBBEAN WOMEN

Surely when history looks at social movements of the 1970s, two of the major ones will be women's liberation and Black liberation. It is important that an accurate portrayal of Caribbean women be recorded in relation to both.

In general, Caribbean women evidenced a decided lack of accurate information about and, in most cases, a lack of interest in the feminist movement in the United States. Their attitudes toward the movement were similar to those of many Black women. Basically they consider Black women's problems to be different from those of white women. They frequently expressed a strong rejection of the women's movement and complained of its inappropriateness for them. Their comments were either disdainful or jocular. In addition, there was an obvious lack of identity with Black American women and their participation in the feminist movement. As a matter of fact, a substantial percentage of Caribbean women did not even identify with the term Black.

In discussing the outcome of the International Women's Year Conference in Mexico of 1975, working-class women expressed indignation, but not surprise. They regarded the conference as being composed of two camps: those women from the imperialist white countries—Eastern and Western Europe and America—and those women from the exploited world—the Caribbean, Latin America, Africa, and Asia. In opposition to the concept of an "international woman who suffers the same problem of male domination wherever she may be," they state the following:

1. White women are now scrambling for equal rights with their men. Caribbean women are living in a worldwide society where there are no rights if you are Black and poor—man, woman or child.

*This explanation was given by a domestic worker who runs this type of lottery in order to make extra money.

2. White women in the liberation movement come from an experience where they were pampered—and still have little to do in their own houses. Their education is used to assist their husbands in climbing the social hierarchy. For most Caribbean working women [who do practically everything in their homes] the only kind of liberation is from the clutches of white economic, political and cultural domination.

3. To our sisters of the Third World, contraceptions and abortions are not solutions to end the hunger of the majority. To control the people's human resources by the people—not just a puppet elite—and equal distribution of the land is part of the solution. In essence, then, the solution is people's control. [9]

There are, however, many middle and upper socioeconomic class Caribbean women who have formed organizations that are akin to the much maligned American women's liberation groups, such as the National Organization of Women. These women do not express the same sentiments articulated by working-class women. Popular media coverage highlights the activities of the middle- and upper-class women's organizations. There are endless women's groups and organizations that purport to be concerned with women's equality. Their ideology, when extricated from their rhetoric, lacked incorporation of the need to strive-fight and struggle in a protracted way against racism, capitalism, and imperialism. Their fight against sexism reflects a selfish sexism (that is, concern for self-advancement, self-aggrandizement, self-satisfaction).

However, it was very enlightening and pleasing to discover the "new Caribbean woman"—a growing number of nonprofessionals, as well as professionals, who have embraced an ideology aimed toward a struggle to eliminate the oppression and poverty resulting from capitalist/imperialist socioeconomic structures. This ideology incorporates a new role for women in recognition of the double standard that exists between the sexes.

New Caribbean women, indeed, recognize that they have real problems as Black women, but they believe that they should deal with them from their own perspectives and historical background—not that of white women. Caribbean women have to organize in order to play a full role beside men for the liberation of the Caribbean. Among the Caribbean women there is a recognizable force growing in awareness of consciousness. These Caribbean women know that they are grossly exploited because of their sex. However, their job categories are inextricably bound to their belonging to the exploited poor, oppressed, working class. Being nonwhite is practically endemic to being exploited in the Caribbean, so race and class are tightly woven. Their sexual identification adds the final strike.

They are mindful of the fact that occupying a top post per se is a superficial achievement for the few women who are in such positions. There is growing awareness of the subtle nefarious influence of the multinational corporation—an awareness that governments must fight against imperialism and people against neocolonialism. New Caribbean women need to lead all Caribbean women in joining the struggle for initiating political and socioeconomic change, so that women can be free and equal citizens in their countries.

The research data revealed two basic and critical facts. First, that the condition of nonwhite Caribbean people is similar to the conditions of those unfortunate persons of societies and countries where oppression and exploitation, agents of capitalism and imperialism, govern. It is within this context that the role of women must be viewed. Women are an exploited population because of biological identity. However, the extent and characteristics of their oppression and exploitation are issues—a direct consequence of economic status.

Second, there is a recognizable basis (as noted, for example, by the "nurse" and the Dominican maid) for a people's liberation struggle. The role of women is critical to the progress of this struggle. Accepting the adage that you can tell the condition of a society by the condition of its women[10] instructs us in the intensity and seriousness of effort, organization, and self-reliance needed. Island by island, the impact of racial, sexual, and economic oppression threatens to create a most chaotic, divisive and onerous situation. Only a people's liberation struggle can eradicate the chaos.

NOTES

1. Anguilla, Yearbook of Statistics, 1976.

2. Frances Henry and Pamela Wilson, "The Status of Women in Caribbean Societies: An Overview of Their Social, Economic and Sexual Roles," Social and Economic Studies (Jamaica), vol. 24, no. 2 (June 1975).

3. Toni Cade Bambara, The Black Woman: An Anthology (New York: New American Library, 1970), p. 7.

4. This theme runs through the works of Bill Riviere, Oppression and Resistance: The Black Condition in the Caribbean, Monograph Series no. 1 (Ithaca, N.Y.: Cornell University Africana Studies and Research Center, 1973), pp. 73–76.

5. Sis. Ayesha, "The Black Working Woman," Black Woman (Trinidad and Tobago) 1 (November 1975): 5.

6. International Labour Office, Year Book of Labour Statistics (Geneva: ILO, 1972).

7. Ibid.

8. Margaret F. Katzir, "The Jamaican Country Higgler," in Work and Family Life: West Indian Perspectives, ed. Lambros Comitas and David Lowenthal (New York: Doubleday, 1973), p. 4.

9. Sis. Asha, "International Women?" Black Woman (Trinidad and Tobago) 1 (November 1975): 20.

10. Quote by Martin Delaney.

REFERENCES

Anguilla, Yearbook of Statistics, 1976.

Asha, Sis. "International Women?" Black Woman (Trinidad and To-bago) 1 (November 1975): 20.

Ayesha, Sis. "The Black Working Woman." Black Woman (Trinidad and Tobago) 1 (November 1975): 5.

Bambara, Toni Cade. The Black Woman: An Anthology. New York: New American Library, 1970.

"The Black Working Woman." Black Woman (Trinidad and Tobago), vol. 2 (June-July 1977).

Comitas, Lambros, and David Lowenthal. Work and Family Life: West Indian Perspectives. New York: Doubleday, 1973.

Creque, Darwin D. The U.S. Virgins and the Eastern Caribbean. Philadelphia: Whitmore, 1968.

Cruzan Satellite (Virgin Islands), vol. 2, no. 6/7 (June-July 1977).

Fanon, Frantz. The Wretched of the Earth. New York: Grove Press, 1968.

Freire, Paulo. Pedagogy of the Oppressed. New York: Herder and Herder, 1970.

Gordon, Shirley. A Century of West Indian Education. London: Longmans, 1963.

Henry, Frances, and Pamela Wilson. "The Status of Women in Caribbean Societies: An Overview of Their Social, Economic and Sexual Roles." Social and Economic Studies (Jamaica), vol. 24, no. 2 (June 1975).

Holbrook, Sabra. The American West Indies: Puerto Rico and the Virgin Islands. New York: Meredith Press, 1969.

Horowitz, Michael M. Peoples and Cultures of the Caribbean: An Anthropological Reader. Garden City, N.Y.: Natural History Press, 1971.

International Labour Office. Year Book of Labour Statistics. Geneva: ILO, 1974.

Jordan, Winthrop. White over Black: American Attitudes toward the Negro, 1550-1812. Baltimore: Penguin, 1968.

Katzir, Margaret F. "The Jamaican Country Higgler." Work and Family Life: West Indian Perspectives, edited by Lambros Comitas and David Lowenthal. New York: Doubleday, 1973.

Riviere, Bill. Oppression and Resistance: The Black Condition in the Caribbean. Monograph Series no. 1. Ithaca, N.Y.: Cornell University Africana Studies and Research Center, 1973.

Smith, Michael Garfield, Roy Augier, and Rex Nettleford. The Rastafari Movement in Kingston, Jamaica. Mona Jamaica: University College of the West Indies, Institute of Social and Economic Research, 1960.

Tannebaum, Frank. Slave and Citizen, The Negro in the Americas. Buenos Aires: Paidos, 1968.

Williams, Eric. Capitalism and Slavery. London: Andre Deutsch, 1964.

8
WOMEN IN CUBA: THE REVOLUTION WITHIN THE REVOLUTION

Johnnetta B. Cole

> And if they were to ask what the most revolutionary aspect of this Revolution is, we'd tell them that the most revolutionary aspect is the revolution that is taking place among the women in our country.
>
> Fidel Castro, December 10, 1966
> Congress of the Federation of Cuban Women

For those of us who live in the Americas, and perhaps on a global scale, the situation among Cuban women today presents, in sharp relief, the complexities, the problems, and the possibilities for the genuine liberation of women. The cultures, histories, and current realities of Third World women involve a range of differences, and yet there are common bases of oppression, whether the physical setting and time period are Alabama in 1860, Cuba in 1958, Mozambique in 1970, or India in 1978. Without denying the influence, and indeed the importance, of tradition and culture, and without minimizing the pain that women can feel from bigoted attitudes and behavior, we can say with overwhelming evidence that the condition of women in a society is fundamentally a reflection of economic structures and relationships. The 1959 Revolution, by radically changing the economic organization of Cuban society, destroyed the overall material basis of inequalities, including the inequalities suffered by women. That revolution did not instantly provide the material means for full incorporation of women into the productive, political, and cultural life of the nation. And that revolution did not (and no revolution can) immediately wipe away centuries old myths and attitudes concerning the "proper places" for men and women. In short, the 1959 Cuban Revolution presented, for the first time, the possibility for all women in Cuba to fully share the rewards and responsibilities of their society.

162

In this brief chapter, we will contrast the conditions of Cuban women in the 1950s before the revolution with the years after, indicating the accomplishments as well as problem areas that still exist.

BEFORE THE REVOLUTION

Before the Revolution of 1959 life for the majority of Cuba's people conformed to the patterns that are repeated in poor, underdeveloped Third World countries all over the world: chronic unemployment, meager health facilities, high rates of illiteracy, and grossly inadequate and unsanitary housing conditions. But while this was the condition for the majority of Cuba's people, the plight of women was particularly harsh.

In the year preceding the revolution, Havana may have been a playland paradise for the North American rich, but it was an inferno for the majority of Cuban women. Approximately 464,000 Cuban women knocked on doors of houses and offices looking for work—but no work existed for them. Over 70,000 eked out a living as servants in the homes of wealthy Cubans and North Americans, receiving between $8 and $25 a month. Of the thousands of beggars on the streets of Havana, at least 25,000 of them were women. In Havana alone, it is estimated that there were 11,500 prostitutes. The Havana of the 1950s had 270 brothels, 700 bars with hostesses (one step away from prostitution), and dozens of rent-by-the-hour hotels. [1]

In 1958 there were only 100,000 working women in Cuba—including all of the servants and the underemployed. [2] Put in slightly different terms, in 1958, 85 percent of Cuban women were housewives.

In the years immediately preceding the revolution, the educational level of Cuban women was dismally low. For example, in 1958, one out of every five women in urban areas could not read or write; two out of every five in rural areas. Of all women over 25 years of age, only 1 out of every 100 had any university education. This generally low educational level prepared the overwhelming majority of Cuban women for their jobs primarily as housewives or maids for rich folks; when all else failed, as prostitutes. Those few Cuban women who did manage to work outside their homes (or someone else's home or "a house"—in 1953 only one out of seven women worked outside) were mainly in tobacco (women formed 37 percent of the tobacco workers in 1953) and textiles (women formed 46 percent of the textile workers). [3]

Housing was particularly poor in Cuba before the revolution: 80 percent of the Cuban people lived in bohios—huts with thatched roofs, dirt floors, and no running water or indoor plumbing. The Cuban and North American bourgeoisie lived in quite different conditions. Their mansions, which before the revolution were private dwellings, are today the national headquarters of organizations like the Federation of Cuban Women. The DuPonts had a home on Varadero Beach, which they occupied for a few months each year, where 122 servants attended the family. Today that mansion is the Las Americas restaurant.

The housing situation as dismal as this was doubly oppressive for Cuban women, since 85 percent of them spent the greatest amount of their time in and around them, performing the drudgery of housework. In 1953 in his speech "History Will Absolve Me," Fidel Castro described the housing situation of the 5.8 million Cuban population:

> There are two hundred thousand huts and hovels in Cuba; 400,000 families in the country and in the cities live cramped into barracks and tenements without even the minimum sanitary requirements; 2,200,000 of our urban population pay rents which absorb between one-fifth and one-third of their income; and 2,800,000 of our rural and suburban population lack electricity.

The situation with respect to health was consistent with that in other areas of services. In 1959 over 60 percent of the population of Cuba (6.5 million) had virtually no access to health care.[4] The people of rural Cuba and the majority of the urban poor lived under "the constant threat of the most serious diseases and epidemics."[5] Before the 1959 Revolution in Cuba, there were high rates of infant mortality, malnutrition, and infectious and contagious diseases such as polio, malaria, tuberculosis, intestinal parasitism, diphtheria, and tetanus.[6]

Again, the nature of an exploitative society is such that women will often suffer additional jeopardies because they are women. For example, health care provided for pregnant women, women in childbirth, and newborns are critical in the prevention of chronic illnesses and death among mothers and infants. Indeed, infant mortality is a particularly good indicator of a nation's health and a very sharp indicator of the condition of women's health. In Cuba before the revolution, 5 out of every 50 children died before their first birthday.

Sports and culture, while not on the same level as health, education, and housing, nevertheless serve as excellent barometers of equality and inequality in a society. In terms of sports before the revolution, Jane McManus notes, "It would be hard to overestimate the importance of basic gymnasium for women in a country like Cuba. At the triumph of the Revolution in 1959, the 'ideal' Cuban woman was pampered and passive. Mild exercise, followed by massages and steam baths, were available only to the wealthy clients of the most

expensive and exclusive beauty salons. The lower classes got their
'exercise' working. Organized, mass physical fitness programs were
unknown."[7] And, even in the highly exploitative professional sports
world of the 1950s, women were not given "a place." In the arts,
while a few women managed to lead respectable lives based on their
talents, too often Cuban women were associated with entertainment
for wealthy Cubans and North Americans.

The conditions of Cuban women in the areas described above—
work, education, health, housing, sports, and culture—were fundamentally outgrowths of the type of economic system in operation in
Cuba. Edward Boorstein has captured the dominant characteristics
of that 1950s economy in these words:

> The central fact about the Cuban economy before the Revo-
> lution was neither its one-crop concentration on sugar nor
> the monopoly of most of the agricultural land by huge latifun-
> dia nor the weakness of the national industry, nor any other
> such specific characteristic. Until the Revolution, the cen-
> tral fact about the Cuban economy was its domination by
> American monpolies—by American imperialism. It was
> from imperialist domination that the specific characteris-
> tics flowed.[8]

In concrete terms this meant that U.S. business interests owned Cuba;
and specifically, these business interests were not concerned with the
plight of Cuban women. There were enough Cuban men to work the
jobs associated with U.S. business interests—indeed, more than
enough since in 1958, 28 percent of the labor force were unemployed
or underemployed.

But in addition to this primary cause of the oppression of women
in Cuba (an inequalitarian economic system designed for the financial
interests of a small national bourgeoisie and a sizable group of foreign
investors), there were certainly a number of traditions, attitudes, and
values in Cuban society that buttressed the notion of women as the
rightful occupiers of the bottom rung of society's ladder. In short,
machismo was a bolster to class oppression. And for some Cuban
women there was racism, too, as yet another instrument for securing
the stratification of Cuban society.

Machismo, as it developed in Cuba, is more complex in derivation and current expression than what is implied in the everyday notion of attitudes of male supremacy among Latin American men, a
legacy from Spanish culture. Cultural sources of male supremacy
attitudes include Africa and the United States as well as Spain.

The Spanish base of machismo was strongly cast in a sexual division of expected and possible behavior within the typical prerevolu-

tionary Cuban family. The husband and father worked, though poor men spent considerable amounts of time as victims of unemployment. The wife and mother seldom worked outside the home—the exceptions being the poor. For women, the control and dominance of their homes and children were often the only outlets they had to express themselves. They cooked heavy Spanish meals and kept spotless homes. Many Cuban men supported a legal family and one or more mistresses. The standard moral code was: "Anything goes for men"; the treasured signs of masculinity were demonstrated in a man's control of his wife and children and his conquering other women. As Margaret Randall notes, "Children grew up with these images of 'man' and 'woman'; proper young girls didn't wear pants and didn't go out unchaperoned."[9]

The African influence in Cuban machismo has received little attention. In part, this is a reflection of the general Western scholarly disregard for African cultural elements in Cuba, elements that, however, do play a part in Cubans' daily lives (art, language, food habits, and the like). Indeed, some scholars and activists in the United States have tended to ascribe egalitarian roles to men and women in West Africa, often mistakenly citing matrilineal societies (usually misnamed matriarchal) as proof. There is an important line of research here, especially since there is an African base to the cultures of the Americas varying in degree and specific cultural origin. Margaret Randall has commented on one African source of machismo in Cuba:

> In Cuba the African religions produced another side to the particular Cuban machismo which has strongly influenced the lives of Cuban women: the abakua. Abakua is a secret society of men who came from religious sects in the Congo and Nigeria that held the age-old beliefs about women being unclean and inferior. The Cuban derivative is often called nanigo. Not only did membership in the abakua (which degenerated from "good husbands, fathers and sons" to include professional killers and other delinquent elements) involve masculine pride; it also became a prerequisite for working in construction, the docks, and port work. At the beginning of this century, approximately 90% of all workers in these sectors were abakua.
>
> The women were proud of the fact that their men were members of this all-male society with its job security and status, and so this false pride based on their own inferiority was deepened in themselves as well as in men. . . . The nanigos were not only Black men, there was a large percentage of whites as well.[10]

The third source of machismo in Cuba—the United States—has received little attention in published sources on Cuba; yet, it takes very little reflection to realize that the very aspects of U.S. society that "went" to Cuba are the most brutally sexist. The same point could be made with respect to racism in Cuba; that is, during the period of U.S. domination, U.S.-styled Jim Crow practices of segregation were brought to Cuba. [11]

Havana, the capital city of Cuba having approximately 1 million inhabitants, was a major site for prostitution and gambling for U.S. vice men. It was also a playground for U.S. sailors and others who had money to spend. And, Cuba developed an international reputation for pornography and dirty movies. As Randall vividly states, in the eyes of the world, Cuban women "were caged in the tourist-poster image of the big-assed, rumba-dancing, bandanna-topped mulatto carrying a basket of tropical goodies belonging to United Fruit and swaying under a palm tree belonging to Eisenhower-via-Batista."[12]

This is not to suggest that the island of Cuba was free of such practices and accompanying attitudes before U.S. penetration. It is to say that the domination of Cuba by the United States increased what were already Spanish- and African-based attitudes of male supremacy. In terms of the practices of vice and prostitution, the patterns can be directly tied to the period of U.S. imperialism.

> As is always the case with this kind of cultural as well as economic exploitation, the worst of American contemporary tradition was exaggerated and made even more grotesque in the colony. . . . Superman and Tarzan became values which filtered from the colonizers through the local ruling class to the population in general, adding a U.S.-edge to Cuban machismo. [13]

AFTER THE REVOLUTION

The triumph of the revolution on January 1, 1959, marks the beginning of fundamental changes in the organization of Cuban society that have deeply affected the lives of the Cuban people. In the same sense that the ills of prerevolutionary Cuba disproportionately affected Cuban women, the benefits of the new political and economic order are dramatically experienced by Cuban women. Those who suffered the most before the revolution—Black people, women, and, in general, the poor—have gained the most. In the specific case of women, this is not to suggest that the total battle has been won; in fact, all evidence suggests that it is the area of Cuban society where old attitudes are particularly rigid. Cuba has managed to eliminate much institutionalized racism and substantially affect racist attitudes in only 20 years. A comparable statement cannot be made about sexism in Cuba—

a reflection, no doubt, of the greater degree of sexism than racism in prerevolutionary Cuba.

Cuba has not eliminated sexist attitudes nor fully incorporated women into the work force and daily life of the revolution. But what has taken place over the past 20 years is a highly impressive series of changes—changes that can be accurately described as a revolution within a revolution. There are two sources of these changes in "women's place" in Cuban society: the revolution itself and specific laws, actions, and organizations within the revolution. We turn now to a discussion of these two sources of change.

Impact of the Cuban Revolution on Women

Of all aspects of the society—health, education, housing, work, culture, and the like—work is clearly the area that has most significantly changed the face of Cuba. In the process of changing its society from one where 25 percent unemployment per year was a constant to one where there is no unemployment, there is a labor shortage. Cuba has become a different place. In concrete terms this means that every adult who wishes to work can do so. Because so much of the society's productive labor is at work (under the priorities of a socialist economy), there are free and modestly priced social services for the entire population.

One of the first massive efforts following the triumph of the revolution was an extensive literacy campaign. In 1961 young boys and girls traveled throughout Cuba, teaching their elders to read and write (in one year 707,000 adults learned to read and write). Of those who learned to read and write, 56 percent were women. The formation of these brigades was a serious challenge to the old ideas of what was proper for young girls to do, and the success of the campaign is measured in the fact that Cuba has virtually eliminated illiteracy.

By 1975 one of every three Cubans was studying something in an educational system that provided free training from the elementary through the university level. In 1975, of the 80,000 university students enrolled, women accounted for 49 percent in science, 47 percent in pedagogy, and 33 percent each in the medical sciences and economics. The aim of "every Cuban with a sixth grade education" is now a realizable goal in a country where women were once the least educated in a sparsely educated population. Women are, of course, the recipients of tremendous improvements in a Cuba where 11 times more resources are put into education than before the revolution; 70 percent of the present school facilities have been built, adapted, or begun since 1959. Finally, with respect to education, we must note the importance in Cuba of the study-work principle. The entire educational system of Cuba has been remolded on this principle—that those who study can simultaneously contribute to the country's economic development through work in the countryside or urban areas. There are important long-range consequences for Cuba when young girls (as is the case with young boys) reach adulthood with the firmly rooted notion of their responsibility to work.

The transformation of health care since the revolution has earned the respect and admiration of even the most severe of Cuba's critics. The transformation is reflected in such measures as the eradication of diseases (for example, polio, diphtheria, and malaria), life expectancy (under 55 years before the revolution but has now gone up to 70 years), expenditure for public health (20 million pesos before the revolution; today over 400 million pesos—a 20-fold increase), and the widespread distribution of free clinics (for example, in 1958 there was not a single free dental clinic in Cuba; in 1976 there were 115 scattered throughout the island). Specifically related to questions of maternity, today pregnant women in Cuba receive an average of 8.5 medical visits each, and 97 percent of all births now take place in a maternity hospital.

Infant mortality is a particularly sensitive indicator of a people's health, Margaret Gilpin and Helen Rodriquez-Trias point out: "Whether children will live or die before they are a year old is determined by a complex interplay of biological and environmental factors such as nutrition, employment income, housing, educational level, the age of the mother, the parents' health, etc. Health care provided for pregnant women, for women in childbirth and for newborn infants is critical in the prevention of illness and death among mothers and infants."[14] Since the revolution, infant mortality has been reduced from 5 out of 50 children before the first birthday to 1 out of 50, the lowest rate in Latin America.

Of the three fundamental services, health, education, and housing, it is the latter that has been the most difficult challenge for Cubans to meet, a reflection, in part, of the severe labor and capital-intensive requirements to eradicate a situation where 80 percent of the Cuban people lived in huts before the revolution. In 1961 the revolution began to reverse its emphasis on home ownership and began to provide for the renting of new housing built by the state for a rent of not more than 10 percent of the family's income. This was a decisive move toward the ultimate goal of free housing for all Cubans. However, the attainment of this goal requires mass mobilization of Cuban men and women. Beginning in 1971 the Cuban people formed microbrigades, a system whereby a percentage of the workers of a work center (factory or a port) spend one and a half to two years constructing houses, while the other workers in the center keep up production by extra effort. The homes built belong to the work collective, and it makes the decision on distribution. It is, of course, particularly striking that Cuban women have incorporated themselves into this process, for the idea of women doing such work is a sharp challenge to prerevolutionary notions of womanhood.

Because of the persistent association of women with housework, these new housing units with running water, electricity, and many modern conveniences bring the greatest relief to those who still do most of the housework.

The priority given to the construction of adequate housing for the Cuban population is captured in the allocations of the national budget:

> Housing and social service construction has a national budget twice that for defense purposes, and the annual investment in housing alone is some 184 million pesos. By comparison, housing and community development allocations in the United States represent less than 2% of the national budget, compared with over 30% for defense. Housing expenditures per capita in the U.S. are less than half of Cuba.[15]

The explosion in participation in cultural activities and sports includes monumental increases in the involvement of women. In the "amateur arts movement" of Cuba, women are actively involved in musical, community-based theater and art groups. And on a national level, women have taken major responsibilities in ballet, theater, literature, and the graphic and plastic arts.

In the area of sports, Fidel Castro was able to report to the First Party Congress of Cuba in 1975: "People have been encouraged in every possible way to do physical exercises and to go in for sports. The diversification of sports has been promoted to include sports in which the country had no tradition or experience. Sports have been encouraged at work centers and in units of the Armed Forces and the Ministry of the Interior. Women's participation has grown considerably."[16] Sports and culture have been defined by the revolution as rights, not privileges, of every Cuban. The material means for participating in these rights have been provided. What is left is the destruction of the age-old attitudes and prejudices against women's participation.

Before the revolution in a typical year, 25 percent of the work force would have been unemployed. Today, Cuba has totally eliminated unemployment (indeed, Cuba suffers from a labor shortage). The effects of such a dramatic change are to be found throughout Cuban society. Men and women can walk with dignity, knowing that they will never again have to beg for work and "be good" in order to keep work when they have found it. The elimination of unemployment has also meant that with the intensive use of Cuban productive labor, the social services described above are available to all for free or at modest costs to individuals. The incorporation of women into the Cuban work force has steadily improved since the triumph of the revolution; however, there are still far too many Cuban women who choose not to work. In 1953 women occupied 9.8 percent of the total labor force (which included the 70,000 domestics); today close to 30 percent of the work force are women.

For some percentage of Cuban women (it is difficult to be more precise), the opportunity to work was all that was needed to bring them into the work force. However, for the majority of Cuban women it has taken more than mere opportunity. First, the provision of basic social services at free-to-minimal cost has meant that many Cuban women chose not to work because they could remain in their homes and still enjoy the fruits of the revolution (for example, free health care and education). For many Cuban women who chose to work, the material conditions to support that choice did not (and still do not) exist. As Vilma Espin, president of the Federation of Cuban Women (FMC), has said, "Obtaining the participation of women in work requires overcoming numerous obstacles of a material nature such as day nurseries, workers' dining rooms, student dining rooms, semiboarding schools, laundries and other social services which would make it possible for the housewife to work."[17] And, finally, for many women attitudes and prejudices about women working keep them out of the work force.

The Cuban Revolution Moves on the Question of Women

The incorporation of Cuban women into the work force, and indeed into the full productive life of Cuban society, has required more than the availability of jobs and statements by the leadership. We turn now to a brief review of the major steps taken by the revolution.

When the revolution triumphed in 1959, it immediately took measures to incorporate women into the work force. Approximately 20,000 women began to study in special "Schools for the Advancement of Domestic Servants." Many of these women became the staff workers of day-care centers. In those early days of the revolution, much of the door-to-door work of talking with women and urging them to join the work force was done by the FMC. In 1969/70 members of the FMC reached 400,000 women in their door-to-door conversations. That was a crucial year for Cuba with the thrust to harvest 1 million tons of sugarcane. Through the work of the FMC, as well as the work by the Committee for the Defense of the Revolution, thousands of women volunteered to cut cane. But as women moved into the work force, they also moved out again. For example, in the last three months of 1969, 140,000 women entered the labor force; but 80,000 left; so there was a net gain of only 27,000. Major reasons for this enormous turnover were, as Fidel Castro noted, "all the residual male chauvinism and supermanism and all those things that are still a part of us." Many men were encouraging their wives not to work; and many women grew tired of the double burden of working outside the home and then coming home to dishes, laundry, and cooking.

This period, 1959 to 1970, has been described as the period when the revolution moved on long-standing notions of the home (casa) as the place for women and the streets (calles) as the place for men. Carollee Bengelsdorf and Alice Hagerman characterize this period:

> Although it had now been made clear that women had the "social duty" to work, and although they were entering the labor force in increasing numbers, no nationally organized attempt was made during this period to challenge the assumption that children, laundry, and cooking were women's work. The expectation remained firm that women would be relieved of this work to the extent that the society could take on those responsibilities. In conditions of underdevelopment this has meant a de facto "second shift" for most women who work. For, given the scarcity of resources, the full services to relieve women of household tasks simply could not be immediately provided. [18]

In the years since 1970, the Cuban revolution has more seriously attacked the problem of "the second shift." The government of Cuba has placed a great emphasis on the construction of day-care centers, for it is clear that the absence of sound day care for their children is a major deterrent to many women working. By 1974 the revolution had constructed 610 day-care centers caring for over 50,000 children —but these still were not enough.

Since 1972 the shopping bag plan (plan jaba) has been in effect in order to give working women priority service at their local grocery stores. They may either drop off their lists in the morning and pick up their groceries in the evening, or they may immediately go to the front of each counter. In a country where the realities of underdevelopment and the U.S.-imposed blockade create long lines, this is a means of saving time for working women. Working women have also received preferential access to a variety of goods and services. For example, working women have preferential access to medical appointments, dry cleaners, shoe stores, hairdressers, and tailors.

The revolution has also worked to extend laundry services for workers at their work places and hot meals in workers' cafeterias.

Although all workers benefit by these services, it is working women who benefit most, for it means that these "household" tasks are done outside of their homes. The basic problem with all of these efforts is that the needs of the Cuban people exceed their capabilities at the present time.

The problem of the second shift has also put women at a disadvantage within their workplaces. "Women who must pick up children at day care centers and take care of their household often cannot stay at their work place to attend assemblies or do voluntary work. Therefore, they have less chance to develop and display attitudes which might lead to their selection by workers' assemblies to leadership positions or for special material rewards."[19]

A structure was created to attempt to ease and, where possible, eliminate some of these jeopardies. In 1969 the Feminine Front was incorporated into the Cuban trade union structure—a secretariat within the Central Trade Union Federation to focus on problems of women in their work centers. The Feminine Front is now known as the Department of Feminine Concerns.

There are also problems in the area of women's participation in political leadership. Today, as throughout the history of Cuba, there are many examples of the heroism and strong leadership qualities of individual women. However, in a more general way, there is much work to be done in this area. Women comprise only 13 percent of the membership of the Communist party of Cuba; 2.9 percent of the leadership at a base level and 0 percent at the top level of the politburo.

This problem is also expressed in the involvement of women in leadership roles in popular power, the municipal, provincial, and national assemblies in charge of all the service and production units operating at those various levels (schools, courts, hospitals, and the like); on the national level, it is the body with the authority to pass all laws and discuss and approve the general outlines of foreign and domestic policy. Before this new system of popular power went into effect, an experiment was carried out in the province of Matanzas. In the Matanzas experiment, women comprised only 7.6 percent of the individuals nominated as candidates and only 3 percent of those elected to municipal assemblies in the province. In a speech in which he discussed the results of the elections, Fidel Castro emphasized that these figures demonstrate how "we still have residues of cultural backwardness and how we still retain old thinking patterns in the back of our minds." And, he continued, "There are certain theories alleging that women don't like to be led by women. . . . If there is a speck of truth to it, it will serve to show that a hard struggle must be waged among women themselves." As a result of the efforts of many organizations in Cuba, but most especially the efforts of the FMC, the percentage of women candidates for municipal assemblies in 1976 rose to 13.6 percent, a doubling of the Matanzas figure for 1974.[20] This increase in female participation in the most important organs of mass political power in Cuba represents important changes in the attitudes of certain women and men who make the nominations as well as some of those women who agree to accept nomination.

In the past few years, Cuba has passed substantial legislation that deeply affects women. In 1975 the Maternity Law was passed, and in that same year the Family Code went into effect. These laws have the potential to cut away the very fiber of discrimination against women.

The Maternity Law of Cuba is based on certain assumptions: that every adult Cuban is a worker, that children will be borne by working women, and that children represent the future of the revolution. These assumptions, within the context of the Cuban revolution, have led to one of the most far-reaching maternity laws in the world:

> The Maternity Law requires that pregnant women take an eighteen week paid leave of absence—six weeks prior to the birth and three months after. Pregnant women are granted six full days, or twelve half days, off for pre-natal care. Mothers are entitled to one day per month during the first year after the birth for the child's medical care; in practice, the father can also take responsibility for this assignment. At the end of the paid maternity leave, if the mother feels she needs or wants to continue to care for her child full time, she can take up to one year's leave without pay; at the end of the year she can return to her former position.[21]

With respect to the Family Code, it is important to note that for one year preceding its adoption there was constant dialogue on the code—on buses and in work centers, homes, and shops. Then, following discussion by the people and approval by more than 98 percent of the participants in meetings and assemblies, the Family Code went into effect on International Women's Day in 1975.

The Family Code is a comprehensive piece of legislature that goes a long way toward bringing equality into social relationships that were hitherto considered "too private" for the law. Today, as a result of the Family Code, divorce is far easier than in the past; illegitimacy is no longer a viable concept. But certainly the most significant aspect of the law, and that which will take the longest to put into full effect, is the stipulation that men are required to shoulder 50 percent of the housework and child care when women work. The difficulty with such a law is, of course, in the necessity of women bringing legal action against their husbands. However, the immediate positive result is that the case for equal responsibilities and rights is given public sanction.

Margaret Randall describes the code in this way: "The sense of the new Code rests entirely on mutual respect between women and men, and respect on the part of parents for their children. The family nucleus as we know it is in fact strengthened, but its private property or bourgeois capitalist-sexist aspects are largely removed."[22] Today, because of the availability of free education, jobs for all, and legal provisions (such as the ease with which divorces can be obtained), no woman in Cuba need put up with an exploitative personal situation in a relationship with a man. But this does not mean no woman does.

Since its founding in August 1960, the Federation of Cuban Women has played instrumental roles in the range of efforts to incorporate women more fully into the productive and active life of their society. In order to carry out this work, the FMC continues to be a center for analyzing the problems women face and creating and suggesting solutions. Each of the specific activities or laws described here have been closely associated with the FMC: from the literacy campaign in 1961 to the passing of the Family Code in 1975; from incorporating women into the work force to suggesting the shopping bag plan. At present the FMC has a membership of over 2,264,000 or 81.5 percent of all Cuban women above the age of 14.

CONCLUSION

Without question, the Cuban revolution has brought enormous changes in the position of women, and it has done so in the short period of 20 years. Serious problems remain, however—problems that grow out of Cuba's legacy of underdevelopment and that are the result of the tenacity of prejudices about women. As Cuba develops its economy, those problems that stem from the lack of a material base to support the integration of women into the work force and life of Cuba will tend to disappear. For example, by the end of the Five-Year Plan (1976-80), Cuba will have 400 new day-care centers, raising the national capacity from 50,000 to 150,000 children cared for and educated in these centers. Similarly impressive growth in other areas suggests that the objective conditions that tie women to hours of housework and child care are being steadily removed.

The subjective problems—machismo and sexism—that keep women out of the workplace, leadership, and full participation in the life of their country are more difficult to root out. There is one particularly protective cushion for attitudes of male supremacy in Cuba, which appears all the more powerful when we realize that it never existed in the same way for racial prejudices. The perpetuation of sexist attitudes is aided by the fact that the setting for so many of the interpersonal relations between men and women is the home. Women may experience tremendous gains in their workplaces but return to situations within the privateness of the household that are filled with old myths and prejudices. Children are taught and practice equality of the sexes in schools but may come home in the evenings, or on weekends, to see their mothers, sisters, and other female relatives in statuses "reserved for women."

The Family Code is a dramatic challenge to the attitude that housework and child care are tasks for women and not for men. The code states that working men and women in a household must share these tasks equally. But these tasks take place, by and large, in the privateness of one's home. It must take an extremely confident woman to bring her husband to public sanction for failure to honor the code. (In contrast, the most frequent settings for racial discrimination were public ones: beaches, clubs, schools, hospitals, and work centers. Because the offenses were committed in public, they were rather quickly dealt with and eliminated by the revolutionary government.)

Clearly, it will not be easy to eliminate the sexist attitudes that stand as barriers to the full liberation of Cuban women. It will take time, perhaps generations. But it will happen because the Cuban people are openly discussing the problem. Women and men are demonstrating a commitment to the ongoing struggle against those myths and attitudes, which block the full movement of Cuban women into the march of their society.

NOTES

1. "Women in Cuba," Granma, March 5, 1978, p. 6.
2. Ibid.
3. Carollee Bengelsdorf and Alice Hagerman, "Emerging from Underdevelopment: Women and Work," Cuba Review 9, no. 2 (1974): 4.
4. Margaret Gilpin and Helen Rodriquez-Trias, "Looking at Health in a Healthy Way," Cuba Review 7, no. 1 (1978): 4.
5. Ibid.
6. Ibid.
7. Jane McManus, "Stretching Out," Cuba Review 7, no. 2 (1977): 29-30.
8. Edward Boorstein, The Economic Transformation of Cuba (New York: International, 1968), p. 1.
9. Margaret Randall, Cuban Women Now (Toronto: Canadian Women's Educational Press, 1974), p. 27.
10. Ibid., p. 28.
11. Ibid., p. 7.

12. Ibid.
13. Ibid.
14. Gilpin and Rodriquez-Trias, "Looking at Health," p. 4.
15. Tony Schuman, "Housing, Progress and Prognosis," Cuba Review 5, no. 1 (1975): 17.
16. Fidel Castro, First Congress of the Communist Party of Cuba (Moscow: Progress, 1976), p. 165.
17. Sheila Rowbotham, "Colony within a Colony," in Women, Resistance and Revolution: A History of Women and Revolution in the Modern World (New York: Vintage, 1974), p. 227.
18. Bengelsdorf and Hagerman, "Emerging from Underdevelopment: Women and Work," p. 8.
19. Ibid., p. 11.
20. "Women in Cuba."
21. Bengelsdorf and Hagerman, "Emerging from Underdevelopment: Women and Work," p. 11.
22. Margaret Randall, "Introducing the Family Code," Cuba Review 4, no. 2 (1974): 31.

REFERENCES

Bengelsdorf, Carollee, and Alice Hagerman. "Emerging from Underdevelopment: Women and Work." Cuba Review 4, no. 2 (1974): 3-18.

_____. "Emerging from Underdevelopment: Women and Work in Cuba." In Capitalist Patriarchy and the Case for Socialist Feminism, edited by Zillah R. Eisenstein, pp. 271-96. New York: Monthly Review Press, 1979.

Boorstein, Edward. The Economic Transformation of Cuba. New York: International, 1968.

Castro, Fidel. First Congress of the Communist Party of Cuba. Moscow: Progress, 1976.

_____. "History Will Absolve Me." In Revolutionary Struggle, edited by Rolando Bonachea and Nelson Valdes. Cambridge: Massachusetts Institute of Technology Press, 1972.

Fox, Geoffrey E. "Honor, Shame, and Women's Liberation in Cuba: Views of Working Class Emigre Men." In Female and Male in Latin America, edited by Ann Pescatello, pp. 273-90. Pittsburg: University of Pittsburg Press, 1973.

Gilpin, Margaret, and Helen Rodriquez-Trias. "Looking at Health in a Healthy Way." Cuba Review 7, no. 1 (1978): 3-15.

King, Marjorie. "Cuba's Attack on Women's Second Shift 1974-1976." Latin American Perspectives 4, nos. 1 and 2 (Winter and Spring 1977): 106-19.

McManus, Jane. "Stretching Out." Cuba Review 7, no. 2 (1977): 29-30.

Nelson, Lowry. "The Cuban Family." In Rural Cuba. Minneapolis: University of Minnesota Press, 1950.

Purcell, Susan K. "Modernizing Women for a Modern Society: The Cuban Case." In Female and Male in Latin America, edited by Ann Pescatello, pp. 257-71. Pittsburg: University of Pittsburgh Press, 1973.

Randall, Margaret. Cuban Women Now. Toronto: Canadian Women's Educational Press, 1974.

_____. "Introducing the Family Code." Cuba Review 4, no. 2 (1974): 31.

_____. " 'We Need a Government of Men and Women. . . .' Notes on the Second National Congress of the Federación de Mujeres Cubanos, November 25-29, 1974." Latin American Perspectives 4, nos. 1 and 2 (Winter and Spring 1975): 111-17.

Rowbotham, Sheila. "Colony within a Colony." In Women, Resistance and Revolution: A History of Women and Revolution in the Modern World. New York: Vintage, 1974.

Schuman, Tony. "Housing, Progress and Prognosis." Cuba Review 5, no. 1 (1975): 17-19.

Sutherland, Elizabeth. "The Longest Revolution." In The Youngest Revolution: A Personal Report on Cuba. New York: Dial, 1969.

"Women in Cuba." Granma, March 5, 1978, p. 6.

9

ANCIENT SONG, THE NEW MELODY IN LATIN AMERICA: WOMEN AND FILM

Nora Jacquez Wieser

Latin American women differ according to their country of origin and socioeconomic status. Yet social classes across geographical boundaries have many similarities. Differences between Argentine and Paraguayan women, for example, are assumed, though the elite and poorer-class women from each of these countries might have features in common. Certain luxuries might be necessities for the elite, whereas necessities might well be luxuries for the poor. This study will focus on poor and working-class women in Latin America, outside of the Caribbean area, which is the topic of Chapter 7. This chapter concentrates on four films in which these women speak for themselves about their situations. The content of their discussions correlates with studies by social scientists on Latin American women, including a visual-type study described later.

The main purpose of this chapter is to integrate several of the studies with the films' contents. The films are important because the sensitive viewer is able to perceive a great deal intuitively. The tone of voice, eye expressions, and gestures of these women enhance our perception of their situation. While the viewers' impressions may not be empirical data, they irrefutably add a dimension that is seldom acquired by a printed-page study alone. The films and the studies complement each other. The studies reveal findings on topics selected by the researcher, and the films portray individuals or groups in women's situations selected by the film makers.

Both the studies and the films support the fact that the women's role in Latin America continues to be defined principally within the limits of home and family. We see in them the effects of this "domestic" definition on a woman in the work force, the educational system, the political sphere, her media image, and her social relationships.

In communal prewage labor societies it is often accepted that both men and women have had equal importance in the family maintenance effort, since the man's role is also defined with the home, family, and immediate community. These societies may have, however, a division of labor according to sex; and with changing social conditions, male superiority results, as is evident in the film Andean Women. The colonial period and the Spanish influence in Latin America have firmly established the patriarchal family. The influence can be seen in the civil codes of most Latin American countries. The patria potestas (paternal authority) provision, with Roman origins dating back to 450 B.C., guarantees the father/husband authority over his wife and children. The husband determines the residence of the family, has his wife's power of attorney, and can dispose of her property without her permission.[1] Isabel Larguía and John Dumoulin assert that the patriarchal family brought with it the division of social life into two spheres, the public and the domestic, whose evolution was unequal. Historical changes occurred in the public sphere.[2] The division became a clear-cut division of work. The Chilean Jorge Gissi Bustos indicates how the division of work gives rise to a legitimating ideological and judicial structure. This structure is perpetuated by accepting, as natural, characteristics for men and women that are not natural but exist as a result of the division of work. By this division, Gissi Bustos says, "The man grants himself more rights than duties and does the opposite with the woman, who in general, accepts it."[3]

SELF-IMAGE: FILMS AS EVIDENCE

A woman's acceptance of her inferiority to the man forms a basis for her self-image. The image women have of themselves is an area that has received little independent study. It is ignored or incorporated into studies on broader issues. Often women's feelings as women are interpreted by an intermediary. To better understand their position, it is important to seek sources where these women speak for themselves. The films and the visual research technique are such sources.

It is one thing to write about Latin American women and interpret their self-image in the light of studies that have only recently begun to proliferate. It is quite another matter to see these women, listen to them talk, and understand them in an audiovisual context. All of the films help us to see the women as they see themselves.

Three films specifically focus on women. Andean Women[4] depicts women in an agricultural community. The Double Day[5] focuses on work conditions and women's status in the society. Simplemente Jenny[6] concentrates on the socialization of women by tradition and the modern values in a consumer society. A fourth film, The Brickmakers,[7] examines women within an exploited social class.

All four films reflect women's inferiority to the male. This reality has greater impact when the women themselves express it, because they have internalized and incorporated it into their self-image. "A son is security—support for us," says an Aymara woman in Andean Women. "As a woman you'll serve the man, nothing more," another Bolivian woman in The Double Day says. In Simplemente Jenny, Juana, an Indian woman from Mexico, would rather have boys because "girls grow up; someone takes them away and often mistreats them." Maria in The Brickmakers tells her daughter simply, "Let it be, what can we do?" A frequent reflection of a negative self-image is the woman's view that it is easier or better to be born a man. [8]

A woman's self-image becomes a legacy for younger generations. In this way women themselves play an active part in the perpetuation of their role. In the Andean Women we understand how educational opportunities for women are limited when a mother explains that she did not go to school and that she did not consider it important for her daughters. A young girl from Puerto Rico in Simplemente Jenny explains that women are expected to be feminine as part of a tradition that her grandmother, her mother, and she, herself, have maintained.

Two additional aspects of the self-image issue are important. First, among poor and working-class women, a negative self-image is related to economic oppression of their social class. Psychological liberation in the U.S. or European sense is meaningless to women whose basic needs for survival are not met—The Brickmakers illustrates this pervasive effect of poverty. Second, a negative self-image would not be a characteristic of the following groups of women:

1. The small minority of women who have achieved self-fulfillment through education and a consequent rewarding profession. Frequently they can afford to have other women do their housework and take care of their children.

2. The women who see as convenient and less demanding their role in the domestic sphere under the husband's authority. These women are predominantly from the middle and upper class, and they have a relative life of leisure if they do not work outside the home, since they also have domestic help for the household. In Simplemente Jenny the camera focuses on an extreme example, an upper-class woman with soft, bottle-blonde hair and studied feminine gestures. "Well," she says flippantly, "I believe women would have fewer conflicts and more success if they tried to look attractive for men, and used their feminine wiles." It is obvious she views herself in terms of her biological potential and has the leisure to use her energies accordingly.

3. There are also younger women who have been influenced by current thinking on the woman's role. These women often must face

the conflict between their own positive image of their potential and the prevailing cultural and economic reality of their country. In The Double Day a group of women openly discuss the need for a new type of family structure. A young Mexican girl questions marriage and a family as the only alternatives for women. Venezuelan women talk about political activity as a vehicle for change. They underline the difficulty of women's political participation within the prevailing cultural norms.

Cultural norms that establish women's exclusive domestic role affect not only a woman's political participation but also her work conditions outside the home, educational patterns, social relationships, and her own view of herself. The films will be analyzed individually to illustrate how women are affected in their daily lives and, most important, how they feel about it.

ANDEAN WOMEN

Bolivian Aymara Indians, primarily women, speak in their native Quechua, which is translated into English subtitles. An all-male film crew was directed by Hubert Smith under the auspices of a National Science Foundation Grant. It is a documentary with no sound effects or narration.

The community of Vitocotos exists as an agrarian/barter economy. The film underscores an inferior position for women, even though they play an essential part in agricultural production, perform all the domestic duties, and barter at the local market. The division of tasks according to sex is quite clear from the men and women interviewed. This division appears to be based on the male's greater strength. Yet, it is the women in the film who cross the boundaries and perform the denoted "male" tasks, such as butchering. In their relationships with men, the women view their role as supportive, since men are the stronger ones and can carry heavy packs. Despite the women's multiple duties, one woman concludes, "Men work a lot, women don't."

A group of women of varied ages are involved in a communal effort of shelling corn. Such tasks apparently form a basis for social interaction. In these scenes the women air their views on education for girls. It seems most of this film's women have not attended school. In 1970 the illiteracy rate for adult women in Latin America was 27 percent as opposed to 19.9 percent for adult males.[9] A higher illiteracy rate is found in rural areas, where men are often accorded preference in educational opportunities. But in most rural areas in Latin America, both sexes suffer from a critical shortage of schools, libraries, teachers, and textbooks. Educational expenditures average 14 percent of the total national budgets. In contrast, an average of 25 percent is allotted for defense budgets.[10]

One woman in the film talks about her daughters' recriminations toward her for their not going to school. She sent them to work in the fields and care for the sheep, pigs, and llamas. "They wanted to read and write," she says, "so that they could live a life without problems, and . . . in La Paz the houses have numbers."

A community market shows the women busily exchanging dried foodstuffs. This type of activity gives the women experience that they can use as street vendors, should they migrate to urban areas. Women street vendors sell the edibles (fruit, candy, gum, or food) they have prepared themselves. It is a marginal, low-status occupation for women in the cities. But it is one of the few occupations women may have "trained" for in their native communities.[11] In the film the men observe the women's barter activities and visit with each other. Two such men discuss a recent fiesta. One says, "We overdid it a bit last night by coming home drunk." "Good," the other man replies, "men deserve their fun."

Courtship patterns are discussed next by the group of women shelling corn. It seems they have had little say in the choice of their mates, despite the fact that the conversation is punctuated by gleeful laughter at the memories. One woman was ordered by her parents to marry her husband. Another maintains she never talked to her husband and "suddenly, we were married." A third women says her husband was her father's friend. A Colombian study indicates the most frequent reason for marriage by women was to achieve security and the respect of others.[12] The film illustrates that Vitocotos women also need a husband to be assured a respectful status in the society.

These women view childbearing as an important part of their role. Two of the women refer to the fact that they have each produced 12 "apostles." The religious implication is obvious, despite the fact that the church exerts diminished influence on women in the area of birth control, according to recent studies.[13] One of the women in the film adds that her husband hated her last two boy babies. "Why do you breed like an animal?" he asked. The remark indicates the male's superiority because he is able to negate his own role in the act when he wishes to do so. The children then become the emotional as well as physical responsibilities of the women.

The film scene takes a sharp emotional turn when a woman begins to sob and speak of the abuse she has suffered from her husband: "I want to leave here, my children are grown. I've raised my family. . . . Some husbands are good and faithful; others beat and abuse us, little by little killing the woman." Each of the four films makes reference to men's physical abuse of their wives. The Latin American woman's sense of duty to her children predominates, since she is conditioned by her society to think of herself last. Frequently, she tolerates abuse and mistreatment because she feels the family must stay together. Often she has no other economic alternatives. The woman in this film would like to leave her husband since her children are grown. But it is difficult for a woman alone. The other women react to her outpouring of emotion with a moving blend of embarrassment, pain, and compassion.

These women's views on work, education, courtship patterns, birth of children, and husband-wife relationships have underlined the weight of tradition on the women's inferior position.

THE DOUBLE DAY

The Double Day (and Simplemente Jenny) was the result of editing 16 hours of film footage shot in Mexico, Bolivia, Argentina, Venezuela, Brazil, and Puerto Rico. The film crew were all women, with the exception of Affonso Beato, the photographer. Helena Solberg Ladd, from Brazil, directed both films. In a recent interview she stated:

> The shooting of both films was preceded by a visit to several countries in Latin America, where I made contacts in preparation for the production. The women interviewed were not selected in advance, only the scope of different situations which we thought were important to examine. Consciousness raising is probably the first objective of films like these. However, the only countries in Latin America where the films are being used right now are Mexico, Venezuela, and Colombia, due in part to censorship, but also to the lack of 16mm facilities.
> I would not use the term "feminist" for the women in my two films. I think these women are very aware that women have specific problems and that they deserve attention as that. . . . Most people are surprised to see how articulate these women are. People often ask me if I had to brief the women before the interviews. The truth is that I was surprised myself by their perceptions of their situation as women. They had a tremendous need to talk and they had a lot to say."[14]

A first reaction to The Double Day is one of surprise, because there are so many women who do have "a lot to say." A young woman from Mexico clearly states that women have to understand their oppression as women to realize "the system is stuck—doesn't work and has to change." This is the broadest socioeconomic interpretation by a woman in the film. The rest of the women, in talking about their own lives, illustrate prevailing social norms and educational patterns and their effects on work conditions for women.

Women in factories in Argentina are shown in the film doing tedious routine work. This is justified by male supervisory personnel who claim that women adapt better to routine. The camera catches one of these men full-face as he says unabashedly: "In general, men are more restless than women, and this type of work tires and bores them easily." One of the women workers explains that women are excluded from the high-level jobs in her factory. The control of personnel is entirely male dominated.

Factory work promises stability and regular hours. But, in Latin America industrialization has not kept pace with a burgeoning work force. Therefore, opportunities for the proletariat women in this area are relatively few. In addition, with little or no skills, these women are relegated to the lowest strata of the factory system. The benefits of regular work hours and relative monetary stability are offset by the need for someone else to care for the children, thereby effecting a change in the family organization. In some countries day-care nurseries must be established in factories as a legal prerequisite. But an Argentine worker in the film says only 52 percent of the factories in her country have complied with the law. Others hire only up to 49 women since 50 women employees would mandate the establishment of a day-care center. Several women indicate that "protective legislation" reputedly makes the hiring of women more expensive and fuels the resistance to hire them.

Historically, the advance of industrialization is characterized by a decreasing need for workers. If women remain at the lowest job status and pay level in the industrialization process, it is reasonable to assume that they form the most expendable part of the labor force. In the late stages of industrialization, the need for more technically and scientifically trained workers again prescribes a condition unfavorable to women. As a rule, women are not the recipients of this training, because the educational patterns operate within the traditional concept of women's role in the domestic sphere.

With their low pay and strong socialization as wives/mothers, it is not surprising that women do not consider themselves as workers in a working class.[15] The Mexican social scientist Maria del Carmen Elu de Leñero indicates that a women often works within a temporary framework. The single women works until she marries and the married woman works until her husband obtains work or better pay.[16] The latter woman works in a purely supportive role within the tradition as wife and mother when there is the economic necessity.

The irony is that this economic necessity is perpetual, due to inflation, decreased earning power, and unemployment for the men.

Elu de Leñero points out that a woman often works with an overriding guilt complex. Her work becomes the cause of whatever negative situations occur within the home. Elu de Leñero adds, "The worst is not that others say so, she, herself believes it."[17] This attitude can create resistance to the collective organization of women's domestic work in the form of day-care centers, laundries, workers' dining rooms, and other activities, which would facilitate women working outside the home. Any resistance from women themselves can also legitimate government failures to promote these types of services. One working mother in The Double Day speaks of the resistance by women because of a tradition of privacy.

Argentine domestics in the film speak of the low pay and the high cost of bus transportation. But most of all, they speak of the insult to their human dignity because of the superior attitude of their employers, women of the middle or upper class who often do not deem it necessary to offer their servants even a cup of tea. One of these woman employers indicates her alienation from working women's lives when she blithely states that women probably work for the nonessentials "to give themselves pleasure." Her attitude evidences the lack of solidarity among women across social classes. Elsa Chaney maintains there is little such evidence. Privileged women, she says, "have an obvious stake in maintaining the status quo and great anxiety at the prospect of losing their servants. It is ironic that the political activity even of radical women depends upon a servant class."[18] Yet, there are other women in the film, psychologists and social workers, middle-class women, who speak with great clarity about working women's inferior status.

Two out of five women in Latin America are within the services sector of the economy, as domestic servants. The pay is minimal, the hours are long, and the situation is often ripe for abuse. The domestics form the large part of the female informal-work sector—that is, work not regulated by contract. It is important to note that in terms of work career, domestic service is a "dead end" with no advancement or additional training opportunities. Margot L. Smith, in her study of female domestics in Lima, points out that if a new skill is learned it is most often one with no value in the labor market.[19]

Who are the domestics? Studies have indicated that the majority of newly arrived rural migrant women in the younger age group work as domestics. Among others, the 1970 study by Juan C. Elizaga of Latin American migration indicates that more women migrate than men.[20] Migration is encouraged by the availability of jobs as domestics and the relative security rural parents might feel having their daughter in the city with assured bed and board. The economic contribution the daughter might provide the family would probably be more than that by a girl in a depressed rural economy.

Smith's study indicates that the typical career of a resident domestic lasts seven years. By the age of 24, she has begun to raise a family of her own.[21] She then does her family's domestic work without pay. Often her bed and food are not assured, but she has a totally different tie to her "consumers." There is also the unmarried or separated mother for whom life in domestic service is a means of supporting her children. These children are cared for by family members or other informal arrangements. Live-in domestics usually may have no more than one child living with them on the job.

A more desirable type of work is daytime domestic service, particularly for women with families because they can return to their own homes at the end of the day. Lourdes Arizpe indicates that in Mexico "these jobs are sought after and found through friends and relatives."[22] Even if they do not make more money, as the women in The Double Day indicate, the advantages for the women and her family are obvious. It is important to note Arizpe's observation for Mexico that the availability of positions in "domestic service is used as a shield against protest over women's high unemployment rate and over the government's unwillingness to do anything about it."[23]

Another area of women's work discussed in The Double Day is the work within the home. Women talk about the "double day" of working women; they also refer to the invisible nature of housework. The latter is in accord with the view that as the public sphere develops for the male, the woman's work is reproducing, "refueling," and maintaining the labor force for the public sphere. Her work becomes an invisible, interior, and, therefore, more inferior part of the societal process.[24]

A Bolivian miner's wife talks about a woman's third place in the family behind the husband and children. She also relates the deplorable working conditions of the men to their drinking problems. The abuse of the women is a result. "Our people are dragged down by their pain," she adds. It is clear that the economic exploitation leads to social degradation. As a consequence the women are doubly oppressed. They suffer the economic deprivation with their husbands and the physical and emotional abuse the economic deprivation engenders.

The Bolivian miner's wife also tells how women are frequently widowed at an early age, left with several children to support and no possibilities for employment. A sewing cooperative in the area seldom has openings. Sometimes there is the dangerous work of sorting minerals in the slag heaps. A woman working the slag heaps rests briefly on her shovel and stresses the importance of having sons who can work in the mines and be a source of support. The dependency relationship of women is entrenched further by the economic situation in a country like Bolivia. Poor women's job opportunities are either nonexistent or pay too little for subsistence without a male.

On a more positive note, the miner's wife speaks of women's gradual recognition by the miners as a force in strike activities. She has witnessed inhuman government repression of such activities, and she has been jailed various times for her participation. Another part of the film also evidences women's political force. A group of women from the slums in Buenos Aires relate how they effectively mobilized to demand better health care, milk for their children, and water for their neighborhood. Thefilm is a rare document of women's force in community mobilization efforts that appear and reappear all over Latin America. Most studies would have one believe these efforts are made exclusively by men. On the other hand, women have proved extremely useful in Latin America as political ploys. They were granted the right to vote, according to Elsa Chaney, "by conservative male leaders who saw women as a conservatizing force in the electorate, or at least believed their vote would prove no threat to the status quo.[25] The Allende era in Chile is a recent example of the use of women as a political force.[26]

Educational patterns are also revealed through the interviews in The Double Day. A scene at a school indicates the socialization process. "In sports," says the director, "girls work more on form and rhythm while the boys work on strength and agility." One group of mothers indicated that their children's education is a prime motivation for their own work outside the home. The dropout factor for girls is evidenced by a young girl who speaks of working as a maid at the age of 13 because of the family's financial situation. "It felt awful seeing my mother work so hard so I decided it was better for me to work too," she says.

The dropout rate is considerably higher for girls than boys. Among the reasons are: (1) because of limited family resources, priorities are established that favor the male as the recipient of educational opportunities; (2) regardless of sex, the family needs the additional income the minor might provide for the family's subsistence; and (3) girls are needed to fill the mother's role at home while the mother goes out to work. In The Double Day the viewer ponders the dropout potential of a 12-year-old girl who must cook, clean, take care of her brothers, and study while her mother works as a daytime domestic.

Despite an entrenched system particularly unfavorable to women, The Double Day is, nevertheless, a positive film about women in Latin America. It is positive because it exposes the system, and the revelations are eloquently expressed by the women themselves. It portrays women who are very much aware of their own reality. Many of them express dissatisfaction, which is a first step toward change.

SIMPLEMENTE JENNY

Helena Solberg Ladd's second film is constructed around a more theoretical framework of women's socialization patterns, specifically the image of women as effected in the society by traditional and consumer-oriented values.

A 13-year-old child named Jenny in a girls' reformatory school in Bolivia gives the film its title. Jenny's bright red sweater sharply contrasts her black hair and black eyes, which look shyly at the camera. In a quiet voice she says, "I want to be myself, that's all. I want to be simply Jenny." The camera closes in on her arm in the red sweater and, gradually, on her hand picking at small tufts of grass as she says these last words. The interminable blades of grass seem to symbolize the obstacles she faces in order to be "simply Jenny." In addition to her low socioeconomic status, Jenny is not a virgin. She was raped at the age of 12 by an older man. Virginity is traditionally held in esteem by women in her society, and Jenny herself says, "It's also a beautiful thing when a girl is a virgin."

Traits relating to "femininity" are also part of the traditional image for women. In the opening scenes, a group of middle-class adolescents in Puerto Rico discuss femininity. A boy already secure in the truism of his words says, "A feminine woman behaves as society expects her to." Girls chime in with maxims such as "She shouldn't talk loudly or scream."

The film then turns to the role of the church and the Spanish Conquest as a measure of white male supremacy. A letter to the king of Spain from Amerigo Vespucci establishes the conquerors' thirst for gold, their deceit of the Indians, and their base opinion of native women as sexual objects. During the narration of the letter, the strident sounds of Handel's "Hallelujah Chorus" lend an ironical note.

Two little girls in flowing white dresses are seen being prepared for First Communion. Their mother, Juana, an Indian woman from Mexico, talks quietly as she sews the finishing touches on her daughters' white veils. Her own negative self-image is evidenced as she speaks of her aspirations for her children's education: "I want them to know, so that they are not, well, for example, like myself, who knows nothing. At least now they'll know and understand as much as their father." In Mexico 1970 statistics indicate that 42 percent of the adult women over 25 had no primary instruction.[27] Lack of education is a factor in the socialization process that perpetuates women's inferiority.

More recently, another socialization factor, the media image of women, has been superimposed on traditional values. Any visitor to Latin America can quickly sense the extent of influence from the United States, which permeates the commercial advertising field. In regard to women this influence most often reinfroces the tradition of women in the domestic sphere and, in addition, superimposes new values related to a consumer society. The new values essentially equate acquisition with success. Also important, as June Nash points out, the media images can give the woman the sense that she is the most important facet of the consumer sector, camouflaging the fact that she has little importance in the production sector.[28] Women have little or no role in decisions concerning what is going to be produced and who is going to produce it, since they are absent from the decision-making hierarchies.

Hilda Araujo Camacho informally categorizes images of women in the media, which she says are a result of "imperialist penetration." There can be little doubt that the origins are foreign and, at this time, particularly U.S. inspired. But self-serving commercial sectors within the countries are quick to capitalize on foreign influences. She delineates the categories as follows:

a) Woman defined as sexual object—through her body, which then receives the most attention.
b) Images which perpetuate racial discrimination. Women in the media who have nothing to do with the indigenous people who constitute the majority of the population.
c) Images of women who represent the esthetic values of the ruling class or of Europeans and/or North Americans.
d) Images of women whose only preoccupation is to buy, propagating consumerism which, at its worst, is consumerism for its own sake and not because of real necessity.
e) Images of women who are not concerned with national problems. Their world revolves around the means of acquiring more material comforts for their families.[29]

Cornelia Butler Flora's study of magazine fiction directed toward Latin American and U.S. middle- and working-class readers indicates a two-way relationship between the readers and the fiction. She says reader response and demand determine the type of fiction, and the fiction, in turn, shapes and reinforces reader values.[30] The relationship might better be termed cyclic, self-perpetuating, and negative since the magazines studied in both cultures emphasized women in a passive role.

The magazines studied for Latin America were edited in Mexico and Colombia. They included foto-novelas ("photo-novels"), which are extremely popular among the working class and have almost a cartoon format, making them accessible to a semiliterate readership.

In addition to the emphasis on women in a passive role, the magazines, according to Butler Flora, help to maintain the status quo by divorcing the reader from her reality and helping her to identify with an unattainable social class. In this way the magazines contribute to thwarting the establishment of a class identity that would recognize the oppression inherent to that class.[31]

Ximena Bunster says that television sets are to be found even in the poorest house of the cities of Latin America. Families will go into long-term debt to buy a television set. She reports that the programs most frequently watched are soap operas produced in Mexico, Venezuela, Argentina, and Peru. The heroine is often from the working class, who achieves social mobility by having a child with a man from the higher social class. She convinces him to marry her after a long process of proving her worth and refusing to marry would-be suitors from her own social class.[32] Obviously, the television viewer of such programs is subjected to the same class alienation forces as the reader of the magazine fiction. The need for fantasizing among these poor and working-class women might be studied to understand further the supply-demand phenomenon and how that serves to perpetuate the established system.

In the film Simplemente Jenny both consumer images and the idealized love-romance images are skillfully attacked by contrasting them to the lives of women like Rosa in the slums of Buenos Aires, Jenny in the reformatory in Bolivia, or Juana in her substandard house in Mexico. By way of contrast, there is the perfume beauty in billowing chiffon, the "Mrs. Clean" in Spanish amidst labor-saving appliances, and the 18-year-old model who claims to represent all Bolivian women. We see examples of foto-novelas and hear the languishing tones from a soap opera, which inevitably concludes in perpetual bliss.

The dangerous subtlety of media impact is felt when Jenny, in the reformatory school in Bolivia, says, "I would like to be a professional. Or somehow rich, rich, and buy a nice house for my sister and care for my brother, all the beautiful things they want." The media coupled with traditional norms have passively removed her from recognition of her reality and effectively socialized her for maintaining the status quo.

THE BRICKMAKERS

The black and white photography is so powerful it could almost function as a silent film. The film was directed by the Colombian husband and wife team, Jorge Silva and Marta Rodriquez. It is an important statement about exploitation and how it affects every member of a family. The mother's burden is particularly underlined to stress the extent of the oppression.

Alfredo and María Castañedas work as brickmakers with their
12 children on a latifundio (large plot of land held by one owner) near
Bogotá. There are, according to the narration, some 50,000 such
brickmakers. The production system is threefold: the landowner who
receives a monthly income for his land, which contains the clay from
which the bricks are made; the production boss who pays the landowner the monthly rental and hires the brickmakers; and the brick-
maker and his family who live in squalid huts on the land where they
get the clay to make bricks.

Their jobs are threatened if they do not vote according to the
mandate of the production boss or the landlord. Both use the workers
as a political ploy to sustain their own exploitive systems. The workers' total lack of political leverage is demonstrated in the beginning
of the film when Alfredo explains that he has always belonged to the
liberal party whose color is red—"noble like the blood of the battlefields," he says with pitiful pride. But he concedes that neither political parties nor presidents have ever done anything for him.

The brickmaking process is extremely laborious, as much of
the film indicates. The men stand in pits of damp mud to work the
clay. In one scene a woman kneels to form the bricks with a primitive wooden mold. A transistor radio blares a soap opera where the
heroine will marry her man despite his humble salary, since love
conquers all. The scene is even more ironical when the program is
interrupted by a commercial for laxatives, which claims to cure any
stomach disorder. The abyss between the people's lives and the propaganda from the media is remarkable.

The bricks are left to dry in the sun before they are carried to
the ovens on the backs of women and children, using head slings.
Even children four or five years old are a part of the family's work
force. Their only advantage is that they carry fewer bricks. It is
deeply moving to see these tiny creatures scurrying along the narrow
paths to the ovens like little animals weighted down with bricks. One
is reminded that the Nazi genocide ovens were certainly a quicker
form of extinction.

The work cycle for the men is some 20 to 30 years before crippling illness or death interrupt. In the meantime, there is pain from
illnesses like arthritis and lung disease. But illness is not the workers only burden. In bad times the only source of money is a loan
from the production boss, which further establishes the dependency
relationship.

The entire family must bear the emotional pain of degradation.
María speaks about her husband's drinking and provoking fights. He
then returns home to abuse his wife and children physically. When
the younger daughter asks, "Why?" the mother's response is, "Let it
be, what can we do?" It is the mother who must remain the unwaver-

ing pillar for the family. Lack of alternatives forces her to accept the mistreatment fostered by the frustration in her husband's life.

Her views on the birth of her children are extremely revealing. Clearly she does not view birth control as an alternative; yet Latin America's current growth rate would double the population every 23 years. "Why does the Lord give so many children to the poor? The rich who can afford them have only five or six. But what can I do? I can't kill them," she says.

There are some pathetic scenes of her maternal tenderness. She stops her work, and with her clay-covered hand reaches into her blouse to nurse her youngest child. The look of contentment on the little girl's face has a universal appeal. It is the setting, the clay-soaked hands, the dirty blouse, the piles of brick in the background that jolt the viewer into realizing that some of the "mothering" in Latin America takes place in the most adverse circumstances.

The scenes with one of the oldest daughters, Leonor, are also poignant. They get up from a bed where perhaps six or eight children have slept with the mother. The father has his own single bed. The mother and daughter go out to the patio to wash their faces and comb their hair to prepare for another day. One senses that despite the circumstances María does her best to inject a thread of dignity. The mother is clearly dominant as the children's source of emotional and physical support.

Leonor's First Communion celebration is a break in the drab routine. The mother lovingly helps the daughter dress, as wistful little brothers and sisters watch. At the party each child is carefully handed his ration of cake. The camera lingers on one little brother who vigorously scrapes even the last crumbs from his plate. But the celebration is marred when Alfredo wants his daughter to dance in the street. After she refuses, he strikes her and throws beer on her new dress.

In the film Leonor makes a symbolic walk in her First Communion finery among the dismal huts. She passes two women dressed in black who come toward the camera. The next few scenes are of a funeral for one of the men, and the parallel between the women in black and Leonor's future are evident. The moans of the widow are intermittent cries for help from God and pleas for the husband to return to take care of the family. A sermon is heard in the background: "Do not give up hope. Life doesn't end, it only changes; our real home is in heaven." A woman mourner indicates that for the wife and children left behind, begging is the most probable alternative. Without a man, these women, like the miners' widows in Bolivia, are virtually defenseless.

The brickmakers and their families do not even constitute a statistic in the work force. They are denied the right of collective orga-

nization, social security, and protective labor laws. Any form of
protest would mean the workers' dismissal by the production boss.
The bricks are sold for 260 to 340 pesos per thousand. Of this amount
the worker and his family receive 35 pesos. They work from 5 A.M.
to 6 P.M. or longer if the production boss demands it. If it rains
before the bricks dry, prior to being baked, all the work is lost without compensation. The ovens have a capacity of 30,000 bricks and
they bake from four to six weeks giving off deadly carbon monoxide
fumes to the surrounding huts.

The Castañedas are an example of political, economic, and cultural deprivation. Poverty as an all-pervasive force affects the entire
family. The viewer senses the despair that must drive Alfredo to his
vices, the hopeless future for the small children who look wide-eyed
at the camera, and the terrible emotional burden for María. The
true meaning of marginalized becomes evident by seeing the oppressed
woman's position within the exploited class. By realizing the extent
of her struggle, the class struggle becomes evident to the viewer.

VISUAL RESEARCH TECHNIQUE

In research it would seem there is a need for what June Nash
terms "empathetic comprehension" for studies on women.[33] The
Chilean political scientist Ximena Bunster, with a team of women
social scientists, has utilized what she terms a "talking pictures"
technique for a study of Peruvian working-class women.[34] The women
were shown pictures of women from their social class in daily life
situations (that is, a factory mother nursing her child, a woman street
vendor, a family at home gathered around the table). These pictures
formed the basis for eliciting responses to the interviewer's questions.
Bunster describes the effects of such a study on both the women and
the researchers:

> We tried to understand the patterned ways in which prole-
> tarian women—in our case Peruvian—saw, felt, labeled,
> and experienced their many worlds. Experiencing the
> photographs, they released and discovered hidden dimen-
> sions of the ways in which they structure and conceptualize
> their life cycle. As researchers, we were invariably over-
> whelmed by their suffering. The constant reaching out to
> them during critical moments of the interview gave us
> added insight into their lives and exposed us . . . to
> hitherto stifled dimensions of their suffering.[35]

The "talking pictures" approach is significant because, as Bunster indicates, it has the potential for exploring an inner world of thoughts and feelings that might well escape the purely empirical researcher.

The Bunster study as well as the other studies cited in this chapter support the content of the films in regard to the women's situation in Latin America. The studies and the films indicated an inferior work status, fewer educational opportunities, and relationships of dependency for women. In addition the film The Brickmakers places the struggle of women within a larger class struggle due to economic deprivation.

All of the films illustrate how women see themselves. The self-image issue, elusive in sociological studies, is underlined in an audio-visual context. The viewers learn from the women's facial expressions, voice tones, and gestures. These are added insights for understanding women's legacy and the self-perpetuation of their role. In The Double Day women express their dissatisfaction with that role and their desire for change. Seeing and listening to the women in all the films make their reality more convincing and more meaningful. To have data from studies coincide with the film content increases the value of the films as learning tools. But more important in a human way, the films and Bunster's "talking pictures" do not permit the women to remain faceless or ignored statistics in the computation of data.

NOTES

1. Nora Scott Kinzer, "Priests, Machos, and Babies: Or Latin American Women and the Manichaean Heresy," Journal of Marriage and the Family 35 (May 1973): 302.

2. Isabel Larguía and John Dumoulin, Hacia una ciencia de la liberación de la mujer (Caracas: Universidad Central de Venezuela, 1975), p. 7.

3. Jorge Gissi Bustos, "Mitología sobre la mujer," in La mujer en América Latina, ed. María del Carmen Elu de Leñero, vol. 1 (Mexico City: SepSetentas, 1975), p. 93. (The translation from the Spanish in this and subsequent Spanish texts are my own.)

4. Andean Women is 19 minutes in length, in color, and distributed by Wheelock Educational Resources, P.O. Box 451a, Hanover, New Hampshire 03755.

5. The Double Day is 53 minutes in length, available in color, and distributed by Cinema Incorporated, P.O. Box 315, Franklin Lakes, New Jersey 07417.

6. Simplemente Jenny is 33 minutes in length, available in color, and distributed by Cinema Incorporated, P.O. Box 315, Franklin Lakes, New Jersey 07417.

7. The Brickmakers is 42 minutes in length and available in black and white from Tricontinental Film Center, 333 Avenue of the Americas, New York, New York 10014.

8. Ximena Bunster B., "Talking Pictures: Field Method and Visual Mode," Signs Journal of Women in Culture and Society 3 (Autumn 1977): 288.

9. International Labour Office, Equality of Opportunity and Treatment for Women Workers, International Labour Conference, 60th sess., Geneva, 1972, p. 22.

10. María Gladys de Mena Guerrero, "Educación para la libertad," Universidad, January-February 1976, p. 60.

11. Lourdes Arizpe, "Women in the Informal Labor Sector: The Case of Mexico City," Signs Journal of Women in Culture and Society 3 (Autumn 1977): 33.

12. Virginia Gutierrez de Piñeda, "Imagen y papel de hombres y mujeres en Colombia," in La mujer en América Latina, ed María del Carmen Elu de Leñero, vol. 1 (Mexico City: SepSetentas, 1975), pp. 62-64, 138-65.

13. Scott Kinzer, "Priests, Machos, and Babies," pp. 300-1; and Mayra Buvinic, "Women and Catholicism in Latin America" (Paper prepared for the Pacific Basin Conference, "East Meets West: Culturally Conditioned Views of the Role of Women," East-West Center, Honolulu, February 28-March 5, 1977).

14. Written interview received by the author on June 10, 1978.

15. See the studies on Puerto Rican women by Helen Safa, "Conciencia de clasa entre las trabajadoras en Latinoamérica: Un estudio de casos," vol. 1, pp. 166-90, and on Brazilian women by Heleith Saffiotti, "Relación de sexo y de clases sociales," vol. 2, pp. 35-59, both in La mujer en América Latina, ed. María del Carmen Elu de Leñero (Mexico City: SepSetentas, 1975).

16. María del Carmen Elu de Leñero, "Trabajo de la mujer y fecundidad: Especial referencia a Mexico," in La mujer en América Latina, ed. María del Carmen Elu de Leñero, vol. 1 (Mexico City: SepSetentas, 1975), p. 67.

17. Ibid.

18. Elsa Chaney, "Old and New Feminists in Latin America: The Case of Peru and Chile," Journal of Marriage and the Family 35 (May 1973): 340.

19. Margot L. Smith, "Domestic Service as a Channel of Upward Mobility for the Lower-Class Woman: The Lima Case," in Female and Male in Latin America, ed. Ann Pescatello (Pittsburgh: University of Pittsburgh Press, 1973), p. 200.

20. Juan C. Elizaga, Migraciones a las areas metropolitanas de América Latina (Santiago: Centro Latinoamericano de Demografía, 1970), p. 21.

21. Smith, "Domestic Service," pp. 195-96.

22. Arizpe, "Women in the Informal Labor Sector," p. 34.

23. Ibid., p. 35.

24. Larguía and Dumoulin, Hacia una sciencia, pp. 9-14.

25. Chaney, "Old and New Feminists," p. 341.

26. Gabriela Plankey, "Las mujeres pobladores y el proceso revolucionario," in La mujer en América Latina, ed. María del Carmen Elu de Leñero, vol. 2 (Mexico City: SepSetentas, 1975), pp. 121-31; and Michele Mattelart, "La mujer y la linea de masa de la burguesía: El caso de Chile," in La mujer en América Latina, ed. María del Carmen Elu de Leñero, vol. 2 (Mexico City: SepSetentas, 1975), pp. 133-54.

27. Elu de Leñero, "Trabajo de la mujer," p. 79.

28. June Nash, "Perspectiva de la mujer Latinoamericana y en las ciencias sociales," in La mujer en América Latina, ed. María del Carmen Elu de Leñero, vol. 2 (Mexico City: SepSetentas, 1975), p. 17.

29. Hilda Araujo Camacho, "Criterios y lineas de investigación en la problemática de la mujer," in La mujer en América Latina, ed. María del Carmen Elu de Leñero, vol. 1 (Mexico City: SepSetentas, 1975), p. 21.

30. Cornelia Butler Flora, "The Passive Female and Social Change: A Cross-Cultural Comparison of Women's Magazine Fiction," in Female and Male in Latin America, ed. Ann Pescatello (Pittsburgh: University of Pittsburgh Press, 1973), p. 61.

31. Ibid., pp. 82-83.

32. Bunster, "Talking Pictures," p. 279.

33. Nash, "Perspectiva de la mujer," p. 11.

34. Bunster, "Talking Pictures," pp. 278-93.

35. Ibid., p. 290.

REFERENCES

Arizpe, Lourdes. Indígenas en la ciudad de México: El caso de las "Marías". Mexico City: Secretaría de Educación Pública, 1975.

_____. "Women in the Informal Labor Sector: The Case of Mexico City." Signs Journal of Women in Culture and Society 3, no. 1 (Autumn 1977): 25-37.

Boserup, Ester. Women's Role in Economic Development. London: George Allen and Unwin, 1970.

Chaney, Elsa M. "Old and New Feminists in Latin America: The Case of Peru and Chile." Journal of Marriage and the Family 35 (May 1973): 331-43.

Chinchilla, Norma S. "Industrialization, Monopoly Capitalism, and Women's Work in Guatemala." Signs Journal of Women in Culture and Society 3 (Autumn 1977); 38-56.

Elmendorf, Mary Lindsay. Nine Mayan Women: A Village Faces Change. Cambridge, Mass.: Schenkman, 1975.

Elu de Leñero, María del Carmen, ed. La mujer en América Latina. 2 vols. Mexico City: SepSetentas. (Some of the essays are available in English in a volume entitled Sex and Class in Latin America, edited by June Nash and Helen Safa. New York: Praeger, 1978.)

_____. Perspectivas femeninas en América Latina. Mexico City: SepSetentas, 1976.

International Labour Office. Equality of Opportunity and Treatment for Women Workers. International Labour Conference, 60th sess., Geneva, 1975.

Larguía, Isabel, and John Dumoulin. Hacia una ciencia de la liberación de la mujer. Caracas: Universidad Central de Venezuela, 1975.

Lavrin, Asunción E. Women in Latin America: Historical Perspectives. Westport, Conn.: Greenwood Press, 1978.

Nash, June. "The Aztecs and the Ideology of Male Dominance." Signs Journal of Women in Culture and Society 4 (Winter 1978): 349-62.

_____. La Concientización de una minera Boliviana. Mexico City: Instituto Interamericano Indigenista, 1975.

Pescatello, Ann., ed. Female and Male in Latin America: Essays. Pittsburgh: University of Pittsburgh Press, 1973.

Portes, Alejandro, and John Walton. Urban Latin America. Austin: University of Texas Press, 1976.

Scott Kinzer, Nora. "Priests, Machos and Babies: Or, Latin American Women and the Manichaean Heresy." Journal of Marriage and the Family 35 (May 1973): 300-6.

II

MINORITY WOMEN IN
THE UNITED STATES

INTRODUCTION TO PART II

Beverly Lindsay

To view the status of American racial minority women is to examine many comparable features that have affected the lives of women in developing nations. Triple jeopardy—race, sex, and class—are perhaps more clearly visible in the United States than in the developing nations. Distinguishing people as a minority group—Native American, Chicano, Afro-American, or Asian American—is based upon race, not ethnicity or national origin (as is usually the case with white ethnic groups). Race is a constant and immutable fact of life. Laura Waterman Wittstock and Sylvia A. Gonzales depict in Chapters 10 and 11, respectively, how racism served as an initial justification for the colonization of minorities in the United States. The extremely arduous condition of slavery for Black Americans was based upon racism, as Gwendolyn Randall Puryear states in Chapter 12. Internal colonialism buttressed by racism has oppressed the status of the most recent Asian immigrants, the Vietnamese, as explained by Gail P. Kelly in Chapter 13 on the schooling of Vietnamese immigrants, which examines internal colonialism and its impact on women.

What appears, however, during the contemporary period is that institutional racism has become so intertwined with class and sex that for minority women the three cannot be separated. Wittstock, Gonzales, Puryear, and Kelly find it difficult to discuss one institutional component of triple jeopardy without discussing the other two, despite the fact that in each instance triple jeopardy is not always discussed in direct relation to colonialism, internal colonialism, or neocolonialism.

Wittstock maintains that the colonial subjugation of Native American people, based on racism, justified by religion, and perpetuated by the views of social scientists (particularly anthropologists), altered and/or established new roles for Indians.

Gonzales briefly describes how the Mexican social structure, which strongly influences contemporary Chicano society, was effected during the colonial period by introducing different roles for males and females. In the case of Black Americans, Puryear presents views of writers who describe how Afro-American life was altered during slavery, which was certainly more repressive than many features of colonialism. Many views associated with a Black matriarchy can be traced to this period.

The education of minorities in the United States was influenced by racism and sexism. These writers depict how the education of and for minority people was designed to socialize them into accepting prevalent societal norms and to fit them into particular economic niches, which were lower than those for most whites. Education for women was more restrictive than that for male minorities. For example, Wittstock depicts how the curriculum at the Carlisle Indian School was different for boys and girls. In a similar vein, the education of Afro-Americans has evinced such differences. Undoubtedly, socialization was perpetuated via the curricula differences and many attitudes were internalized by minority females. Hence Puryear suggests that many contemporary Black female college students express preferences for traditional female areas of study; their preferences cannot be explained solely in terms of envisioned future socioeconomic roles. If the perception of future socioeconomic roles was the sole factor, then we might expect to observe relatively restrictive choices for males as well. (Socialization is at work, as we observed earlier in Wang's study on Chinese females in Malaysia.)

Several writers portray how minority females consistently occupy the lower rungs of the employment ladder. Their positions, which are frequently confined to teaching and service areas (due, in some part, to their academic majors), and their compensations are lower than those for white and minority males and white females. In her discussion of employment trends for Black American women, Puryear presents data that accurately portray this situation. Information regarding full- and part-time employment (rather than simply observing average annual incomes) illustrates the lower economic position of Black American women. (Of course, one could contend that compensation for white American female employees is consistently lower than that for white men, meaning that sexism also affects American women.) However, racism coupled with sexism are the employment realities for minority women. It might be argued that not all minority females experience noticeably lower economic differentials in comparison with whites. However, the majority of minority women do not fall within this rather select category, as the presentations by Wittstock and Puryear indicate.

Perhaps one of the most crippling effects of triple jeopardy for minority women in the United States is observable in terms of family life and/or male-female relationships. The harsh effects of triple jeopardy are devastating effects on the family since it is a most fundamental social institution. All four of the contributors to this section express profound concern with the tenseness that is sometimes manifested in family relations.

Gonzales attributes part of this tenseness to Chicanas' internalization of their proper sex roles as wives and mothers. The internalization of ideas regarding sex roles prevents, to some degree, their seeking additional roles outside the home and family. If they seek outside roles, despite racial and economic oppression (or perhaps because of such phenomena), they often encounter resistance from Chicano males. According to Gonzales, Chicano men need to change their machismo attitudes. However, in a society where males are usually viewed as the providers, Chicano men's domination in the domestic realm may be the only area in which their self-esteem appears to be loosely intact. They frequently cannot establish their position outside the home since racism and economic oppression prevent this.

Wittstock's discussion on Native Americans indicates how the roles of Indian men and women were altered during the epoch when Indians were being subjugated through treaties and other political and economic procedures. Some tenseness is still caused by this; however, Indian women have sometimes made concerted efforts to be quite supportive of male political endeavors—witness their roles in various contemporary social and political movements for Native American people.

The status of Vietnamese men and women has been drastically altered during the orientation and resettlement period in the United States. According to Kelly, Vietnamese men, for example, were taught English, to purchase household items, and to prepare for lower-echelon service positions. Men were to be the providers. Kelly indicates that the preparation of men for positions that are usually reserved for U.S. women means that as Vietnamese men occupy such positions, the role of Vietnamese women is pushed into oblivion. Since Vietnamese women occupied viable social and economic roles in Vietnam, they find this lack of direction difficult to accept. Domestic tensions were in evidence in the refugee camps, fostered in orientation classes and activities. As the refugees leave the camps, the domestic tensions may be compounded.

That Black American women hold a favored position in the labor force is a myth, according to the material presented by Puryear. Nevertheless, this myth has been perpetuated and has sometimes caused Black men to have unrealistic views of Black women. Arguments are voiced that Black women do not need liberation. That is, their socioeconomic roles do not need improvement, particularly in relation to Black men. Puryear presents data from the Department of Labor, the Department of Commerce, and other sources that clearly belie this myth. Black American women work due to economic necessity to help support their families and themselves. Even when they work, racism and sexism force them to occupy lower-echelon positions, and they receive lower compensation than white men, white women, and Black men. Black American women hold traditional views in that they are committed to the world of work, in contrast to the career world, simply because economic necessity forces them to make this choice. Despite such evidence, the myth of the Black American matriarch—that is, the liberated woman—continues to exist. Black men have expressed the view that Black women are too liberated and should be more supportive of Black men. Tense relations have sometimes existed due to faulty perceptions.

Hopefully, these chapters will provide insight into the problems confronting minority women in the United States. Identifying racial, sexual, and class oppression is a first and necessary step toward their eradication. Equality for Third World women is a primary goal in this struggle for basic human rights. We hope these chapters will make a contribution to the cause in this country.

10
NATIVE AMERICAN WOMEN: TWILIGHT OF A LONG MAIDENHOOD

Laura Waterman Wittstock

HISTORICAL CONSIDERATIONS

For 9,000 miles along the longitudes that score the Western hemisphere, the tribes and nations known as American Indians and Eskimos live in a broad diversity of economic surroundings from almost primeval forests to densely populated cities bulging with the worst of modern humankind's technological detritus. Within the tribes and nations, sweeping change has taken place since recorded alien contact 500 years ago. Each century has brought wave upon wave of colonization and economic exploitation. And each wave has been brought in the name of, or perhaps in spite of, progress. Surprisingly, this is a history that has repeated itself on all the great continents of earth and is one that has apparently taught no lessons that futurists might include in their plans.

There is today a patchwork of native life along the longitudes that is at once earthbound and chaotic—true to ancient curricula and yet portrayed as stepchildren to the wicked industrial parents. The deaths and horrors of the nineteenth century colonialist rule visited upon native people is being recorded again in South America today, without, it seems, much notice of the fact by the rest of the world. Human rights are for those strong enough to defend their humanity. Today, white men are being acquitted of butchering Indians in the jungles of the Amazon because the men did not know that to do so was a crime. And not without some decalogue juggling, the colonization of the Western hemisphere has taken place with the aid of at least two major religions.

Thus, there are two great connecting threads that tie the hemisphere's Indian populations to one another: forced cultural change from alien political powers and forced social change from alien or-

ganized religious powers. As the colonizing process spread east to
west, pushing northward toward the Arctic and southward to Tierra
del Fuego, not one tribe was allowed to escape the will of the conquerors. The distinction between the political and religious power of
the Roman Catholic and later Protestant churches in the Americas was
often indistinguishable and, more often, merged. In the United States,
for example, "religious freedom" from the tribal point of view was in
the nineteenth century no more than a facade for the blending of faith
and government. This is easily seen even today on U.S. coinage that
includes the script: "In God We Trust." The "We" of course, did
not include nonbelievers, it must be assumed. Indeed, in due course,
government-sponsored missionary schools made superhuman efforts
to bring tribes within the context of the trustees.

Sciences and particularly the social sciences, branching forth
in the nineteenth and early twentieth centuries, contributed much to
the chronicles of native decline. Anthropology owes much of its shape
to the studies of Indians all over the hemisphere,[1] especially North
America. Here, in the beginnings of a science with a colonialist and
male-dominated center, was born the Indian woman's image—name-
less and faceless, so uniformly second to man. The supreme self-
confidence of the times allowed for detailed records of every phase
of native life, including its destruction, to fill the reports of viceroys
and vicars alike. The penchant for records as well as the assumption
that close examination of native peoples is the scientist's right are
exemplified in the following passage:

> When the unmarried of opposite sexes were casually
> brought together, there was little or no conversation
> between them. No attempts by the unmarried to please
> or gratify each other by acts of personal attention were
> ever made. . . . A solution to this singular problem, is,
> in part, to be found in the absence of equality in the sexes.
> The Indian regarded woman as the inferior, the dependent,
> and the servant of man, and from nurture and habit, she
> actually considered herself to be so.[2]

Lewis H. Morgan, quoted above, represents to American anthropology,
perhaps, the prototypal field researcher. As an example of comparison, Mary Elmendorf describes a Mayan village today:

> Women's work is sex-stereotyped, as illustrated by such
> ceremonies as the Hetzmek, a kind of baptismal rite.
> This ceremony is performed when girls are three months
> old—its symbolism likened to the three hearth stones that
> are the center of a woman's activities.[3]

Citing three centuries of virtual enslavement during the period of Spanish colonial rule and the nineteenth century Wars of the Castes, Elmendorf goes on to describe the women of the village of Chan Kom as confident and self-assured, sometimes venturing successfully into the market place as small business managers and vendors. The author explains that women in such traditional communities enjoy far more equality with men because subsistence agricultural life makes a marriage a union of two specialists. The traditional community in this sense is alien-influenced but still based in the ancient corn culture of the area.

For North American Indian women, observations of their courting and marriage customs coincided oddly with Victorian white concepts of the late nineteenth century:

> The young maidens of the Chippewa were closely guarded and were modest in their behavior toward the young men of the tribe. If a young man wished to call upon a young woman he talked first with the older people who lived next to the door of the lodge.[4]

Frances Densmore is by far a more typical ethnographer of the North American Indian family, as the passage shows. Her books were widely renowned in the Bureau of American Ethnography's circle of membership. It was thus that these painfully romantic passages were repeated over and over, following a pattern established by Lewis Henry Morgan in Ancient Society, which inspired Frederick Engels to author The Origins of the Family, Private Property, and The State in the Light of the Researches of Lewis H. Morgan (1892). The basis of Engels's hypothesis was the concept that humankind had experienced stages of development throughout history: savagery, barbarism, and civilization.[5] Engels had based his hypothesis that matrilineal descendancy preceded patrilineal descendancy on Morgan's work, including histories of Iroquoian tribal life.[6] While both views have subsequently been discarded by anthropologists of later times, there has been great difficulty in completely shaking off these archaic views, particularly since they are found throughout the histories and observations of Indian tribes. These views, having much to do with descriptions of property, the concept of property and ownership of material wealth, and the classification of household work and child rearing as drudgery, persist even today, complicated by the difficulty of anthropologists in differentiating customs before alien contact and after:

> Discussion of the family has also suffered from a one-discipline approach. If historians have tended to ignore the

important materials on prehistoric times, or more accurately, history before written language, if we tend to
cut out of our view anthropology and archeology, the same
limitation is true of anthropologists: their view of humankind could use some perspective. [7]

The point bears repeating that "decontamination" of the mate-
rialist approach to history

has never been consistently applied across the range of
phenomena with which anthropologists are familiar, despite the fact that anthropologists have played a crucial
role in discrediting this option. . . . and in view of the
passion with which anthropologists have argued that they
have remained free of ideological bias. [8]

Priscilla Giddings Buffalohead points out that there are current
inconsistencies that have taken an even more subtle turn with the
emergence of the "feminist anthropologist." Buffalohead, while noting
that Morgan and others treated the subject of the lack of male Indian
chivalry toward Indian women as if chivalry were a worldwide custom,
also points out the faulty arguments of women anthropologists who
argue for the need for more studies of women by women who are
"similarly oppressed":

Given their argument, I think it must be noted that although
they suggest that data on women is just beginning to come
in, they have already concluded that women's lives universally are subordinate to those of men. [9]

While the historical framework is necessary to any discussion
of American Indian women, an examination of the overall oppression
of the histories of the people in dealing with tribal custom is needed
for a balanced picture. It must be noted that colonialism as a phenomenon performs distortions of native people's destinies that are so
inextricably interwoven with native expression that, as with many recently recorded tribal customs, life comes to imitate art. [10] Contemporary discussions, such as this work, of native women in terms
of social, educational, and career patterns must take that perspective
into account.

THE COLONIALIST OVERVIEW

The discussion of the effects of colonialism are limited here
to the United States, although, in many cases, the outcomes of colo-

nialist rule are much more severe in other countries with specific respect to native women:

> For one hundred and nine years Indian women in Canada
> have been subject to a law which discriminates against
> them on the grounds of race, sex and marital status.
> The Indian Act, which regulates the position of Indians in
> Canada, provides that an Indian woman who marries a
> non-Indian man ceases to be an Indian within the meaning
> of any statute or law in Canada.[11]

By comparison, the United States hoped to diminish steadily the numbers of Indians by various means outside of warfare. These means extended to conferring citizenship on Indians who left Indian land and lived as whites. Various treaties and laws came along to focus specifically on the Indian woman. These provided for the status of the woman with respect to holding tribal rights, land, and whether her children would be considered henceforth Indians. Typically, there were no provisions for the status of Indian men who married white women, perhaps because such a possibility would have been considered impossible in practice. This specificity is exemplified in the act of June 7, 1897:

> That all children born of a marriage heretofore solemnized
> between a white man and an Indian woman by blood and not
> by adoption, where said Indian woman is at this time, or
> was at the time of her death, recognized by the tribe shall
> have the same rights and privileges to the property of the
> tribe to which the mother belongs.[12]

Only women who fell exactly within the definition were able to have their children recognized as having tribal rights and property privileges. The law did not extend to Indian men nor women married after the date of the act nor to members by adoption. Children were viewed as taking the "habits" of the white father, and only in cases where the husband fails to discharge his duty are the children then viewed as Indians if they remain on the reservation and the mother is an enrolled tribal member.

From a general viewpoint, the entire hemisphere was subjected to the process of European political dominance and the imposition of a male-dominated socialization effort:

> The ascendancy of the chief was a phenomenon that ac-
> companied European invasion everywhere. The Europeans
> needed some one responsible official to deal with in Indian

negotiations, and if no real chief existed, as was usually the case, they invented one. Sometimes the fictitious power thus invested in these "treaty chiefs" was accepted by the other Indians and became actual. More often it led to discord. [13]

This practice of conferring chieftainship had been carried on quite vigorously throughout Canada and the United States from earliest contact on through President Harry S. Truman, who selected a chief of the Cherokee Nation of Oklahoma, as was his reserved right. It gave rise to a pronounced fiction, even among tribes, that there never were any female chiefs or heads of state by a sort of Orwellian[14] sleight of hand performed deftly by zealous recorders and willing informants.

The "white man's burden" concept seemingly was less pronounced in Black slave-owning America than in middle and South America where plantations depended on native labor, but perhaps this was only owing to the political differences between southern European influence compared with northern European influence. There are, after all, many acceptable comparisons between treatment of Blacks and coloreds in Kenya and South Africa by British and North American treatment of Indians, whereas Portugese Angola compares more closely with Spanish rule in middle America. This is further seen in the fact that, in North America, Britain and then the United States insisted on a federal relationship with Indians, making note of this privilege in the Articles of Confederation and the U.S. Constitution. However, as the years passed and a Department of the Interior was needed to regulate lands in the United States, this federal privilege was transferred from the Department of War to the Interior as the office responsible for carrying out the federal trust responsibility, which stemmed from treaty obligations between the government and Indian tribes. Various laws have come under this office for administration, but not exclusively so. Other departments administer a number of laws affecting tribes, but custom has come to dictate that the trust responsibility is within the Interior. The primary agency within the Department of Interior for administering Indian affairs was, and is, the Bureau of Indian Affairs (BIA).

Historically, the post of superintendent of Indian Affairs was first established with the War Department in 1789 and was transferred to the Interior Department in 1849. The new administrative agency was at the same time involved in settling land claims and determining the uses of public lands, placing the department in a conflict of interest from which it has not to this day emerged. The department's sub-agency the Bureau of Indian Affairs today lists 482 federally recognized tribal entities: 205 organized under the Indian Reorganization

Act, the Oklahoma Welfare Act, or the Alaska Native Act; 51 officially approved organizations outside specific federal statutory authority; and 225 traditional organizations having recognition without formal approval of their structure. The trust lands for which the United States is responsible, according to the BIA, total 50.4 million acres —39.7 million acres tribally held and 10.7 million acres individually held.

Population estimates identify about 1 million Indians and Alaska Natives, with about half being deemed eligible for services from the BIA. Services for which eligibility must be established include education, social services, road programs, credit, housing assistance, health services, nontaxable land allotment or assignments, law enforcement, technical assistance in all areas of the BIA's expertise, and preference with regard to employment in the BIA and the Indian Health Service. Eligibility, however, is not easy to determine. Persons of Indian descent who meet the membership criteria for federally recognized tribes are assured of consideration for services provided by the BIA. Membership does not, however, ensure entitlement, which may be dependent upon the specific language of the statute upon which a specific program is based.

In 1934 the Indian Reorganization Act was passed as a means of helping Indians recover from the devastating effects of the Allotment Act of 1887. The Allotment Act provided for the division of Indian lands to individual Indians under a 25-year trust arrangement. Under this act, 17.4 million acres of Indian land were declared surplus and purchased by the government for non-Indian settlement. By 1935, 90 million acres had been lost. The Reorganization Act ended land allotments and established tribally chartered administrations with community electorates. While the act ended allotments, it often became the vehicle by which existing tribal governments (chiefs, headmen, councils, clans, societies) broke up into peevish elected councils, with no system of balancing their legislative, interpretive, and enforcement powers. In this we can see the development of internal colonies or neocolonialism, if tribes are also seen as retaining somewhat their original national identities.

Early efforts at "civilizing" Indians carried forth the European blueprint: domestic work for women, field work for men. Several federal laws attest to the chronology: July 22, 1790, the Intercourse Act regulating traders in licensing; April 18, 1796, establishing government trading houses; March 30, 1802, restricting liquor consumption among tribes; March 3, 1819, appropriations for civilizations of Indians by persons of "good moral character" to "improve the habits and conditions" of Indians; and March 3, 1883, authorizing use of revenues from pasturage, timber, and mining to be used by tribes, with approval of the Department of Interior. An example of this civilizing effort is seen in the vigorous work of Richard Henry Pratt, former U.S. Army Indian fighter and founder of the Carlisle Indian School. Pratt was quite enamored with the military life and style and designed his school along those lines. During the four hundredth anniversary world exposition celebrating the "discovery" of America, held in Chicago in 1891, he could not resist the opportunity to show his civilizing effort with Indian children in his school. Arranging the students in ranks he marched them in the preexposition parade held in New York City. Two hundred seventy boys and 52 girls marched under a silk banner that proclaimed: "United States Indian Industrial School, Carlisle, Pennsylvania," with the slogan underneath, "Into Civilization and Citizenship." In Chicago:

> The boys were divided into ten platoons, each representing a characteristic of the school, through which we expected them to attain civilization qualities and citizenship. The first platoon carried school books and slates. The second represented printing; the front rank carried sticks, galleys, cases, etc. and the rear rank papers and pamphlets which they had printed. [15]

The ranks described totaled ten, each carrying implements of baking, carpentry, blacksmithing, shoemaking, harness making, tinsmithing, and tailoring. At the school itself, girls' industries were limited to baking and tailoring. The children were put to work over the summers in the neighboring farms.

General Pratt's work was a monumental effort of the period and represented the boilerplate curriculum, which was followed more or less throughout the country by missionaries who were empowered and funded by the act of 1819 to perform the "improvement" of the "habits and conditions" of the tribes, with no regard for individual tribe or culture. Farming tribes and hunters and gatherers alike were "encouraged" into the civilizing process. Thus, very early in Indian affairs, women and girls of all tribes that could be so coerced were molded to the domestic arts by the domineering, mainstreaming process of the times. Indeed, following World War II, the civilizing process took on a technological turn. The BIA instituted an employment policy in the 1950s to relocate families off the reservations to distant cities in order for them to obtain gainful employment. The training programs that accompanied relocation included welding for males and hairdressing and nurses' aide training for females.

To a great extent the civilizing process has become the nadir from which the measure of the colonizers has been taken, and this has been so on both sides of the Atlantic. At the painful expense of tribes and other minorities, the civilizing force laid the groundwork for the coming of age of civil rights in the United States. "For us, the Indian tribe is the miners' canary and when it flutters and droops we know that the poison gases of intolerance threaten all minorities. And who of us is not a member of some minority?" asked Felix Cohen.[16] In the United States, at least to some extent, colonialism and its by-products had grown, spread, and then drooped of their own heavy weight on the populace. But because tribes, even very large ones, are geographically trapped within the political confines of the United States, true independence remains an unanswered and certainly unaddressed question for world opinion and the courts.

THE SISTERHOODS

Just a week prior to the World Conference of the International Women's Year in June 1975, the American Association for the Advancement of Science sponsored a Third World Women's Seminar on Women in Development, which unfortunately included only one American Indian—the author. Ninety-five women from 55 countries attended five workshops and debated the means by which women could bridge the gap between theoretical involvement in world development and actual involvement. In many instances, the sheer diversity of law, custom, economic conditions, and gross national products of the countries removed any possibility of consensus on many, if not most, points. This microcosm of the developing nations disagreed on many issues, but one point bears repeating: there was heated disagreement on the training of women in crafts,[17] particularly the traditional crafts of weaving, pottery, embroidery, and others that are culturally related and expressive of the ethnic arts. Battle lines were quickly drawn with formally educated multilinguals on one side and traditional separatists on the other. The women could agree that all women must face sexual oppression and break into male-dominated decision-making occupations, link employment policies with economic independence, and emphasize learning to learn rather than the acquisition of skills and data; culture was the stumbling block. Instinctively every woman there knew that the cultural blueprint is passed most effectively and thoroughly from mother to child,[18] but few were willing to advocate that women forgo the "woman's work" crafts in favor of technological skills. In the United States, tribes place great importance on the Indian woman's arts, among which are basketry and countless patterns of traditional and interpretive beadwork in addition to those mentioned above. In many societies, these arts are the most profound expressions of cultural creativity to be found. In others, they accompany and complement men's arts: weaving, sculpture, painting, body ornamentation (tattooing, scarring, piercing), and certain types of beadwork and bonework. In some American Indian societies, these arts are the remaining vestiges of transitioning cultures, but in no tribal context, no matter how small the group, are these art forms the singular expression of Indian women's roles. Yet, Indian women are often identified and stereotyped by Western observers as being inextricably tied to these expressions as <u>though</u> they were in fact <u>traits</u>. The noted Indian anthropologist Bea Medicine writes:

> The interplay of the "ideal" as contrasted to "real" culture[;] the structural organization of the Native tribe; the type of family and kinship network; the patterns of socialization or child training practices; the belief system; and the values, explicit and implicit, of the unique tribal group accounted for the variation in women's place within each culture. . . . Becoming, being, and remaining female are aspects of socialization or enculturation which make a female a part of a cultural group and yet allow her to remain an actualized individual woman. . . . Learning to be a person is a process of becoming. It is based upon gender difference and is part of the training practices for children peculiar to each tribal aggregate. [19]

Despite such explanations, the notion persists, as with the women attending the seminar in Mexico City in 1975, that women's art is women's essence. Many there sought to identify sexism by association with women's art and thus to discard both by transition to "education" or "business" occupations. Most sought to retain women's art but disagreed as to whether women should merchandise their art and thus associated sexism with colonialist influence and the male domination of the mercantile classes of Third World countries.

A rather spectacular example of Indian women's art making a successful transition is to be seen in the relocation period of the BIA (1950-68). In cities where Indian families were being relocated across the United States, there was a sudden proliferation of Indian "centers," which served as information and aid centers and social gathering places. The BIA had believed that the further Indians were relocated from their home reservations the less the likelihood that they would return home. And again, the relocation was expected to have a civilizing effect and at the same time diminish the federal responsibility proportional to the numbers being successfully relocated. Los Angeles, California, for example, has a multitribal Indian population of 90,000 by most estimates. Other large populations of Indians can be found in Chicago, San Francisco, Cleveland, Seattle, and others. Indians relocated by the BIA found themselves in truly alien climates. Indian women in many instances began to do what they knew how to do:

they formed craft circles, held bazaars to sell their work, and raised money for the new urban Indian centers—the place away from home where Indians went to be with other Indians. The women's distinctive art proliferated in quilts, beaded articles, ceremonial garb, and new designs in cloth and yarn. These sisterhoods fueled the fires of urban Indian unity and made possible the debut of the urban-born "warrior brotherhoods"[20] that sprang forth in Chicago, Minneapolis, and San Francisco. Women sold their crafts so that the bodies of dead brethren could be shipped home for the last time.[21]

Taking the lead on issues often left to women—education, health, and welfare—the Native American Women's Action Corps formed in San Francisco in 1970. Later that year the North American Indian Women's Association was formed to promote education, health, and family life. In November 1977, out of the National Women's Conference in Houston, Texas, was founded the American Indian-Alaskan Native Women's (AI-ANW) Caucus. This group of women, formed around a core of professional women from many backgrounds (both tribal and professional), took on the "traditional" issues but also proclaimed their advocacy for Indian women's place in society as equal partners. One issue before the caucus now is the compliance among BIA schools with Title IX. The caucus was not surprised to find the situation so lacking:

> Inquiry was initiated in 1975 on educational equity for Indian women and girls in . . . federally funded programs by the National Advisory Council on Women's Education Programs. Testimony from Albuquerque indicated that Title IX, the chief federal law prohibiting sex discrimination in all federally-assisted education programs, was neither understood nor enforced.[22]

The National Advisory Council later contracted with the American Indian Law Center at the University of New Mexico to conduct a study sampling the BIA schools to measure their understanding and compliance. The study results indicated that the schools have not even begun to address the lack of educational equity in the schools.

Historically, of course, we need look no further than General Pratt for an explanation of this malaise so pervasive among the BIA schools. A believer in the education of the whole child, Pratt planned and executed a vigorous physical education program and thereby set the cornerstone for Indian sports participation, which persists today. He built a gymnasium in one of the old cavalry stables at Carlisle and introduced team sports for boys, such as football and baseball, and exercises for girls. He classified teams by grade or industrial shop and played them off against one another. He also played them against other teams. In Pratt's opinion, "Young Indians, seeing their chance for physical development, were quite as ambitious to seize their opportunities as our own youth." None, to be sure, was more ambitious than General Pratt himself, who hired the famous "Pop" Warner to become the Carlisle football coach "at what seemed for us an almost impossible figure," said the General. Thus, as the BIA schools came into being, the curriculum was team sports for men and boys and "physical education" for women and girls, much the same as U.S. public schools of the period.

One other Indian women's organization bears discussing because it alone recognizes the need for Indian women to be portrayed from within their cultural and community milieu. This group was also formed out of a larger concern—the American Indian movement. In 1978, at the movement's conference in South Dakota, issues of cultural identity, education, sterilization, and welfare were identified as the banner topics to be undertaken by Women of All Red Nations (WARN). But also at the forefront of WARN's concerns is the positive image of Indian womanhood: family life, medicine of women, birthing, nutrition, care of the dead, and traditional patterns of life that can be adapted for living anywhere. As often occurs in the politics of confrontation, the machinery necessary to drive the movement loses momentum and focus in times of impasse. WARN has come about at a time when refocusing is greatly needed—thus, their address of the cultural identity of Indians, no matter where they may live, is perhaps the key to the future.

EDUCATION: THE ETHNOCENTRIST'S FRUSTRATION

The AI-ANW Caucus reports information supplied by the U.S. Department of Health, Education and Welfare (HEW) statistics on the lack of vocational choice and how it has impacted earning power.[23] In 1970 the median salary for ethnic women was $6,823 for whites, $3,072 for Hispanics, and $1,697 for Indians. As to educational backgrounds of Indian women, 33 percent of the female population have completed high school, with the average grade completion being 10.5. One year of college was completed by 10.1 percent; 1.2 percent of rural women completed four years of college; and 3.8 percent of urban women have completed four years of college.

Employment is an equally dismal picture: in 1970, 35 percent of Indian women were employed outside the home but only 2 percent were managers and administrators—26 percent were service workers, 25 percent were clerical workers, 7 percent were domestics, and 19 percent were operatives. The 1970 census placed the Indian female population at 388,210. An interesting statistical contortion is that planned for the 1980 census, the basis for U.S. dollar allotments for all federal programs affecting Indians, will be the elimination of data on any Indian who does not actually reside on a reservation. The special form "For Indians Only" will provide information on Indians who live on Federally recognized reservations. National statistics will be at least 50 percent inadequate, using this method. Politically, of course, the action is flagrant and discriminatory.

The AI-ANW Caucus, at its founding in Houston, identified the following resolutions of issues:

Tribal rights, sovereignty, end of treaty termination,
Indian education,
Systematic removal of Indian children from families and communities,
Indian health service,
Involuntary sterilization,
Affirmative action/employment, and
Statistical data gathering based on race.

In 1978 the BIA, pursuant to its mandated reorganization plan, revealed the recommendations of the BIA Reorganization Task Force. The Task Force found that, although over $500 million is spent on Indian education, the educational attainment level of Indian children and adults is poorer than that for any other major group in the United States. Further, 65 percent of Indian children are in public schools, not BIA schools.

Earning power, employment, and education statistics all cast Indian women at a definite disadvantage at home and in the marketplace. But the real question is, What steps do Indian women want to take to ensure cultural intactness while competing for higher educations and better jobs? It is an unresolved question that has eluded definition by the Indian population nationally and that is discussed in meeting rooms everywhere under the aegis of "Indian Education."

It was thought that Indian children could get a good education and be useful citizens if they were subjected to an environmental onslaught: "In Indian civilization I am a Baptist," said General Pratt, "because I believe in immersing the Indians in our civilization and when we get them under, holding them there until they are thoroughly soaked." This had to be done away from the reservation. "If they were brought among our people, placed in good schools, and taught our language and our industries . . . in a little while their children could be made just as competent as the white children," stated the General. And so it was done and is being done to this day. BIA boarding schools operate hundreds of miles from home reservations. BIA training and relocation efforts tried to send Indians as far from home as possible. Through enormous effort—delicately handled so as not to terminate the BIA school system altogether—tribes and groups have sought reforms to the archaic and only domestic federal school system in the United States.

Losing ground in the spoken native languages, tribal religions, and everyday dress categories of cultural intactness, Indians clung tenaciously to what characteristics of ethnicity they could get away with. Languages similar to creole (English, French, Chippewa) and pidgin (various Indian terms mixed with English) took shape in the BIA schools. Today, the Bilingual Education (Title VII) federal regulations have been modified to include "Indian English." Allowable cultural items and activities were powwows or intertribal dances and the special costuming specifically designed for these dances. The costumes have their roots in true tribal traditions—beloved warriors, dog soldiers, beloved women, honored elders, and clans and societies. Today they proliferate without regard to tradition and are worn in dance competitions by all tribes. A particular curiosity of this phenomenon is the "Indian Princess," a comic example of life imitating bad art. Since the post-World War II period, there have been an "Indian Miss America" and numerous "Indian Princesses" who compete at powwows,[24] wearing excessively decorated costumes—a sort of Indian kitsch—topped with hand-beaded tiaras.

Perhaps the greatest disservice done to Indian women and men was the low expectation of federal schools. The schools did not believe in their own system and did not believe that Indians were capable of more than the agricultural and industrial schools of General Pratt's dream.

Then in 1973, at long last, the Indian Education Act was passed into law and had a lifetime of five years, which has now been extended for another five years. The thrust of the reform was to provide local Indian control of education programs on a limited basis—an experiment. At the administrative level of this law and other laws providing $250 million annually on Indian education, HEW's statistics say that there are six Indian women[25] in general schedule (a government service position) employment associated with these funds. The Indian Education Act provides service funds to public schools and demonstration, pilot, and technical assistance funds to tribes and organizations on a competitive basis. The programs range from preschool to higher education, and, although statistics are not available as to benefits, it is contended that Indian women are filling the traditionally female roles: elementary schoolteacher, teacher aides, cooks and other nutrition-related jobs, art instructors, music instructors, and "women's" sports. Early experimentation service programs in public schools, in a struggle to define Indian education, added "culture" and "craft" classes to their programs. Tribal schools, urban schools, and various programs of special emphasis did the same. Native language was taught most successfully in areas where a high fluency rate was already operating. A recent needs-assessment survey completed in the public schools of Minneapolis, Minnesota, shows the Indian community's ranking of the five greatest needs the schools' Indian education must respond to:

1. Indian social worker aides helping Indian students,
2. Indian people working with Indian students who have drug or alcohol problems,
3. Indian parent tutors to give assistance to Indian students who are behind in school,
4. Indian elders coming into the schools to teach about culture and history, and
5. Indian culture and history teachers.

As tribal schools and programs respond, the general hue and cry for competency-based education and "back to basics" role modeling has taken on a new emphasis, as the rankings above indicate. With Indian women filling modeling roles at the elementary grade levels, Indian education will likely be no different than "white" education with respect to sexism and early childhood learning. The ethnocentrist position that the best education for Indians is the same as the current trend being promoted for the general population still prevails, pluralistic or multicultural curricula notwithstanding.

The onus for defining Indian education is on Indians—and because many Indian women who are completing professional training are in the helping professions—likely Indian women, to a great degree. With what the BIA school programs have left to Indian ethnicity, the shape of future Indian education will be initially formed. We know that one key ingredient of culture, language, is exceedingly difficult to regain once it has been seriously eroded. Thus, the future of Indian education also promises to be an uncertain one.

HEALING THE WOUNDS

Owanah Anderson, Indian member of the President's National Advisory Committee on Women, brought the issue of Indian health programs before the president's domestic policy adviser in 1978:

I asked that before the Indian Health Service (IHS) proposed budget cuts were even considered, that it be remembered

that the American Indian has the poorest health, the short-
est lifespan, the greatest mortality rate, and that half the
population group is dependent on IHS for health care. I
further reminded that health care service along with education are obligations honorably assumed by the Federal
system through a series of real estate transactions.[26]

The Indian Health Service (IHS), which operates medical facilities throughout the United States, has functioned under HEW since
1955 when the BIA relinquished control of the services they simply
could not provide. The IHS has done somewhat better. Current budgets estimates of $492.5 million (recommended for fiscal 1979) keep
IHS functioning but not improving. And serious problems have sur-
faced, not the least of which is the sterilization of Indian women.
New regulations becoming effective in 1979 seek to minimize federally
assisted sterilizations. The new regulations include (1) uniform and
detailed informed consent (including interpreters when needed), (2)
mandatory 30-day waiting periods except under certain circumstances,
(3) minimum age of 21, and (4) mentally incompetent alternatives to
sterilization. The following language is added: "Your decision at any
time not to be sterilized will not result in the withdrawal or withhold-
ing of any benefits provided by programs or projects receiving Federal funds." The regulations are stricter, following a General Ac-
counting Office report criticizing the regulations, but policing compliance is quite another matter. As Anderson has pointed out in her
remarks, "In my opinion, this procedure for involvement of the In-
spector General is after the fact."[27]
Since women of childbearing ages are likely to come into contact with the Indian Health Service more frequently than other population segments, the present and future capabilities of the service
are most likely to affect Indian women. An evaluation of the IHS is
planned for 1979, likely a difficult task, because the service has not
benefited from great public pressure to improve its services nor
write about what it does do. It is rather an amorphous bureaucracy,
tucked away within the confines of the sprawling HEW. However,
some enlightenment may come from within—93.5 percent of all Indian
women employed by HEW work at the IHS![28]
Finally, it is worth noting the catalog of Indian ills:

Indians have the highest infant mortality rate in the nation:
32.2 of every 1,000 Indian babies born on the reservations
die during their first year, compared with 23.7 per 1,000
nationally. . . . The life expectancy of Indians on the reservation is nearly one-third shorter than the national average.

Mental illness thrives at an alarming rate. Suicide, alcoholism, glue, paint and gasoline sniffing, delinquency and broken homes all are considerably more common among Indians than among the general population. [29]

Alcoholism and chemical dependency are rapidly becoming problems before Indian people, which some believe are reaching epidemic proportions. The Minneapolis needs-assessment rankings discussed earlier show the need for persons to work with students who have alcohol and drug problems to be the number two need, right behind the need for social worker aides.

On another but related dimension, family intactness relates closely to health and, most assuredly, well-being. In 1978 Public Law 95-608 was passed into federal law. It is called the Indian Child Welfare Act, and it deals with the problem of Indian children who are or could be adopted away from their tribal environments. The law's major provisions grant exclusive jurisdiction to an Indian tribe (except where such jurisdiction is otherwise vested in the state by federal law) for any child custody proceedings involving an Indian child living within the tribe's reservation. There is protection for urban children as well, but the circumstances and remedies are much more complex.

In any state court proceedings for foster care placement or termination of parental rights, the act requires transfer of the case to tribal court if the parents, Indian custodian, or child's tribe so requests and if neither parent objects. The tribal court may decline to hear the case. However, in the event that state court proceedings are not transferred, later intervention is guaranteed, and a series of requirements is set out for notification of parents, tribe, custodian, and Secretary of the Interior. Court-appointed counsel is required in indigency cases. Preference is given to the Indian child's extended family, other members of the child's tribe, and finally to other Indian families in cases of adoptive and foster care placements. The act requires that court records are maintained, which will permit an Indian child, upon reaching 18, to establish tribal identity. The act also authorizes grants to Indian tribes and organizations to establish and operate Indian child and family service programs and prepare and implement Indian child welfare codes.

Healing the body and mending the spirit have been traditional modalities for Indian women, particularly within the family group and with children. The popular notion of the "medicine man" is a sexist image promoted in the same way that the "chieftain" was promoted. An impressive pharmacopoeia, which has now been partially lost, was partly the work of women throughout the hemisphere. Cer-

tainly great healers of both sexes have practiced the healing arts in
ancient times and today as well. But, the limitations placed on sex
that are the biases of alien observers have done much to damage and
distort the true identity of the Indian woman with regard to curative
and preventive medical practices.

TOWARD WOMANHOOD

Feminism has reared a specter before Indians in the United
States as few other social causes have. Many fear it, most do not
understand it, and a few have breathed deeply and decided not to partake. Tribal women in the hemisphere have been inextricably oppressed along with their brother men historically, and yet they find
themselves doubly oppressed contemporarily, as Western sexist
values have been applied to women everywhere. Kinship and clan
systems, when functioning, act as a deterrent to independent action,
especially actions of a critical nature within the group. In the United
States Indian women do not feel the unifying cause as in Canada where
race can be lost by marrying non-Indians. And, because tribal women
have had a long history of struggling survival rather than independent
development, broadly legislated equal opportunity and antisexist laws
have been met with resistance. Such legislation is perceived as being
the majority's solution to the majority's problem, and holding little
relevance for tribal women and their historical and cultural perspectives. But problems do remain to be faced.

A weakening of the traditional religious and cultural fabric by
500 years of Western influence has taken its toll. Indians of all ages
in America are responsive and responding to sexist influences. Di-
luted present-day sermonizing that refers somewhat obliquely to a
mother earth and a father sky lose substance on the uncomprehending
ears of the faithful. Few women are totally assuaged:

> Leaders are particularly sexist, never having learned our
> true Indian history where women voted and participated
> equally in all matters of tribal life. They have learned
> the white man's way of talking down to women and re-
> garding their position as inferior.[30]

Most women are determined to bring change, but only from
within the tribal context and on their own terms, as a sort of separate
peace. The change is also surely to have new advocates. Betty
Friedan, pioneering feminist, has suggested that life-span will have
a greater impact on cultural change than any other single cause.[31]
Indian women in America are benefiting from better health practices,

lower morbidity rates, and generally longer life-spans, although, to be sure, Indian health is nowhere near as good as that of the general population. But in time, with better health, the life-spans of Indian women will edge further and further into old age. The childbearing years will represent a smaller percentage of life's totality than ever before, and in the intervening years change is certain to come. Also, the highly fluid nature of Indian life in America today gives rise to an assumption of cultural change from tribal mingling in cities, diffusion of intact cultural practices in a sweeping or trend effect, and the appearance of revivals and orthodoxies. Indeed, the social and spiritual movements that followed the BIA's relocation programs of the 1950s and 1960s brought cultural changes of sudden and dramatic proportions. These movements have lost momentum in an ennui that is more a comment on the economy than political conditions in the country. While they were in full flower, from 1968 to 1974, their impact was felt all across the land.

What place Indian women will make for themselves in the shifting realities of the technological proliferation that is leaving Third World women around the globe in doubt as to a future course is no one's good guess. But tenacity and faithfulness have done more over time to bring Indian women to the brink of the end of their long maiden hood.

NOTES

1. Margaret Mead, "The American Indian as a Significant Determinant of Anthropological Style," Anthropology and the American Indian: A Symposium (San Francisco: Indian Historian Press, 1973).

2. Lewis Henry Morgan, League of the Hodenosaunee (New York: Dodd, Mead, 1904), pp. 314-15.

3. Mary Elmendorf, "The Dilemma of Peasant Women: A View from a Village in Yucatan," in Women in World Development, ed. Irene Tinker and Michele Bo Bromsen (Washington, D.C., Overseas Development Council, 1976), pp. 88-94.

4. Frances Densmore, Chippewa Customs (Washington, D.C.: Smithsonian Institution, 1929; reprint ed., Minneapolis: Ross and Haines, 1970), p. 72.

5. Ann J. Lane, "Women in Society: A Critique of Frederick Engels," in Liberating Women's History, Theoretical and Critical Essays, ed. Bernice A. Carroll (Urbana: University of Illinois Press, 1976), p. 11.

6. Morgan, League of the Hodenosaunee. There are numerous passages that exemplify attitudes of the period, particularly with respect to comparing Indian cultures unfavorably with European social mores and norms.

7. Lane, "Women in Society," p. 11.

8. Marvin Harris, The Rise of Anthropological Theory: A History of the Theories of Cultures (New York: Columbia University Press, 1968), pp. 4-5.

9. Priscilla Giddings Buffalohead, "American Indian Women: Views of the Anthropologists" (Lecture presented at the University of Minnesota, Minneapolis, 1977), pp. 4-5.

10. Bea Medicine, The Native American Woman; A Perspective (New Mexico: National Educational Laboratories, 1978), p. 17.

11. Katherine Jamieson, Indian Women and the Law in Canada: Citizens Minus (Ontario: Minister of Supply and Services, 1978), p. 1.

12. Felix S. Cohen, Handbook of Federal Indian Law (1970; reprinted, Albuquerque: University of New Mexico Press, n.d.), p. 187.

13. William Brandon, The American Heritage Book of Indians (New York: Dell, 1964), p. 215.

14. The popular meaning of "Orwellian" is the doublespeak of 1984. Here is meant the Animal Farm decalogue of the animals that changed meaning over time until it was reversed—seemingly without the animals ever noticing very much. See George Orwell, Animal Farm (New York: Harcourt, Brace, Jovanovich, 1946), p. 121.

15. Richard Henry Pratt, Battlefields and Classrooms, ed. R. M. Utley (New Haven: Yale University Press, 1964), p. 195.

16. Felix S. Cohen, "Indian Self Government," American Indian 5, no. 2 (1949): 3-12.

17. Elmendorf, "Dilemma of Peasant Women," p. 165.

18. Medicine, Native American Woman, p. 21.

19. Ibid., pp. 21-22.

20. Minneapolis, Minnesota, in 1968 saw the birth of the American Indian movement, originally called the Coalition of Indian Americans. United Indians formed in Chicago. United Native Americans formed in San Francisco. The groups' formations coincided with the pooling of large segments of Indian populations in metropolitan areas during the late 1960s and early 1970s. See also Alvin Josephy, Red Power (New York: American Heritage Press, 1971).

21. Cleo Waterman was president of the San Francisco American Indian Center during portions of the 1960s and 1970s, including during the 1969 occupation of Alcatraz. Her group of Indian women performed logistics for the occupation and, in addition, made and sold Indian women's work items to finance several center activities, including shipment of Indian dead to their home reservations. See also Jane B. Katz, I Am the Fire of Time (New York: E. P. Dutton, 1977).

22. American Indian-Alaskan Native Women's Caucus, Newsletter, ed. Owanah Anderson (Wichita Falls, Tex.: AI-ANWC, January 1979).

23. See the 1970 Census Public Use Sample Tapes. For further study, see also the report of the U.S. Commission on Civil Rights, Social Indicators of Equality for Minorities and Women, 1978.

24. Powwow—Algonkian language stock. A term referring to medicine persons who "dreamed" or "conjured." Webster's New World Dictionary, 2d ed. (College), s.v. "powwow." Common contemporary usage, derivation uncertain, by Indians of American tribes refers to a dance celebration, usually one including dance contests of some kind.

25. American Indian-Alaskan Native Women's Caucus, Newsletter.

26. Ibid.

27. Ibid.

28. Ibid.

29. Edgar S. Cahn and David W. Hearne, eds., Our Brother's Keeper: The Indian in White America (New York: New Community Press, 1970), pp. 55, 58.

30. Medicine, Native American Woman (from an unpublished paper by Kathleen Smith), p. 94.

31. Betty Friedan, Speech to Nebraska Association of Women in Law, national public radio, Washington, D.C., January 15, 1979.

REFERENCES

American Indian-Alaskan Native Women's Caucus. Newsletter, edited by Owanah Anderson. Witchita Falls, Tex.: AI-ANWC, January 1979.

Beck, Peggy V., and A. L. Walters. The Sacred Ways of Knowledge: Sources of Life. Tsaile, Ariz.: Navajo Community College; Albuquerque: Adobe Press, 1977.

Brandon, William. The American Heritage Book of Indians. New York: Dell, 1964.

Buffalohead, Priscilla Giddings. "American Indian Women: Views of the Anthropologists." Lecture presented at the University of Minnesota, Minneapolis, 1977.

Cahn, Edgar S., and David W. Hearne, eds. Our Brother's Keeper: The Indian in White America. New York: New Community Press, 1970.

Cohen, Felix S. Handbook of Federal Indian Law. 1970; reprint ed., Albuquerque: University of New Mexico Press, n.d.

_____. "Indian Self Government." American Indian 5, no. 2 (1949): 3-12.

Densmore, Frances. Chippewa Customs. Washington, D.C.: Smithsonian Institution, 1929; reprint ed., Minneapolis: Ross and Haines, 1970.

Elmendorf, Mary. "The Dilemma of Peasant Women: A View from a Village in Yucatan." In Women in World Development, edited by Irene Tinker and Michele Bo Bromsen. Washington, D.C.: Overseas Development Council, 1976.

Harris, Marvin. The Rise of Anthropological Theory: A History of the Theories of Cultures. New York: Columbia University Press, 1968.

Jamieson, Katherine. Indian Women and the Law in Canada: Citizens Minus. Ontario: Minister of Supply and Services, 1978.

Josephy, Alvin. Red Power   New York: American Heritage Press, 1971.

Katz, Jane B. I Am the Fire of Time. New York: E. P. Dutton, 1977.

Lane, Ann J. "Women in Society: A Critique of Frederick Engels." In Liberating Women's History, Theoretical and Critical Essays, edited by Bernice A. Carroll. Urbana: University of Illinois Press, 1976.

Mead, Margaret. "The American Indian as a Significant Determinant of Anthropological Style." Anthropology and the American Indian: A Symposium. San Francisco: Indian Historical Press, 1973.

Medicine, Bea. The Native American Woman, A Perspective. New Mexico: National Educational Laboratories, 1978.

Morgan, Lewis Henry. League of the Hodenosaunee. New York: Dodd, Mead, 1904.

Orwell, George. Animal Farm. New York: Harcourt, Brace, Jovanovich, 1946.

Pratt, Richard Henry. Battlefields and Classrooms. Edited by R. M. Utley. New Haven: Yale University Press, 1964.

Webster's New World Dictionary. 2d ed. (College).

11

LA CHICANA: GUADALUPE OR MALINCHE

Sylvia A. Gonzales

INTRODUCTION

For the more than a decade of women's movement activities, no figure is more elusive than the Chicana or Mexican American woman. Only recently has Chicana scholarship begun to question the ill-conceived stereotypes of this woman so prevalent in Mexican and American literature. The Chicana, as most women, is a victim of a sexist history. The Mexican American woman, like her Mexican sister, carries the burden of Mexico's past and present. In order to understand her it is necessary to analyze the impact of the Spanish Conquest on the Mexican nation as well as the sociohistorical conditions that have produced further psychological conquests of the Mexican psyche.

The Mexican American woman is allowed two characterizations from Mexican history. One is that of Malinche, the traitor and mistress of Hernando Cortes, and the other is that of Guadalupe, the maternal virgin. These characterizations are not unique to Mexican American women. Most contemporary Western nations either create their own symbols or are inheritors of the Judeo-Christian figures of the Virgin Mary and Eve. However, in the case of the Chicana where historical events have produced three major physical and psychological conquests—the colonial experience, postrevolutionary disillusionment, and contemporary economic instability—the scapegoat attitude and its resultant characterizations allowed the Chicana are exaggerated. Malinche is blamed for the conquest of the Mexican nation and, thus, all contemporary ills of Mexican society. The absurdity of rendering such blame to this female historical scapegoat has gone unchallenged for more than 200 years.

An examination of sexism as the progenitor of colonialism, neocolonialism, and internal neocolonialism hopefully will stimulate the

scholarship that will release Mexican Americans from these debilitating stereotypes. An objective analysis of the characterizations af-
forded Mexican and Mexican American women as either Eves or virgins, Malinche or Guadalupe, will challenge the history of sexism and
its ensuant sexist history, which has weighed so heavily on the Mexican American woman.

THE ECONOMICS OF COLONIALISM

In 1519 Cortes landed in Mexico. The battles described in Bernal Diaz del Castillo's The Discovery and Conquest of Mexico[1] and
the defeat of the Mexican nation led to Mexican colonialism under the
Spanish crown. The Spaniards economically exploited Mexico for love
of God and country. Bernal Diaz describes in rich detail the civilizing
of the Indians of Mexico to Christian values and customs—the Spanish
conquistadores' divine mission. Whatever the rationale behind colonialism, it is an exploitative venture where a nation seeks to acquire,
extend, or retain overseas dependencies.[2] The mother country values
the exploited colony for its great riches and guards them closely.[3]
Therefore, the motivating force behind colonialism is economic and
it exerts a tremendous social impact on those exploited.*

Colonies are investment areas where the rate of profits far ex-
ceeds that from domestic ventures, explains historian W. E. B. Du-
Bois.[4] How, then, does color play a part? The United States was a
colony of Great Britain, but skin color was basically the same—white.
England profited much from its colonies, though, and demanded more
and more in the form of exorbitant taxes. Here was a case in which
sameness of skin color did not prevent exploitation. In contrast, after the defeat of Mexico, Cortes summoned Cuauhtémoc, Indian lord
and prince, to him. Cuauhtémoc told Cortes that he had done his duty
in defense of his city and asked Cortes to kill him. Cortes lauded

---

*The French anthropologist Roger Bastide described the origins
of the social sciences in direct relation to colonialism. It was important in the 1800s to reject social philosophy as a science for social
management for the colonized. The reassessment of social philosophy
as a form of social law actually began in Europe with the migration of
the peasants to the cities, followed by industrialization and its resultant exploitation of the workers and, finally, the French Revolution
(see Roger Bastide, Applied Anthropology [New York: Harper Torchbooks, 1973], for a discussion of the failure of social philosophy and
of the need to create a new science, particularly in relation to the
European crisis of 1789 and colonialism).

Cuauhtémoc for his bravery and told him that he respected him.[5] Apparently, Cortes did not withhold his admiration of Cuauhtémoc because of the Indian's color but rather admired his strengths as a warrior and defender of his people—a case where one man treated another as an equal regardless of color.

Racism, however, seems to be an inherent trait of colonialism and neocolonialism. Colonialism is a result of world exploration and trade. Historically, the white European established himself as a great adventurer and took pride in himself as being the leader in colonizing other lands that would afford him enormous profits at home. As the world grew smaller, it became necessary to revitalize a form of social management at home; and as it is more desirable to exploit those who are less like oneself, color became a leading factor in determining the exploiters from the exploited.

It is necessary to understand the causes and effects of exploitation in order to understand the contemporary status of the Chicana, affected not only by racism but also by sexism. Colonialism and neocolonialism are very much a part of Mexican American history. We can better understand the larger burden placed on the Mexican American female by examining the origins of colonialism. The first indication of economic exploitation of one group over another was the relegation of women to the helpmate role with no monetary compensation. It is this writer's contention that sexism is the oldest form of economic exploitation and colonialism. This chapter will provide data to support this thesis.

WOMAN: MOTHER OR MISTRESS

The two most famous women in Mexican tradition and history are Malinche and the Virgin de Guadalupe. Each symbolizes the culture's dual view of women. Malinche, the Mexican Eve, was the mistress of Cortes. Because she facilitated communication between Cortes and native tribes, she has been blamed for the conquest of Mexico. Octavio Paz writes that the conquest was not only a violation in the historical sense but also in the very flesh of Indian women. Doña Malinche, says Paz, symbolizes this violation. To him, Doña Marina represents the Indian women who were fascinated, violated, or seduced by the Spaniards. Paz concludes that the Mexican people will not forgive La Malinche for her betrayal, just as a small boy will not forgive his mother if she abandons him to search for his father.[6]

The Virgin de Guadalupe, in contrast to Malinche, is the universal mother. Just as the biblical Eve represents mankind's downfall in the Garden of Eden, the Virgin Mary, pure and passive, prepares the way for mankind's salvation through the birth of Christ the Son.

The Virgin or universal mother is also the intermediary between disinherited man and the unknown, inscrutable power—the Strange. [7]

Eves and Malinches are notorious throughout history. While mankind commands the earth and the heavens, man seeks a suitable definition for this person who is a sometime helpmate, sometime spoils of his victories in battle, and, too often, the scapegoat for his failures. Almost every contemporary Western nation can look at its own history and find the characterization of Eve.

At the same time, mankind has also allowed his female the counterimage of virgin, untouched by the frailties of the human race. The virgin image embodies purity of soul, spirit, and body. She is the mother of mankind in its purest form. A God can only be conceived of a woman that has been untouched by another man. Therefore, this God is above all men. This virgin mother becomes the custodian of the germinating fetus, providing her energies and nutritional lifeblood to her son much as Mother Earth does for the entire human race. This virgin mother epitomizes passivity and self-scarifice as she offers her body to mankind in his search for the heights of power and perfection—his conception, free from male intervention, of a pure, passive, and noncompetitive source.

In the case of Cuauhtémoc, the hero of Mexico, the dichotomy is brought to fulfillment. Paz writes that even his relationship with a woman fits the archetype of the young hero, at one and the same time the lover and the son of the goddess. [8] Lopez Velarde further states that Cuauhtémoc went out to meet Cortes, that is, to the final sacrifice, separated from the curved breast of the empress. [9]

As the history of the Spanish Conquest illustrates, history is about men. It is about men, their challenging of each other, their wars, their victories. For this reason, the history of a group's victories or defeats weighs upon men's self-concept. In victory men take the most precious property of their enemy, the women, and rape them. Susan Brownmiller in her monumental work, Against Our Will, documents this custom among men as a ritual of victory. [10] In defeat they reject the property that has been soiled by the raping victors, as did the men of Bangladesh after the vicious raping of their women at the hands of invading soldiers during the Bangladesh war of independence. Oftentimes, men-nations attribute their destruction to the traitorous acts of the female victim, such as is the case of La Malinche.

Through the rape or seduction of the woman, the final psychological victory has occurred. She has betrayed her race by opening herself to the enemy, even though it might be against her will. She is then transformed into the culprit of the conquest, the final giving away of the power and glory of her people—a power and glory she has had no part in defining. According to Judeo-Christian tradition, God the

Father decided that Adam should not eat the apple. And it was Adam's act that determined the future of the entire human race. Eve only assumed importance as the scapegoat of his deed after Adam defied God.

Origins of Sexism

Marvin Harris, a Columbia University anthropologist, has provided a most insightful thesis on why men dominate women. In <u>Cannibals and Kings</u>, Harris maintains that, historically, dominance is a product of the very real problem of population control. Harris describes the patterns of male dominance in all cultures throughout history. Harris writes in "Why Men Dominate Women," an article that appeared in the New York <u>Times Magazine</u>, that it is necessary to investigate the cultural conditions that have nurtured and sustained male sexism. Like most advocates of women's rights, Harris does not hold to the theory that men dominate women because it is natural for them to be aggressive and take control. Male supremacy, says Harris, is not a biological imperative or a genetically programmed characteristic of the human species.[11] Nor is it an arbitrary social convention or a conspiracy among males to degrade or exploit women.

Harris, instead, proposes that the entire complex of male supremacy plus the very definition of <u>feminine</u> as passive and <u>masculine</u> as aggressive can be deduced from one fact—virtually all band and village societies engaged in warfare in which males were the principal if not exclusive combatants. Throughout prehistory, according to Harris, as well as during more recent epochs, warriors fought battles exclusively with spears, clubs, bows and arrows, and other muscle-powered weapons. Under these conditions, the greater average strength and height of the human male, which can be traced back to our primate ancestry, became critically important. Military success, and hence the life and death of whole communities, depended on the relative number of aggressive, brawny men who were psychologically and physically prepared to risk their lives in combat. In preparation for their combat roles, Harris continues, males were taught competitive sports such as wrestling, dueling with spears, and racing with heavy weights. Masculinity was also instilled by subjecting boys to intense physical ordeals such as circumcision, trials of stamina, deprivation of food and drink, and drug-induced hallucinatory encounters with supernatural monsters. But, to get males to risk their comfort and lives on behalf of perfecting masculine personalities, some powerful system of rewards and punishments was needed. Ostracism was the punishment; sex was the reward. Thus, if wives and concubines were to be the chief inducement for men to become masculine, Harris concludes that women had to be trained from birth not for combat but for acquiescence to male demands.[12]

Harris provides provocative and thorough documentation of his thesis. His point is that warfare and sexism are closely linked social inventions, both of which arose to serve the same vital function— namely that of preventing overpopulation and the consequent destruction of the natural resources needed by prehistoric human groups. [13] In any serious study of female politics, it is important to understand this link between warfare and sexism. It is necessary to devise new methods of population control, sophisticate contemporary warfare, and redefine women's role in order to extirpate sexism.

Sexism, Colonialism, and Chicana Oppression

Mexican American sexism requires a look at the history of oppression that the Mexican nation has experienced. Just as some colonialism has its roots in sexism, group oppression is linked to colonialism and/or neocolonialism, whether by internal or external forces. The economics of exploitation have ruled the Mexican psyche since colonial times and this has special significance for Mexican American women.

Although all women share the burden of Eve, in the case of the Chicana, the image of scapegoat or Malinche becomes exaggerated within the reality of the Mexican people's multiple defeats. Paz claims that the strange permanence of Cortes and La Malinche in the Mexican's imagination and sensibilities reveals that they are something more than historical figures; they are symbols of a secret conflict that we have still not resolved. "When he repudiates La Malinche, the Mexican breaks his ties with the past, renounces his origins, and lives in isolation and solitude."[14]

It is this author's contention that the greater the number of physical and psychological defeats of a people in the economics of survival, whether in warfare or social and political development, the greater the oppression of the female members of the group. This oppression is manifested in several ways, one of the most important being the cultural, social, and exclusive definition of women as either Virgins or Eves.

The Mexican psychiatrist Rogelio Diaz-Guerrero, in describing the Mexican family, contends that the wife is not viewed as a sexual object because she may become too interested in sex and, thus, may become a prostitute. The Mexican family, writes Diaz-Guerrero, is founded upon two fundamental propositions. They are the absolute and unquestionable supremacy of the father and the necessary and absolute self-sacrifice of the mother. Abnegation is essential to the Mexican wife and mother. The enjoyment of sex is a selfish aim that is beyond her feminine role and would cast her to a life of Malinche, mistress or prostitute. [15] Through these characterizations by male-controlled social customs, women are allowed no divergence from their acceptable definitions as either Eves or Virgins. They continue to be rewards as either wives or concubines.

It seems that the greater the need to recapture masculine dignity because of social, economic, and political defeat, the greater the curse on the female members of the group. Historically, this has been done in the way most convenient to mankind. This is to dominate women and at the same time blame them for male defeat by the conqueror, thereby placing this loss of masculinity beyond their control. The conquest of Mexico is not evidence of the weakness of the Aztec warriors at the hands of the Spanish conquistadores, then, but the result of an exterior force—the betrayal by the woman Malinche. The burden is even greater on Malinche, considering that in traditional, authoritarian cultures men are viewed to have little control over their sexual drives, whereas women are entrusted with the sexual morality of the group. Women are expected to resist the uncontrollable sexual drives of men and thereby exercise restraint for both. Malinche gave herself to Cortes and with her the entire Mexican nation. According to Paz, there is nothing surprising about the curse that weighs against La Malinche, and he explains the use of the word Malinchistas to describe those who want Mexico to open itself to the outside world. [16]

The Chicana suffers for the defeat of the Aztec nation at the hands of Cortes, successive postrevolutionary disillusionments of the Mexican nation, exasperating social conditions of contemporary Mexico, and finally, the status of the Chicano in the United States as a victim of economic oppression and discrimination—neocolonialism. To further aggravate the burden of the Chicana, the Mexican American has little opportunity to study the history of his heritage, much less engage in serious analysis of its influence on his treatment of the Chicana. The repudiation of Malinche is perpetuated even more so by Chicanos. Armando Rendon writes in Chicano Manifesto that Chicanos have their share of Malinches, which is what they call traitors to la raza who are of la raza. In the service of the gringo, Rendon continues, Malinches attack their own brothers, betray our dignity and manhood, cause jealousies and misunderstanding among us, and actually seek to retard the advancement of the Chicanos, if it benefits themselves. [17]

There is no male group that retains exclusive rights to sexism, although Mexicans and Chicanos have been stereotyped "Macho" or supermale. But these are groups that have experienced great challenges to their manhood. And with such groups, their female counterparts suffer their acts of revenge. Octavio Paz writes that the Macho commits unforeseen acts that produce confusion, horror, and destruction. The Macho, as described by Paz, opens the world and in doing so, he rips and tears it, and this violence provokes sinister laughter. But Paz believes that in its own way this behavior reestablishes equilibrium and puts things in their places, by reducing them to dust, to misery, to nothingness. The humor of the Macho, says Paz, is an act of revenge.[18]

DOÑA MARINA, MALINCHE

The story of Malinche is a simple one. It begins with the state of the Aztec Empire in 1519. The soldier Bernal Diaz described his first glimpse of the Aztec citadel of Tenochitlan on November 8, 1519, as one of surprise at the sight of so many cities and villages. The Spaniards were amazed and said that it was like the enchantments they tell of in the legend of Amadis. Some of the soldiers asked whether the things they saw were not a dream.[19]

The Aztec warriors were among the proudest in the history of Indian civilizations. They were also warlike and bloody, most disdained for their human sacrifices. And these sacrificial rituals also provide witness to the use of women as rewards. According to anthropologist Michael Coe, most famous among the Aztec sacrifices was that of the young captive chosen annually to impersonate the god Tezcatlipoca. For one year he lived a life of honor, worshipped literally as the embodiment of the diety. Toward the end, he was given four beautiful maidens as his mistresses. The four mistresses, along with the other goods and privileges awarded him, prepared him for his sacrifice to the god.[20] Women were sacrificed, too. Although they also were prepared for their sacrifice, they did so as a kind of vestal virgin. So either women served as rewards for the males being sacrificed or were sacrificed themselves. But in either case, they had no part in deciding their roles or social customs.

Because women were not the leaders or determinants of the group's activities, it would be hard to conceive of one female as being responsible for the destruction of so noble and brave an empire. Yet, the legend of Malinche as traitor and the designation of all future "traitors" as Malinchista lives on.

Doña Marina is the first woman with which the Chicana has to identify in history. In order to understand her story, it is necessary to look at the Aztec Empire prior to the arrival of Cortes. Flor Saiz, in her monograph, La Chicana, states that under the rule of Montezuma, the Aztec emperor, a group of men were assigned the duties of tax collectors. According to Saiz, the tax collectors went to all the villages and took what they wished for the emperor. Every year many of the sons and daughters of the village families were demanded for sacrifice or for other services such as work on the plantations or in the palace. If wives and daughters were exceptionally beautiful, the tax collectors oftentimes carried them off and raped them. "They ravished and abused them and then put them to work. The common people lived in terror of Montezuma and especially the tax collectors."[21]

As the conquistadores explored along the coast, Cortes met with several Indian groups. The most impressive meeting was held in Tabasco where Cortes met with Indian chiefs from many surrounding towns. The Indians arrived with gifts for Cortes of gold and other valuable items. Although the gifts were very valuable, Bernal Diaz records that they were nothing in comparison with the 20 women that were given to them. It was an Indian custom to give gifts to strangers, including women. Diaz tells of one excellent woman called Doña Marina, so named when she became a Christian. Cortes gave Doña Marina, who was good looking, intelligent, and proud, to Alonzo Hernandez Puertocarrero, one of his captains. After Puertocarrero went to Spain, Doña Marina lived with Cortes and bore him a son named Don Martin Cortes.[22]

Doña Marina had been the mistress and cacica of towns and vassals since her childhood, records Bernal Diaz. Her father and mother were caciques of a town called Paynala. While she was still a small child, her father died and her mother remarried a young man, another cacique, and bore him a son.[23] Saiz writes that it was the custom to divide an inheritance between sons and daughters.[24] But as Bernal Diaz tells us, it seems that Doña Marina's father and mother decided that the son should receive all of the inheritance. So that there would be no impediment to this, they gave Doña Marina to some Indians from Xicalango, a neighboring village, and reported that she had died.[25]

At the age of 12, Marina was given to the people of Tabasco, and they gave her to Cortes. Saiz writes that she became the interpreter for Cortes because she spoke the common language and could communicate with many different tribes. Historical accounts seem to indicate that Marina strongly opposed Montezuma because of the terror his regime caused.[26] In any case, Marina performed her duties well.

"The Sons of Malinche"

Why have Mexican male historians blamed Malinche for the defeat of the Aztec nation? Marina has taken on the character of legend rather than historical figure. She is a legend that is tainted by her sex. The far-fetched nature of the overwhelming blame placed on Malinche for the defeat of the Aztec Empire is accepted in exchange for unquestioned pride in Aztec prowess. The Mexican people have blinded themselves to reality and logic in seeking a rationalization for their conquest. Even Mexican intelligentsia falters when faced with this sensitive point in the Mexican psyche.

In Octavio Paz's work "The Sons of Malinche," which is contained in his book The Labyrinth of Solitude, Malinche is described as the chingada ("the violated one"). The Mexican peoples are hijos de la chingada madre ("sons of the violated mother"), according to Paz. And who is the violated mother? She is, of course, Malinche. Paz goes on to say that the chingada is the mother who has suffered, metaphorically or actually, the corrosive and defaming slander implicit in the verb that gives her her name.[27]

Paz discusses the several meanings of the verb chingar. He describes the social and psychological implications of the verb. It is always an aggressive verb, he says, and in Mexico the word has innumerable meanings. It is a magical word in that a change of tone, a change of inflection, is enough to change its meaning. It has as many meanings as it has emotions. Because of this, it has as much significance as the various aspects of the Mexican male psyche. Accordingly, a Mexican male can be a chingon, a gran chingon, as in business, politics, or with women, or a little chingon. But whichever he is, Paz writes, the word always implies aggression. It also means to violate bodies, souls, and objects and, ultimately, to destroy.[28] No wonder that, as Paz says, the essential attribute of the Macho, power, almost always reveals itself as a capacity for wounding, humiliating, or annihilating. It is impossible, in Paz's view, not to notice the resemblance between the figure of the Macho and that of the Spanish conquistador. This is the model, more mythical than real, Paz continues, that determines the images the Mexican people form of men in power: caciques, feudal lords, hacienda owners, politicians, generals, or captains of industry. They are all machos or chingones. Mexican literature contains many prototypes of this mythical model, an example of which is Juan Rulfo's Pedro Paramo.[29]

Although the word has sexual connotations, Paz claims it is not a synonym for the sexual act; one may chingar a woman without actually possessing her. And when it does allude to the sexual act, Paz maintains that violation or deception gives it a particular shading. The man who commit it, continues Paz, never does so with the consent of the chingada. "Chingar, then, is to do violence to another. The verb is masculine, active, cruel . . . and it provokes bitter, resentful satisfaction."[30]

Paz sees the victim of the chingon as passive, inert, and open, in contrast to the active, aggressive, and closed person who inflicts the wound. "The chingon is macho, the male; he rips open the chingada, the female, who is pure passivity, defenseless against the exterior world. The relationship between them is violent, and it is de-

termined by the cynical power of the first and the impotence of the
second. The dialectics of the closed and the open thus fulfills itself
with an almost ferocious precision."[31] In studying Paz, it is important to keep in mind that open and closed and passive and aggressive
are descriptions of the male-female state that have evolved through
historical circumstance and social custom. There are those who cite
biological differences and their psychological responses as indicative
of the "open" and the "closed" view of men and women. Most prominent among them is Freud and the early school of psychoanalysis. The
female is viewed as "open" in respect to her sex, the passive recipient
of the male's "closed" sexual structure. However, the "open" sexual
design of the female body does not necessitate passivity nor the male's
"closed" design, aggression. These are interpretations of the body
based on historical convenience and economies.

Octavio Paz has been the scourge of Chicano males and many non-
feminist Chicanas. Chicano males, as they struggle against the effects
of minority status in the United States, are unable to reconcile analysis
of their negative self-image with serious self-criticism. Then too,
they fear that a universal look at Paz's writings will provoke feelings
of guilt and hostility. Such hostility, they argue, will lead Chicanas
to align themselves with the Anglo-feminist movement to the detriment
of the Chicano family and culture. They attack the writings of Paz
with all the skills of a gran chingon.

Some Chicanas shy away from Paz's thesis for several reasons.
Because of its unpopular reception in the Chicano male community,
professional women, especially, fear that to embrace it would instigate
the anger of Chicano male colleagues and thus sever their support and
alliance. Also, to accept the writings of Paz would entail the rejection
of their current identity and cultural role and require their subsequent
embarking on a totally new pattern of personality and role formation.
This is an awesome and frightful task for a group that has barely established a group identity within a heretofore oppressive environment.
Can the Chicana devote energies to her own consciousness raising while
the majority of her group still experience economic exploitation? But
then again, can oppression or internal neocolonialism be attacked
without attacking their origins in sexism? The Chicana feels a real
love and compassion for her male counterpart. She recognizes that
he has suffered oppression in this country as well as in his native
Mexico. She feels dutiful to him at the cost of her own needs, as her
cultural tradition dictates. And she does not want to give the appearance of divisiveness before the Anglo powers.

The Mexican Heroine: Myth or Reality?

This misinterpretation of history continues. The arguments
used by Chicano writers and Chicana nonfeminists against Paz are

that the Chicana has been stereotyped as passive and defenseless.
They point to the Adelitas of the Mexican Revolution and the activist
Chicanas of today as examples of the weaknesses in Paz's thesis.
Rendon writes, "Young girls are relating to the folk heroines of the
Mexican Revolution, La Adelita, subject of a revolutionary corrido,
who exemplified the soldaderas [women who accompanied the rebel
armies as camp soldiers, sometimes taking arms themselves]."[32]
It is fashionable in the contemporary Chicano movement to glorify the
Mexican woman's role in the Revolution of 1910 as having fought along-
side the Mexican male. There were many outstanding women who participated in the revolution.

Elisa Acuña y Rosetti, university educated, joined the forces
of Emiliano Zapata and remained with them until Zapata was assassi-
nated. And Guadalupe Rojo, assumed the responsibility for a controversial antigovernment newspaper upon the death of her husband. She
was jailed for her activities and upon her release returned to the
newspaper to continue in her antidictator activities. Doña Silvina
Rembao de Trejo was given the name La Matrona de la Revolución
("the matron of the revolution") because of her activity on the battlefield.[33] But, these women are exceptions. The prototype of La Adelita was more common. And she was the woman who followed the soldiers from camp to camp, attending to their needs, physically and
emotionally.

Sexism has been a part of Mexican history. Sor Juana Inez de
la Cruz, the seventeenth century Mexican poetess, addresses Mexican
sexism in many of her poems. She accuses "stupid men" of unreason-
able blame of women while oblivious that their acts incite the very
acts they censure. She particularly criticizes male provocation of
female virtue, taunting them to succumb and disdaining them if they
do not. Sor Juana questions, "Or which deserves the sterner blame,
though each will be a sinner: / She who becomes a whore for pay, / Or
he who pays to win her?"[34]

Sor Juana Inez de la Cruz was the outstanding poet in Mexico
during its three centuries of existence as a Spanish colony. The
church censored Sor Juana's writings and prohibited her from writing
more. The cause of the censorship was Sor Juana's critique of a
sermon delivered by a vain but highly acclaimed religious scholar,
Father Vieyra. In admonishing Sor Juana her superior reminded her,
"A las mujeres, a la cocina ['for women, the kitchen']."[35]

Is the Chicano male's need to personalize the discussion reflec-
tive of the series of defeats his Chicano-Mexican psyche has suffered?
Is it that the Chicano male, in trying to recapture his masculinity like
his Mexican ancestors, cannot face the further defeat of self-criticism?
Diaz Guerrero writes that the undisputed authority of the male is explained by the fact that he has the male sex organs. Most often Mexi-

can women who excel scholastically or professionally are viewed by men as becoming male.[36] It would be a great service to the Mexican people to understand this not as a pathology of the Mexican culture but, rather, as a symptom of the social and universal ill of sexism. It is important to investigate the origins of sexism as a root to oppression in order to resolve both. Objective scholarship would release Chicano males from the stereotype of machismo and help them to understand their own attitudes toward the Mexican American woman.

MEXICAN "HISTRICITY" AND THE CONTEMPORARY MEXICAN AMERICAN

The history of most minority groups in the United States seems to indicate that group awareness and self-criticism are dependent on the group's economic, social, and psychological advancement. The Jews, Italians, Irish, and, most recently, the Blacks have all gone through a period of cultural and political insulation as well as isolation. Public analysis of one's own group amounting to group self-criticism was most often forbidden and raised questions as to the writer's loyalty. The familial expression "not to hang one's dirty wash in public" has been used to censure public disclosure of group weaknesses. Group loyalty is equated with family loyalty. The idea of an extended family in the Mexican American community is indicated in the expression familia de la raza ("family of the race"). The members of la raza are known by their Spanish surname, language, and Spanish-derived culture. These elements give them a kind of mystical bond, the importance of which cannot be overemphasized.[37] So, just as Mexican pride protects the family from outside attack and criticism, the Mexican American defends the integrity of la familia de la raza from the exterior world.

There is a fear of group exposure to the outside world and, with it, continued unacceptance. But as the Jewish people have discovered, and now the Blacks with Alice Walker's Meridian and Toni Morrison's Song of Solomon, revelation has often met with acclaim and admiration. It seems, however, that this kind of group introspection may be an indication of mainstreaming. Paz remarks that it is astonishing that a country (Mexico) with such a vivid past, a country so profoundly traditional, so close to its roots, so rich in ancient legends even if poor in modern history, should conceive of itself only as a negation of its origins.[38]

The Brazilian educator Paulo Freire talks about the importance of "human histricity." Humankind learns from the past in order to foresee the future. But, Freire also talks about the fear of freedom and humankind's inability to free themselves from the ghosts of the past.[39] Paz also talks about the phantasms as vestiges of past realities in the Mexican experience. "Their origins are in the Conquest, the Colonial period, the Independence period, and the wars fought against the United States and France."[40]

Samuel Ramos, a Mexican professor of social philosophy, went even further in describing the inferiority complex of the Mexican. He describes this complex in terms of the pelado, a universally familiar social type in Mexico, and the distrust so predominant in the Mexican psyche. The term pelado defies translation into English, but Ramos portrays the pelado as a result of Mexican history, which has given the Mexican a feeling of insignificance. Because of this feeling, the Mexican seeks power in the only suggestive force assessable to him—that of the male animal. When a Mexican compares his void with the character of a civilized foreigner, Ramos writes, he consoles himself in the following way: "A European has science, art, technical knowledge, and so forth; we have none of that here, but . . . we are very manly." Ramos says they are manly in the zoological sense of the term—that is, in the sense of the male enjoying complete animal potency. The Mexican believes this potency is shown through courage. But Ramos feels that this courage is a false image of the real weakness the Mexican is trying to hide. Ramos also points to the Mexican's inferiority complex as a result of his proletarian status. He says that the pelado associates his concept of virility with that of nationality, creating thereby the illusion that personal valor is the Mexican's particular characteristic. The frequency of individual and collective patriotic manifestations is symbolic of the Mexican's insecurity about the value of his nationality, argues Ramos; decisive proof of this affirmation is found in the fact that the same sentiment exists in cultivated and intelligent Mexicans of the bourgeoisie.[41]

Ramos is convinced that these characteristics were present in Mexicans of the colonial era, who for different reasons developed a similar personality. Social life of that time abounded with injustices, which left the Creole at a disadvantage in relation to the penisular Spaniard, who was always a recent arrival. Because of his lowly condition, the mestizo cultivated a kind of reticence in order to cover up his thoughts. There is a similarity, insists Ramos, between the Mexicans of the colonial period and contemporary Mexicans, although Mexicans experienced changes for the better in the eighteenth century. According to Ramos, however, in the agitated atmosphere of the past century and for other reasons already set forth, old attitudes returned.[42]

The idea of historical phantasms is similar to Plato's idea of the shadows on the wall. Mexico's present is made up of shadows of the past. The effects hide the causes. Mexicans then study the effects as independent attitudes rather than the causes. History, then, is the key to clarification of the origins of Mexican ghosts.

The Mexican American:
A Case of Classic Colonialism

The Chicano people, by understanding their own history and
the history of the Mexican nation, can confront the present. A psychology of masculine survival through warfare is one of fierce competition. Competition on the battlefield leads to triumph and national
pride. The United States defeated the Mexican nation and stole much
of their country, albeit by legally disguised means. This blow was
compounded by this neighboring nation's developing into the most powerful country in the world. Even further, today the United States provides the only available escape hatch for the unemployed poor of Mexico. Stop the illegal alien and the Mexican nation will surely falter
from lack of a job market for its explosive population. The degree
of Mexican dependency on the United States is tremendous. An example of this is the recent attempt of Mexico to sell some of its oil to
Russia. Although such a sale would have helped Mexico achieve economic independence, it was canceled because of the U.S. threat that
if such a sale were consummated, Mexico's "favorite nation status"
would be terminated.[43] Mexico is not yet psychologically ready to
endure the sacrifice such economic sanctions would impose on its
people for possible economic independence in the future. So colonial
economics are perpetuated in contemporary U.S.-Mexican relations.

Joan W. Moore writes that the colonial concept, when applied
to the Mexican American, need not undergo the adaptations recommended by sociologists for use with the Black American. Moore, in
fact, describes the Mexican American in terms of "classic colonialism." The initial Mexican contact with Americans, explains Moore,
came by conquest, not by choice. Mexican American culture was
well developed; it was autonomous; the colonized were a numerical
majority. Further, they were—and are—less ghettoized and more
dispersed than the American Blacks. In fact, adds Moore, their patterns of residence (especially those existing at the turn of the century)
are exactly those of classic colonialism, and they were indigenous to
the region and not imported.[44]

Moore discusses three types of colonialism imposed on the
Mexican American. In New Mexico, there was a situation of com-
paratively "pure" colonialism, whereas outside of New Mexico, the
original colonial conquest was overlaid, particularly in the twentieth
century, with grossly manipulated voluntary immigration. Moore
notes that a continuity of elite participation in New Mexico from the
period of Mexican rule to the period of American rule paved the way
for a high level of conventional political participation. The fact that
village social structure remained largely intact, she says, is in some
measure responsible for the appearance of the Alianza, a Mexican
American mass movement. But even this movement, according to

Moore, is an outcome of colonialism—the expropriation of the land by large-scale developers and federal conservation interests led ultimately to the destruction of the village economic base and the movement of the dispossessed into the cities. Living together in a closer environment than that of small, scattered villages allowed them to unite in response to the anticolonialist protests of a charismatic leader. [45]

The Texas experience is categorized by Moore as "conflict colonialism." She explains this as a reflection of the violent discontinuity between the Mexican and American periods of elite participation and the current struggle for the legitimation of ethnic politics on all levels. Moore compares conflict colonialism to the Black politics of the Deep South, although it comes from different origins. [46]

Moore applies the term economic colonialism to the colonial concept in California. The destruction of elite political strength by massive immigration and the comparative absence of local political organization meant a political vacuum for Mexican Americans. Extreme economic manipulation inhibited any attachment to the reality or the ideals of American society and, Moore continues, indirectly allowed as much intimidation as was accomplished by the overt repression of such groups as the Texas Rangers. [47]

The Effects of Colonialism
on the Mexican American Woman

What, then, is the solution to the dilemma of the Chicano that will alleviate the Chicana's situation? Self-criticism is important, not only for Chicanos but for all men and women. But, most important to Chicanos is understanding sexism and its historical origins. If the Mexican past is that of a colonized people, and colonialism has its roots in warfare and sexism, then the Chicano must look at this history and determine how it has influenced the characterizations he has allowed his female counterpart.

When a Mexican male is asked why he must marry a virgin, he commonly answers, "Porque nos gusta estrenar ['because we like to break in our women']." This response connotes ownership, possession, and disregard for the sentiments of the woman. Traditionally in Mexico a woman is either a prostitute or virgin, mistress or wife, with no in-between. A woman's engaging in sexual activity outside marriage makes her a prostitute, while for a man it makes him a gran chingon, or supermale. The virgin image remains with the woman throughout her life. If she enjoys sex, her husband fears her potential for being a Malinche.

Paz explains that Mexican Catholicism is centered around the cult of the Virgin of Guadalupe. He reminds us that she is an Indian virgin, and the scene of her appearance to the Indian Juan Diego was on a hill that formerly contained a sanctuary dedicated to Tonantzin, "Our Mother," the Aztec goddess of fertility. The conquest, writes Paz, coincided with the apogee of the cult of two masculine divinities: Quetzalcoatl, the self-sacrificing god, and Huitzilopochtli, the young warrior god. It was the defeat of these gods—which is what the Spanish Conquest meant to the Indian world, because it was the end of a cosmic cycle and the inauguration of a new divine kingdom—that caused the faithful to return to the ancient feminine dieties. Paz believes that this phenomenon of a return to the maternal womb is without a doubt one of the determining causes of the swift popularity of the cult of the Virgin. He tells us that the Indian goddesses were goddesses of fertility, linked to the cosmic rhythms, the vegetative processes, and agrarian rites. The Catholic Virgin is also the Mother (some Indian pilgrims still call her Guadalupe-Tonantzin), but contrary to the early goddesses, her principal attribute is not to watch over the fertility of the earth but to provide refuge for the unfortunate. The Mexican Virgin, according to Paz, is the consolation of the poor, the shield of the weak, the help of the oppressed. "In sum, she is the mother of orphans." All men are born disinherited and their true condition is orphanhood, writes Paz, but this is particularly true among the Indians and the poor in Mexico.[48]

If all men are born disinherited and their true condition is orphanhood, then it would seem that there is no physical connection between man and man, only the intermediary, woman. But it is not women who disinherit; it is the male lineage that determines inheritance in most cultures. It is the man who decides to give a child a name. The bastard child becomes the son of a bitch, angry at that mysterious father, comforted by the unwanted mother, and driven to a certain masculinity of acceptance. This is a language among men where once again the woman is peripheral.

Nevertheless, there seems to be a certain mysticism centered around women. Just as mother nature is to be tamed, so must women. As Mother Earth gives life, so does woman. The male must conquer nature. In this he is one with himself. This creates a bond of masculinity among men that women cannot penetrate. At the same time men have been mystified by the life-giving nature of women. How befitting that the savior of mankind should be born of a virgin. According to Paz, in reality all Mexicans are born of a virgin because they all are orphans and disinherited. Is this, then, a result of the conquest and their disinherited claim to masculine victory?

This results in an especially cruel interpretation of the female in the Mexican mentality. Paz says that in a certain sense all Mexicans, by the simple fact of being born of woman, are hijos de la chingada, sons of Eve, or Malinche. But the singularity of the Mexican resides, according to Paz, in his violent, sarcastic humiliation of the mother and his no less violent affirmation of the father. Paz writes that there is a special admiration for the father, which is expressed when men want to show their superiority by the pronounement "I am your Father." The question of origins, then, is at the core of the Mexican's anxiety and anguish.[49]

The Chicano has little access to origins. He lives in a country where he feels and displays cultural remnants while not wholly understanding their source. While the Mexican may at least examine the effects of the causes of his history, the Mexican American is barely cognizant of the effects. He tries to distinguish them within a maze of cultural conflict to determine which are truly of Mexican origin, Anglo origin, or a mixture of them both. Those that he determines to be Mexican must be verified and understood from the resources of Mexican scholarship, which is outside his immediate experience. It is difficult for him to resolve the compounded effects of Mexican history and the contemporary experience of the Chicano in relation to the Chicana woman.

Perhaps the solution can be found in Harris's work. If sexism is universal and stems from man's natural need to survive, contemporary groups, regardless of their psychological and physical defeats, can study sexism in its most primitive form. While Harris's theory holds that anatomy destines males to be trained to be fierce and aggressive if there is war, it denies that anatomy or genes or instinct or anything else makes war inevitable. Merely because all human beings in the world today and in the known past have lived in war-making sexist societies or societies affected by war-making sexist societies is not reason enough, concludes Harris, to cast human nature in the image of the savage characteristics required for war. "The fact that warfare and sexism have played and continue to play such prominent roles in human affairs does not mean they must continue to do so for all time."[50]

Harris suggests that the development of safe contraceptive methods has eliminated the need for warfare as a form of population control. He also argues that as military technology becomes more and more computerized and as hand-to-hand combat becomes obsolete, women may very well achieve full sexual parity. Harris sees no reason to doubt that sexism will eventually die out, provided, of course, that our culture does not die out first. If it does, he claims, it will not be the fault of our genes but of our intelligence.[51]

If Harris is correct and sexism can be eliminated, then my thesis holds that colonialism, neocolonialism, and racism, too, can be eliminated. However, no form of discrimination can be overcome without attacking it at its source—sexism. Chicanos argue that Chicana feminism will lead to the destruction of the family and, thus, Chicano culture. This need not be so. As a matter of fact, Chicana feminism may well provide the vehicle for serious scholarship, cultural analysis, and group self-criticism. If Chicano males can free themselves of the phantasms of the past and their sexist causes and effects, will and intelligence can guide their lives instead and Chicano people will survive.

NOTES

1. A description of the conquest and the Spanish defeat of the Mexican Indians is contained in the original Spanish version of Bernal Diaz del Castillo's Historia de la conquista de Nueva España (Mexico: Editorial Porrua, 1974); and the English translation, Bernal Diaz del Castillo, The Discovery and Conquest of Mexico, trans. A. P. Maudslay (New York: Farrar, Straus, and Giroux, 1973).

2. Funk & Wagnalls Standard College Dictionary, 6th ed., California State Series, s.v. "colonialism."

3. Rudy Acuna, A Mexican American Chronicle (New York: American, 1971), p. 54.

4. Beverly Lindsay discusses W. E. B. DuBois in Chapter 1. Her reference is W. E. B. DuBois, Color and Democracy: Colonies and Peace (New York: Harcourt, Brace, 1945), p. 130.

5. Diaz del Castillo, Discovery and Conquest of Mexico, p. 454.

6. Octavio Paz, "The Sons of Malinche," in Introduction to Chicano Studies, ed. Livie Isauro Duran and H. Russell Bernard (New York: Macmillan, 1973), p. 27.

7. Ibid., p. 27.

8. Ibid., p. 26.

9. Ibid., p. 26.

10. Susan Brownmiller, Against Our Will (New York: Simon and Schuster, 1975).

11. Marvin Harris, "Why Men Dominate Women," New York Times Magazine, November 13, 1977, p. 115.

12. Ibid., pp. 116, 117.

13. Ibid., pp. 117, 118.

14. Paz, "Sons of Malinche," pp. 27, 28.

15. Rogelio Diaz Guerrero, Estudios de la psicología del Mexicano (Mexico: Editorial Trillas, 1972), pp. 23-38.

16. Paz, "Sons of Malinche," p. 27.

17. Armando Rendon, Chicano Manifesto (New York: Collier, 1971), pp. 96, 97.

18. Paz, "Sons of Malinche," p. 24.

19. Michael Coe, "The Post-Classic Period: The Aztec Empire," in Introduction to Chicano Studies, ed. Livie Isauro Duran and H. Russell Bernard (New York: Macmillan, 1973), p. 64.

20. Ibid., p. 73.

21. Flor Saiz, "La Chicana," 1973, pp. 11-15.

22. Diaz del Castillo, Discovery and Conquest of Mexico, p. 64.

23. Ibid., p. 66.

24. Saiz, "La Chicana," pp. 11-15.

25. Diaz del Castillo, Discovery and Conquest of Mexico, pp. 66, 67.

26. Saiz, "La Chicana," pp. 11-15.

27. Paz, "Sons of Malinche," pp. 20, 21.

28. Ibid., p. 21.

29. Juan Rulfo, Pedro Paramo (Mexico: Fondo de Cultura Económico, 1971).

30. Paz, "Sons of Malinche," pp. 21, 22.

31. Ibid., p. 22.

32. Rendon, Chicano Manifesto, p. 184.

33. Saiz, "La Chicana," pp. 42, 43.

34. Antonia Castaneda Shular, Tomás Ybarra-Fausto, and Joseph Sommers, Literature chicana, texto y contexto (Englewood Cliffs, N.J.: Prentice-Hall), pp. 8, 9.

35. Noemi Atamoros, Sor Juana Ines de la Cruz y La Ciudad de México (Mexico City: Colección Popular Ciudad de México, 1975), pp. 90-92.

36. Diaz Guerrero, Estudios de la psicología del Mexicano, pp. 23-38.

37. Nancie L. Gonzales, The Spanish Americans of New Mexico: A Distinctive Heritage, Mexican American Study Project Advance Report 9 (Los Angeles: University of California Press, September 1967), p. 52.

38. Paz, "Sons of Malinche," p. 28.

39. For a discussion of Freire's ideas on fear of freedom and man's "histricity" see Paulo Freire, Pedagogy of the Oppressed (New York: Seabury Press, 1970).

40. Paz, "Sons of Malinche," p. 19.

41. Samuel Ramos, "Psychoanalysis of the Mexican," in Introduction to Chicano Studies, ed. Livie Isauro Duran and H. Russell Bernard (New York: Macmillan, 1973), p. 242.

42. Ibid., p. 245.

43. Bill Waters, "Mexico Moscow Oil Stymied by Gringo Stomp," Arizona Daily Star, June 11, 1978, p. 3F.

44. Joan W. Moore, "Colonialism: The Case of the Mexican American," in Introduction to Chicano Studies, ed. Livie Isauro Duran and H. Russell Bernard (New York: Macmillan, 1973), p. 364.

45. Ibid., p. 370.

46. Ibid.

47. Ibid., p. 371.

48. Paz, "Sons of Malinche," p. 26.
49. Ibid., pp. 23, 24.
50. Harris, "Why Men Dominate Women," p. 123.
51. Ibid.

REFERENCES

Acuna, Rudy. A Mexican American Chronicle. New York: American, 1971.

Atamoros, Noemi. Sor Juana Ines de la Cruz y La Ciudad de México. Mexico: Colección Popular Ciudad de México, 1975.

Bastide, Roger. Applied Anthropology. New York: Harper Torchbooks, 1973.

Brownmiller, Susan. Against Our Will. New York: Simon and Schuster, 1975.

Diaz del Castillo, Bernal. The Discovery and Conquest of Mexico. New York: Farrar, Straus, and Giroux, 1973.

Diaz Guerrero, Rogelio. Estudios de la psicología del Mexicano. Mexico: Editorial Trillas, 1972.

DuBois, W. E. B. Color and Democracy: Colonies and Peace. New York: Harcourt, Brace, 1945.

Duran, Livie Isauro, and H. Russell Bernard, eds. Introduction to Chicano Studies. New York: Macmillan, 1973.

Freire, Paulo. Pedagogy of the Oppressed. New York: Seabury Press, 1970.

Gonzales, L. Nancie. The Spanish Americans of New Mexico: A Distinctive Heritage, Mexican American Study Project Advance Report 9. Los Angeles: University of California Press, September 1967.

Harris, Marvin. Cannibals and Kings. New York: Random House, 1977.

Paz, Octavio. The Labyrinth of Solitude. New York: Grove Press, 1961.

Rendon, Armando. Chicano Manifesto. New York: Collier, 1971.

Rulfo, Juan. Pedro Paramo. Mexico: Fondo de Cultura Económica, 1971.

Saiz, Flor. "La Chicana," 1973.

Shular, Antonio Castañeda, Tomás Ybarra-Fausto, and Joseph Sommers. Literatura chicana, texto y contexto. Englewood Cliffs, N.J.: Prentice-Hall, 1972.

Waters, Bill. "Mexico Moscow Oil Stymied by Gringo Stomp." Arizona Daily Star, June 11, 1978.

12
THE BLACK WOMAN:
LIBERATED OR OPPRESSED?

Gwendolyn Randall Puryear

THE BLACK WOMAN
IN THE ECONOMIC MARKET

Economic oppression is a major concern of colonized people throughout the world. The United States is no exception. Note that economic concerns are major issues in both the Civil Rights and Women's Liberation movements in the United States. Consequently, an accurate perception of any group of people in society must incorporate economic issues. The economic position of the Black woman in the United States will be reviewed by examining labor force participation rates, reasons for work, work remuneration, and the nature of occupations entered.

It has been contended that Black women are disproportionately represented in the labor force and that this overrepresentation is an indication of favored position in the job market. An examination of labor statistics indicates that there is indeed a large number of Black female workers. In 1978, for example, there were over 5 million minority women 16 years of age or older in the civilian labor force. Of all nonwhite women 16 years of age or older, 53.3 percent were in the civilian labor force, while the percentage was 49.5 percent for white women. [1]

The gap between Black and white women in labor force participation rates, however, has narrowed markedly. In past decades participation rates for Black women were as much as 12 percentage points higher than for white women. In 1976 the difference between the two groups was only 3 percentage points. Black females' participation rates have shown little change over the last ten years, but the rates for white women have risen at a slow but steady pace. [2]

Janice Gump examined employment rates for Black and white women for the decades of 1890 through 1970 (excluding 1910) and 1974

251

and concluded: "Black women have always worked more than white women, and though labor force participation has increased for both groups, the increment has been dramatic only for white women."[3]

Labor force participation alone is no indication of favored position in the economic market. Other factors must be considered. When work remuneration is examined, it becomes evident that the Black woman holds no enviable position. She, like her white counterpart, earns substantially less than men, either Black or white. And although the earnings gap has narrowed appreciably, fully employed Black women continue to earn less than white women. In 1977 Black women who worked year round at full-time jobs had a median earnings income of $8,290—93 percent of that of white women, 78 percent of that of Black men, and 54 percent of that of white men.[4]

In addition to holding the least enviable position in terms of work remuneration, Black women are most affected by unemployment. In 1978 the unemployment rate for women was 7.2 percent compared with 5.2 percent for men. The rate for Blacks was 12.6 percent, compared with 5.2 percent for whites. Black women had a jobless rate of 13.7 percent.[5] An examination of occupations entered again highlights the constraints on the Black woman in the economic market:

> Although the disadvantaged economic status of women and minority groups can be blamed partly on high unemployment, it is also associated with their underrepresentation in better paying jobs. While half of all white men are in professional, managerial, or skilled craft occupations—those paying relatively high wages—less than one-fourth of white women and about 30 percent of minority men and 15 percent of minority women are so employed.[6]

Nonwhite women workers tend to be more heavily concentrated in service occupations (including private household worker) than are white women—33 and 19 percent, respectively, in 1978.[7] Since 1960, however, significant changes have occurred in the occupational distribution of minority women. The proportion of minority women in professional and technical occupations increased from 7 percent to over 14 percent between 1960 and 1976; the proportion employed as clerical workers increased from 9 to 26 percent. The percentage of private household workers, however, dropped from 35 to 9 percent. These changes have greatly contributed to the improvement in salaries of minority women.[8]

At this point, some clarification in terminology is necessary. The Bureau of Labor Statistics uses the terms White and Black and Other to describe the race of workers. In this chapter, the "Black and Other" category is referred to as nonwhite or minority for purposes of brevity. It includes all persons who identified themselves in the enumeration process of the 1970 census to be other than white. At the time of the 1970 census, 89 percent of the "Black and Other" population group were Black; the remainder were American Indians, Alaskan Natives, Asian and Pacific Islanders, and all other nonwhite groups. The term Black is used when the data refer exclusively to the Black population. According to the 1970 census, approximately 96 percent of the Hispanic population is white. Therefore, persons of Hispanic origin are included in the white population.

It should be pointed out that most minority race women employed in professional occupations are concentrated in the areas of teaching or nursing, occupations traditional for women and generally low-paid professions. When other professional occupations are examined, the Black woman is greatly underrepresented. In 1978 only 2.9 percent of all employed minority race women were employed as administrators or managers; this is about half the proportion of white women (6.5 percent) in that occupational group. [9]

Compared with Black men in professional occupations, a disproportionate number of Black women are found to work in lower-status professions. Patricia Gurin and Anne Pruitt compared the proportion of Black women and Black men in the six highest paying professions in 1970 and found that more Black men than women were doctors, lawyers, nonhealth technical professionals, engineers, and physical and social scientists. The only area in which Black women had achieved parity with Black men was college teaching. Summarizing this data as well as data on occupational and income standards for men and women, they noted that fewer Black women work in the top professions (and earn the least) of the four sex and race groups. [10] Their conclusion mirrors that of Gump who noted that within the professional occupations, Black women are concentrated in fewer professions than are Black men, white women, or white men. [11]

Why then is there this erroneous assumption that Black women hold a favored position in the labor market? Gurin and Pruitt explained that the typical presentations of sex and race differentials in wages and occupational position are partly responsible. This distortion, they noted, has occurred because sex and race discrimination have been treated as totally separate phenomena, with analyses of race discrimination comparing the earnings and job classifications of Blacks and whites, controlling sex, showing that Black men experience more discrimination than Black women. Likewise, analyses of discrimination by sex compare the earnings of men and women, controlling race, and generally show that Black women experience less discrimination than white women. These relative comparisons of race discrimination between men and women and sex discrimination between Blacks and whites have resulted in a distorted depiction of the employment status of Black women. An accurate picture depends on using white men as the normative group for all comparisons. [12]

Gurin and Pruitt also noted that wage comparisons of Black and white women typically have not been presented with work history adjustments, again distorting the picture of the Black woman's position in the labor force. They noted that by controlling number of weeks of employment in a given year the comparisons of Black and white women show evidence of race discrimination at every level of education in every age cohort. This is in contrast to the usual picture (not controlling for work history) in which income parity between white and Black women is reached at the high school graduation level and in which Black women with at least some college earned more than comparably educated white women:

> Among women 25 to 34 years of age the following reversals occur by controlling for number of weeks of employment. With one to three years of college, black women earned $168 more than white women when amount of employment was not controlled but $180 less when full time workers were compared. With four years of college black women earned $235 less instead of $215 more than white women when weeks of employment was controlled. And even with education beyond the baccalaureate degree, black women earned $171 less instead of the $355 more in the usual uncontrolled comparisons. [13]

It is important to examine the myth of the Black woman's favored position in the labor market in its proper perspective. Perpetuating this myth has served only to uphold the patriarchal system dominated by white males. It has caused internal strife among Blacks (men against women) and women (Black against white). The fact is that the Black woman holds no favored position in the marketplace. She is most oppressed, experiencing both sex and race discrimination.

In order to assess accurately the economic status of the Black woman and relate her market position to sex role issues, it is necessary to understand the reasons for the Black woman's past and continued presence in the labor force. It is also important lest we infer that Black women's labor force participation indicates special freedom or opportunity:

> Black women have long been accustomed to working outside the home. . . . To marry was not to become fully employed as a housewife as was the case for many white women. Black women were expected to continue to work because, in a society that measured a black worker's worth as less than

that of whites, it was necessary that both partners be employed to make ends meet. [14]

The Black woman works because she must. The income that
she provides is crucial to the family's well-being. Two-parent Black
families with wives in the labor force had a median income of $15,703
in 1976, 82 percent of the median income ($19,047) of similar white
families. Black husband-wife families without wives in the labor force
had a median income of only $9,219, 65 percent of the median income
($14,288) of their white counterpart. [15]

Another major factor indicating the importance of the Black
woman's income is the large proportion of Black families headed by
women. In 1977, 39 percent of all Black families were headed by
women compared with 12 percent of all white families. Moreover,
the median income of a Black family headed by a woman was only
$5,598 in 1977, less than half of the poverty level for a nonfarm family
of four ($6,191). In 1977 Black families headed by women were almost
twice as likely to have incomes below the poverty level as similar
white families (51 and 24 percent, respectively). Among families
headed by women working full-time year round, the incidence of poverty was more than four times greater for Black families (16.2 percent) than for white families (3.6 percent). [16]

The National Urban League in their publication The State of
Black America 1978 stated that among adult workers in the United
States, Black women in general and Black female family heads in particular are receiving the brunt of the continuing recession/depression.
Yet, current government policies fail to assign high priority or ur-
gency to their employment situation. [17] Again the conclusion reached
is that Black women hold no favored position in the marketplace.

SEX ROLE CONSIDERATIONS

The labor force participation rates of Black women have been
used as an indicator of liberated sex role ideology. The preceding
statistics, however, clearly illustrate that a major reason for Black
female employment is necessity—not liberated sex role ideology,
special freedom, or need to achieve. It should not be assumed that
labor force participation is of no importance when examining the sex
roles assumed by Black women. In fact, the political and economic
oppression in the United States that made it necessary for the Black
woman to work was probably a major factor in shaping her sex role.
However, labor force participation is not the only factor involved,
nor does it imply liberated sex role ideology. In order to assess accurately the sex role ideology of the Black woman, it is necessary to

examine the relationship between work and the woman's role as well as other factors such as aspirations and expectations.

Work outside the home has been an integral function for Black women since they were brought to the United States. Moreover, women played a crucial role in the economy of West African society through their active involvement in both agriculture and the retailing of merchandise. [18] Since the largest group of slaves was brought to the United States from West Africa, it is most probable that the sex role of the Black American woman was highly influenced by that of her West African predecessor.

For the Black woman in the United States, then, work outside the home was and still is a vital function. Gump noted:

> The historical fact of the black woman's labor efforts in this country provides partial explanation for why her sex role ideology may be different. For the black woman work has been neither opportunity nor novelty. . . . Work outside the home is not exceptional to the role of wife or mother but rather is an integral and accepted part of what it may mean to be a black woman. [19]

Given the place of work in the sex role ideology of the Black woman, it is no surprise that a large percentage of Black women are committed to a lifetime of work. In a study examining dimensions of career choice, motivational factors, attitudes toward career choice, commitment, and other sex role issues, Martha Mednick and Gwendolyn Randall Puryear collected data from approximately 300 college senior and sophomore women at five predominantly Black schools in the southeastern and Middle Atlantic States. The high level of commitment to work was revealed in answers to the question: "When would you return to work after children?" By the time their children reached first grade, 87 percent of the women expected to return to work, or in other words, did not plan to remain absent from the labor market while they had children. [20] These findings mirror those of other investigators of Black women. [21]

The high level of commitment to work found in studies with Black women is in marked contrast to findings on the future plans of white women. Joseph Fichter, in his study of college graduates, found that almost one-half (47 percent) of the Black women, compared with one-fourth (24 percent) of the white women wanted to continue to work after marriage, combining a family with a career or steady job. More white (31 percent) than Black (13 percent) women wanted to work only after their children were grown. [22]

In a five-year study of the educational and labor market experiences of young women, over 7,000 white and 1,000 Black women aged

18 to 24 years were asked the following question: "Now I'd like for you to think about a family where there is a mother, a father who works full time, and several children under school age. A trusted relative who can care for the children lives nearby. In this family situation, how do you feel about the mother taking a full-time job outside the house?"[23] Results showed that more Black than white women held permissive attitudes toward the mother's working, and nearly twice as many white (27 percent) as Black women (15 percent) were opposed. The authors suggested that these differences between Black and white women reflected rather deeply rooted variations in the role expectations of young women growing up in the two communities.

Differences in role expectations were also found by John H. Scanzoni in his national study of 3,096 men and women. He found that Black women were significantly more modern than their white counterpart on "traditional mother role" orientation. Modernity was assessed by responses to questions such as: "Do you think that a working mother can establish just as warm and secure relationship with her children as a mother who does not work?" and "Do you feel a preschool child is likely to suffer if the mother works?"[24]

Janice Gump and Wendell Rivers found that the proportion of Black women who planned to combine full-time employment with the traditional role of wife and mother was approximately twice that of white women.[25] Note that U.S. Department of Labor statistics indicate greater labor force participation for minority mothers. In 1978, 67.6 percent of minority women with children 6 to 17 years of age were workers, as were more than half (55.4 percent) of those with children under 6. For white women comparable rates were 58.9 and 41 percent, respectively.[26]

Congruent with their plans for combining roles, Black women were also more likely than their white counterparts to see full-time employment and the traditional role of wife and mother as compatible life goals.[27] This absence of conflict or minimal conflict around the marriage-career choice was also found in the Mednick and Puryear study of Black college women. Approximately 72 percent of the women sampled indicated an absence of marriage-career conflict.[28]

Another area typically examined to assess sex role conflicts is that of fear of success. Matina Horner described fear of success as a psychological barrier to achievement in women.[29] She defined this construct as a

> stable characteristic of personality acquired early in life in conjunction with sex-role standards. It is conceived as a disposition (a) to feel uncomfortable when successful in competitive (aggressive) achievement situations because such behavior is inconsistent with one's femininity, an inter-

nal standard, (b) to expect or become concerned about social rejection following success.[30]

Horner found that women showed significantly more fear of success imagery than men when responding to Thematic Apperception Test (TAT) cues.[31] In fact, 65 percent of the women as compared with 10 percent of the men showed such imagery in their fantasy productions. Recent studies have also demonstrated high fear of success levels for white college women.[32]

Studies with Black women have generally found low levels of fear of success imagery relative to that generally found for white women.[33] These findings have usually been interpreted as an indication that success does not arouse negative concerns for Black women and that success is less threatening to them. However, in one of the first studies appearing since 1970, which directly compared Black and white women, Mednick and Puryear found no significant race differences in fear of success.[34] The level of fear of success imagery for Black women was the same as that found in previous studies, but there was a significantly lower level of fear of success for white women than that found earlier. These findings seem to indicate that Black women, now as in the past, experience very little role conflict in achievement or success situations. White women, on the other hand, appear to be accommodating intellectual mastery and professional achievement into their options as women, experiencing much less conflict than in the past. This change can probably be attributed to the Women's Liberation movement as well as to economic pressures in U.S. society, which have made employment for white women both acceptable and necessary in many households.

Gurin and Pruitt have also noted a reduction in differences between Black and white women. They found an increase in the number of white women who expect to continue working after they have children. Their data, collected in 1971 from women attending the University of Michigan and in 1970 from women at predominantly Black colleges, showed that the plans of Black and white senior women were reasonably similar. Virtually all of both groups expected to work after getting married but before having children. In addition, close to the same proportion of both groups (50 percent Black and 42 percent white) stated that they expected to work after having children as well.[35] Again, however, Black women have not changed appreciably. It is the white woman who has changed. She has been able to incorporate work as one of several options available to her.

When attempting to assess whether the Black woman is "liberated," we again must conclude that she is not. Her work involvement evolves, not from any liberal sex role ideology, but from necessity. Concomitant with the necessity for work, the Black woman's role incorporates that of worker, and she feels little if any marriage-career conflict. The white woman in this instance seems to be becoming liberated in that the Women's Liberation movement and current economic pressures have provided her with options—options to stay at home and carry out the traditional role and/or to work outside the home if she so desires. This option has not been and still is not available to the majority of Black women. They must work and they see this work in terms of responsibility—not self-fulfillment. Support for this view can be found in several studies. B. F. Turner found that for Black college women high career expectations were related to what appeared to be the women's perceptions of the expectations of men they knew, their parents, and other significant persons in their lives. [36] Gump found that white women were significantly more adopting of the view that identity, a sense of self-worth, and satisfaction would result from the woman's pursuit of her own abilities rather than from fostering the interests and abilities of those emotionally close to her. She suggested that Black women's high expectations for work derive not so much from an achievement ethic as from a sense of responsibility—this sense of responsibility being deeply ingrained in Black female sex role ideology, a responsibility that includes economic provision for the family as well as provision of the more traditional functions. [37]

Gump further suggested that this sense of responsibility has often become detached from economic necessity. Although most Black women who work must do so in order to ensure the survival of the family, the sense of responsibility—of having to give in this manner —remains, even when the need to work in an absolute sense is no longer present. This sense of responsibility, Gump suggested, has become autonomous.

This sense of responsibility or "other" orientation was also found in the Mednick and Puryear study of Black college women. When asked why they would return to work after having children, the majority of the women gave other-oriented responses such as "to help my people" or for "financial reasons." An example of a self-oriented response would be "for self-fulfillment." This absence of concern for self or self-fulfillment was also seen when the women were asked about the type of satisfaction their future career would offer. Very few women made responses relating to self-fulfillment. [38]

We see then that, although the sex role ideology of the Black woman includes a strong commitment to work, she has a strong sense of responsibility to the needs of her family and sees her role in terms of meeting those needs. It should be clear that the Black woman holds no radical sex role ideology. In fact, she is very traditional in her educational and occupational aspirations, expectancies, and motivations, as well as in her attitude about the woman's role, marriage, and children.

The traditionality of the Black woman's aspirations and expectancies are illustrated in a study by Gurin and her colleagues. They examined motivations and aspirations of Black students attending ten predominantly Black colleges in the South in 1964/65 and conducted a repeat study of students attending six of the original colleges in the spring of 1970. They found sex differences in educational expectancies, with women being less certain than men that they would eventually go to graduate or professional school. Moreover, fewer women than men expected to go immediately after college. These differences in educational expectancy were evident at the senior level but not at the freshman level. This was attributed to the fact that the educational expectancies women held as freshmen decreased more than the expectancies held by men. Sex differences were evident in degree plans, with more women than men seeing the master's degree as terminal. More men gave the doctoral or professional degrees as their goal. These differences in degree plans were observed at the freshman and senior levels. The researchers concluded that in terms of educational aspirations, Black women held lower expectations than did Black men.[39]

Patricia Gurin and Edgar Epps examined occupational attractiveness and choices and found striking sex differences. They asked Black college students to judge 150 occupations and found that men and women held identical opinions on which occupations carried the greatest prestige, demanded the most ability, and were most difficult for Blacks to enter because of racial discrimination. They differed, however, on which jobs would be most personally desirable. Both men and women agreed that the jobs judged by men to be most desirable (masculine occupations) accorded greater prestige and demanded greater ability than did the jobs women found most desirable (feminine occupations). The jobs women identified as most desirable were viewed by both men and women as according less status and requiring less ability and talent than the jobs men found most attractive. These sex differences were also found in actual job choices—women's job choices carried significantly lower prestige and ability demands and fell within more traditional areas of achievement for Blacks. They found this pattern of lower aspirations among women in every college that participated in the study and as marked in 1970 as in 1964.[40]

The traditionality of Black women's career choices has been found in other studies. In one such study[41] career choice was categorized as traditional or innovative, with traditionality defined as the proportion of women in a field. Those fields having fewer than 30 percent women were designated nontraditional. Of the group as a whole, 32 percent were role innovators. However, the pattern of career choice varied drastically from school to school. In one school (a state school in a Middle Atlantic state), a highly traditional pattern was seen. At the other extreme was the group at a large urban university with 58 percent responding innovatively. It is of interest that an earlier study conducted at this school and data from the American Council on Education Freshman Survey Questionnaire revealed a very similar proportion of innovative women. The second most innovative group attended a small private women's college.

The overall pattern appeared to indicate greater innovativeness on the part of women in this study than those reported in the study by Gurin and D. Katz[42] or in studies of white women.[43] The great variation from school to school, however, cautioned against generalizing about Black college women as a homogenous population in this regard. Moreover, the concentration of innovators in only two of the five schools led the authors to concur basically with previous research— that when it comes to career choice, the Black woman tends to aspire to traditionally female occupations.

The traditionality of the Black woman in terms of occupational aspirations is also seen in the openness with which she considers future jobs. Gurin and Epps found that Black college women indicated that they had seriously considered significantly fewer occupations than men and that the occupations listed by women reflected a narrower range of prestige, ability, and nontraditionality than those of the men. They concluded that women's job and educational horizons were more foreclosed and less open to the influence and potential challenge offered by the college experience.[44] Comparing these results with those from similar studies with white students, Gurin and Pruitt reported that the whole pattern of sex differences in aspirations was very similar and that women, both Black and white, are influenced by conventional views of appropriate educational and occupational roles for women.[45]

The conventional sex role ideology held by the Black woman is also seen in her definition of the woman's role. A large number of Black women indicate that they would prefer to stay home and not work, work only before the birth of children, or only after their children are grown.[46] In a survey of college freshmen, more Black (30.4 percent) than white (19.6 percent) women agreed strongly with the statement: "The activities of married women are best confined to the home and family."[47] Moreover, in a survey in which college women were asked to respond to an open-ended question about the role of Black women, the largest proportion of the sample stressed the idea of being in a supportive role to their men.[48]

Gump also noted the traditional sex role ideology of the Black woman. In her 1972 study of college women she found that Black women significantly more than white women endorsed the position that identity and happiness would derive from pursuit of the traditional role. She cited the following example: "No matter how successful a woman may be in utilizing her intelligence and creativity she can never know true happiness unless she marries and has a family."[49]

It appears, then, that the Black woman has been very much affected by sex role stereotypes and constraints. Her occupational and educational choices and aspirations are those traditional for women. Her perception of the woman's role is that of wife and mother and being in a supportive role to the man—very traditional indeed. The only area in which the Black woman was shown to differ appreciably from the traditional white woman's role was that of labor force participation and commitment to work. This commitment to work must be differentiated from commitment to career. Black women seem to be committed to a lifetime of work but not to career. They seem to be in the labor market primarily to obtain money. This is in contrast to career, which connotes a profession, a desire for achievement, self-development, and self-fulfillment. The Black woman's strong commitment to work does not come from a desire to fulfill herself or from a feminist ideology, as it is assumed to represent when held by white women. The Black woman's expectations for employment and actual participation in the labor force do not so much reflect an embracing of the achievement ethic but a realistic assessment of survival needs and a sense of responsibility to fulfill those needs.

The Black woman is very traditional indeed in terms of her sex role ideology. Her role, however, because of history and necessity, is broader than that of her white counterpart, encompassing both labor force participation and a commitment to work. The Black woman, however, has never played the role of the traditional woman in U.S. society—the housewife. She still does not have the option because, as Mae C. King noted, the exercise of the traditional housewife role by white women is contingent upon the assumption by white males of the traditional breadwinner role. U.S. society has systematically denied Black men the job opportunities necessary to fulfill this "American male" role, and it has, consequently, not been possible for Black women to assume the housewife role. The realization of "American femininity" for the Black woman was contingent upon the actualization of "American masculinity" for the Black man. [50]

King noted further that the roles of Black men and women have differed little in this society since oppression is no respecter of sexes. Today Black women continue to shoulder responsibilities that are considered male in white U.S. society:

> Her race shaped her role, and America contemptuously
> withheld from her the gauze of "American femininity."
> She, like her male companion, was forced to serve the
> American order in any manner that the white rulers
> deemed essential for the maintenance of a system which
> rewarded whites and degraded blacks. Any variation in
> the tasks performed by male and female was hardly based

on consideration of or respect for the "femaleness" of the black woman. In other words, the black woman was "defeminized" by the American system and was routinely forced to assume responsibilities that were otherwise incompatible with "woman's place."[51]

PSYCHOLOGICAL ISSUES
AFFECTING THE BLACK WOMAN

While the Black woman is defeminized and forced to assume responsibilities usually defined as within the male domain, she is also seen as the personification of the rejected domestic component of woman—the antithesis of the idealized "ultrafeminine" woman in society.[52]

To see herself portrayed as the antithesis of the ultrafeminine woman in society has exacted a heavy toll on the Black woman. As if this were not enough, the Black woman has also been criticized and ostracized for the strength and fortitude that she was required to possess for survival in a hostile society.

The 1960s and early 1970s were times of ferment for Black men and women but also a time of attack upon the Black woman from the establishment and from within her own group. One form was that taken by Daniel Moynihan in his thesis on the Black matriarch; one expression was the exhortation by Black males that she step aside. These two movements will be examined briefly and an effort made to determine their effect on the Black woman.

The term matriarch is usually negatively toned and implies anything from successful, dominant and/or masculine to powerful and castrating. The two major overlapping definitions generally employed, however, focus primarily upon family power or authority vested in females in the presence or absence of male heads or simply upon the sex of the family head. By the latter definition, some white and Black families are matriarchal and most Black families, at least during this century, have been headed by males.[53] The Black woman's position in this society, relative to that of the Black man in occupations entered and work remuneration, was documented in preceding pages, and the Black man was found to be in the better position. When matriarchy is viewed in terms of family power, however, other factors must be considered and the conclusion is not as clear-cut.

Deloris Mack, studying patterns of spouse power in Black and white families, noted that research has failed to yield consistent results, partly because of differences in indexes used and partly because of failure to deal adequately with the class factor. She used several different indexes of power and found class differences in two out of three power situations examined. She found no comparable racial differences. [54] Jacquelyne Jackson, summarizing findings on spouse power, stated that insufficient data are available to make definitive statements about the patterns of spouse power for all Black families. However, available data suggest that in husband-wife families, most lower socioeconomic status (SES) and upper SES tend to be patriarchal, while most middle SES tends to be egalitarian. [55]

As noted previously, many Black households are headed by women, and these families are faced with serious financial problems. Jackson noted that policy makers and authors discussing the Black family (for example, Moynihan)[56] regard the absence of a male head of household as the primary cause of poverty in female-headed families and see as the primary solution a male's presence as an economic provider and ultimate source of family authority and power. They emphasize Black male employment and income needs and ignore Black female unemployment and underemployment. [57] While increasing the number of male-headed households may be an ideal solution, the present state of affairs finds many Black female-headed households, and emphasis must be placed on removing the race and sex discrimination experienced by these women.

The National Urban League, in its publication The State of Black America 1978, stated:

> Current governmental employment policies fail to assign high priority or urgency to providing meaningful jobs to female heads of families, especially among minority groups. Most recommendations tend to center on youth or male breadwinners. Those that do revolve about female heads of families almost totally focus on families that are already on welfare. Apparently, little attention is given to providing jobs to female family heads to prevent them from having to go on welfare in the first place. [58]

There must be a firm commitment to significantly improving the educational, occupational, and income status of Black women and men and, consequently, their families. Again, it is obvious that the Black woman is not liberated but oppressed. Robert Staples noted:

> But the matriarchy concept implies some advantage for women in the society. Instead of having any particular privileges under the slave system, Black women were, in reality, burdened with the dual role of laborer and mother. Here is the origin of her two-pronged oppression, which has.been labeled the notorious Black matriarchy. [59]

Although unfounded, the idea of the Black matriarch has been believed and perpetuated, consequently painting a negative portrait of the Black woman. Elizabeth F. Hood noted that their image is of critical concern to Black women in U.S. society. Yet

> history books, the media and scientific racism send out the stereotyped message: black women as matriarchs emasculate black men and thereby prevent the formulation of healthy black family and community structures. From these unhealthy families and pathological communities flow the diseases of poverty, low educational achievement, prostitution, drug abuse, and unemployment. This line of reasoning established the black woman as the "evil one," rather than the victim.[60]

Myths of Black women as matriarchs and emasculators of Black men were believed by Blacks and whites, men and women. Of greatest importance, however, is that these myths were accepted by Black women. As Michele Wallace noted, the Black woman is angry but paralyzed by her feeling that she has no right to be. She has attempted to be supportive of the Black man in all he has done, even that which has been abusive of her. This has created within the Black woman inestimable emotional devastation.[61]

Myths of the Black matriarchy also influenced the role Black women were requested to play in the Black Liberation movement. The rhetoric of many organizations in the 1960s and early 1970s was exhorting the Black woman to change, to redefine her role from a position of dominance and success to one more supportive and ancillary to that of the man. She was told that she must be more passive and traditionally female—that is, to accept the woman's role as defined in white middle-class terms. For example, the Student Nonviolent Coordinating Committee (SNCC), the Republic of New Africa, and other Black organizations were known to advocate a more domestic and secondary role for women.[62]

Although the rhetoric has been reduced, the effects on the Black woman have persisted. These ideas have caused many Black women, especially those involved in the Black Liberation movement, to reassess their roles and have engendered a great deal of conflict. One area in which this conflict is evident is that of fear of success. Puryear and Mednick found that women who ascribed to a militant philosophy exhibited more fear of success than nonmilitant women. Militancy was defined as degree of concern with the struggle for Black liberation. This finding indicated that achievement in intellectually competitive situations is associated with the anticipation of negative consequences for women concerned with the struggle for Black liberation. Moreover, the findings indicate that many Black women have been seriously affected by the questions concerning their achievement —was it at the expense of the achievement of the Black man and did it have negative consequences for the maintenance of the Black family?[63]

The Black woman indeed holds no favored position. Moreover, she is caught in the bind of being scorned for the role she has had to play for her survival and that of her family. She has been made to feel guilty and conflict-ridden for her limited achievements because of myths saying her progress was made at the expense of the progress of Black men.

Joyce Ladner noted that the Black woman has been considered liberated because she has not been privy to the protectiveness of society—of men—as has been the white woman.[64] But is this liberation? To be truly liberated would mean to have the option of protectiveness available when needed:

> For there are those who would assert too quickly the freedom of the black woman and they must be reminded of her bondage. If black women have not been subordinated, neither have they been cherished; if they have not been limited, neither have they been protected. If they have gained independence, they have done so at the great price of too little dependency.[65]

The Black woman, therefore, is by no means liberated. She is oppressed—more so than the white woman who has no element of racial oppression to contend with; the white woman who now has options —the option to fulfill herself at home or in the labor market. The Black woman has no options and will thus remain oppressed until race discrimination ceases and allows her man to support her and the Black family; until race discrimination ends and allows all Black people in this country, both male and female, to be equal and enjoy the full rights of human beings. This fact is one of the major reasons for the absence of large numbers of Black women in the Women's Liberation movement.

THE BLACK WOMAN AND WOMEN'S LIBERATION

The Black American woman has been reluctant to embrace the Women's Liberation movement. One reason is that many Black women see the alleviation of racial oppression as their major priority. This view has been expressed by several writers. Frances Lucas stated that obtaining liberation as a female is not the Black woman's first order of business; rather, it is obtaining liberation for her people.[66] Mary Dennison commented that an organized effort to "liberate" Black women is, at best, premature, for should we liberate her and leave Black men and children to their own salvation, each seeking his own road to freedom?[67] Nikki Giovanni made this point most elegantly when she stated: "Black people consider their first reality to be Black and given that reality we know from birth that we are going to be oppressed—man, woman or eunuch."[68]

The Black woman is also concerned that active involvement in the Women's Liberation movement would adversely affect her relationship with the Black man. She does not want to compete with the Black man who for so long was denied the privilege of caring for his wife and children. Ladner voiced this sentiment when she noted that Black men are not our enemy—it is the oppressive forces in the larger society that subjugate Black men, women, and children.[69]

Another very real factor influencing Black participation in the women's movement is that some of the major concerns of white women do not apply to their Black counterparts. And even those Black women who support the movement admit that many of the goals are class-bound. Addressing this issue, Robert Staples stated:

> At the root of the Black woman's rejection of the women's liberation movement are the different historical experiences she has encountered and the fact that forms of oppression that the white woman has suffered are symbolic and have never applied to Black women. Many white women, for instance, are protesting the sheltered lives they have led—being put on a pedestal and being confined to suburbia with all its gadgetry. But Black women historically were the sex objects that white men used in order to preserve the white woman's place on that pedestal.[70]

Many of the "freedoms" now sought by the white woman have for a long time been thrust upon her Black counterpart—not as "freedom" but as a burden. While white women have tired of being cherished and protected and choose to try their independence, many Black women long for these experiences. They already know independence and responsibility.

Although the large majority of Black women are not actively involved in the Women's Liberation movement, there is a significant group of Black women who are involved in, if not women's lib per se, a Black feminist movement. These women, however, accept a "limited sisterhood" with white women, fighting for equal pay for equal work, federally subsidized day care, the right to choose abortion, legal protection against domestic violence and rape, affirmative action in training programs and employment, more representation in the media, and entry into traditional male structures of the world of work.[71] These are major issues affecting all women.

In the final analysis, the oppressor in U.S. society is the patriarchal system run by the white male. This system is both racist and sexist, and Black women bear the brunt of oppression. Yet, they are termed liberated.

NOTES

1. U.S., Department of Labor, Bureau of Labor Statistics, Office of Current Employment Analysis, Employment and Earnings, vol. 26, no. 1 (Washington, D.C.: Government Printing Office, January 1979).

2. U.S., Department of Labor, Bureau of Labor Statistics, U.S. Working Women: A Databook (Washington, D.C.: Government Printing Office, 1977).

3. Janice Gump, "Reality and Myth: Employment and Sex Role Ideology in Black Women," in Psychology of Women: New Directions for Research, ed. Julia Sherman and Florence Denmark (New York: Psychological Dimensions, 1979, in press).

4. U.S., Department of Commerce, Bureau of the Census, Money, Income and Poverty Status of Families and Persons in the U.S., Advanced Report Series P-60, no. 116 (Washington, D.C.: Government Printing Office, 1978).

5. U.S., Department of Labor, Bureau of Labor Statistics, Employment and Earnings.

6. U.S., Commission on Civil Rights, The State of Civil Rights: 1977 (Washington, D.C.: Government Printing Office, 1977).

7. U.S., Department of Labor, Bureau of Labor Statistics, Employment and Earnings.

8. U.S., Department of Labor, Women's Bureau, Minority Women Workers: Statistical Overview (Washington, D.C.: Government Printing Office, 1977).

9. U.S., Department of Labor, Bureau of Labor Statistics, Employment and Earnings.

10. Patricia Gurin and Anne Pruitt, "Counseling Implications of Black Women's Market Position, Aspirations and Expectancies" (Paper presented at the meeting of the National Institute of Education's Conference on the Educational and Occupational Needs of Black Women, Washington, D.C., December 1975).

11. Gump, "Reality and Myth."

12. Gurin and Pruitt, "Counseling Implications."

13. Ibid., p. 3.

14. Deloris Aldridge, "Black Women in the Economic Market: A Battle Unfinished," Journal of Social and Behavioral Sciences 21 (1975): 50.

15. Robert B. Hill, "The Economic Status of Black Families and Children," in The State of Black America 1978, ed. the National Urban League (New York: National Urban League, 1978), pp. 21-39.

16. U.S., Department of Commerce, Bureau of the Census, Money, Income and Poverty Status.

17. Hill, "Economic Status."

18. For a detailed discussion, see Gump, "Reality and Myth"; and Melville Herskovits, The Myth of Negro Past (Boston: Beacon Press, 1958).

19. Gump, "Reality and Myth," p. 16.

20. Martha Mednick and Gwendolyn Randall Puryear, "Motivational and Personality Factors Related to Career Goals of Black College Women," Journal of Social and Behavioral Sciences 21 (1975): 1-30.

21. Joseph Fichter, Graduates of Predominantly Negro Colleges, Class of 1964, prepared for the National Institutes of Health, Contract PH 43-63-1173 (Washington, D.C.: Government Printing Office, 1967); and Janice Gump and Wendell Rivers, "A Consideration of Race in Efforts to End Sex Bias," in Issues of Sex Bias and Sex Fairness in Career Interest Measurement, ed. Esther E. Diamond (Washington, D.C.: Department of Health, Education and Welfare, National Institute of Education, Spring 1975).

22. Fichter, Graduates.

23. U.S., Department of Labor, Years for Decision: A Longitudinal Study of the Educational and Labor Market Experience of Young Women, vol. 1, Manpower Research Monograph no. 24 (Washington, D.C.: Government Printing Office, 1971), p. 34.

24. John H. Scanzoni, Sex Roles, Life Styles, and Childbearing (New York: Free Press, 1975), p. 51.

25. Gump and Rivers, "Consideration of Race."

26. U.S., Department of Labor, Bureau of Labor Statistics, Marital and Family Characteristics of the Labor Force (Press release no. USDL 78-638, Washington, D.C., March 1978).

27. Gump and Rivers, "Consideration of Race."

28. Mednick and Puryear, "Motivational and Personality Factors."

29. Matina Horner, "Sex Differences in Achievement Motivation and Performance in Competitive and Non-competitive Situations" (Ph.D. diss., University of Michigan, 1968).

30. Ibid., p. 22.

31. Ibid.; and Matina Horner, "Toward an Understanding of Achievement-Related Conflicts in Women," Journal of Social Issues 28 (1972): 157-75.

32. Lois Hoffman, "Fear of Success in Males and Females: 1965 and 1972," Journal of Consulting and Clinical Psychology 42 (1974): 353-58; and Lynn Monahan, Deanna Kuhn, and Phillip Shaver, "Intrapsychic versus Cultural Explanations of the 'Fear of Success' Motive," Journal of Personality and Social Psychology 29 (1974): 60-64.

33. Peter Weston and Martha Mednick, "Race, Social Class and the Motive to Avoid Success in Women," Journal of Cross-Cultural Psychology 1 (1970): 284-91; and Mednick and Puryear, "Motivational and Personality Factors."

34. Martha Mednick and Gwendolyn Randall Puryear, "Race and Fear of Success in College Women: 1968 and 1971," Journal of Consulting and Clinical Psychology 44 (1976): 787-89.

35. Gurin and Pruitt, "Counseling Implications."

36. B. F. Turner, "Socialization and Career Orientation among Black and White College Women," cited by Janice Gump, "Reality and Myth."

37. Janice Gump, "A Comparative Analysis of Black and White Women's Sex-Role Attitudes," Journal of Consulting and Clinical Psychology 43 (1975): 858-63; and Gump, "Reality and Myth."

38. Mednick and Puryear, "Motivational and Personality Factors."

39. Patricia Gurin and Edgar Epps, Black Consciousness, Identity and Achievement (New York: John Wiley and Sons, 1975).

40. Ibid.

41. Mednick and Puryear, "Motivational and Personality Factors."

42. Patricia Gurin and Daniel Katz, Motivation and Aspiration in the Negro College (Ann Arbor, Mich.: Institute for Social Research, 1966).

43. Sandra Tangri, "Role-Innovation in Occupational Choice among College Women" (Ph.D. diss., University of Michigan, 1969).

44. Gurin and Epps, Black Consciousness.

45. Gurin and Pruitt, "Counseling Implications."

46. Fichter, Graduates.

47. Gwendolyn Randall Puryear, "A Profile of Freshman Students at Howard University, Fall 1976," mimeographed (Washington, D.C.: Howard University, 1977).

48. Mednick and Puryear, "Motivational and Personality Factors."

49. Gump, "Comparative Analysis," p. 859.

50. Mae C. King, "Oppression and Power: The Unique Status of the Black Woman in the American Political System," Social Science Quarterly 56 (1975): 116-28.

51. Ibid., pp. 122-23.

52. Eldridge Cleaver, Soul on Ice (New York: Dell, 1968).

53. Jacquelyne Jackson, "A Critique of Lerner's Work on Black Women," Journal of Social and Behavioral Sciences 21 (1975): 63-89.

54. Deloris Mack, "The Power Relationship in Black Families and White Families," Journal of Personality and Social Psychology 30 (1974): 409-13.

55. Jackson, "Critique of Lerner's Work."

56. Daniel Moynihan, "The Negro Family, The Case for National Action," Report prepared for the Office of Planning and Research (Washington, D.C.: U.S. Government Printing Office).

57. Jackson, "Critique of Lerner's Work."

58. Hill, "Economic Status," p. 38.

59. Robert Staples, The Black Woman in America (Chicago: Nelson Hall, 1973), p. 14.

60. Elizabeth F. Hood, "Black Women, White Women: Separate Paths to Liberation," The Black Scholar 9 (1978): 45-56.

61. Michele Wallace, "Black Macho and the Myth of the Superwoman," Ms, January 1979, p. 87.

62. For a detailed discussion of the matter, see Staples, Black Woman in America.

63. Gwendolyn Randall Puryear and Martha S. Mednick, "Black Militancy, Affective Attachment, and Fear of Success," Journal of Consulting and Clinical Psychology 42 (1974): 263-66.

64. Joyce Ladner, Tomorrow's Tomorrow: The Black Woman (New York: Doubleday, 1971).

65. Gump and Rivers, "Consideration of Race," p. 134.

66. Frances Lucas, "Miles to Go Before We Sleep," Right to Treatment: The Magazine of the National Association for Mental Health, Spring 1975, pp. 14-16.

67. Mary Dennison, "Total Liberation," quoted in Staples, Black Woman in America.

68. Nikki Giovanni, as quoted in Helen King, "The Black Woman and Woman's Lib," Ebony 26 (March 1971): 75.

69. Ladner, Tomorrow's Tomorrow.

70. Staples, Black Woman in America, pp. 168-69.

71. Hood, "Black Women, White Women."

REFERENCES

Aldridge, Deloris. "Black Women in the Economic Market: A Battle Unfinished." Journal of Social and Behavioral Sciences 21 (1975): 48-62.

Cleaver, Eldridge. Soul on Ice. New York: Dell, 1968.

Dennison, Mary. "Total Liberation Comes Before New Roles." Quoted in Robert Staples, The Black Woman in America. Chicago: Nelson Hall, 1973.

Fichter, Joseph. Graduates of Predominantly Negro Colleges, Class of 1964. Prepared for the National Institutes of Health, Contract PH 43-63-1173. Washington, D.C.: Government Printing Office, 1967.

Gump, Janice. "A Comparative Analysis of Black and White Women's Sex-Role Attitudes." Journal of Consulting and Clinical Psychology 43 (1975): 858-63.

_____. "Reality and Myth: Employment and Sex Role Ideology in Black Women." In Psychology of Women: New Directions for Research, edited by Julia Sherman and Florence Denmark. New York: Psychological Dimensions, 1979, in press.

Gump, Janice, and Wendell Rivers. "A Consideration of Race in Efforts to End Sex Bias." In Issues of Sex Bias and Sex Fairness in Career Interest Measurement, edited by Esther E. Diamond, pp. 123-40. Washington, D.C.: Department of Health, Education and Welfare, National Institute of Education, Spring 1975.

Gurin, Patricia, and Edgar Epps. Black Consciousness, Identity and Achievement. New York: John Wiley and Sons, 1975.

Gurin, Patricia, and Daniel Katz. Motivation and Aspiration in the Negro College. Ann Arbor, Mich.: Institute for Social Research, 1966.

Gurin, Patricia, and Anne Pruitt. "Counseling Implications of Black Women's Market Position, Aspirations and Expectancies." Paper presented at the meeting of the National Institute of Education's Conference on the Educational and Occupational Needs of Black Women, Washington, D.C., December 1975.

Herskovits, Melville. The Myth of Negro Past. Boston: Beacon Press, 1958.

Hill, Robert B. "The Economic Status of Black Families and Children." In The State of Black America 1978, edited by the National Urban League. New York: National Urban League, 1978.

Hoffman, Lois. "Fear of Success in Males and Females: 1965 and 1972." Journal of Consulting and Clinical Psychology 42 (1974): 353-58.

Hood, Elizabeth F. "Black Women, White Women: Separate Paths to Liberation." The Black Scholar 9 (1978): 45-56.

Horner, Matina. "Sex Differences in Achievement Motivation and Performance in Competitive and Non-Competitive Situations." Ph.D. dissertation, University of Michigan, 1968.

_____. "Toward an Understanding of Achievement-Related Conflicts in Women." Journal of Social Issues 28 (1972): 157-75.

Jackson, Jacquelyne. "A Critique of Lerner's Work on Black Women." Journal of Social and Behavioral Sciences 21 (1975): 63-89.

King, Helen. "The Black Woman and Woman's Lib." Ebony 26 (March 1971): 68-76.

King, Mae C. "Oppression and Power: The Unique Status of the Black Woman in the American Political System." Social Science Quarterly 56 (1975): 116-28.

Ladner, Joyce. Tomorrow's Tomorrow: The Black Woman. New York: Doubleday, 1971.

Lucas, Frances. "Miles to Go Before We Sleep." Right to Treatment: The Magazine of the National Association for Mental Health, Spring 1975, pp. 14-16.

Mack, Deloris. "The Power Relationship in Black Families and White Families." Journal of Personality and Social Psychology 30 (1974): 409-13.

Mednick, Martha, and Gwendolyn Randall Puryear. "Motivational and Personality Factors Related to Career Goals of Black College Women." Journal of Social and Behavioral Sciences 21 (1975): 1-30.

_____. "Race and Fear of Success in College Women: 1968 and 1971." Journal of Consulting and Clinical Psychology 44 (1976): 787-89.

Monahan, Lynn, Deanna Kuhn, and Phillip Shaver. "Intrapsychic versus Cultural Explanations of the 'Fear of Success' Motive." Journal of Personality and Social Psychology 29 (1974): 60-64.

Moynihan, Daniel. "The Negro Family, The Case for National Action." Report prepared for the Office of Planning and Research. Washington, D.C.: U.S. Government Printing Office.

Puryear, Gwendolyn Randall. "A Profile of Freshmen Students at Howard University, Fall 1976." Mimeographed. Washington, D.C.: Howard University, 1977.

Puryear, Gwendolyn Randall, and Martha S. Mednick. "Black Militancy, Affective Attachment, and Fear of Success." Journal of Consulting and Clinical Psychology 42 (1974): 263-66.

Scanzoni, John H. Sex Roles, Life Styles, and Childbearing. New York: Free Press, 1975.

Staples, Robert. The Black Woman in America. Chicago: Nelson Hall, 1973.

Tangri, Sandra. "Role-Innovation in Occupational Choice among College Women." Ph.D. dissertation, University of Michigan, 1969.

Turner, B. F. "Socialization and Career Orientation among Black and White College Women." Cited by Janice Gump. "Reality and Myth: Employment and Sex Role Ideology in Black Women." In Psychology of Women: New Directions for Research, edited by Julia Sherman and Florence Denmark. New York: Psychological Dimensions, 1979, in press.

U.S., Commission on Civil Rights. The State of Civil Rights: 1977. Washington, D.C.: Government Printing Office, 1977.

U.S., Department of Commerce. Bureau of the Census. Money, Income and Poverty Status of Families and Persons in the U.S. Advanced Report Series P-60, no. 116. Washington, D.C.: Government Printing Office, 1978.

U.S., Department of Labor. Years for Decision: A Longitudinal Study of the Educational and Labor Market Experience of Young Women, vol. 1. Manpower Research Monograph no. 24. Washington, D.C.: Government Printing Office, 1971.

U.S., Department of Labor. Bureau of Labor Statistics. Marital and Family Characteristics of the Labor Force. Press Release no. USDL 78-638, Washington, D.C., March 1978.

_____. U.S. Working Women: A Databook. Washington, D.C.: Government Printing Office, 1977.

U.S., Department of Labor. Bureau of Labor Statistics. Office of Current Employment Analysis. Employment and Earnings. vol. 26, no. 1. Washington, D.C.: Government Printing Office, 1979.

U.S., Department of Labor. Women's Bureau. Minority Women Workers: Statistical Overview. Washington, D.C.: Government Printing Office, 1977.

Wallace, Michele. "Black Macho and the Myth of the Superwoman." Ms, January 1979, pp. 45-89.

Weston, Peter, and Martha Mednick. "Race, Social Class and the Motive to Avoid Success in Women." Journal of Cross-Cultural Psychology 1 (1970): 284-91.

13

THE SCHOOLING OF VIETNAMESE IMMIGRANTS: INTERNAL COLONIALISM AND ITS IMPACT ON WOMEN

Gail P. Kelly

In April 1975, 129,000 Vietnamese came to the United States as the long and bloody war ended. These individuals came for a variety of reasons. The most common one—and one given by Vietnamese of all classes (of rural and urban origins) and almost all occupations— was that they feared that with the fall of the Thieu government they would be unable to continue living as they had in the past.[1] Vietnamese Catholics, close to half of the immigrants, believed their churches would be closed and their priests (in rural villages, also mayors, judges, and teachers) killed.[2] (Vietnamese Catholics and the government of North Vietnam had a long history of mutual animosity.) South Vietnamese government officials and wealthy businessmen feared their social and economic positions would be undermined by the new Vietnamese government. Vietnamese who came to the United States, in short, were motivated by a desire to maintain cultural, religious, social, and economic patterns as they had known them in the cities and countryside of Vietnam. They expressed little interest in adopting new ways.

When Vietnamese first arrived in the United States, they were placed in four camps: Camp Pendleton in California, Fort Chaffee in Arkansas, Eglin Air Force Base in Florida, and Fort Indian Town Gap in Pennsylvania. The purpose of the camps was to resettle Vietnamese according to U.S. government guidelines. In the camps the U.S. government conducted health, security, and financial screening

Research for this chapter was made possible by grants from the University of Buffalo Foundation, State University of New York at Buffalo Institutional Funds, the SUNY (State University of New York) Foundation, and the New York State Council for the Humanities.

as required by immigration law and resettled Vietnamese with American sponsors. Sponsors were individuals or organizations willing to take moral and financial responsibility for individuals or family units until they became self-supporting. Government policy was to spread Vietnamese resettlement throughout the country. The sponsorship program encouraged such a diaspora, because the financial commitment that the program required Americans to make to Vietnamese was so great that few individuals or organizations could afford to undertake sponsorship. Within any one community a handful of individuals or groups stepped forward to provide full financial support for the two to three years that the government required of sponsors. As a result, Vietnamese were initially relocated in parts of the United States where Americans wanted them. By the time the camps closed in late 1975, they were scattered throughout the country, isolated for the most part from other Vietnamese.

The resettlement camps were the first points of entry into the United States for Vietnamese. The camps were removed from American society: they were ringed by white lines and guarded by Military Police, and Vietnamese could not leave them; neither could Americans have free access to the camps. Admission to the camps was contingent on approval by the government agencies administering them. Americans who were granted permission to enter the camps could do so only during daylight hours and were restricted to certain camp areas (recreation halls, school offices, and resettlement agency headquarters).

In the closed atmosphere of the camps Americans readied Vietnamese for entry into U.S. society. Much of this preparation consisted of formal and informal education aimed specifically at adults. The largest single activity in the camps, other than finding sponsors for Vietnamese, was education. At Fort Indian Town Gap, Pennsylvania, for example, 38 classes in the English language were conducted simultaneously for three hours, morning, noon, and night, five days a week. As of September 1975, 9,700 individuals over age 18 out of a total camp population of 16,000 attended such classes daily. Over $3.7 million was expended on education in the camps.[3]

These educational programs provided instruction in the English language. A stated aim of the classes was to prepare Vietnamese for what Americans called the refugees' "New Life" in their "New Land."[4] The nature of that preparation is the focus of this chapter. I will analyze formal and informal education of adults in the camps. Specifically, I will dwell on English language instruction, cultural orientation programs, and bilingual written materials for adults.

The analysis presented here is based on materials I collected at Fort Indian Town Gap, Pennsylvania, while doing fieldwork there in 1975. These include curriculum guides, books, and instructional materials used in adult education classes; interviews with teachers, curriculum specialists, and persons who participated in cultural orientation and language programs; and camp newspapers. Additionally, I have used classroom observations where appropriate in describing the types of occupational and social roles for which the camps prepared Vietnamese women and men.

INTERNAL COLONIALISM: A FRAMEWORK
FOR ANALYZING CAMP PROGRAMS

Internal colonialism is the framework I will use in analyzing U.S. educational and resettlement policies. Internal colonialism has, in the main, been taken as the process by which one nation has subjugated another nation, taking control over its territories, polity, economy, and cultural institutions. It can be distinguished from classical colonialism in that classical colonialism entails the domination of peoples outside the boundaries of the colonizer's nation-state. Internal colonialism by this definition grows out of classical colonialism. The Indians of Latin America, for example, became internal colonies only after they were parts of overseas colonies.

Many conceptualizations of internal colonialism emphasize the fact of nation-to-nation domination, arguing that internal colonialism exists only in relations between nation-states.[5] This view distinguishes between oppression having differing roots. According to this view, the oppression born out of racial or cultural differences would not be the same as oppression whose origins lie in national differences. The above definition of internal colonialism would preclude from consideration colonized racial and ethnic minorities. That definition would exclude them simply because they did not at a point in the past hold territory within the nation-state that currently oppresses them.

To define nation only in terms of territoriality is to define nation on Western terms and not on the terms that many Third World peoples define nationhood. Chinese, for example, do not tie nationality to being born in China, or to its land, but rather to being literate in Chinese and versed in its culture.[6] Because of the Western-centric notion of colonialism when confined to relations between territorially defined states, a literature on internal colonialism has evolved that focuses less on the origins of the relation than on the nature of the relationships that emerge between cultural and racial groups.[7] Thus, peoples who are minorities within a nation-state who may or may not have territorial claims or have constituted a nation-state in the past can be considered colonized. By this definition, Blacks, Native Americans, and immigrant communities are internal colonies in the United States. They are internal colonies because their relationship to white,

Anglo-America is analogous to that of overseas colonies to the metropole. Characteristic of that relationship is forced entry into the society and culture of the colonizer; creation of a labor force that is differentiated by caste (defined by race, culture and/or language) and controlled by and dependent on the colonizer; sharing of a single polity with the colonizer, which the colonizer dominates; and racial and cultural oppression. [8]

The relations between educational systems and internal colonialism are multifaceted. Education traditionally has been the means by which individuals are taught prevailing social norms and prepared for a place within the society. As long as the norms and behavior the school teaches are shared by all members of society, the school cannot be considered an instrument of internal colonialism, especially if relations in the society are not determined along racial/cultural lines. However, when oppression is based on racial/cultural distinctions and when the schools perpetuate them through teaching children values that are at variance with or foreign to those of their family and culture, and when it prepares students for narrow, submissive roles allocated to them by the dominant group, then the schools function to extend the internal colonial relationship. In nations where schooling is compulsory, like the United States, education becomes for the colonized the first instance of forced entry into the society and culture of the colonizer. It is the colonizer—in the United States, the white majority—who controls schools, determines educational content and the culture the schools transmit, and decides the uses of education in the society.

Schools are not only the major entry point for the colonized into the cultural and social systems set by the colonizer; schools also prepare individuals for the world of work. This the schools do not only by teaching individuals skills that are bought and sold on the labor market but also by orienting individuals to the values that employers find desirable in employees at different levels of the labor force. For some, the schools teach punctuality, respect for property not their own, obedience; for others, the schools encourage initiative and innovation and encourage students to control their means of livelihood. In internal colonies, the schools prepare individuals for the world of work according to occupations at which the schools (or more precisely those who control the schools) presume the colonized will work. Sometimes differential preparation occurs by students' achievement and presumed intelligence, as measured by tests designed by the colonizer, based on the colonizer's own cultural norms. Those who score poorly receive generalized vocational training; those who score better end up receiving technical or crafts training, while the high achievers are channeled to academic training and the managerial/professional jobs within the economy. The colonized, racially and/or culturally different from the colonizer, are trained for occupations that are both the lowest in terms of pay and prestige in the labor force. These occupations are ones that are dependent on the colonizer. In the world of work as well as of culture, the schools deny the autonomy of the colonized.

Similarly, the schools prepare the colonized for a political system dominated by the colonizer. In internal colonies, the schools teach that there is but one nation, indivisible, and that nation is presided over by the colonizer. In the United States, for example, the teaching of history and social studies emphasizes the names of presidents and their terms of office. This accustoms children to a nation ruled by white men, for all presidents have been white and male. The Civil War serves to remind students that there is but one nation, not many colonies. Freedom from oppression, additionally, is possible only with the help of the white man. Lincoln freed the slaves, most history texts point out—the slaves did not free themselves. History teaching, then, not only denies the existence and autonomy of the colonized; it also fosters the dependency of the colonized on the colonizer within the polity the colonizer dominates.

Education for the colonized perpetuates racial and cultural oppression not only through dependency teaching but also by denying, if not deprecating, the culture and race of the colonized. For example, U.S. schools have long ignored Native American cultures, except to distort them and label them as primitive.[9] The schools define how the colonized can survive within the society, for they show how income and status are tied to accepting the norms, culture, and language of the colonizer. It is not without reason, for instance, that U.S. schools, when they present Native Americans as heros to emulate, choose those who to some degree exemplify the dominant culture's values—they either made peace with the White Man or brought aspects of white culture to the colonized. In portraying Black Americans, texts written since the 1960s chose to portray Booker T. Washington and Martin Luther King, and not Malcolm X. They praise those who accept the colonizer's rules of the game and not those who exert the autonomy of the colonized.

Internal colonialism, then, can be seen as that set of relationships that fosters the dominance of groups definable by race and/or culture over a racially, culturally, and/or linguistically different group. Internal colonialism involves forced entry of the colonized into the society and culture of the colonizer, a division of labor based on race and culture in which the colonized are placed in dependency relations with the colonizer, the sharing of polity between colonizer and colonized that the colonizer dominates, and cultural oppression. Schools can become instruments of internal colonialism—they are the first point of forced entry for the colonized into the society and culture of the colonizer; they prepare the colonized for economic roles determined by the colonizer; they legitimate and normalize the polity as one that the colonizer rules for the colonized; and they become a means of cultural oppression. In short, in internal colonialism the schools teach roles and behavior appropriate to the colonized in a political, social, and economic order controlled by the colonizer. The roles the schools teach are ones that the colonizer, not the colonized, chooses, and these roles are imposed if not by the school by the economic and political order.

While there has been much theorizing and research on colonialism, classical and internal, its educational manifestations, and impact, little work has been done relating to its impact on women. Indeed, much of the literature on colonialism, especially on internal colonialism, assumes that its impact on men and women is identical.[10] Educational systems in this literature are seen to differentiate solely on the basis of culture and race—not on the basis of gender as well as culture and race. Scholars of Third World women, however, have made it abundantly clear that systems of stratification in Latin America, Asia, and Africa have been grounded on gender as well as race and nationality.[11] How education has contributed to this has not been a major research focus either in the study of classical or internal colonialism.

In this chapter I will use the framework of internal colonialism to analyze education in the resettlement camps for Vietnamese. My analysis will show how these programs prepared Vietnamese for entry into the American lower classes while, at the same time, attempting to change their life-styles. While this is the case, I will also demonstrate that the process of internal colonialism that the programs initiated were differentiated along gender lines. Particularly striking is the degree to which the establishment of male domination within the family and the usurpation of women's roles was essentially given as compensation for the Vietnamese males' loss of class status and power in their transition from Vietnam to the United States. This phenomenon, which I shall describe at length in this chapter, is a characteristic of internal colonialism, which has long been overlooked in our analyses. In order to understand the extent to which male domination is offered as a substitute for class dominance in the process of internal colonialism in the case of the Vietnamese, it is first necessary to understand the class origins of the Vietnamese who came to the United States and the role of women within the Vietnamese family and society.

VIETNAMESE WHO CAME TO THE UNITED STATES

Vietnamese who came to the United States represented their nation's political and economic elite. As Table 5 shows, over 24 per-

TABLE 5

Primary Employment Skills of Heads of Households
(N = 30.628)

Skill Category	Number	Percent
Medical professions	2,210	7.2
Professional, technical, and managerial	7,368	24.0
Clerical and sales	3,572	11.7
Service	2,324	7.6
Farming, fishing, forestry	1,491	4.9
Agricultural processing	128	0.4
Machine trades	2,670	8.7
Benchwork, assembly, repair	1,249	4.1
Structural and construction	2,026	6.6
Transportation and miscellaneous	5,165	16.9
Did not indicate	2,425	7.9

Note: Reports skills only, not individual's prior employment.

Source: Interagency Task Force for Indochinese Refugees,
"Report to the Congress" (Washington, D.C.: Interagency Task Force
for Indochinese Refugees, December 15, 1975), p. 13.

cent of heads of households were professionals, managers, and technicians; 7.2 percent were medical doctors or dentists; while another
11.7 percent were employed in clerical or sales industries (a category
made up largely of lower-level government officials and businessmen).
In all, about 45 percent of Vietnamese entering this country were part
of the small Vietnamese ruling class, which had fought hard against
social revolution. The elite nature of the Vietnamese immigrants becomes even clearer when their educational backgrounds are taken into
account. About 82 percent of all Vietnamese over age 18 had secondary or better education (in Vietnam, less than 64 percent of the
school-age population entered primary school). Over 20 percent of
the immigrants were university-educated (2.5 percent in Vietnam received higher education). [12]
    While the Vietnamese entering the United States were, taken as
a whole, the elite of South Vietnam's society, there were some who
had more humble origins. As Table 5 shows, about 5 percent were
engaged in rural occupations. Additionally, most Vietnamese with
skilled trades tended to be former soldiers, who gained their skills
from the army or navy, but who were neither affluent nor powerful in

Vietnam (about 4,500 Vietnamese rank-and-file soldiers and sailors came to the United States).

Men outnumbered women among the immigrants. About 45 percent were women[13] whose class origins one can only presume are similar to the men who came. The women clearly had been gainfully employed in Vietnam. Only 14 percent reported their occupations as "housewife."[14] In Vietnam urban as well as rural poor and middle-class women were in the work force, entering in increasing numbers since the war's escalation in the 1960s and the inflation that accompanied it.

In the Vietnam of the 1960s most women worked for wages out of economic necessity. Peasant women for centuries have worked the land and have been petty traders; in the forced urbanization during the war, these peasant women worked in the cities as petty traders, bar girls, laundresses, maids, and prostitutes to sustain themselves and their families. Middle-class women came into the job market in the inflation of the 1960s, as men's salaries on which they had been supported no longer were adequate to sustain their families in the life-styles to which they had become accustomed.[15] Immigrants whom I interviewed at Fort Indian Town Gap told me how wives of prominent civil servants, university professors, and the military opened knitting factories, began working as teletype operators, secretaries, and the like to supplement family income. In short, Vietnamese women who came to the United States had a history of working outside the home.[16]

Not only were immigrant women of all classes working women, many were the sole support of their families since the men either had been killed in the war or disabled by it and unable to work. About 21.6 percent of all immigrant households were headed by women who were their major breadwinners.[17]

Vietnamese immigrants, men and women alike, had few expectations or experiences of a life in which women were not involved in the economy and did not play a major role in both economic and family life.

ENGLISH LANGUAGE INSTRUCTION:
DIFFERENT ROLES FOR DIFFERENT SEXES

English language classes, without question, were a formal point of entry for Vietnamese into U.S. society and culture. To some extent that entry was forced, at least for men, as camp authorities pressured men into attending classes. At Fort Indian Town Gap, camp authorities pointed out in the daily newspaper, Dat Lanh, that learning to speak English was the key to getting a good job and income in the

United States. Those who found this incentive lacking were visited by camp administrators and urged to go to class. Vietnamese barracks leaders, appointed by Americans, were also enlisted to convince recalcitrant Vietnamese that they needed to go to class.

While Americans concentrated on encouraging men to go to English classes, they made no such effort to bring women to class. In fact, women were initially discouraged from attending. When classes began, women flooded the classrooms expecting to become better equipped to enter the work force. However, camp authorities and teachers discouraged their presence. They then reduced class size by eliminating women from classes. School officials proclaimed the classes open only to heads of households since, they argued, it was they alone who would enter the work force. [18] In practice, this meant that women were excluded from class, for Americans assumed women were not heads of household. This policy, which was in effect from June to late August 1975, was justified by school personnel on several grounds. First, they argued that men, not women, would be breadwinners and, therefore, had priority in learning English. Second, they believed that permitting women in class would disrupt the Vietnamese family. Women, they said, might learn the language faster than men, and men would "lose face" because of this. This then would lead to marital conflicts and divorce. Further, they argued that there were other types of classes for women that would suit them for life in the United States: classes in birth control, child care, sewing, and cooking, as well as, after September, the Pennsylvania Commission for Women's sessions called "Women in America." Women gained free access to the language classes at Fort Indian Town Gap three months later when the camp population had diminished as refugees were resettled in the United States.

The English language classes were introductions to U.S. culture and Vietnamese potential roles, both occupational and social, within it. This was evident in the curricular materials used in class, the conduct of class, and in teacher attitudes. It was explicit in interviews I held with school personnel.

Two types of curricular materials were used in teaching English at Fort Indian Town Gap: the Survival English course developed by the Department of Health, Education and Welfare and, as a supplement, the Macmillan English Language 900 Series texts. The Survival English course, taught at three levels, had 16 lessons that covered topics (in the order presented) that included meeting strangers, finding a place to live, occupations, renting apartments, shopping, John's interest, and applying for jobs. [19] The first lesson began with greetings and sex identifications. Students were drilled on phrases such as "Hello," "Good afternoon," "My name is . . . ," "I'm a boy," "I'm a girl," and "Do you speak English?" Subsequent vocabulary taught locations of lavatories, days of the week, numbers, food, time, parts of the body, and job titles. Once vocabulary was introduced as words in isolation, lessons centered on patterned sentences and conversations. In all but 2 of the 16 lessons the conversations took place between a mythical "Mr. Brown" and "Mr. Jones," with Mr. Brown responding to Mr. Jones's questions. For example, Mr. Jones (no doubt the Vietnamese refugee) inquired in a lesson on numbers how he might go about buying a house. In the lesson on occupations, Mr. Jones asked what kind of job he might get to support his wife and two children. Mr. Jones was told that he could work as a room clerk, salesman, cashier, laborer, plumber, bricklayer, cook, cleaning person, secretary, typist, seamstress, or nurses' aide.

Women were present in the 16 units of Survival English only in two instances: in a lesson on budgeting and shopping and in one called "Conversation." One lesson contained two lines about a Miss Jones. These lines were: "Miss Jones missed the bus to the Miss Universe competition" and "She is an attractive girl."[20] The only other reference to women in the curriculum was in a set of drills on shopping that depicted women shopping for small items. In the basic classes teaching persons who knew no English, a Mrs. Brown shopped for dresses, shoes, food, aspirins, baby needs, and cosmetics, while Mr. Brown shopped for shirts, houses, cars, and furniture.[21] In the advanced classes the division of labor between the sexes was elaborated. A women named Marie compared prices of food and other commodities, thereby saving her husband his hard-earned money. Marie was wise and would buy nothing but food without consulting her husband, Tim. In the lesson she found out where the cheapest sofa and sewing machine in town could be bought, but took her husband to the stores for him to decide whether the items should be purchased.[22]

The Macmillan English Language 900 Series, used as a supplement to the Survival English course, was not written specifically for Vietnamese refugees. It is a series of texts designed for non-English speakers, be they Italian, Arab, Chinese, German, or French. These texts, interestingly enough, are quite different from the materials devised specifically for Vietnamese. Women are not absent in the text nor so inactive. They travel, they work, go to the doctor, shop, ask questions. Despite this, the roles portrayed for women are limited to that of wife and mother. In Lesson One, Book Three (intermediate level), for example, Judy talks with John about buying a new sofa.[23] In Unit 2, Barbara and Ella talk about baking a cake for Harry, while Frank and Tom discuss hammers and nails; in Unit 4, marriage is discussed as are bridal dresses; in Unit 5, Mr. James buys a house and Mabel has coffee klatches with her new neighbors; in Unit 8, on health and sickness, Dr. Smith and his female nurse give Mrs. Adams advice on her children's health and Mr. Lewis advice on his own health and in Unit 9, mother puts children to bed and wakes them up, while father goes off to work.[24]

The curriculum materials used in teaching Vietnamese the English language, in sum, emphasized a strict division of labor between the sexes, preparing Vietnamese women not for the workplace but for narrow social roles. In many course materials, women simply did not exist. When they entered the texts, their roles were depicted solely as that of wife, mother, and shopper. In the Survival English course, designed specifically for refugees, occupations suggested for Vietnamese men often were those reserved for U.S. women. Vietnamese men were presented as qualified to become typists, seamstresses, or nurses' aides. Further, these jobs were at the very lowest ends of the occupational and salary scales in the United States. The programs were not only allocating Vietnamese men into lower-class and female occupations, they also presented immigrant men with roles traditionally reserved for U.S. women. It is Mr. Jones in the Survival English course who finds out where stores are, gets a doctor, selects a church, locates the children's school, and the like. In the Survival English materials women seemingly had no role.

The teaching materials were not the only elements in formal English instruction that attempted to rob Vietnamese women of their social and economic roles and put Vietnamese men into lower-class and female work-force jobs—teacher-student interaction in class worked similarly. An incident in an English class designed for illiterates illustrates this best. This class had more women in it than any other class I observed at Fort Indian Town Gap. (The other classes appeared to be predominantly male; advanced English classes had almost no women in them.) Because the students were illiterate, written materials could not be used. The six-week course had but three units—parts of the body and their names, foods, and jobs. All this was constructed by the teachers with the assistance of the curriculum coordinator. Vocabulary was introduced by pointing to an object or a picture of it and learning the English name for it. When pictures of objects were not available, charade was used. In one class the teacher clucked and flapped his arms like a chicken to introduce the term chicken. He then drilled the class on the phrase, "I want some chicken to eat."[25]

The major emphasis in the classroom was on occupations—teaching Vietnamese how to describe their work skills to prospective employers. In several classes, the teacher began with the phrase, "What kind of work do you do?" He then drew stick figures showing different kinds of work—ditch digging, selling, and the like, naming them all. After introducing phrases like "I am a ditch digger" or "I am a mechanic," he asked each of his 30 or more students, "What kind of work do you do?" The first student to respond was a young man, obviously a former soldier. He responded by imitating a gun with his fingers and replied, "I rat-a-tat-tat." The teacher corrected him with "I work with my hands." Next to recite was a middle-aged woman, who had lacquered teeth (indicating she came from a rural lower-class family). She made a motion that looked like casting nets (I found out later that she came from coastal Vung-Tau and had fished for a living). The teacher responded with "I am a housewife." The woman looked puzzled. The teacher then drew a stick figure on the blackboard representing a woman with a broom in her hand inside of a house. He repeated, "I am a housewife," pointing to the woman. She and the women sitting with her began a lively discussion in Vietnamese and started laughing. The teacher then drilled all the women as a group repeatedly with the phrase "I am a housewife."

The United States, it has often been claimed, is a plural society with little consensus over roles, values, and behavior. In the camps, not all programs Americans developed for Vietnamese attempted to deny women roles in the economy as well as in the household or prepare the Vietnamese elite for lower-class status. Programs that did so, however, were not compulsory as was English language instruction and were not the crucial entry point into U.S. society that the schoolroom was.

WOMEN IN AMERICA:
A COUNTER TO ENGLISH CLASSES

"Women in America" represented an alternative to the types of occupational and social roles fostered in English language classes for women. Those who designed this program firmly believed in women's rights and fluidity of sex roles. They also felt their mission was to liberate Vietnamese women who were living in a state of bondage similar to that of women in nineteenth century China.[26] The program coordinator, an American woman in her late twenties, had lived several years in Taiwan, Hong Kong, and Japan and saw the Vietnamese family and women's roles within it in light of her limited observations abroad. To her, it was only recently that these women had stopped having their feet bound. According to her, their role was only to produce male heirs for the family and to accede to the wishes of their mothers-in-law and husbands within the household where they were confined. Camp authorities, she told me, through their educational programs and practices (specifically the practice of not intervening in known cases of wife beating at Indian Town Gap) reinforced Vietnamese women's traditional roles, which, she believed, were both oppressive and impractical in the United States. The "Women in America" programs were set up to explain to Vietnamese women their rights in the United States and the roles they could assume.

"Women in America" was initially designed as a series of meetings dealing topically with life in the American family, women's rights (right to hold property, abortion, birth control, and so on), women at work, and organizations that assist women in whatever they choose to do. What was planned as a series of meetings became six single evening presentations covering the same ground each time. This occurred because few of the same people came to more than one session, either because they had found sponsors and left the camps, lacked interest, or had difficulty in finding someone to care for their children.

The content of the meeting varied each time, depending on responses to them. At several, discussion centered on snow or shopping, as Vietnamese women sought out information about the United States in general and took the opportunity to meet Americans to ask questions that intrigued them the most. Generally, the class organizers tried to cover the four topics each night before their audience changed the subject. Four women from the Pennsylvania Commission for Women spoke at each meeting, assisted by a Vietnamese language translator. The first speaker usually talked about family life. She stressed men's participation in housework and child care and showed pictures of men bathing children, doing dishes, shopping, and the like. No pictures were shown of women engaged in these tasks. The second speaker discussed women's right to abortions on demand, to divorce, to vote, to own property, and to work if they chose. She emphasized women's rights to plan family size. The third presentation was on jobs and explained to Vietnamese women that some U.S. women worked—some chose not to work. With the aid of photographs, the speaker surveyed the world of work for women, showing photos of women as bulldozer operators, nurses, teachers, librarians, salesladies, karate teachers, beauticians, and the like. The person giving the presentation paused when she showed the picture of a nurse at work and told the class that it was an excellent occupation for women. At this point at one meeting a middle-aged Vietnamese woman asked if women could be butchers. The American presenter told the immigrant that she knew of no women butchers in the United States. The final talk was on women's organizations. This was primarily a detailed enumeration of groups like the YWCA, Planned Parenthood, the National Welfare Rights Organization, and the League of Women Voters.

These classes tried to present women with work possibilities quite different from those of other formal education programs. Unlike the English language classes, "Women in America" portrayed the woman working and financially independent. The series, however, did not have as much an impact as did the English language classes, for no more than 30 persons attended the meetings. Several of those who attended were men who, in the discussions following the presentations, made speeches claiming that men in the United States had no rights at all. The impact of the programs was all the more limited because there was no real incentive for Vietnamese to attend them or take them seriously. Camp authorities and schoolteachers openly disapproved of the meetings and ran movies and English classes during the times they were scheduled. Further, camp authorities made it clear to Vietnamese that only by learning English would they be prepared to survive in the United States. Area coordinators who were responsible for barrack sections of the camps by September, when the "Women in America" series began, pressured adults into going to English language classes; they did not exert any such pressure for persons to attend the series. Most openly resenting the classes, they believed "Women in America" would disrupt the Vietnamese family, make Vietnamese men anxious about resettling in the United States and having to cope with aggressive women, and in the long run, make camp authorities' task more difficult.

THE WRITTEN WORD AND INTEGRATION INTO U.S. SOCIETY

While English language classes and "Women in America" focused primarily on work roles appropriate to Vietnamese, informal education in the camps concentrated on the uses of leisure and attitudes of those who lived in the United States. This informal education was integral to camp life. Every day Vietnamese shopped at the camp post exchange (PX); they attended the various recreation centers in the camps; they flocked to the nightly movies; many hung around resettlement agency offices, and others chatted with U.S. soldiers and refugee workers about snow, Montana, dating, and hot dogs. In the camps Vietnamese had little to do but wait and attend functions Americans set up for them and learn as much as possible about the country. The major source Vietnamese had about the United States was Dat Lanh ("Good Land"), the daily bilingual camp newspaper published by the U.S. Army Psychological Operations Unit. Dat Lanh was not merely a news sheet summarizing national, international, and camp events (which it did), it was also a journal intended to supplement the work of schools in preparing Vietnamese to live in the United States. It was the only bilingual reading material at Fort Indian Town Gap other than camp notices and government documentary information.

Dat Lanh, which began publication on May 28, 1975, carried three types of articles: camp announcements (meeting and mealtimes, lists of incoming refugees, notices of sponsorships available to refugees, barrack rules, immigration laws), how-to articles (how to work a telephone, register for sponsor, buy a car), and informational articles about the United States and its culture. (The informational pieces about the United States will be the focus of this section.) Two types of articles appeared: those on U.S. history and geography and those providing information on social behavior. The history/geography articles appeared almost daily. They consisted of atlastype descriptions of each of the 50 states and the lives of U.S. presidents. On holidays, Dat Lanh ran two-to-three-page stories explaining the significance of the day, particularly Memorial Day, Flag Day, the Fourth of July, Labor Day, Armed Forces Day, Halloween, and Thanksgiving. The purpose of these stories was to orient Vietnamese to U.S. society. Their presentation of the society was one that emphasized its cultural and political unity. Neither ethnic communities nor nonwhites appeared in the columns of Dat Lanh. The articles were acclimatizing Vietnamese for entry into a society ruled by white Americans and seemingly inhabited exclusively by them. This becomes clearer when taken against the contents of Dat Lanh as a whole. Dat Lanh (as well as the newspapers of all the holding centers) omitted any mention of Vietnam except to announce briefly the departure of several thousand Vietnamese from Guam for Vietnam and to include one item on food shortages and unemployment in Saigon. Not only did the paper ignore news of Vietnam, it also ignored the development of Vietnamese communities in the United States, notably in Los Angeles and Washington, D.C., preferring instead to focus attention on Vietnamese settling happily with U.S. families in rural Vermont or Pennsylvania or on the birth of Vietnamese children given American names like "Mary" or "John."

While the news items and information articles prepared Vietnamese for a society in which they would become Americans, Dat Lanh also proposed male and female roles for Vietnamese similar to those English language classes promoted, almost obliterating women's roles outside the nuclear family. Daily, the paper contained a column entitled the "American Way of Life." This column invariably was addressed to heads of households who were presumed to be male. The column explained tipping in restaurants (when the man takes the family out), getting insurance for his car and family, buying his family clothes, cars, houses, and the like. Other installments explained to men how they should behave toward women. They advised men to take their wives on trips, to rise when a woman enters the room, to open doors for women, to help them push revolving doors, to pay the bills at restaurants, to buy tickets, and the like. Further, it told them not to be "frightened" by American women who seem "noisy, aggressive, dominating" and reassured them that most women in the United States are "quiet, content and gentle" and enjoy being taken care of.[27] In the six-month life of Dat Lanh only two articles in the series were addressed to women. Both of them were about dating.

They counseled women on how to find single men, urging them to join sports clubs and photography or ballroom dancing classes. Girls should not ask men out, Dat Lanh advised its readers: "In this country, the man does the inviting out and the planning." The column told girls to ask men to their homes for dinner, if they really wanted to impress them.

While the "American Way of Life" was addressed to men, Dat Lanh often printed items addressed to women. Most were entitled "Attention Mothers" and contained short tips on pregnancy, child care, child health, toys, and the like. A front-page article in that series on July 31, for example, described mother's duties in getting health care for their children.

Dat Lanh, then, prepared Vietnamese differently for American society on the basis of sex. Through its column "The American Way of Life," it informed Vietnamese men of the behavior expected of them if they were to be integrated into American society. Women, however, were not so informed; Dat Lanh, rather, chose only to advise them on carrying out minimal household and mothering tasks, neither of which was necessarily tied to integrating them into American social life.

THE SCHOOLING OF VIETNAMESE
IMMIGRANTS AND INTERNAL COLONIALISM

This chapter has shown how educational programs for Vietnamese immigrants have contributed to the process of internal colonialism. Further, it has demonstrated that the process is different for women than it is for men.

The educational programs in the camps were instruments of internal colonialism: English language programs, Dat Lanh, and the "Women in America" programs, regardless of their points of disagree ment, were directed toward getting Vietnamese to enter the society and culture of Americans regardless of their desires. Most Vietnamese were ambivalent about becoming integrated into American society; they opposed the U.S. resettlement policy, openly expressing their desire to remain Vietnamese within the United States. Of this Americans were well aware. Article after article in Dat Lanh derided Vietnamese unwillingness to leave the "Little Vietnams" of the camps and become Americans. After the camps closed, Vietnamese opposition to U.S. policies became overt, as they abandoned their original places of resettlement to form Vietnamese communities.[28]

While the camp educational programs were a point of entry of Vietnamese into the society and culture of Americans, they did not serve this purpose for men and women alike. Except for "Women in

America," the educational programs did not so direct Vietnamese women. Rather, they prepared Vietnamese men for integration into the U.S. work force and society—Vietnamese women were not the focus of integration efforts. "Women in America" alone tried to prepare the women for entry into the U.S. work force. However, like the other educational efforts, they impinged upon Vietnamese culture and set U.S. terms for Vietnamese adjustment to the society.

The educational programs were also instruments of internal colonialism in the way they allocated Vietnamese into the U.S. labor market. English language classes taught Vietnamese (for the most part, the professional and managerial elites of their country) to expect to become unskilled laborers, laundresses, secretaries, seamstresses, dishwashers, and the like, with marginal incomes. These were, to some extent, the jobs that Vietnamese ended up with after the camps closed. A year after the camps closed, 73 percent of the immigrants who had once been professionals, technicians, managers, and businessmen found themselves blue-collar workers; another 17 percent became clerical and sales personnel. Only 10 percent went into jobs equivalent to those they had held in Vietnam. Most worked in jobs paying minimum wages; many of these jobs were temporary. Yearly income was so low that close to 50 percent of all Vietnamese families in the United States received some form of welfare. The school programs prepared the Vietnamese for these lower-class roles.

While the educational programs fostered the lowering of Vietnamese expectations, they did so by preparing men for occupations usually reserved for women in U.S. society. However, while preparing men for women's roles, they also prepared Vietnamese men to usurp women's roles within the family. The schools taught Vietnamese men to take care of schooling, medical care, shopping, and the like. To some extent internal colonialism was providing Vietnamese men with power within the household in exchange for their loss of power within their society and nation.

A third characteristic of internal colonialism mentioned in the introduction to this chapter was the sharing of a single polity by colonizer and colonized, ruled solely by the colonizer. Education in the camps tried to normalize such relationships. Dat Lanh particularly functioned in such a manner by omitting news from and about Vietnam or about the then-developing Vietnamese community in the United States. To some extent this served to break Vietnamese ties with their country of origin and to downplay Vietnamese expectations that they could organize their own community in this country and thereby exert autonomy. Dat Lanh paraded U.S. presidents—all white and all male—through its pages, accustoming Vietnamese, male and female alike, to the realities of who holds power in the United States.

A final aspect of internal colonialism outlined earlier is racial and cultural oppression. In education, this has long been documented vis-à-vis Native Americans, Blacks, and Chicanos. Racial oppression has taken several forms—outright discrimination in education, either by providing separate and unequal education or by denying educational opportunity; overt cultural and racial slurs, or omission. In U.S. education oppression through omission is more often the rule than the exception today. This entails simply ignoring the internal colony. In the curriculum, often, Blacks, Native Americans, and the like simply do not exist. The actors in the world are white, male, and American. Oppression takes the form of denial. The education of Vietnamese in the camps represented cultural oppression by denial. No Vietnamese existed in the world presented to the immigrants, despite the fact that the Survival English course and "Women in America" were designed specifically for Vietnamese. In Survival English, Mr. Jones and Mr. Brown speak to one another, seek jobs, health care, apartments, and the like—the Vietnamese in these courses were not Mr. Ngo or Mr. Duc but Mr. Jones, an American.

The oppression implicit in the programs in the camps was best summed up by T.V.Q., a journalist who spent five months at Fort Indian Town Gap. "Let me say this," he remarked in an interview about the educational programs. "The Americans have done a lot for me, but whatever we think we need, they don't provide, and whatever we don't need, they provide."[29]

NOTES

1. Gail P. Kelly, From Vietnam to America: A Chronicle of the Vietnamese Immigration to the United States (Boulder, Colo.: Westview Press, 1978).
2. Le-Thi-Que, A. Terry Rambo, and Gary D. Murfin, "Why They Fled: Refugee Movement during the Spring 1975 Communist Offensive in South Vietnam," Asian Survey 16 (September 1976): 855-63.
3. U.S., Department of Health, Education and Welfare, Task Force for Indochinese Refugees, "Report to the Congress," unpublished (Washington, D.C.: HEW, 1976).
4. Kelly, From Vietnam to America, chap. 4.
5. Pierre Van den Berg, "Education, Class and Ethnicity in Southern Peru: Revolutionary Colonialism," in Colonialism and Education, ed. P. G. Altbach and G. P. Kelly (New York: Longmans, 1978), pp. 270-300.
6. Joseph Levenson, Liang Chi Ch'ao and the Mind of Modern China (Berkeley: University of California Press, 1970).
7. John Liu, "Toward an Understanding of the Internal Colonial Model," in Counterpoint: Perspectives on Asian America, ed. Emma Gee (Los Angeles: University of California, Asian American Studies

Center, 1976), pp. 160-68; and Philip G. Altbach and Gail P. Kelly, Colonialism and Education (New York: Longmans, 1978).

8. Liu, Counterpoint, pp. 160-68.

9. Jeanette Henry, "Textbook Distortion of the Indian," Indian Historian, December 1967, pp. 244-50.

10. Martin Carnoy, Education as Cultural Imperialism (New York: McKay, 1974).

11. I. Safa and J. Nash, Sex and Class in Latin America (New York: Praeger, 1976).

12. Interagency Task Force for Indochinese Refugees, "Report to the Congress" (Washington, D.C.: Interagency Task Force for Indochinese Refugees, December 15, 1975); Kelly, From Vietnam to America; and Joseph Dodd, "Aspects of Recent Educational Change in South Vietnam," Journal of Developing Areas 6 (July 1972): 55-71.

13. Interagency Task Force for Indochinese Refugees, "Report to the Congress," p. 11.

14. Ibid., p. 13.

15. Ngo Vinh Long, Vietnamese Women in Society and Revolution: The French Colonial Period (Cambridge, Mass.: Vietnam Resource Center, 1974); and Arlene Eisen Bergman, Women of Vietnam (San Francisco: People's Press, 1974).

16. Vietnamese Immigration Collection, State University of New York at Buffalo Archives, taped interviews, nos. 32, 33, 42, 73, 75, 78, September 1975-October 1976. These are interviews with school officials, immigrants, resettlement workers, and camp officials.

17. Interagency Task Force for Indochinese Refugees, "Report to the Congress," p. 13.

18. Vietnamese Immigration Collection, tapes nos. 9, 10, 29, 30.

19. Vietnamese Immigration Collection, State University of New York at Buffalo Archives, Survival English, Box 3, 1975.

20. Vietnamese Immigration Collection, Survival English, Unit 1, Lesson 1.

21. Ibid., Level 2, Intermediate, Lesson 4, p. 4.

22. Ibid., Level 1, Unit 4, Lessons 3, 4.

23. Ibid., Advanced Class, Unit 5, "How to Stretch Your Dollar."

24. English Language Services, English 900, 16th ed. (New York: Collier Macmillan, 1975), Books 1-3, p. 8; Unit 2, p. 19; Unit 4, pp. 38-42; Unit 5, p. 49; Unit 8, pp. 77-86; Unit 9, p. 93.

25. Vietnamese Immigration Collection, tape no. 30.

26. Ibid.

27. Dat Lanh, September 7, 1975, p. 1.

28. Kelly, From Vietnam to America, chap. 7.

29. Vietnamese Immigration Collection, tape no. 5, side 1.

REFERENCES

Altbach, Philip G., and Gail P. Kelly. Colonialism and Education. New York: Longmans, 1978.

Bergman, Arlene Eisen. Women of Vietnam. San Francisco: People's Press, 1974.

Carnoy, Martin. Education as Cultural Imperialism. New York: McKay, 1974.

Dodd, Joseph. "Aspects of Recent Educational Change in South Vietnam." Journal of Developing Areas 6 (July 1972): 55-71.

English Language Services. English 900. 16th ed. New York: Collier Macmillan, 1975. Books 1-3.

Henry, Jeanette. "Textbook Distortion of the Indian." Indian Historian, December 1967, pp. 244-50.

Interagency Task Force for Indochinese Refugees. "Needs Survey, 1976." (A copy of this survey is contained in the Vietnamese Immigration Collection, State University of New York at Buffalo Archives, Box 2.)

_____. "Report to the Congress." Washington, D.C.: Interagency Task Force for Indochinese Refugees, December 15, 1975.

Kelly, Gail P. From Vietnam to America: A Chronicle of the Vietnamese Immigration to the United States. Boulder, Colo.: Westview Press, 1978.

Le-Thi-Que, A. Terry Rambo, and Gary D. Murfin. "Why They Fled: Refugee Movement during the Spring 1975 Communist Offensive in South Vietnam." Asian Survey 16 (September 1976): 855-63.

Levenson, Joseph. Liang Chi Ch'ao and the Mind of Modern China. Berkeley: University of California Press, 1970.

Liu, John. "Toward an Understanding of the Internal Colonial Model." In Counterpoint: Perspectives on Asian America, edited by Emma Gee, pp. 160-68. Los Angeles: University of California, Asian American Studies Center, 1976.

Liu, William F., and Alice K. Murata. "The Vietnamese in America." Bridge: An Asian American Perspective 5 (Fall–Winter 1977): 31–39, 42–50.

Montero, Darrel, and Marsha I. Weber. Vietnamese Americans: Patterns of Resettlement and Socio-Economic Adaptation in the United States. Boulder, Colo.: Westview Press, 1979.

Ngo Vinh Long. Vietnamese Women in Society and Revolution: The French Colonial Period. Cambridge, Mass.: Vietnam Resource Center, 1974.

"Nhian Dinh cua HEW ve Tinh Tran Cinh Cu." Doi Song Moi 2 (October 1976): 1, 15.

Safos, I., and J. Nash. Sex and Class in Latin America. New York: Praeger, 1976.

U.S., Department of Health, Education and Welfare. Task Force for Indochinese Refugees. "Report to the Congress." Unpublished. Washington, D.C.: HEW, 1976.

_____. "Report to the Congress." Unpublished. Washington, D.C.: HEW, 1975.

Van den Berg, Pierre. "Education, Class and Ethnicity in Southern Peru: Revolutionary Colonialism." In Colonialism and Education, edited by P. G. Altbach and G. P. Kelly, pp. 270–300. New York: Longmans, 1978.

Vietnamese Immigration Collection, State University of New York at Buffalo Archives. Survival English. Box 3, 1975.

_____. Taped interviews, nos. 5, 9, 10, 29, 30, 32, 33, 34, 42, 64, 72, 73, 75, 78, 79, September 1975–October 1976.

14
THIRD WORLD WOMEN AND
SOCIAL REALITY: A CONCLUSION

Beverly Lindsay

> The mark of a . . . contribution, whether in the natural
> or the social sciences, is not that it reveals some eter-
> nal truth. It is, rather, that existing knowledge and
> analysis are put together in new ways, raising questions
> . . . which allow and force friends and enemies alike to
> push their own research and analysis into different areas.
> André Gunder Frank,
> "Dependence Is Dead, Long Live
> Dependence and the Class Struggle"

The preceding chapters provide avenues for examining basic
sociocultural issues that affect the lives of Third World women,
whether in Africa, Asia, the Caribbean, Latin America, or the United
States. These issues revolve around the oppressive effects manifested
throughout various social, educational, and economic institutions, as
discussed in the introductory chapter. All of the writers in this volume have examined the status of Third World women under these
three umbrella institutional influences. The purpose of this final
chapter is to discuss conceptual nexuses among the various chapters,
despite what sometimes appeared to be different views expressed
about Third World women. It will be contended that triple jeopardy
—race, sex, and class—forms common bonds among women of color.
This chapter will discuss these linkages in relation to conceptual views
of colonialism, neocolonialism, internal colonialism, internal neocolonialism, dependency, and development.

TRIPLE JEOPARDY—RACE, SEX, AND CLASS

We have observed that the concepts of race, sex, and class help
to explain the position of oppressed females. Particular views help us

to understand some social phenomena more so than others. For example, if we examine the position of women in developing nations in terms of internal or domestic conditions in their respective countries, class and sex provide considerable insight. The position of Indians in Latin America and Blacks in the Caribbean involves the additional dimension of race. For minority women in the United States, race, sex, and class are so intertwined that manifestations of their presence constantly permeate the lives of these Third World women.

We must constantly bear in mind that the manner in which women experience the adverse effects of race, sex, and class can and does differ among the groups of Third World women. Differences may also be observed among women in the same country. For example, differences in social class can affect Caribbean and Latin American women in different ways. Racial differences between Vietnamese and Black American women can also be observed. Distinctions in linguistic and cultural patterns may account for part of the differences. Yet both groups are victims of race, sex, and class. The daily lives and activities of many African, Asian, and Latin American women may not be <u>directly</u> affected by race. Yet race and racism, which buttress many international economic and political negotiations, policies, and programs, influence the lives of women in politically sovereign nations. In this sense, triple jeopardy is a reality.

CONCEPTUAL VIEWS:
A CRITICAL REEXAMINATION

The material presented in the introductory chapter and that of several writers (Lewis, Joseph, Wittstock, Gonzales, Puryear, and Kelly) explains the status of Third World women in terms of various conceptual views of colonial exploitation. Some writers (Adams, Lindsay, and Wieser) examine their status in terms of variables that are components of the overall conceptual views, while still others (Wang, Devon, and Cole) examine particular variables without relating them to the conceptual views. This last group of writers implicitly argued that perhaps colonialism, internal colonialism, neocolonialism, and internal neocolonialism may not be the most appropriate paradigms for examining particular groups of Third World women. Nevertheless, all writers contended that the <u>oppressive</u> effects of race, or sex, or class, or a combination of the three adversely affect Third World women. The central question may very well be: What conceptual view(s) most adequately provides an explanation of the relative status of Third World women?

From a historical perspective, traditional or classical colonialism models appear to have considerable applicability for women in

Africa, Latin America, the Caribbean, and the United States, as Lewis Wieser, Joseph, Wittstock, and Gonzales point out. Basic structural changes in economic, social, and educational institutions became evident under colonialism. Various views have been offered to explain the origins of colonialism, with economic variables being one major factor that is often cited. Works by W. E. B. DuBois, Stokely Carmichael, Charles Hamilton, Samuel F. Yette, Martin Carnoy, and H. V. Savitch support this thesis.[1] In her chapter on Chicanas, Gonzales contends that sexism is a fundamental reason for economic exploitation and colonialism. While this writer does not completely support this position, it is clear that ascribed characteristics such as race and sex historically served as justifications for the systematic subjugation of nations and racial groups.

Women may have already been subjugated by males in their own traditional societies by sexist practices prior to colonialism—if so, then women were further exploited under colonialism. This writer agrees with Ester Boserup, Leith Mullings (see Chapter 1), and Lewis that different roles existed for males and females prior to colonialism; however, it is a moot point whether equality or inequities existed in all traditional societies. Wang contends that in Chinese society colonialism did not apply—that is, if we view colonialism as it was manifested in many parts of Africa, Latin America, and the Caribbean. However, Wang's chapter did not focus on Vietnam or India, for example, which were French and British colonies. *

The historical origins of four American racial groups—Native Americans, Chicanos, Afro-Americans, and Vietnamese Americans —differ somewhat. Undoubtedly, all these groups are linked by racial oppression in both a historical and contemporary sense. Native Americans were defeated in wars, subjugated through treaties, and relegated to specified territories or reservations as a conquered people. Their historical status approximates that of traditional or classical colonialism. Chicanos trace their historical origins to Mexico, which was defeated as a nation in its attempts to maintain and expand its possessions in what is now the United States. Treaties were signed between the two nations. Yet, Mexicans who remained or migrated to the United States were usually not covered by political agreements between the two sovereign nations. Slavery was the orig-

---

*The Japanese attempted to expand their economic influence by engaging in colonialist practices, but they were defeated in what is now the People's Republic of China, and their colonial domination was short-lived in Taiwan. Yet, the Japanese's attempted penetration was fostered by ethnic distinctions. In short, ascribed characteristics such as race and/or ethnicity were inextricably linked to economic motives for colonial expansion and subjugation.

inal plight for Black Americans, and socioeconomic forces and racism generated during that period are still present today. The recent Vietnamese immigrants are the latest example of a group experiencing racism and economic oppression.

It has been contended that the structure of oppression characterizes internal colonies. Moreover, the structure of oppression is inextricably interwoven with racial and/or cultural distinctions, which is the domestic face of imperialism.[2] Gilbert G. González argues (as Philip G. Altback and Gail P. Kelly also suggest)[3] that what identifies a nation (or a former nation) is its economic, cultural, historical, and territorial unity. If one of these characteristics is absent, then the group is not a nation; hence the concept of a colony is incorrect in discussing a group that is not a nation. Instead Chicanos and Black and Vietnamese Americans must be considered national minorities, since all four of these characteristics are not present.[4] González further asserts that a national minority differs from a nation in two principal respects:

> First, a national minority, as opposed to a nation, has
> no common or continuous territory, but is usually dis-
> persed in small or large settlements; second, a nation
> has its own economy (autonomous or not), whereas a na-
> tional minority is usually economically integrated into the
> economy of the nation within which the minority resides.[5]

This writer concurs with Gonzáles that Chicanos, Black Americans, and Vietnamese Americans do not have a continuous territorial base in the United States, which they had in their original countries. González's second contention raises questions. A nation has its own economy whether it is autonomous or not, while a national minority is usually integrated economically into the economy of the nation where it resides. What are the real distinctions between a nation that may not have an autonomous economy and a national minority that may not be economically integrated into the nation where it resides? Using González's economic argument, we are tempted to ask: Why and how is Liberia an independent nation? Liberia has used the U.S. dollar as its currency, and its national economy is closely linked to the United States and many multinational corporations that are based in America.

There are various writers (such as Sidney Wilhelm, Michael Reich, and Robert L. Allen)[6] who maintain that Black Americans and other racial minorities are not fully integrated into the U.S. economic system. If they were, they would not be the economic "rejects" of U.S. society. It appears, then, that racial minorities in the United States may precisely fit neither all the characteristics of a nation nor all the characteristics of a national minority. Nevertheless, the conditions and status of minorities in the United States have been characterized by the same types of harsh oppression that were present in the historical colonial areas, as documented in Chapter 1 as well as several other chapters of this volume. In the historical sense, there may be few discernible differences among the lives of minority Americans and people in Africa, Asia, Latin America, and the Caribbean. They are the victims of institutionalized oppression.

In an examination of what are currently referred to as "developing nations," we frequently encounter the term neocolonialism. Many countries of Africa, Asia, Latin America, and the Caribbean have recently (or during an earlier historical period) earned "flag" independence. Many countries of the developing world are still characterized by economic, social, and cultural ties to the former colonizer or another major world power. The sociocultural aspects of neocolonialism are tied to economic imperial bonds. Minorities in the United States also have similar linkages with the white ruling class in America. Thus, the concept of internal neocolonialism seems applicable.

It appears, however, that the concepts of neocolonialism and internal neocolonialism still cling to a historical explanation of socioeconomic conditions regarding the subjugation and oppression of colored people. During the contemporary period, oppression of people is occurring in more sophisticated modes than those witnessed in the past, since there are few remaining colonies. Many Latin American nations have been politically independent for over 100 years. Over 20 years have elapsed since Ghana became independent in 1957, which helped to set in motion the appearance of formal independence for most sub-Saharan African nations. Yet many "independent" nations and racial minorities in the United States are in a dependent state relative to the major world powers and/or former colonizers. Hence, we turn to the views postulated in dependency theory. Dependency theory incorporates many features of neocolonialism and internal neocolonialism; but dependency views push our current analysis and explanation even further than the former concepts.

As mentioned in Chapter 1 dependency relationships exist between the Third World and developed nations, between the ruling elite and the general populace in developing nations, and between racial minorities and the white majority in the United States. To a great degree, dependency theory was formulated and refined to explain the continuous exploitative economic relations between the ruling elite and the subordinate populace. Samari Amin, Walter Rodney, James Cockcroft, André Gunder Frank, Dale L. Johnson, and Joseph C. Jorgensen contend that the world powers developed economically, politically, socially, and culturally at the expense of Third World nations and people.[7] Or, in the terms of the dependency theorists, the metropole or center developed at the expense of the satellite or periphery. For example, the economic development of Great Britain was possible because this nation was the metropole or center of economic activity. Former British colonies, currently Third World nations in the Commonwealth, were at the periphery or simply satellites for economic activities at the metropole. The greater economic benefits still continue to accrue here. This is a current economic and sociopolitical reality that was set in motion by earlier historical economic forces. Many of these historical forces were fostered and buttressed by racism, which is a major reason why we contend that race and racism are still significant variables in understanding the dynamic relationships involved in international economic orders.

Jorgensen has further developed conceptual views regarding dependency relationships for domestic or internal activities of a metropole and satellite within one nation. He focuses on the economic and sociopolitical conditions of Native Americans. Yet, much of his discussion, if examined in terms of contemporary conditions, applies to other U.S. minorities despite the fact that their historical origins in the United States are not precisely the same. According to Jorgensen, the metropole and the satellite are interdependent since they can be both nexus and locus of different degrees of socioeconomic activity:

> The metropolis-satellite concept (however) does not reflect a simple two member relationship where one locus is metropolis and the other is satellite. Rather it deals with a pyramidal structure of political and economic power positions (nexus), and these power positions comprise a discernible ordering in space (locus). . . . Areas that concentrate less political and economic power are satellite to those that concentrate more. . . . The pyramidal structure wherein practically all nations, regions within nations, and urban areas are metropolises in some relations and satellites in others is a product of (1) the expropriation of surplus value created by producers and its appropriation by capitalist; and (2) the historical persistence of the structural features of capitalist . . . development whose dominant feature is the simultaneous creation of underdevelopment. It is [a] contradiction in the mode of production where the metropolis, for its own growth, expropriates the surpluses of the satellites.[8] [Emphasis added]

The metropole is the nexus because it is the center of concentration for economic, political, and social power and influence. The satellite is a nexus; but it is peripheral to the center. Providing resources and labor and consuming goods that are owned and produced by the metropole is a function of the satellite. The satellite does not share proportionately in the economic surpluses from its own area nor does it have concentrated political and economic power relative to a metropole.[9] Native Americans concentrated on reservations and urban enclaves are the satellites for economic and political power for the white ruling class. So are Chicanos, Black Americans, and Vietnamese Americans. Federal legislation and regulations ostensibly ensure that those who are U.S. citizens receive at least minimum economic benefits. Yet economic consumption by these several minority groups occurs in situations where they have limited, if any, choice on where they can purchase goods. Or, they purchase low quality goods at high prices. Such consumption generates considerable profit for the ruling majority.

To a degree, class or economic patterns are discernible within various racial groups. For example, in the United States there is the racial minority bourgeoise whose position is not as economically depressed as the majority of those in a particular racial group.[10] In this sense, there can be a metropole-satellite relationship for one racial group. Quite recently William Julius Wilson discussed the economic and sociopolitical role of rather select groups of Black Americans. Wilson maintains that race is of declining significance in the lives of some Black Americans, since their class or economic status is more important than race. The gap between the middle class and affluent Black Americans and poor Black Americans is widening.[11] Undoubtedly, there is some merit in Wilson's argument; however, an examination of current Department of Labor, Department of Health, Education and Welfare, and Bureau of Census data (for example, the material briefly presented by Puryear in this volume) do not indicate that the majority of Black Americans are in the affluent class or what might be viewed as an authentic middle class. For Black Americans, national unemployment figures are continually twice the rates for whites, and salaries or economic compensation is consistently lower than that for whites. Puryear provides references in this volume for these statements concerning the economic position of Black Americans—and particularly, Black women—and Wittstock provides data on Native American women. These differences can only be explained by institutional racism, which is not a factor for working-class whites.[12] For the latter group, class is a factor. For the former group, race and class are the realities.

If one examines the strictly internal domestic relations in terms of dependency theory in many countries of Africa, Asia, Latin America, and to a lesser extent, the Caribbean (but usually excluding Cuba from the Caribbean and Latin America), it is found that class or economically dependent relations exist between the ruling elite and the majority of the populace. This is a contention regarding domestic aspects of dependency relations, if race is not interjected. In some instances, the Indians and Blacks of Latin America and the Caribbean immediately bring the issue of race into the picture. Domestic and international dependency relationships continue because the ruling elite in the metropole, or center, benefit <u>and</u> the ruling elite in the satellite, or periphery, also benefit. Various social, educational, and economic institutions are used to sustain the position of the ruling class whether in the metropole or the satellite.

A major purpose of capitalist economic relations (the focus of dependency theory) is to generate profits by what appear to be the most efficient means. One manner of ensuring this is to attempt to keep wages and related benefits at a minimum level. Of course, some U.S. workers must be paid more than minimum wages in order to engage in moderate consumption activities to perpetuate the economic cycle. Hence, there is stratification in the working class. Who will be paid the lower wages? And who will constitute the reserve labor force to help maintain low wages? In the United States, race and sex become criteria for determining who falls into the category of lower-paid workers and who constitutes the reserve labor force. [13] Similar criteria are at work in international economic relations. It is no accident that many products are manufactured in Caribbean (as discussed in Joseph's chapter) or Asian nations where wages are lower than what they would be in the United States. The workers in these nations comprise part of the international reserve labor force.

How do the status and position of Third World women fit into the tenets expressed in dependency theory? Third World women are people of color. Hence, race and racism affect their lives as they do those of men. Women have the additional ascribed characteristic of sex. There are obvious biological distinctions between the sexes, which means that women bear children or reproduce the labor force. [14] The social patterns of most societies dictate that women will be responsible for raising children and providing for young children's socialization. Women also reproduce labor power and manage family consumption. Cooking the food, cleaning the house, purchasing the food, and other household activities are usual duties for women. That women may be confined to these roles or basically responsible for them is a result of different socialization for males and females.

Males are also socialized to believe that housework is a sole legitimate sphere for women, and, given the <u>male-dominated power structure</u>, their sexist views usually result in actions that perpetuate the oppressed position of women. The portion of the Cuban Family Code that stipulates that males shoulder 50 percent of the domestic chores and responsibilities when their spouses work becomes quite significant when viewed in the context of sexist views. The material in the chapters on Kenyan, Indian, Chinese, and Chicano women clearly illustrates socialization patterns and use of power to enforce the resulting sexist views. The political and economic roles from which women are excluded are the very roles that would allow them to allocate resources and values. In other words, they are excluded from the roles of power. In short, a social and ideological worldview or cultural hegemony is imposed by men—usually males of the dominant class. Cultural hegemony "is an order in which a certain way of life and thought is dominant, in which one concept of reality is diffused . . . in all institutional and private manifestations."[15]

Third World women constitute a cheap or unpaid labor force and a reserve labor force for both international and domestic economic needs.[16] Wang's material on women in the People's Republic of China indicates how Chinese women constitute a reserve labor force in a country that is striving toward a socialist society where invidious distinctions based upon class and sex should have been eliminated. Wang portrays how political ideology in the People's Republic of China glorified the role of the housewife during the early 1950s and after the Great Leap Forward of the late 1950s, when the national economy slumped, so there was a shortage of jobs for men. Women were to be housewives and contribute their domestic talent and support to men and the socialist nation. Cultural hegemony was being imposed by males in a socialist nation.

All Third World women do not directly perform household duties. Women domestic servants in Latin American societies or women and men servants in African societies may perform some of the household duties. Yet, it is women as wives or mothers who are responsible for their administration—that is, sex still determines where the responsibility falls. The social class of women determines how household responsibilities will be performed. Women are members of the social class of their husbands, fathers, or other significant males in their lives. Thus, Helen Safa states that:

> Women themselves are not a class, but members of another class, depending on their socioeconomic position in society. . . . The class position of women is defined not by women themselves, even when they are working, but by their husbands or fathers, whose status they assume. While this is another clear reflection of women's dependency on men, it does not mean that women cannot acquire class consciousness independently. It does suggest that the process by which women acquire class con-

sciousness will be <u>different and more difficult than it is for men</u>. [17] [Emphasis added]

Class distinctions exist among groups of Third World women that in the internal social arrangements of a nation may equal or exceed those based on sex and/or race. That is, the relative social position of Third World women within a particular country is influenced by class. So, the social and economic positions of affluent or professional women may appear to have limited relation to working-class or peasant women of the nation, as chapters on Latin American, Caribbean, and African women succinctly state. Whether women are members of an affluent, working, or peasant background, a large part of their socioeconomic status is determined by men, since the male worldview is prevalent. Sexism is a constant factor. Women consistently hold lower social and economic status than men of the same class—that is, "liberation" by class does not mean liberation by sex. Still, peasant and unskilled women in developing nations and many minority women in the United States are "the oppressed of the oppressed!"

Socialist countries have made some concerted attempts to introduce a worldview, espousing equality among people, through the introduction of policies to eradicate invidious distinctions based upon class, sex, and race. Some examples may be witnessed in Cuba and the People's Republic of China. What remains to be seen is how successful the policies of these socialist nations will be. If successful, some of the policies may be incorporated by other nations.

Basic structural changes for eliminating inequities between the sexes must occur in various institutions. If these changes were to occur for the contemporary developing nations of Africa, Asia, Latin America, and the Caribbean, double jeopardy—sex and class—would not be internal domestic realities; in international relations, racism would not be a factor; in the United States triple jeopardy—race, sex, and class—would no longer be the reality for minority women. In the meantime, dependency relationships, based upon race, sex, and class, are being perpetuated through social, educational, and economic institutions. These are the linkages among Third World women.

NOTES

1. W. E. B. DuBois, <u>Color and Democracy: Colonies and Peace</u> (New York: Harcourt, Brace, 1945); Stokely Carmichael and Charles Hamilton, <u>Black Power: The Politics of Liberation</u> (New York: Random House, 1967); Samuel F. Yette, <u>The Choice: The Issue of Black Survival in America</u> (New York: Putnam, 1971);

Martin Carnoy, ed., Education as Cultural Imperialism (New York: David McKay, 1974); and H. V. Savitch, "Black Cities/White Suburbs: Domestic Colonialism as an Interpretive Idea," The Annals 439 (September 1978): 118-34.

2. Gilbert G. González, "A Critique of the Internal Colony Model," Latin American Perspectives 1 (Spring 1974): 154-55. Please note that González is citing the arguments of Ronald Bailey and Guillermo Flores in their joint article, "Internal Colonialism and Racial Minorities in the U.S.: An Overview"; also Ronald Bailey, "Economic Aspects of the Black Internal Colony"; and Guillermo Flores, "Race and Culture in Internal Colony: Keeping the Chicano in His Place." These papers were presented at the Stanford University Seminar on Dependency, Winter Quarter, 1972. Bailey's and Flores's papers are also part of a collection edited by Frank Bonilla and Robert Girling, Structures of Dependency (Stanford, Calif.: Stanford University, 1973).

3. Philip G. Altbach and Gail P. Kelly, eds., Education and Colonialism (New York: Longman, 1978), chap. 1.

4. González, "Critique of the Internal Colony Model," p. 156.

5. Ibid.

6. Sidney Wilhelm, Who Needs the Negro? (Cambridge, Mass.: Schenkman, 1970); Michael Reich, "The Economics of Racism," in The Capitalist System, ed. Richard C. Edwards et al., 2d ed. (Englewood Cliffs, N.J.: Prentice-Hall, 1978); and Robert L. Allen, Black Awakening in Capitalist America (New York: Doubleday/Anchor, 1970).

7. Samari Amin, "Underdevelopment and Dependency in Black Africa: Their Historical Origin and Contemporary Form," Journal of Modern African Studies 10 (1972): 503-24; Walter Rodney, How Europe Underdeveloped Africa (Dar es Salaam, Tanzania: Tanzania Publishing House, 1972); James Cockcroft, André Gunder Frank, and Dale L. Johnson, Dependence and Underdevelopment: Latin America's Political Economy (New York: Doubleday/Anchor, 1972); and Joseph C. Jorgensen, "A Century of Political Economic Effects on American Indian Society, 1880-1980," Journal of Ethnic Studies 6 (Fall 1978): 1-82.

8. Jorgensen, "Century of Political Economic Effects," p. 4.

9. Ibid., pp. 2-4.

10. Class distinctions within a racial group were discussed by E. Franklin Frazier in Black Bourgeoisie: The Rise of a New Middle Class in the United States (New York: Collier, 1957), chaps. 2, 5, and 6, in particular.

11. William Julius Wilson, The Declining Significance of Race: Blacks and Changing American Institutions (Chicago: University of Chicago Press, 1978), chaps. 1, 6, and 7, in particular.

12. Robert L. Allen, "Racism and the Black Nation Thesis," Socialist Revolution 27 (January-March 1976): 145-50; and Jasper

Mims, Jr., "Race and Class: Determinant Factors in Urban Society," Negro History Bulletin 42 (January-March 1979): 20-21.

13. Ibid.

14. Gayle Rubin, "The Traffic in Women: Notes on the 'Political Economy' of Sex," in Towards an Anthropology of Women, ed. Rayna Reiter (New York: Monthly Review Press, 1975), pp. 160-64.

15. John Cammett, Antonio Gramsci and the Origins of Italian Communism (Stanford, Calif.: Stanford University Press, 1967), p. 204.

16. Gayle Rubin, "The Traffic in Women," pp. 160-64; Martha Mueller, "Women and Men, Power and Powerlessness in Lesotho," Signs: Journal of Women in Culture and Society 3 (Spring 1977): 154; and Harriet Sibisi, "How African Women Cope with Migrant Labor in South Africa," Signs: Journal of Women in Culture and Society 3 (Spring 1977): 167.

17. Helen Icken Safa, "Class Consciousness among Working-Class Women in Latin America: Puerto Rico," in Sex and Class in Latin America, ed. June Nash and Helen Icken Safa (New York: Praeger, 1976), p. 70.

REFERENCES

Allen, Robert L. Black Awakening in Capitalist America. New York: Doubleday/Anchor, 1970.

_____. "Racism and the Black Nation Thesis." Socialist Revolution 27 (January-March 1976), 145-50.

Altbach, Philip G., and Gail P. Kelly, eds. Education and Colonialism. New York: Longman, 1978.

Amin, Samari. "Underdevelopment and Dependency in Black Africa: Their Historical Origin and Contemporary Form." Journal of Modern African Studies 10 (1972): 503-24.

Bailey, Ronald. "Economic Aspects of the Black Internal Colony." In Structures of Dependency, edited by Frank Bonilla and Robert Girling. Stanford, Calif.: Stanford University Press, 1973.

Bailey, Ronald, and Guillermo Flores. "Internal Colonialism and Racial Minorities in the U.S.: An Overview." In Structures of Dependency, edited by Frank Bonilla and Robert Girling. Stanford, Calif.: Stanford University Press, 1973.

Cammett, John. Antonio Gramsci and the Origins of Italian Communism. Stanford, Calif.: Stanford University Press, 1967.

Carmichael, Stokely, and Charles Hamilton. Black Power: The Politics of Liberation. New York: Random House, 1967.

Carnoy, Martin, ed. Education as Cultural Imperialism. New York: David McKay, 1974.

Cockcroft, James, André Gunder Frank, and Dale L. Johnson. Dependence and Underdevelopment: Latin America's Political Economy. New York: Doubleday/Anchor, 1972.

DuBois, W. E. B. Color and Democracy: Colonies and Peace. New York: Harcourt, Brace, 1945.

Flores, Guillermo. "Race and Culture in Internal Colony: Keeping the Chicano in His Place." In Structures of Dependency, edited by Frank Bonilla and Robert Girling. Stanford, Calif.: Stanford University Press, 1973.

Frazier, E. Franklin. Black Bourgeoisie: The Rise of a New Middle Class in the United States. New York: Collier, 1957.

Gonzáles, Gilbert G. "A Critique of the Internal Colony Model." Latin American Perspectives 1 (Spring 1974): 154-61.

Jorgensen, Joseph C. "A Century of Political Economic Effects on American Indian Society, 1880-1980." Journal of Ethnic Studies 6 (Fall 1978): 1-82.

Mims, Jasper, Jr. "Race and Class: Determinant Factors in Urban Society." Negro History Bulletin 42 (January-March 1979): 20-21.

Mueller, Martha. "Women and Men, Power and Powerlessness in Lesotho." Signs: Journal of Women in Culture and Society 3 (Spring 1977): 154-66.

Reich, Michael. "The Economics of Racism." In The Capitalist System, edited by Richard C. Edwards, 2d ed. Englewood Cliffs, N.J.: Prentice-Hall, 1978.

Rodney, Walter. How Europe Underdeveloped Africa. Dar es Salaam, Tanzania: Tanzania Publishing House, 1972.

Rubin, Gayle, "The Traffic in Women: Notes on the 'Political Economy' of Sex." In Towards an Anthropology of Women, edited by Rayna Reiter. New York: Monthly Review Press, 1975.

Safa, Helen Icken. "Class Consciousness among Working-Class Women in Latin America: Puerto Rico." In Sex and Class in Latin America, edited by June Nash and Helen Icken Safa. New York: Praeger, 1976.

Savitch, H. V. "Black Cities/White Suburbs: Domestic Colonialism as an Interpretive Idea." The Annals 439 (September 1978): 118-34.

Sibisi, Harriet. "How African Women Cope with Migrant Labor in South Africa." Signs: Journal of Women in Culture and Society 3 (Spring 1977): 167-77.

Wilhelm, Sidney. Who Needs the Negro? Cambridge, Mass.: Schenkman, 1970.

Wilson, William Julius. The Declining Significance of Race: Blacks and Changing American Institutions. Chicago: University of Chicago Press, 1978.

Yette, Samuel F. The Choice: The Issue of Black Survival in America. New York: Putnam, 1971.

INDEX

abakua, 166
Acuña y Rosetti, Elisa, 240
Adams, Lois, 15, 25, 26, 29, 298
Affirmative Action, 1
African Training and Research
  Center for Women, 46
African women, 25-26, 31-95
Alaska Native Act, 212-13
All-China Democratic Women's
  Federation, 100
Allen, Robert, 300
Allende era, 188
Alliance Girls' School, 85
Allotment Act, 213
Altbach, Philip, 9-10, 300
amah, 110
American Association for the Ad-
  vancement of Science, 215
American Indian-Alaskan Native
  Women's (AI-ANW) Caucus, 214,
  218, 219
American Indian Law Center, 217
American Indian movement, 5, 218
Amin, Samari, 33-34, 301
Anderson, Owanah, 221-22
antitraditionalist perspective, 35-
  36, 37
anti-Western perspective, 36, 37-
  38
Arizpe, Lourdes, 187
Asian women, 26-27, 96-142
Atlanta University, 11
Aztec Empire, 236

Balaguer, Joaquin, 151
Bambara, Toni, 145-46
Bandung Conference of Colored
  Peoples, 5
Bastide, Roger, 230
Belgrade Conference of Non-
  aligned Powers, 5

Bengelsdorf, Carollee, 172
Bilingual Education federal regu-
  lations, 220
Black feminist movement, 267
Black Liberation movement, 157,
  265
Black Power movement, 5
Black women in the United States,
  251-75
Bokamba, Georges, 66-67
Boorstein, Edward, 165
Boserup, Ester, 13, 14, 299
Brown, H. Rap, 145
Brownmiller, Susan, 232
Buffalohead, Priscilla, 210
Bunster, Ximena, 191, 194-95
Bureau of American Ethnography,
  209
Bureau of Indian Affairs (BIA),
  212-13, 214, 216-18, 219-20,
  221; Reorganization Task Force,
  219
Business and Professional Wom-
  en's Club, 155
Bustos, Jorge, 180
Butler Flora, Cornelia, 190-91

Camacho, Hilda Araujo, 190
Cameroon Constitution, 43
Caribbean women, 27-28, 143-61
Carlisle Indian School, 204, 214
Carmichael, Stokely, 9, 299
Carnoy, Martin, 9, 299
Castro, Fidel, 162, 164, 170, 173
Central Trade Union Federation,
  173
Certificate of Primary Education
  exam, 86
Chandbibi, 124
Chaney, Elsa, 186, 188

311

ABOUT THE EDITOR AND CONTRIBUTORS

BEVERLY LINDSAY presently is an Assistant Professor of Education Policy Studies at The Pennsylvania State University, University Park, Pennsylvania. She holds an Ed.D., M.Ed., and M.A. from the University of Massachusetts, Amherst. Her B.A. (Magna Cum Laude) was awarded from St. Mary's University in San Antonio, Texas. Her major areas of research and publication focus on socio-cultural and educational issues influencing Third World people. She has received grants from the Ford Foundation, the National Fellowship Fund, and The Pennsylvania State University to conduct research in Africa, the Caribbean, the People's Republic of China, and the United States. Her publications have appeared in the International Education Journal, The Kenya Education Review, Educational Leadership Journal, the Urban League Review, the Journal of Modern African Studies, the Journal of Thought, and the Journal of Black Studies.

LOIS ADAMS has a B.A. from Clark College, Massachusetts, an M.A. from Columbia University, and is completing her Ph.D. at the University of Wisconsin, Madison, in African languages and culture. She has conducted research in Francophone Africa.

JOHNNETTA B. COLE is a Professor of Anthropology at the University of Massachusetts, Amherst. Her Ph.D. and M.A. were earned at Northwestern University. She has conducted field research in Liberia, Cuba, and other Caribbean Islands. Her publications have appeared in The Black Scholar, Freedomways, The Massachusetts Review, and The American Anthropologist.

TONIA K. DEVON has a Ph.D. from the University of California, Berkeley, an M.A. from the University of Wisconsin, Madison, and a B.A. from Grinnell College, Iowa. She conducted field research in India through a Fulbright-Hays Grant. Her publications have appeared in the Comparative Education Review.

SYLVIA A. GONZALES, a Ford Foundation Fellow, has an Ed.D. from the University of Massachusetts in educational administration. She also holds an M.Ed. from Antioch College and a B.A. from the University of Arizona. Currently, she is an Assistant Professor at San Jose State University and Co-Coordinator of the National Women's Studies Association. She has written articles for the Los Angeles Times, La Luz Magazine, Latin American Literary Review, De

Colores: A Journal of Emerging Raza Philosophies, U.S. Civil Rights Journal, and the Social Science Quarterly.

GLORIA I. JOSEPH is currently a Professor of Social Sciences at Hampshire College in Amherst, Massachusetts, and has held previous professorships at the University of Massachusetts, Cornell University, and College of the Virgin Islands, St. Croix. Her Ph.D. in psychology is from Cornell University and she has an M.S. and a B.A. from the City College of New York and New York University, respectively. She has conducted extensive research in the Caribbean Islands on the roles of women, psychology in the Caribbean, and political development. Publications on these and related subjects have appeared in the Bill of Rights Journal, Science, Journal of Afro-American Studies, Journal of the National Association of Women Deans and Counselors, Educational Opportunity Forum, and the American Sociological Review.

GAIL P. KELLY is currently an Associate Professor of Social Foundations of Education at the State University of New York in Buffalo. She received her A.B. from the University of Chicago, her M.A. from the University of Indiana, and her Ph.D. from the University of Wisconsin. Her major research and writing interests lie in comparative education with special emphasis on Southeast Asia and Vietnam in particular. Articles on these general areas and women have appeared in the Journal of Ethnic Studies, Journal of School Health, Comparative Education Review, and New Politics. Two of her books are From Vietnam to America and Education and Colonialism (coedited).

SHELBY LEWIS is an Associate Professor of Political Science at Atlanta University. She holds a Ph.D. from the University of New Orleans, an M.A. from the University of Massachusetts, Amherst, and a B.A. from Southern University. She has conducted extensive research in Africa through Ford Foundation Grants and also taught there. She is on the executive boards of the African Heritage Studies Association and the National Conference of Black Political Scientists.

GWENDOLYN RANDALL PURYEAR, a clinical psychologist, is Coordinator of Research and Institutional Testing at Howard University. She holds a Ph.D. and an M.S. from Howard University and a B.A. from Bennett College, Greensboro, North Carolina. Her publications on motivations, aspirations, and perceptions of women have appeared in the Journal of Consulting and Clinical Psychology and the Journal of Social and Behavioral Sciences.

BEE-LAN CHAN WANG holds an A.B. (Cum Laude) from Harvard University and a Ph.D. from the University of Chicago in sociology with specialities in Asian social issues. A native of Malaysia, she has been a lecturer at the Science University in Penang, Malaysia. Presently, she is an Assistant Professor of Sociology at Wheaton College, Wheaton, Illinois. Publications on her areas of focus have appeared in Comparative Education Review and Sociology of Education.

NORA JACQUEZ WIESER has a Ph.D. from Case Western Reserve University, an M.A. from Middlebury College, and a B.A. from Loretto Heights College, Denver. She is an Assistant Professor of Romance Language and Culture at Oberlin College. She has presented scholarly papers on Latin American women in Latin America and the United States.

LAURA WATERMAN WITTSTOCK is a member of the Seneca Nation of New York, Heron Clan. She is a journalist, a founder and developer of MIGIZI Communications, a native news service in the Midwest, and an independent Indian education and programs consultant. She has been the editor of the Legislative Review and her publications have appeared in Media Bulletin, Civil Rights Digest, and Indian Voice.